Kenneth Burke in the 1930s

Studies in Rhetoric/Communication
Thomas W. Benson, Series Editor

Kenneth Burke IN THE 1930s

Ann George and Jack Selzer

THE UNIVERSITY OF SOUTH CAROLINA PRESS

© 2007 University of South Carolina

Published by the University of South Carolina Press
Columbia, South Carolina 29208

www.sc.edu/uscpress

Manufactured in the United States of America

16 15 14 13 12 11 10 09 08 07   10 9 8 7 6 5 4 3 2 1

Library of Congress Cataloging-in-Publication Data

George, Ann, 1957–
    Kenneth Burke in the 1930s / Ann George and Jack Selzer.
        p. cm. — (Studies in rhetoric/communication)
    Includes bibliographical references and index.
    ISBN-13: 978-1-57003-700-9 (cloth : alk. paper)
    ISBN-10: 1-57003-700-0 (cloth : alk. paper)
    1. Burke, Kenneth, 1897–1993—Criticism and interpretation. 2. Burke,
Kenneth, 1897–1993—Political and social views. 3. Nineteen thirties. I. Selzer,
Jack. II. Title.
    PS3503.U6134Z667 2007
    818'.5209—dc22

                                                                              2007007332

This book was printed on Glatfelter Natures, a recycled paper with 50 percent
postconsumer waste content.

Concerning the matter of my "orthodoxy": having heard so much about the many difficulties which many sincere and enterprising men have met with, I made peace with myself by the following formula: I would think of myself simply as anti-capitalist and pro-communist, and let all the rest go hang. Insofar as the various warring groups will accept me as an ally on that basis, I am with them.

Letter from Kenneth Burke to
Sidney Hook, December 27, 1933

My interests are, as always, a concern for the reversal of splintering rather than for its intensification.

Letter from Kenneth Burke to John Brooks Wheelwright,
December 7, 1933; to Joshua Kunitz, December 7, 1936

Burke is a man of the 1930s.

Frank Lentricchia, *Criticism and Social Change*

Contents

Illustrations

Series Editor's Preface

In *Kenneth Burke in the 1930s* Ann George and Jack Selzer reread the major and shorter works Kenneth Burke wrote during an extraordinary period of productivity and influence. In this decade Burke published *Counter-Statement* (1931), his novel *Towards a Better Life* (1932), *Permanence and Change* (1935), *Attitudes toward History* (1937), and *The Philosophy of Literary Form* (1941). He also wrote another book, *Auscultation, Creation, and Revision*, which was completed in 1932 but not published for more than sixty years. In addition he produced dozens of reviews, essays, and articles; engaged in a wide-ranging correspondence with leading intellectuals and writers; and participated in various political and publication ventures, including the 1935 American Writers' Congress.

George and Selzer present vigorous new interpretations of Burke's works in the 1930s, bringing a reflective, generous, and judicious perspective that gives them fresh significance. At the same time, through their wide reading and archival research, they bring to their readings a detailed account of Burke's interactions with the movements of the time, including activist writers, leftist intellectuals, Chicago pragmatists, the southern Agrarians, and the New Critics, corresponding and debating with such figures as Malcolm Cowley, John Dewey, Mike Gold, Sidney Hook, Marianne Moore, Katherine Anne Porter, John Crowe Ransom, Allen Tate, Robert Penn Warren, William Carlos Williams, and Edmund Wilson. George and Selzer's placement of Burke in the literary and political history of his time and their reading of Burke in the context of his own life and correspondence permits the authors to articulate how Burke's rhetorical theory from the 1930s is itself thoroughly rhetorical. The result is a vastly enriched reading of such works as *Permanence and Change*, *Attitudes toward History*, and *The Philosophy of Literary Form*. While demonstrating how deeply these works are embedded in and motivated by the intellectual and political ferment of the 1930s, George and Selzer at the same time reveal how Kenneth Burke again and again transcended old, stalled debates with radical and compelling new formulations.

THOMAS W. BENSON

Preface

I t almost goes without saying that a book about Kenneth Burke's intellectual and social affiliations in the 1930s must itself be the product of conversations with many individuals, especially when that project has taken shape over many years. Those conversations and the new relationships that developed around them have made our academic lives tremendously richer and this project unusually rewarding. We offer the product of those conversations here: a more-or-less linear narrative about Kenneth Burke's thinking among fellow thinkers during the decade of his most remarkable productivity, the 1930s. In 1931 Burke published his first collection of essays (*Counter-Statement*), and his novel *Towards a Better Life* appeared in the first days of 1932. By April 1941 he had come out with another such collection (*The Philosophy of Literary Form*); published two influential treatises (*Permanence and Change* and *Attitudes toward History*) and written a third (*Auscultation, Creation, and Revision*), which was published half a century later; participated in the most important leftist cultural events of the period in New York City, including the famous writers' congresses sponsored by the League of American Writers; and contributed dozens of essays and reviews (and satires) to the *Nation*, the *New Republic*, the *Southern Review*, *New Masses*, *Direction*, and any number of other important magazines. Along the way he won a Guggenheim, participated in John Reed Club and Popular Front rallies and lectures and other performances, was arrested for political rabble-rousing, debated every civic issue during a volatile period of national upheaval, was divorced and remarried—and consorted with innumerable writers, artists, editors, and other significant cultural workers, among them Malcolm Cowley, Edmund Wilson, John Dewey, William Carlos Williams, Sidney Hook, James T. Farrell, I. A. Richards, Allen Tate, Cleanth Brooks, John Crowe Ransom, and Robert Penn Warren. This book is a record of the interactions among those people and periodicals as they were filtered through the considerable intellectual capacity known as Kenneth Burke.

    While we take responsibility for our formulation, warts and all, we must also acknowledge the outstanding scholarship from which we have drawn and the substantial advice we have received. We hope our notes and citations begin to give credit where it is due, but we also want to express here our respect, admiration, and appreciation to the many scholars whose work on Kenneth Burke and on the 1930s has been both instructive and sustaining. In particular we acknowledge those who listened patiently and responded productively to numerous lectures and conference presentations by us on one or another aspect of Kenneth Burke in the 1930s, especially panels sponsored by the Conference on College Composition and Communication and the Rhetoric Society of America, and the participants in the seminar on art and politics (ably chaired by Kathleen Farrell) conducted at the 1999 Kenneth Burke Conference in Iowa City. Members of the Kenneth Burke Society have generously supported our research in many additional tangible and intangible ways; we especially acknowledge the encouragement and assistance of David Blakesley, Bernard Brock, Tim Crusius, Greig Henderson, William Rueckert, and David Cratis Williams. More particularly, in Skaneateles John Crowley shared personal insights at a memorable dinner, and Jacqueline Mott Brown recalled lakeside childhood encounters between Kenneth Burke and her father. We have benefitted as well from expert and conscientious research assistance from Christopher Malone, Andrew Alexander, Dana Anderson, Marika Seigel, and Matt Newcomb. Brandy Bower (Penn State) and Carol Lipson (Syracuse) provided invaluable assistance with artwork. For financial support that helped us to gain access to various archives, we thank the Institute for the Arts and Humanities at Penn State, the College of the Liberal Arts at Penn State, and the Addran College of Humanities and Social Sciences and the Office of Research and Sponsored Projects at Texas Christian University. The assistance of our department chairs at Penn State and TCU was indispensable as well: thanks to Don Bialostosky, Robert Caserio, Fred Erisman, Alan Shepard, Dan Williams, and Richard Enos.

    More personally, for essential moral and intellectual support along the way, we thank our many generous and accomplished colleagues at Penn State, TCU, and elsewhere, particularly Don Bialostosky, Greg Clark, Sharon Crowley, Rosa Eberly, Richard Enos, Lester Faigley, Cheryl Glenn, Christina Haas, Charlotte Hogg, Becky Howard, Caren Irr, Carrie Leverenz, Brad Lucas, Jennifer Jackson, Steve Mailloux, Jon Olson, Ron Pitcock, Robin Schulze, Marie Secor, Stuart Selber, Gary Tate, Jeff Walker, Tilly Warnock, Elizabeth Weiser, Sue Wells, and Janet Zepernick. Janice Arvin lent needed serenity. The reviewers of the manuscript for the University of South Carolina Press, David Blakesley of Purdue University and Barry Brummett of the University of Texas, made many helpful suggestions, as did Ben Giamo and

Andrew Feffer. A succession of spectacular student colleagues in unforgettable graduate seminars lent their insights to various parts of the manuscript at various stages; seeing some of their work develop in part out of our efforts has been the most satisfying experience of our careers. And from the beginning our work has been nurtured, encouraged, assisted, improved, and sustained by the personal warmth, professional expertise, and intellectual generosity of Charles Mann, Sandra Stelts, Michael Burke, Julie Whitaker, and other members of the Burke family.

Sandra Stelts and Charles Mann, and their colleagues in Penn State's Special Collections operation in Paterno Library, stand in as well for the many other librarians and staff members around the country who assisted us with unfailing courtesy, expertise, and patience, notably at the following institutions: the New York Public Library; the Newberry Library; Butler Library, Columbia University; Bird Library at Syracuse University; the Hoover Institution, Stanford University; the Jean and Alexander Heard Library, Vanderbilt University; Joseph Regenstein Library, University of Chicago; Hornbake Library at the University of Maryland; Princeton University Library; Van Pelt Library at the University of Pennsylvania; John Hay Library at Brown University; the Beinecke Rare Book and Manuscript Library at Yale University; Olin/Chalmers Libraries at Kenyon College; the Rosenbach Museum and Library; Southern Illinois University Library; the Library of Congress; and the Smithsonian Archives of American Art.

Finally we wish to thank and acknowledge the following for their permission to reprint materials and to quote from books, articles, and correspondence: Jacqueline Mott Brown, for permission to reprint a photo of Kenneth Burke; Michael Burke, trustee of the Kenneth Burke Literary Trust, for permission to quote Kenneth Burke's works and correspondence and to reprint photographs; Robert Cowley, for permission to quote Malcolm Cowley's correspondence; Roderick H. Craib, for permission to quote materials related to Granville Hicks; Cleo Paturis, for permission to quote from correspondence by James T. Farrell; Carl Josephson, for permission to quote from Matthew Josephson's correspondence; Marianne Craig Moore, literary executor for the Literary Estate of Marianne Moore, for permission to quote correspondence by Marianne Moore; Barbara Thompson Davis, trustee for the estate of Katherine Anne Porter, for permission to quote correspondence by Katherine Anne Porter; Lucy Dos Passos Coggin, for permission to quote correspondence by John Dos Passos; Ernest B. Hook, for permission to quote correspondence by Sidney Hook; Carol A. Leadenham, for permission to quote writings in the Joseph Freeman Papers at the Hoover Institute, Stanford; Patrick Gregory, for permission to quote from Horace Gregory's correspondence; Nicholas Jenkins, for permission to quote from a previously unpublished letter by Lincoln Kirstein (copyright 2006 by the New York Public Library, Astor, Lenox and Tilden Foundations); Helen Tate, for permission to quote from Allen Tate's correspondence, and Martha Briggs, Lloyd Lewis Curator of Midwest Manuscripts at the Newberry Library, for permission to quote Tate's letter to Cowley of December 19, 1930 (Malcolm Cowley Papers, box 65, folder 3974); Declan Spring, agent for the estates of William Eric Williams and Paul H. Williams, for permission to quote letters from William Carlos Williams to Kenneth Burke; Alexandra Dorinson, for permission to quote the correspondence of Richard McKeon; Sadie DeWitt, for permission to reproduce work by Shirley Jackson and correspondence by Stanley Edgar Hyman; Donn Zeretsky, with assistance from John Callahan, for permission to quote correspondence by Ralph Ellison; Helen Ransom Forman, for permission to quote from John Crowe Ransom's correspondence; and the Cartoon Bank, for permission to reproduce a *New Yorker* cartoon by Alain.

Our deepest gratitude goes to our families, local and extended, for their support, patience, love, and understanding. To David and Katie, to Linda and Molly and Maggie we owe just about everything. We dedicate this book to them, with love. As the song goes, "At Last. . . ."

Kenneth Burke in the 1930s

Introduction

K enneth Burke once (and famously) remarked that he was "not a joiner of societies" (letter to Malcolm Cowley, June 4, 1932). And scholarship on Burke has in the main reinforced that self-assessment: his body of work has nearly always been considered apart from social movements and political affiliations. Those literary critics who have looked to Burke for theoretical and practical guidance have typically regarded him as "a kind of eccentric New Critic" whose "vast [interpretive] system based on a metaphor of drama" won him but a few (if devoted) disciples, whose positions fit only uneasily with mainstream New Critical dogmas and personalities dominant after World War II, and whose political and social investments, particularly the ones from the 1930s, had little to do with his thought (Denning, 435–36). Those in the fields of rhetoric and communication who have been drawn to Burke have regarded his (oft-noted) difficulty and iconoclasm as evidence of a radical individuality, have taken his autodidacticism and originality as signs of intellectual independence, and have interpreted certain biographical details of his life as additional signs of inspired insularity (e.g., his status as an independent scholar unattached to a regular university living; his long residency at an off-the-beaten-path New Jersey farm; even his alcoholism). Rhetoricians and literary critics alike, discounting Burke's political and aesthetic commitments, have been drawn especially to "dramatism" (and the succeeding "logology": the study of the ontology of language) as Burke's core project, have consequently attended most carefully to *A Grammar of Motives*, *A Rhetoric of Motives*, *The Rhetoric of Religion*, and *Language as Symbolic Action* (the books associated with dramatism and logology that were written in the 1940s, 1950s, and 1960s), and have therefore regarded Burke's 1920s and 1930s works as mostly preliminary and peripheral. Moreover, as Michael Denning has also noted (437), Burke's Depression-era books have been available to readers through editions that he revised in the 1950s to make his commitments to other thinkers in general—and to left-wing politics in particular

—more circumspect. While those revisions did succeed in lending currency and freshness to Burke's theoretical insights, and while the new editions made his ideas available to generations of new readers, they also covered most of his political and social tracks and gave readers the impression that Burke's 1930s experiences left little permanent mark on his work.

The record from the 1930s, however, shows something very different. If Kenneth Burke was not a joiner of every society (particularly if a membership fee was expected), he certainly belonged to a great many of them; the fact is that Burke was anything but unaffiliated, anything but marginal to the political and intellectual radicalism of the 1930s. During that decade Burke regularly attended meetings of the New York City John Reed Club until it was succeeded by the League of American Writers. Then he became a loyal, long-term, active member of the league, and a featured participant in important writers' congresses sponsored by the league in 1935, 1937, and 1939. He taught courses at three different universities. He took part in political rallies and demonstrations, one of which led to his arrest. Just as during the 1920s he was identified with most of the important modernist literary magazines (most notably the *Dial*, which ceased publication in 1929), Burke in the 1930s was closely associated with several important literary and cultural magazines, including the *Nation*, the *New Republic, Partisan Review, Direction, Poetry*, and the *Southern Review*, and he wrote for a number of others as well. And, as the record of his remarkable correspondence indicates, he had productive personal and professional relations during the 1930s with individuals who belonged to a number of interconnected intellectual circles: self-described "aesthetes" whose commitment to the religion of art remained very roughly intact from the 1920s (e.g., Marianne Moore, Katherine Anne Porter, William Carlos Williams); committed leftists associated with the Communist Party and with the Popular Front (e.g., Malcolm Cowley, Matthew Josephson, Waldo Frank, Joseph Freeman, James T. Farrell); Southern Agrarians and proto–New Critics (e.g., Allen Tate, Robert Penn Warren, John Crowe Ransom, Cleanth Brooks); Chicago School critics and intellectuals (e.g., R. S. Crane and Richard McKeon); and pragmatists and social scientists such as John Dewey and Sidney Hook. Even the letter to Cowley that seemingly concedes that he "is not a joiner of societies" actually proclaims quite the opposite: angry and impatient with Cowley's charge that he should "do something" to avoid becoming someone like the isolated John Neal of his recently published novel, *Towards a Better Life*, Burke after several drafts disavowed to Cowley any identification with the reclusive Neal; resisted with no small sarcasm Cowley's "put[ting] him in a narrow house . . . facing the wall"; announced his "full agreement . . . with the Communists as to objectives" ("private wealth must be confiscated for the good of the community") and reminded Cowley of his presence at a recent political meeting at Edmund

Wilson's place to meet the Communist Party presidential candidate, William Z. Foster; described his life as "crowded" and full of "conversations"; mentioned forthcoming writings in the *New Republic* and two other works in progress (one a bit of ghostwriting, the other to become *Auscultation, Creation, and Revision*); and along the way mentioned his congress with a host of current friends and colleagues (e.g., Williams, Josephson, Robert Cantwell, John Chamberlain, Edmund Wilson, Granville Hicks).

In short, while Burke may not have "joined" the Communist Party or every other political action committee that he was invited to be a part of, he was indeed affiliated with a variety of fascinating groups and individuals during the Great Depression. Moreover Burke's extensive writing projects in the 1930s fundamentally emerged from and contributed to the cultural conversations enacted within and among those various groups and publications: as "the major cultural theorist of the Popular Front" (Denning, 445), he devoted considerable energy and intellect to drawing from and fashioning that Front. This book, something of a sequel to Selzer's *Kenneth Burke in Greenwich Village* (a subsequent volume is planned to consider Burke's work after 1940), is the record of those conversations and their interanimations as they are manifest in many of Burke's essays and his four books of the period: *Auscultation, Creation, and Revision* (completed in 1932 but first published in 1993); *Permanence and Change* (1935), *Attitudes toward History* (1937), and *The Philosophy of Literary Form* (1941). Building on the recent emphases of Michael Denning, John McGowan, and Frank Lentricchia, among others, all of whom have called attention to the vitality of Burke's 1930s writings, *Kenneth Burke in the 1930s* reports what we have learned from immersing ourselves in the literary and cultural magazines that Burke read during the 1930s and from examining Burke-related archives at Stanford, Princeton, Penn, the University of Chicago, the Newberry Library, Yale, Penn State, Syracuse, Columbia, the Library of Congress, and the New York Public Library (among others). By considering these extensive and mostly unexplored repositories of Burke letters and manuscripts, by looking at other primary materials, by studying the magazines where Burke's works appeared—the *Nation*, the *New Republic*, *Partisan Review*, *Hound and Horn*, *New Masses*, the *Southern Review*, *Science and Society*, *Direction*, *Poetry*, and so forth—and, most important, by reading Burke carefully against the ideological conversations of the time, we are able to offer a context for understanding the works Burke produced during a period when he was most productive and highly influential—when he was, in Denning's words, "the most important communist cultural theorist in the United States" (436). Indeed it is our contention that the books Burke wrote during the 1930s ought to be regarded as contributions as important and compelling as his later volumes, including *A Grammar* and *A Rhetoric*; that the insights and critical apparatuses in *Permanence and Change*,

Attitudes toward History, and *The Philosophy of Literary Form* are as suggestive, original, useful, and enlightening as those in the later works; and indeed that some of the most important concepts in those later works—most notably dramatism itself—ought to be understood in the context of Burke's 1930s commitments.

Chapter 1, "April 1935," therefore introduces the cast of characters, groups, and magazines that the rest of the book will elaborate on. In passing it offers a thick description of Burke's controversial participation in the famous first American Writers' Congress, held in New York on the last weekend of that remarkable April: the event highlights the importance of Burke's participation in forming the leftist literary and cultural agenda and illustrates the personal and intellectual complexities involved in that participation. Chapter 2, focusing on *Auscultation Creation, and Revision*, details Burke's efforts to retain an appreciation for the aesthetic during a cultural moment when artists and intellectuals in New York were stampeding to embrace the values of proletarian art. Just as it was appearing that the 1920s aesthetes had been "routed" (to use the phrase from *Auscultation*), Burke paused to assign to aestheticism a leading role in the reintegration of contemporary culture. The chapter connects Burke with little magazines operating in the aesthetic tradition of the *Dial*, such as *Pagany*, *Hound and Horn*, *Poetry*, and the *Criterion*, and to the artistic and cultural values that they promulgated—and documents his own uneasy turn toward what Edmund Wilson in "An Appeal to Progressives" called "a new manifesto and new bill of rights" derived from communist ideals.

Chapter 3, on *Permanence and Change*, is in many ways the central chapter of the book. It traces Burke's thinking and his affiliations from 1933 to 1935, the years when he wrote and published *P&C*, placed in magazines a great many other essays and reviews (as well as a portion of *P&C*), and especially defended his thinking in the *Nation*, *New Masses*, and the *New Republic*. The chapter includes an account of how the genre of *P&C* (which we call "the cultural history") associates the book with both aestheticist and leftist tracts, and it indicates how the argument of *Permanence and Change* offers a salient corrective to both aesthetes and doctrinaire Communists. Ever independent and able to contain contraries, Burke could not help critiquing Marxists almost as much as he was criticizing capitalist formulations, and so *Permanence and Change*, in its appropriations of Thorstein Veblen and Dewey—and in its support for the same "poetic orientation" that is summoned in its own way in Burke's "Revolutionary Symbolism in America" and in *Auscultation*—demonstrates his mature critical sensibility. *Permanence and Change* argues for communism, but "more at the level of culture than economics, and never uncritically" (to borrow Robert Wess's formulation): "Marxism does provide some necessary admonitions as to our faulty institutions," Burke wrote to

Matthew Josephson, "but as I understand it, it is exactly 180 degrees short of being a completely rounded philosophy of human motivation" (September 11, 1935).

Chapter 4, on *Attitudes toward History*, embeds that too-seldom-read book in the politics of the Popular Front and its opposing parties, as those political positions were drawn in *Direction* (a semiofficial organ of the League of American Writers), *Science and Society*, and *Partisan Review* (whose political orientation shifted away from Stalinism after 1936). This chapter also includes an account of the 1937 second American Writers' Congress (where Burke addressed a resolutely Popular Front gathering on "The Relation between Literature and Science"), and an explanation of Burke's famous (and telling) feud with Sidney Hook. Chapter 5 recalls Burke's participation in the third American Writers' Congress in 1939, when he presented his prophetic and much admired "The Rhetoric of Hitler's 'Battle.'" But mainly it concentrates on a discussion of *The Philosophy of Literary Form:* without abandoning the Left or an insistence that art was part of rather than apart from society, Burke in that book nevertheless spoke to new constituencies—to the New Critics associated with the *Southern Review*, to social scientists associated with pragmatism and a new movement known as semantics, and to intellectuals of several sorts who were seeking an accommodation between Freud and Marx. We also offer "An Informal Chronology," a supplement that will document Burke's activities and thus make it easier for readers to negotiate the arguments that we present.

Finally the text includes sidebars that are intended to dramatize Burke's engagements with his intellectual and cultural peers. These unpublished or seldom published letters, articles, photos, caricatures, and cartoons, together with some of our own short essays, interrupt the narrative slightly so that our version of history does not come off as inappropriately smooth and uncomplicated. Together, the chapters and sidebars are intended to cooperate in creating a picture of Kenneth Burke as operating within the astonishing mixture of writings, personalities, and cultural particulars that constituted the 1930s. Kenneth Burke was not a gadfly marginalized by all sorts of establishments, we argue, so much as he was an indefatigable genius whose brilliance emerged out of particular material sites and intellectual circles whose presence can be measured and felt in his work—*must* be measured and felt, we would contend, if we are to understand Kenneth Burke well at all.

One   April 1935

An Overview

For many Americans enduring the Great Depression, April 1935 was indeed the cruelest month. Since unemployment was still stuck at around 25 percent, where it had dropped to in 1932–33, President Franklin Roosevelt was obtaining final approval for a five-billion-dollar relief appropriation that was designed to stimulate public works projects and to alleviate some of the nation's suffering. The heady first days of the New Deal two years behind him now, Roosevelt was coping as best he could with a number of grim realities, including the continuing banking crisis that had accompanied his inauguration (private currencies were developing in many areas where all the banks had failed) as well as persistent labor turmoil. There were frustrating strikes in progress by autoworkers in Toledo, by subway construction crews in New York, by the factory workers of the National Biscuit Company, and by miners in Wilkes-Barre, where at least twenty-six and perhaps as many as forty labor leaders were jailed that April (depending on the account)—the climax of two years of bloody and literally explosive conflicts between the Glen Alden Coal Company and the United Anthracite Miners. Thirty thousand miners across the nation were threatening to walk out in sympathy, encouraged by Paul Muni's film *Black Fury*, which re-created the tensions surrounding a Pennsylvania miners' strike. A textile strike had idled 400,000 additional workers across the country. Amid the turmoil the new Congress of Industrial Organizations—the CIO—was in the process of being founded by John L. Lewis. Ever since walkouts by San Francisco longshoremen several months before had led to violence, a general strike, and sensational trials, a Red Scare had been spreading throughout the nation; and so violence between left-wing and right-wing Americans was also erupting in polarized Chicago, Minneapolis, Portland, Toledo, and other cities. When a young African American Communist labor leader named Angelo Herndon, seeking to overturn his 1932 conviction on trumped-up charges of rabble-rousing in Georgia, wrote letters to solicit support for his appeal to the

Supreme Court (one letter went to Kenneth Burke), the *New Republic* responded on April 10 with an editorial championing Herndon's cause.

Meantime the nation's birthrate was plunging as young marrieds despaired of feeding new mouths. Farm failures were so rife that over 50 percent of the nation's farmers were forced into tenancy (75 percent in Deep South states such as Mississippi and Georgia): that was the estimate of Alabama senator John Bankhead (*New York Times*, April 14, 1935), who was recommending a bill to enable more tenant farmers to obtain their own land over time and who hoped thereby to stave off additional violence in the heartland. Even the physical elements seemed to be in revolt: Dust storms in Kansas, Oklahoma, Texas, and Colorado destroyed millions of acres of wheat, reported the *New York Times* on April 12, ruining the lives of thousands of farmers, killing scores of them, making it dangerous even for the healthy to breathe, and sending thousands off to seek better fortune in California. Indeed a dust bowl eruption on April 10, 1935, made the few scattered thunderclouds over the heartland literally rain mud that forced down a pilot out to top Amelia Earhart's record for transcontinental air travel. Another dust storm on Sunday, April 14 (reported the *Times*), had the effect of driving down temperatures more than fifty degrees in a matter of a few hours and of choking to death millions of farm animals.

In New York City the *Times* was advertising Clifford Odets's new one-act play, *Waiting for Lefty*, its action centered about a prospective taxi drivers' strike in New York. Audiences of up to 1,400 people typically rose to their feet at its conclusion to shout with fervor, "Strike! Strike!!" The April 6 issue of the *New Yorker* commended the "special eloquence of violence and desperation" of the play, which featured proletarian set pieces, the image of research chemists and surgeons forced into driving cabs, and Elia Kazan materializing from the audience to editorialize on the underclass—but the same magazine ridiculed Odets's short undercard presentation, *Til the Day I Die*, as a "hopeless melodrama . . . dealing with the Nazi persecution of the Communists." A front-page story in the *Times* on April 7 surveyed the broader development of the "theatre of the Left" and of the New Theatre League (formerly the League of Workers' Theatres) that had spawned Odets and other proletarian playwrights. George Gershwin was putting the finishing touches on his *Porgy and Bess*, which would begin its Broadway run on October 10.

Readers of the *New Republic* (most of them New Yorkers) were wondering how to respond to a riot in Harlem late in March that developed out of unemployment among African Americans in New York of at least 50 percent to 60 percent (the April 1 issue of *Time* magazine estimated that more than 100,000 of the 250,000 Negroes in New York were on relief) and out of badly overcrowded housing circumstances (unemployment was driving people to share living quarters, while segregation artificially inflated rents). When a committee reported to Mayor Fiorello LaGuardia that a third of all New York families were being victimized by unemployment and that 400,000 New Yorkers were destitute, the mayor reorganized the city's $240 million relief office under a new director of emergency relief, Oswald Knauth (*New York Times*, April 7). Eighteen percent of the 7.5 million New Yorkers were receiving some form of government relief—from four to ten dollars a week plus rent, depending on the size of the family (Markey, "Relief")—and New York newspapers advertised precious few open jobs apart from the army of clerks needed to manage the relief effort itself. Instead employment pages were filled with "Situations Wanted" ads, especially columns and columns of notices placed by women seeking jobs as cooks, chambermaids, stenographers, governesses, housekeepers, and laundresses. An April 14 graphic in the *Times* dramatized the extent of the crisis: it estimated that national income after taxes had plummeted from more than $61 billion in 1929 to less than $40 billion in 1934. Even more dramatic were stories about the city's eighteen emergency nursing schools, which treated children aged two to four who were rendered ill from starvation; about the 80,000 free lunches served to New York City schoolchildren each day; and about the 40,000 white-collar unemployed who were working for seventy-five dollars a month under the supervision of the works director as sign painters, recreation supervisors, librarians, lab workers, music teachers, museum personnel, and actors.[1] There was a general consensus among New York and *New Republic* intellectuals, therefore, that radical change was needed, probably on a Marxist model, if the nation was to endure.

Meantime, away from the Northeast, Senator Huey Long of Louisiana was belittling Roosevelt's efforts to achieve national economic recovery, including the relief appropriation. Touting his resolute support for education in Louisiana in an April 12 speech to Louisiana State University faculty, promoting his own "Share the Wealth" plan, and ridiculing "Prince Franklin" in an April 22 Senate speech "in the third year of our reigning empire of St. Vitus" that he regarded as no better (and more corrupt) than the Hoover administration, Long, amid charges of corruption in his own political machine, was nevertheless expected to lead a third-party challenge to Roosevelt in the 1936 election. He immediately flew to Iowa after the Senate speech to promote his presidential possibilities. There Long attacked Roosevelt's "Lord High Chamberlain," Interior Secretary Harold Ickes, as "the chinch bug of Chicago" and mocked the attempts of New Dealers to outdo what was being done in Louisiana to combat the Depression ("There Was Once a Tea Party"). A *Time* magazine profile published April 1, 1935, speculated that Long might be able to attract up to 10 million votes from FDR in 1936—enough to give victory to the Republican candidate. Father Charles

Coughlin in Detroit was also denouncing the National Recovery Act and Roosevelt on his frequent radio broadcasts—and organizing more than eight million Americans into his own political organization, the National Union for Social Justice. The subject of an April 1935 *Reader's Digest* feature ("When Father Coughlin Comes to Washington"), Coughlin in his March 11 broadcast scored Roosevelt's NRA; attacked the Federal Reserve System and the nation's bankers (particularly Jewish ones such as Bernard Baruch) as the source of all economic problems; vowed chillingly "to drive the moneychangers from the temple"; and defended the right of the descendants of "the Nordic nations to teach the world the story of commerce and to carry the glory which they inherited." On May 22, 1935, Coughlin would fill Madison Square Garden to overflowing as a rousing conclusion to his month-long speaking tour to promote the National Union and criticize the New Deal (Brinkley, 177).

In sympathy with Coughlin, reactionary Hearst-family newspapers were fanning the Red Scare. For example, when more than one hundred thousand college students across the nation, concerned about developments in Europe, demonstrated on April 12 on behalf of international peace, Hearst papers carried a photo of banner-waving University of Chicago students above the caption "Young Communists" and applauded editorially when the University of Pittsburgh subsequently forced the resignation of progressive professors. Drugstore impresario Charles Walgreen on April 10 notified the Board of Trustees of the University of Chicago (and the Hearst-sponsored *Chicago Herald Examiner*) that he was withdrawing his niece from the university because he was "unwilling to have her absorb Communist influences," and on April 20 the *New York Times* reported that Hearst newspapers had "been diligently heaping faggots under the pot" of subsequent investigations at Chicago that would last through June (McNeill, 63; Mayer, 150). (Walgreen was impressed and satisfied when university president Robert Hutchins on April 18 denounced the *Herald Examiner* for "silencing the voice of reason" and compromising academic freedom.) On April 2, 1935, when the Supreme Court overturned the notorious conviction of the nine "Scottsboro boys," who had been sentenced to death for the March 1931 assault of two white women on an Alabama train, on the grounds that Negroes had been barred from the jury, American Communists rejoiced, since the Scottsboro case had long been a leftist cause célèbre. As *New Masses* reported on April 16, the Communists sponsored an all-day Scottsboro Victory Celebration at the Fifth Avenue Theatre on April 13 that featured newsreels, "prominent speakers," and a showing of "*Harlem Sketches*, the film that startled the Mayor's Investigating Committee on Racism." But the Alabama attorney general, meanwhile, vowed to retry the case, and so editorialists north and south, left and right, speculated at length on the impact of the case on southern politics.

Leftists and rightists were lining up in Europe too, of course. Many nations were trying to respond to the threat newly posed by Adolf Hitler, who, having solidified his political position two years before, was in the early but unmistakable stages of his reign of terror. Bells were kept silent in German churches on April 7 to protest the arrest of Protestant pastors; Nazis shut down performances of Schiller's *Don Carlos* (the April 4 *Times* reported) because audiences were applauding so vigorously the line "Sire, give us freedom of thought!"; Catholic nuns and clergymen were arrested in order to intimidate dissenters; newspaper and magazine editors were required to heel to the Nazi line or go out of business; and Jews were being forced out of schools and into their own segregated institutions. (The Nuremberg Laws depriving Jews of citizenship would be enacted in September.) When Hitler began building airplanes and submarines and announced plans to reinstate conscription to raise his army to 800,000 men—"Hitler Liquidates Versailles!" screamed a March 27 editorial in the *Nation*—the other European powers quickly took what countermeasures they could. On April 1 Anthony Eden and Joseph Stalin announced in Moscow that Great Britain and the Soviet Union had agreed to cooperate in foreign affairs against their developing common enemy, and a similar pact between France and Russia was forged a few days later with the approval of Turkey, Rumania, and Yugoslavia. On April 2, 1935, anti-Nazi rallies were reported in Lithuania and in the free city of Danzig. On his way back to London, Eden made additional stops in Poland and Czechoslovakia to attempt to enlist additional cooperation. Then on April 11–15, representatives from Britain, France, and Italy met at Stresa in northern Italy to discuss a unified response to Hitler's actions. Benito Mussolini was still in the midst of an estrangement from Hitler, but he was also massing troops for imminent military action in Ethiopia.

April 1935 was also eventful for Kenneth Burke, as eventful as any month in his long and amazing career. With his thirty-eighth birthday approaching, Burke was engaged in a whirlwind of activities centering about the New York City intellectual, political, and literary circles that sustained and animated him and his work. On April 1 the Guggenheim Foundation announced in the *New York Times* that it was making its annual awards to forty-seven distinguished artists, scholars, and writers. Among those awarded fellowships were Lola Ridge, Edmund Wilson, Langston Hughes—and Kenneth Burke ("for the writing of a book studying the effect which ideas and social values have had upon the practical and material aspects of different cultures" throughout history [Burke to Moe, undated, late March 1935]). Like the other Guggenheim Fellows, Burke would receive two thousand dollars, in his case to support what would become his *Attitudes toward History* (published in 1937) and to recognize his recently published novel, *Towards a Better Life* (1932), and treatise *Permanence and Change*, the latter of which was announced in a full-page ad in the March 27, 1935, *New Republic* and presented in the New Republic Dollar Series ("pioneering light-cloth binding of a new durable material which renders jackets unnecessary . . . since it combines the flexibility of paper covers heretofore used with the permanence of a library binding").

For Burke the Guggenheim announcement and the *New Republic* ad began a month that was for him as personally sensational as national and international events. For the next ten days, Burke, living now at 121 Bank Street in Greenwich Village and commuting to his Andover farm whenever possible to prepare for spring planting, was receiving congratulations from members of his various circles: from his old friend the incendiary Allen Tate and his new (and temporary, as it would turn out) friend the proletarian novelist James T. Farrell, whose Studs Lonigan novel *Judgment Day* Burke was then reviewing for publication in June; from poets William Carlos Williams, Horace Gregory, James Daly, and Marianne Moore; from the artist Peter Blume and the erstwhile Dada novelist Robert Coates; from the critics Joseph Wood Krutch (the *Nation*), Malcolm Cowley (the *New Republic*), Lewis Mumford, Isidor Schneider (*New Masses*), Henry Hazlitt (*New York Times*), John Erskine (Columbia University), and Austin Warren (Boston University). Burke also heard from his old *Dial* colleague Ellen Thayer, who complimented the music columns he was writing for the *Nation;* from the novelist-professor Edgar Johnson and the philosopher Sidney Hook; and from any number of others. On April 5 Burke was invited to speak to the Brooklyn College chapter of the National Students' League, and he was guest lecturing in Hook's philosophy course at New York University. On April 25 Burke presided over the annual Boar's Head Poetry Reading at Columbia University and added a few introductory remarks of his own, taken from a review he was writing of poems by Horace Gregory. Burke was considering an offer to join the advisory council for the new "Book Union," a scheme to initiate a book-of-the-month club dedicated to the propagation of leftist works (Hart to Burke, March 28, 1935; Klopfer to Burke, May 14), which would later cause him some grief. On Tuesday, April 23, Burke went to a party to celebrate the opening of a New York exhibit of paintings by his old Provincetown Players friend Charles Ellis, and he was making plans to have dinner with another longtime friend from the early 1920s, the writer-turned-mystic Jean Toomer. Reviews of *Permanence and Change* were beginning to appear—by Joseph Wood Krutch in the *Nation* (April 17), by Norman Guterman in *New Masses* (April 16), and by Henry Hazlitt in the *New York Times Book Review* (May 5).

And, as usual, Burke was also pursuing regular, ambitious, and varied writing projects. In addition to beginning work on what would become *Attitudes toward History*, the project he had proposed for his Guggenheim award, he was developing a number of publication possibilities. On April 19 he had lunch with the publisher Thomas Crowell and the editor-critic Gorham

Munson; the three discussed prospects for a book on contemporary American authors because Burke was beginning work on a long essay about recent
American poetry for the newly founded *Southern Review* and had some ideas
that he thought might be expanded into a book-length study. Burke's regular
music criticism column appeared as usual in the *Nation* in the last days of
March—this one the one praised by Ellen Thayer, on "The 'Problems' of the
Ballet"—as did his review of *Dostoevsky: A Life*, by Avrahm Yarmolinsky. Featured in the April 23 *New Republic* was Burke's lengthy overview article on the
novels of Erskine Caldwell ("Maker of Grotesques," six years later collected
in *The Philosophy of Literary Form*), in which Burke psychoanalyzed *Tobacco
Road* and *God's Little Acre* and treated Caldwell less as a proletarian realist
than as a Dadaist. Burke also finished his review of Gregory's book *Chorus for
Survival*, and mailed it off to *Poetry* on May 1; and he was working on the Farrell review and another on Edmund Wilson, which he was unable to complete
(Cowley to Burke, April 18, 1935). On April 17 Burke went to an editorial
board meeting for a leftist publication known as *Action*, intended for the Jewish working class, because he had been asked to join its editorial board (Rady
to Burke, April 11).

Amid this dizzying list of projects, like nearly every prominent New York
City leftist writer, Burke was also involved in the preparations for the first
American Writers' Congress, scheduled for the final days of the month. Having been involved in the initial drafting of the call for the congress (it first
appeared in *New Masses* on January 22 above the signature of Burke and sixty-
three others), Burke was invited to the planning meetings for the congress
(Calmer to Hicks, Hicks Papers, February 23, 1935). On March 23 he was
formally invited to give a paper (Johns to Burke), and he was summoned to
an April 12 meeting "of all who will read reports at the Writers' Congress"
(Johns to Burke, April 9, 1935). Beginning as early as April 6, he was helping Henry Hart to edit the papers of the congress into a published volume,
eventually entitled *American Writers' Congress* (Hart, "Introduction," 17; Calmer to Hicks, March 13 and 23, 1935). Burke also wrote an item for a "Discussion Issue" of *Partisan Review* that anticipated the congress and that
included pieces by Farrell, Hart, Gregory, and Schneider, though for some reason Burke's piece never appeared. (The article—see sidebar—promoted his
view that "a completely mature Marxian criticism will refuse to 'burn the
books,' either literally or metaphorically; that it vows the critic to survey the
whole scene.") On April 18 he attended a planning meeting for the congress
and began polishing the speech that he was preparing and that has since
become one of his best-known pieces, "Revolutionary Symbolism in America."

In short, in April 1935, Kenneth Burke was at one very high point in his
amazing productivity, influence, and prestige. And he was in the midst of various overlapping circles that gave his work intellectual encouragement, shape,

Call for an
American Writers' Congress

THE capitalist system crumbles so rapidly before our eyes that, whereas ten years ago scarcely more than a handful of writers were sufficiently far-sighted and courageous to take a stand for proletarian revolution, today hundreds of poets, novelists, dramatists, critics, short story writers and journalists recognize the necessity of personally helping to accelerate the destruction of capitalism and the establishment of a workers' government.

We are faced by two kinds of problems. First, the problems of effective political action. The dangers of war and Fascism are everywhere apparent; we all can see the steady march of the nations towards war and the transformation of sporadic violence into organized fascist terror.

The question is: how can we function most successfully against these twin menaces?

In the second place, there are the problems peculiar to us as writers, the problems of presenting in our work the fresh understanding of the American scene that has come from our enrollment in the revolutionary cause. A new renaissance is upon the world; for each writer there is the opportunity to proclaim both the new way of life and the revolutionary way to attain it. Indeed, in the historical perspective, it will be seen that only these two things matter. The revolutionary spirit is penetrating the ranks of the creative writers.

Many revolutionary writers live virtually in isolation, lacking opportunities to discuss vital problems with their fellows. Others are so absorbed in the revolutionary cause that they have few opportunities for thorough examination and analysis. Never have the writers of the nation come together for fundamental discussion.

We propose, therefore, that a Congress of American revolutionary writers be held in New York City on May 1, 1935; that to this Congress shall be invited all writers who have achieved some standing in their respective fields; who have clearly indicated their sympathy to the revolutionary cause; who do not need to be convinced of the decay of capitalism, of the inevitability of revolution. Subsequently, we will seek to influence and win to our side those writers not yet so convinced.

This Congress will be devoted to exposition of all phases of a writer's participation in the struggle against war, the preservation of civil liberties, and the destruction of fascist tendencies everywhere. It will develop the possibilities for wider distribution of revolutionary books and the improvement of the revolutionary press, as well as the relations between revolutionary writers and bourgeois publishers and editors. It will provide technical discussion of the literary applications of Marxist philosophy and of the relations between critic and creator. It will solidify our ranks.

We believe such a Congress should create the League of American Writers, affiliated with the International Union of Revolutionary Writers. In European countries, the I.U.R.W. is in the vanguard of literature and political action. In France, for example, led by such men as Henri Barbusse, Romain Rolland, Andre Malraux, Andre Gide and Louis Aragon, it has been in the forefront of the magnificent fight of the united militant working class against Fascism.

The program for the League of American Writers would be evolved at the Congress, basing itself on the following: fight against imperialist war and Fascism; defend the Soviet Union against capitalist aggression; for the development and strengthening of the revolutionary labor movement; against white chauvinism (against all forms of Negro discrimination or persecution) and against the persecution of minority groups and of the foreign-born; solidarity with colonial people in the struggles for freedom; against the influence of bourgeois ideas in American literature; against the imprisonment of revolutionary writers and artists, as well as other class-war prisoners throughout the world.

By its very nature our organization would not occupy the time and energy of its members in administrative tasks; instead, it will reveal, through collective discussion, the most effective ways in which writers, as writers, can function in the rapidly developing crisis.

The undersigned are among those who have thus far signed the call to the Congress.

Nelson Algren
Arnold B. Armstrong
Nathan Asch
Maxwell Bodenheim
Thomas Boyd
Earl Browder
Bob Brown
Fielding Burke
Kenneth Burke
Erskine Caldwell
Alan Calmer
Robert Cantwell
Lester Cohen
Jack Conroy
Malcolm Cowley
Edward Dahlberg
Theodore Dreiser
Guy Endore
James T. Farrell
Ben Field
Waldo Frank
Joseph Freeman
Michael Gold
Eugene Gordon
Horace Gregory
Henry Hart
Clarence Hathaway
Josephine Herbst
Granville Hicks
Langston Hughes
Orrick Johns
Arthur Kallet

Herbert Kline
Joshua Kunitz
John H. Lawson
Tillie Lerner
Meridel Le Sueur
Melvin Levy
Louis Lozowick
Grace Lumpkin
Edward Newhouse
Joseph North
Moissaye Olgin
Samuel Ornitz
Myra Page
Paul Peters
Alan Porter
Harold Preece
William Rollins
Paul Romaine
Isidor Schneider
Edwin Seaver
Claire Sifton
Paul Sifton
George Sklar
John L. Spivak
Lincoln Steffens
Philip Stevenson
Bernhard J. Stern
Genevieve Taggard
Alex. Trachtenberg
Nathaniel West
Ella Winter
Richard Wright

357

Call for an American writers' congress, 1935. From the *New Masses*, January 22, 1935

and sustenance: leftists planning the Writers' Congress and imagining the various roles that writers might play in the development of American Communism and socialism; literary and artistic "aesthetes" that Burke had worked with in the 1920s; and, outside New York, Agrarians and other southern intellectuals as well as acquaintances and intellectual forces associated with the University of Chicago.

Burke's Precongress Commentary for *Partisan Review*

In March 1935, in order to hype the event and sharpen the intellectual exchanges that were anticipated in the first American Writers' Congress, editors William Phillips (a.k.a. Wallace Phelps) and Philip Rahv produced a Writers' Congress Discussion Issue of the Partisan Review. In addition to carrying ads for the congress and an editorial touting it, the issue included three core essays—Edwin Seaver's "What Is a Proletarian Novel?"; Phillips and Rahv's own essay, "Criticism"; and Edwin Rolfe's essay "Poetry"—as well as three responses to each. Kenneth Burke was asked to write a response to Rahv and Phillips, and he produced the following essay when Rahv's letter of March 22 reminded him that his essay was due by April 3. But for some reason Burke's contribution was not included when the PR issue actually appeared. Was it because he sent his work in after the deadline? Was his argument too iconoclastic, anticipating the politics and reception of Burke's Writers' Congress speech? Or was there some other impediment? In any case, we reprint the essay here for the first time, not least because its appropriation of the terms "push away from" and "pull towards" will appear in his later work.

There is an obscurantist, anti-intellectualist trend observable among the Marxians (though wholly foreign to Marx himself)—and what I like particularly in this essay on Criticism by Phelps and Rahv is their freedom from this trend. Our culture needs strong stomachs, which can get food values out of almost anything. The cultural adjustments which the world is making are too manifold for absolute acceptance and rejection on strict political grounds. Culturally, we are fighting on *two* fronts. First, there is the problem of socializing ownership. But as all-important as this is, even if it were settled, we should still face a momentous issue, the adjustment of people to machinery in general. Socialization of ownership must be established before we can tackle the second problem with rationality. But though problem one must be solved before we can solve problem two, the solution of problem one does not automatically guaranty the solution of problem two.

The relation of the individual to his group, the idiosyncrasies that rise out of specialization, the great percentage of abstractness required for the management of an industrial plant under any conditions, the industrial instability of methods, with attendant shiftiness of population, the age-old difficulties of making people at home in artificial environments much different from the state of "mild savagery" for which they are neurologically endowed, the ways in which disease, death, obsession, and hypochondria remain vital psychological factors despite lack of official recognition—such elements demand that we be not over-prompt in deciding what literature is "right" and what is "wrong." For the complete artist will be seeking formulas which have a bearing upon all this great complexity, much of it extending beyond the immediate struggles to end capitalism.

To say that people are primarily involved in matters of adjustment is to say that they are forever solving problems. Incentives, in other words, are fundamentally negative. We adopt an expedient (either in political action or in the writing of a poem) as a way of *avoiding* something. Thus, as a critical instrument I should particularly recommend a distinction, in Bertrand Russell's *Analysis of Mind,* between the "push away from" and the "pull towards." Communism, Fascism, and the reassertion of *laissez-faire* all represent a "push away from" the same general set of dissatisfactory conditions. They differ in their selection of the particular "pull towards" by which the negative incentive gets its positive matching. Similarly, food is not initially an incentive to eating. Hunger is the incentive and food is found by experience to be the thing we should "move towards" in order to "move away from" hunger. It is probably because the negative thus precedes the positive that in history the nihilistic attitude precedes the revolutionary one. The infant quickly learns that food is the correct "solution" for its problem because its range of experiment is extremely limited. It can shout, squirm, and eat. It tries them all, and discovers that the third expedient is the most effective. Did it have a greater opportunity for experiment on this important subject, it might require years to find the accurate positive to match its negative, and in the course of its trial-and-error process might try courses as widely different as praying, reading success stories, and listening to Father Coughlin.

In time we come to associate the image of food so naturally with hunger that we reverse the process, thinking that the desired thing determines the desire. Or, as Russell puts it, by the common sense view, "what comes first in desire is something imagined with a specific feeling related to it, namely, that specific feeling which we call 'desiring' it. The discomfort associated with unsatisfied desire, and the actions which aim at satisfying desire, are, in this view, both of them effects of the desire." Over against this, he holds: "The primitive non-cognitive element in desire seems to be a push, not a pull, an impulsion away from the actual, rather than an attraction towards the ideal." The errors of naive criticism consist (a) in assuming that when you establish the validity of the "push away from" you automatically argue in behalf of the correct "pull towards," and (b) in assuming that the "push away from" can be defined once and for all in a few explicit economic terms.

I take it that a completely mature Marxian criticism will refuse to "burn the books," either literally or metaphorically; that it vows the critic to survey the whole scene, always with the desire to find how broad or deep the "push away from" that stimulates to art and action might be. It will know that a poet's myths are as "real" as anything else in the universe, since they are constructed to serve as psychological devices in the business of living. A sequence of symbols is as truly a tool as any tangible thing in metal, though its ends meet a more thorough-going test of utility, utility of a kind which Phelps and Rahv would probably prefer not to call utility at all. Until everything is settled, poets are engaged in throwing forth every imaginable kind of "pull towards" in the hopes that it will adequately match the "push away from" lying at the bottom of their "inspiration." Insofar as their medium of expression is a socializing one (even under capitalism we have the communal ownership of speech, but only because private preemption is very hard to manage), their symbols will tend to be socialized.

For any given work to completely fulfill in itself all revolutionary needs, I should think that it would have to embody not only the "push away from" but the "pull towards" which revolutionary politics advocates. In this sense I should seem to disagree with some of the latitude which Phelps and Rahv would permit. However, in a cooperative social texture where short comings can easily be remedied by conversation or by the reader's prior knowledge, such a demand becomes the purest pedantry. One may hear people who are absolutely convinced of Communism complain because a given play did not corroborate every last minutia of their beliefs. Yet why should it be required to, when they can themselves so easily supply the missing elements?

In sum: I believe that in judging contemporary art, we should think of socialized ownership as the next step, not the ultimate step, in the matching of "push away from" and "pull towards" that stimulates a writer's imagery. We should be right in demanding that the author's general attitudes fall in with our current purposes— but we should tend to doubt the sticking powers of a work that faithfully and completely served these purposes and none other. Men are politicians only in part— and their non-political ingredients must also figure in their artistic symbols.

Burke and the First American Writers' Congress

Almost everyone, it seems, has heard the story of that now-again-famous event, the first American Writers' Congress, held from April 26–28, 1935 (in proximity to May Day), at the Mecca Temple and the New School for Social Research in New York City. The congress was attended by 216 of the most politically engaged literary figures in America (such as Granville Hicks, Isidor Schneider, Corless Lamont, Waldo Frank, Horace Gregory, Richard Wright, Robert Cantwell, Genevieve Taggard, Josephine Herbst, Malcolm Cowley, Mike Gold, Tillie Lerner [Olson], James T. Farrell) and many others from Europe and Latin America (e.g., Louis Aragon, André Gide, André Malraux, Emilio Enricos, and Ford Madox Ford). Sixty-four of the writers were from twenty-four states other than New York. Thirty-six were women, and twenty-one were Negroes. Langston Hughes was unable to attend but sent a paper that was read at the opening session (*New Masses*, May 7, 1935, 7).

What exactly happened at that meeting? Frank Lentricchia has recounted the basic story of the congress:[2] One manifestation of that flowering of the arts, entertainment, and political thought known as the Cultural Front, the

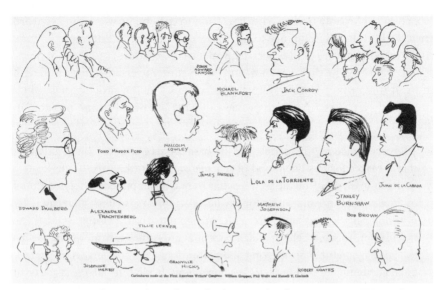

Caricatures of Kenneth Burke and others at the first American Writers'
Congress, April 1935. Burke is in the group of six (upper right). From *New
Masses*, May 7, 1935

meeting was called, Lentricchia says, to extend the reach of the John Reed
Clubs by helping radical writers to band together in the cause of the destruc-
tion of decaying capitalism and the establishment of a workers' government
(*Criticism*, 21).

One of the speakers at the meeting was Kenneth Burke. "Revolutionary
Symbolism in America," presented on the morning of Saturday, April 27,
examined in hardheaded, pragmatic terms the semiotics then associated with
the revolutionary movement in the United States, the "myths" and "symbols"
around which the Left was seeking to create "areas of allegiance"—particularly the terms *the masses* and *the worker*. "Considering the matter purely from
the standpoint of propaganda," taking into account the demagogic "procedures of men like Huey Long and Father Coughlin," and borrowing explicitly from the logic of "advertising men," "sales organizations," and Hollywood,
Burke urged the substitution of the term *the people* for *the masses* and *the workers* because it seemed to him closer to American values. A term such as *the
worker* tended to exclude the very elements that Communist propaganda
hoped to recruit, whereas for Burke "the symbol of 'the people'" contained
"connotations both of oppression and of unity": "In suggesting that 'the
people,' rather than 'the worker,' rate highest in our hierarchy of symbols, I
suppose I am suggesting fundamentally that one cannot extend the doctrine
of revolutionary thought among the lower middle class without using middle-class values." In keeping with the general tenor of the congress, Burke's

talk attended broadly to the writer's relation to society; by using the key word *propaganda* even with reference to highbrow or avant-garde "literature," Burke constructed literature (and especially proletarian literature) as a form of propaganda that was in dialogue not only with the converted leftists but with the still unconvinced. Moreover Burke was also in the process of arguing strenuously for a less-than-narrow view of what might constitute proletarian literature:

> The acceptance of "the people" as the basic symbol also has the great virtue that it makes for less likelihood of schematization on the part of our writers. So far at least, the proletarian novel has been oversimplified. . . . The symbol of "the people" should make for greater breadth in a writer's allegiance. By informing his work mainly from the standpoint of his positive symbol, he would come to see, I believe, that a poet does not sufficiently glorify his political cause by pictures of suffering and revolt. Rather, a poet makes his soundest contribution in this wise: He shows himself alive to all the aspects of contemporary effort and thought. . . . The complete propagandist, it seems to me, would take an interest in as many imaginative, aesthetic, and speculative fields as he can handle. . . . The writer's best contribution to the revolutionary cause is implicit. If he shows a keen interest in every manifestation of our cultural development, and at the same time gives a clear indication as to where his sympathies lie, this seems to me the most effective long-pull contribution to propaganda he can make. . . . I am suggesting that an approach based on the positive symbol of "the people," rather than upon the negative symbol of "the worker," makes more naturally for this kind of identification whereby one's political alignment is fused with broader cultural developments.

Lentricchia builds his discussion of Burke's speech in rather sensational fashion, in keeping with legends of Burke's marginalization: his version emphasizes how reaction to the talk was so hostile that Joseph Freeman, one of the conference organizers, was moved to shout, "We have a traitor among us!," and that someone else explicitly linked Burke's thought to Hitler's; and he repeats the famous account of how Burke reacted to those responses to his speech by having hallucinations of "excrement . . . dripping from [his] tongue" and of his name being shouted as "a kind of charge" against him, "a dirty word"—"Burke!" (Yagoda, 67).[3]

Why was the reaction to Burke's address so negative? Lentricchia offers his own explanations, based on his meticulous and powerful reading of the speech and his own formidable knowledge of leftist texts and contexts. He speculates, with reason, that Burke must have been vilified for a series of ideological deviances: To use a phrase such as "revolutionary symbolism" was "to confuse mere superstructural effect with the directive . . . motor principle of revolution." To add the phrase "in America" was to put on blinders of nationalism that tended to mask the historical inevitability of revolution. To offer "the people" in place of "the worker" was to employ naively the rhetorical methods of Hitler (who was appealing analogously to "the folk").[4] To critique Marxist dogma in any way was to part with the pure Marxism of the true believers there gathered and to promote a "deviant" Marxism attentive not to theory but to the practical implications of ideology within culture. To offer only a general critique of capitalist culture was to shift attention away from the proper focus of Marxist attention, economics. And to recommend that the Left might appropriate, even speak through, some of capitalism's key mechanisms of repression—to claim that the socialist cause in America could triumph if it could only infiltrate the powerful language of liberty so central to American ideology—was to recommend heresy. Burke, according to Lentricchia, "was asking his radical auditors to resist thinking of social doctrine as separable from its medium of dissemination," was "telling them that right social action, for a literary intellectual, was preeminently a literary act because it was grounded in . . . the rhetorical textures . . . and structures of discourse." Burke's intellectual listeners had trouble making an integral connection between radical social vision and literary discourse: they could not accept his insistence that the literary is always a form of social action, could not appreciate that the proletarian novel was an indulgence because, while it was applauded by the already convinced, it was also unread by the working class, alienating to the unconvinced, and hence risked no real dialogue with non-Marxists (*Criticism*, 22–28).[5] And so the congress, concludes Lentricchia, was hostile in its response to Burke: "We can see Burke's participation . . . [as] an intellectual theatre, with Burke enacting the father's role of historical materialist and his hostile respondents playing the parts of purists, sons anxious to purge . . . all fascist misappropriations of the master's word" (*Criticism*, 23). Within Lentricchia's theater Burke played the role of the righteous soul in a morality play, beset by an audience of mean-spirited and single-minded antagonists.

But the complete story of the speech, its claims and circumstances, and reactions to it is, to quote Burke himself from another context, "more complicated than that," particularly because Lentricchia was reading Burke—naturally enough—against his own project in *Criticism and Social Change* (wherein Burke is something of a stand-in for Gramsci) and was interpreting it under the influence of Burke's later selective recollection of its circumstances. But when the congress and Burke's role in it are measured against other contemporary and not-so-contemporary accounts of the event, including those in Burke's unpublished manuscripts and in other archives of the American Left, it is possible to flesh out the episode and the speech more fully and to understand Burke's position as less marginal though not less controversial.[6]

What exactly was the Writers' Congress all about? And what was Kenneth Burke's role in it? First, the congress was not in fact an effort to extend the influence and agenda of the John Reed Clubs, although it was indeed developed by many of the members of the John Reed Club of New York, founders of *Partisan Review*. John Reed Clubs had been established in the first years of the Great Depression in New York and other cities to develop a cadre of revolutionary artists who would have the power to promote a proletarian revolution. Loosely but intimately tied to the American Communist Party, founded by the editors of *New Masses* in the same month that the stock market crashed, modeled after Soviet cultural organizations such as the Proletarian Artists and Writers League, and sporting the motto "Art Is a Class Weapon," John Reed Clubs discovered and encouraged young artists and writers, exposed those young writers to industrial settings to add to the authenticity of their proletarian writing, organized and promoted art exhibits, supported little magazines, and held dances, concerts, and shows to enhance proletarian appreciation for art even as that art moved the masses toward revolution. In other words, as Malcolm Cowley succinctly summarized, John Reed Clubs were organized "to clarify the principles and purposes of revolutionary art and literature, to propagate them, and to practice them" (*Dream*, 135–36). There were JRC classes and lectures on poetry, fiction, Marxism, and many other topics. Kenneth Burke in fact participated in the John Reed Club of New York, spoke formally before the group on several occasions (Dupee to Burke, November 28, 1931; Rahv to Burke, December 26, 1933), and offered a course on "English Prose" under its auspices—his first formal effort at teaching.[7] In 1934 club membership expanded greatly both in New York and elsewhere. As the Depression hardened, novices were joining JRCs in droves, attracted by the prospect of publishing their work in *Partisan Review* or *New Masses* or the *Hammer* or *Left Front* or *Dynamo* or *Anvil* or *Blast* or *Red Spark* or one of the many other leftist magazines that were springing up, and active chapters were becoming well established in Boston, Philadelphia, Chicago, San Francisco, and a great many other cities—even seemingly unlikely ones such as Oklahoma City, Chapel Hill, and Davenport. By the end of 1934 there were at least 1,200 members in thirty clubs across America (Klehr, 350; Homberger, 129). In September 1934 representatives of the John Reed Clubs met in Chicago to assess their considerable progress and chart their future.

But even as the John Reed Clubs were prospering, they were also being put out of business as a result of larger world events. A November 1930 conference in Kharkov, Russia, an effort by the Communist Party to formulate a unified program for revolutionary culture, had already directed John Reed Clubs and similar groups to be somewhat more inclusive; delegates from the United States, including Mike Gold, Josephine Herbst, and

Matthew Josephson, were encouraged to reach out to Negroes and to workers (as opposed to just the intellectuals), to increase contacts with other
socialist groups, and to recruit new writers (Aaron, 223; Schwartz, 42–45;
Homberger, 136–38; Cowley, *Dream*, 136). Then Stalin and his allies, in the
face of the very real threat being posed by Hitler in 1934–35, moved toward
the formation of a United Front or People's Front or Popular Front (depending on the translation),[8] an effort at a still broader, more inclusive and powerful leftist membership capable of aligning with other socialist and workers'
groups ("Thirty Years Later," 498). It was Stalin's wish to counter the
strength of the increasingly intimidating Right by establishing international
ties—alliances with every kind of Western Left. Instead of emphasizing strict
orthodoxy, instead of persisting further in his progressively notorious policy
of exclusion and expulsion, Stalin now out of necessity was encouraging a policy of relative openness and toleration.[9] Hence, it was decided in September
1934, at the urging of Alexander Trachtenberg (the leader of the Communist
Party's American publishing house), that the John Reed Clubs were to be dis-
solved in 1934–35 and replaced by an organization that would come to be
known as the League of American Writers. The John Reed Club of New York
accordingly folded in February 1935 (Cooney, 80). As John Chamberlain
explained in *Saturday Review* on May 11, 1935, "since last autumn . . . the literary 'line' has changed; the threat of war and reaction has had its effect.
Exposed on the extreme Left, the communists, and the writers sympathetic
to communism, have seen the need of making common cause against the
forces of reaction with all who more or less agree with them" ("Literary
Left," 3).

   In fact the Writers' Congress was actually the occasion for forming the
League of American Writers (as the official call for the congress made
clear);[10] the LAW was formally instituted at the final session of the congress
as a broadly based "united front manoeuvre, with only fascists and 'out and
out' reactionaries excluded. Membership in it [did] not imply acceptance of
the Communist political position" (Chamberlain, "First," 4), though Communists and fellow travelers of course dominated. The LAW and the congress even officially muted their criticisms of FDR, as the proceedings make
clear: "I think the Communist Party had reached the point of being neutral
on the New Deal but dead against Fascism," noted Granville Hicks. "It was
on those grounds that the Congress stood" ("Thirty Years Later," 504). May
Day observances two days after the congress were literally to the tune of
the United Front, reported *New Masses* on April 30, calling attention to
"the excellent song 'United Front' by J. Fairbanks just published in the Workers' Song Book, Number 2" (30). The first American Writers' Congress,
then, was something of an olive branch (Wess, 57), an effort not so much at
John Reed Club–style solidarity but at reaching out to a broader range of

writers—particularly established writers, not the new finds of the John Reed Clubs—and recruiting them to a broadly proletarian cause. The invitation to speak to Burke was a part of that olive branch, given Burke's critical stance toward the party in his *Auscultation, Creation, and Revision* (which remained unpublished until much later), and in *Permanence and Change* itself, which recommended a "poetic" orientation as a gentle leaven to the hardcore Marxist interpretive slant. And so the content and thesis of Burke's speech were constrained by the occasion: in it Burke was simply suggesting strategies for reaching out that were in moderate keeping with the official theme of the congress and that anticipated the Comintern's official declaration of the People's Front strategy two months later. A historian of the Communist Party of the United States remembers the congress as an opportunity to show that "cultural activities should be less sectarian, and that sympathetic writers should not be confronted with either joining the party or perceived as a outcasts."[11] When, in January 1935, Granville Hicks drafted for *New Masses* and *Partisan Review* an "official call for an American Writers' Congress" that invited "all writers who have achieved some standing in their respective fields [and] who have clearly indicated their sympathy to the revolutionary cause" to gather for the event, Kenneth Burke was an appropriate signer.

But of course maintaining a consensus about this official mission for the congress was not easy, especially given the infighting characteristic of American intellectual leftists in New York. Not without reason did the April 1935 issue of *Vanity Fair* poke fun at members of the radical Left for being "proverbial for their marplot mischief" and "incapable of cooperating with any other radical at any time" (Franklin). Many of the writers at the congress in fact felt betrayed by the decision to dissolve the John Reed Clubs in favor of the League of American Writers, to reach for a broader constituency (Kutulas, *Long War*, 90). Cowley reported that radical writers from the bottom of the social spectrum, those originally recruited by the John Reed Clubs, were especially alienated by the Popular Front policy ("Thirty Years Later," 512–13), a perspective that is supported by Richard Wright's sardonic reminiscence in *The God That Failed*.[12] Incipient Trotskyists were already opposing the People's Front on the grounds that it obscured the class issue, and many sectarian younger and old guard leftists alike wanted to maintain the resolutely avant-garde, politically committed nature of the John Reed Clubs. When hardcore leftist critics of the party leadership (e.g., Max Eastman, Edmund Wilson, V. F. Calverton, Sidney Hook) were excluded from the list of those invited, their allies objected loudly: what was a United Front without them? Mike Gold, Joseph Freeman, and other hardliners explicitly and bitterly protested the moderation of the planned proceedings and argued strenuously in their talks that artists should portray without compromise or exception the lives of workers so that workers would be inspired to protest and revolt. "The proletarian novel has got to be . . . a novel that deals with the working class," noted Martin Russak. "In the working class we have a distinct kind of human being" (Hart, 165). Novelist Jack Conroy agreed. In an uncompromising paper delivered just after Burke's,[13] "The Worker as Writer," Conroy (lately the editor of *Anvil* and author of *The Disinherited*, one of the most acclaimed proletarian novels) countered the broad definition of proletarian writing favored in Burke's speech: "the works of too many contemporary writers are imbued with a false conception of working class life and what really matters to the worker. . . . As Michael Gold has pointed out [in his opening address at the congress], American proletarian fiction must of necessity deal with prophesy, with hopes, with the decay of society and the manifestations of such decay in the lives of people" (Hart, 84). The poet Robert Gessner agreed: "The proletarian poet has not been sufficiently revolutionary. . . . Workers have appeared at this Congress and asked us to come and see them as they actually are. . . . One thing that keeps revolutionary writers from doing so is the fear that their technique would be lost. Leave your technique on the fence. It will come trotting after you with its tail between its legs" (Hart, 177–78).

Some less established but firmly committed leftist writers attending the congress, like Wright, were put off by what they interpreted as respectable, almost polite proceedings. In any event, according to Cowley, "the effect on the younger writers was to alienate them from the Communist Party. Some of them became Trotskyites, some became independent radicals, and some sheared off from the movement entirely. There was a new war between literary generations that started at this first American Writers' Congress" ("Thirty Years," 513).[14] In short, then, the congress occurred at a moment of heated debate within the Left that evinced its broad strength and appeal— and yet that proved disastrous in creating the unity that it sought. Some (such as Gold, Conroy, and Freeman) wanted to retain ideological purity and intellectual heft even at the expense of practicality, while others less devoted to the Communist Party and more committed to a People's Front (including Burke, Edwin Seaver, and Matthew Josephson) were adopting a more outward-looking, pragmatic stance. The controversy in and about the John Reed Clubs and the American Writers' Congress, then, is a representative anecdote that stands for the larger discussion about revolutionary culture that was going on outside club and congress meeting rooms; it is a vehicle for marking some important positions and personalities in the conversation around Kenneth Burke. What becomes obvious from a study of this conversation is that not only were writers on the left anything but monolithic in their views in 1935— that is no doubt one reason why postmortem summaries of the event differ so much in their accounts—but that each point on the spectrum within the leftist position itself represented and recommended a complex and uneasy (and

FIRST AMERICAN WRITERS CONGRESS
April 26-28, 1935
New York

PRESIDING COMMITTEE

SOVIET UNION
Maxim Gorki
Fedor Gladkov
Mikhail Sholokov
Sergei Tretyakov
Sergei Dinamov

GERMANY
Heinrich Mann
Ludwig Renn
Theodor Plivier
Anna Seghers
Johannes R. Bechor

JAPAN
Kirohata Kurahara

CHINA
Fu Lan Chi
Li Sing
Hwa Han
Liu Fen-Shu

MEXICO
Jose Mancisidor
Juan de la Cabada

HAITI
Jacques Roumain

CUBA
Juan Marinello
Rojino Pedroso

ITALY
Giovanni Germanetto

SPAIN
Rafael Alberti

FRANCE
Henri Barbusse
Romain Rolland
Andre Gide
Andre Malraux
Louis Aragon

DENMARK
Martin Anderson-Nexo

P R O G R A M

April 26th

8:15 P.M. - Opening Session of the Congress
Mecca Temple, 131 West 55th Street, N.Y.C.

Chairman: Granville Hicks

Speakers:
Malcolm Cowley - Josephine Herbst - Hays Jones - Waldo Frank -
Friedrich Wolf - Earl Browder - M. Nadir - Langston Hughes -
Michael Gold

April 27th
Morning Session - 9 A.M. to 1 P.M.
Auditorium New School of Social Research
66 West 12th Street, N.Y.C. (near 6th Ave.)

Speakers:
Joseph Freeman - "Tradition of American Revolutionary
Literature
Kenneth Burke - Revolutionary Symbolism in America

Harry F. Ward - The Writer's Part in the Struggle Against War

Jack Conroy - The Worker as Writer

(over)

-2-

Edwin Seaver - The Proletarian Novel

Isidor Schneider - Proletarian Poetry

Discussion

April 27th
Afternoon Session - 2 to 5:30 P.M.
New School

Edward Dahlberg - Fascism and the Writer

Eugene Gordon - Social and Political Problems of the Negro Writer

John Howard Lawson - Technique and the Drama

Michael Blankfort and Nathaniel Buchwald - Social Trends in the Modern Drama

Josephine Herbst - Industrial and Agrarian Struggles and the Novel

Corliss Lamont - The Writer and the Soviet Union

Discussion

April 27th - 8 P.M. - Sessions of Commission of the Novel, Poetry and the Drama.
Other commissions will be arranged by request. Meeting places will be announced.

April 28th - Morning Session 9 A.M. to 1 P.M.
New School

Meridel Le Sueur - Proletarian Literature in the Middle West

James T. Farrell - The Short Story

Clarence Hathaway - The Revolutionary Press and the Writer

Mathew Josephson - The Role of the Writer in the Soviet Union

Joshua Kunitz - Literary Fellow Travellers

Eugene Clay - The Negro in Recent American Literature

Joseph North - Reportage

Discussion

-3-

April 28th
Afternoon Session - 2 P.M. to 5:30 P.M.
New School

M. J. Olgin - The Soviet Writers Congress
Malcolm Cowley - What the Revolutionary Movement Can Give the Writer
Granville Hicks - Development of Marxist Criticism
Albert Halt - The Working Class Theatre
Henry Hart - Contemporary Publishing and the Revolutionary Writer
Alexander Trachtenberg - Publishing for Workers

Discussion

April 28th
Evening Session - 7 to 9 P.M.
John Reed Club - 430 Sixth Avenue, 2nd Fl.

Speaker:
Orrick Johns - Creation of the League of American Writers
Report on organization and constitution

Presiding Committee Report on nomination as for National and Executive Committee for the League

Discussion

E L E C T I O N S

9 P.M. - RECEPTION

Program of the first American Writers' Congress. From the Joseph Freeman Collection, Hoover Institution Archives, Stanford University often unstable) negotiation between politics and aesthetics. Response to Burke's speech, therefore, was bound to be conflicted no matter what he said. And so resistance he got.

That resistance was intensified by Burke's history with his colleagues who were gathered at the congress. Burke's uneasy affiliation with the Left in the years before 1935 is easy enough to document. It is apparent as early as *Counter-Statement*, a 1931 book that is deeply conflicted over the claims of the aesthetic versus the claims of the social in art. It is also apparent in the response to *Counter-Statement:* late in 1931, for example, Granville Hicks (speaking for many others) reviewed *Counter-Statement* as the work of an aesthete more interested in technique than in social criticism, and Burke and Hicks traded counterblasts on the issue of Burke's social relevance throughout 1932.[15] It is apparent in Burke's 1932 novel, *Towards a Better Life*—as stylized, artistically experimental, and aestheticized a piece of fiction as anyone could find, and something of an antithesis to the proletarian novel according to just about everyone except Burke.[16] *Auscultation, Creation, and Revision* (also 1932) is another record of Burke's uneasy negotiation between the political Left and the aesthetic Right. Documents in Burke's personal archives make clear that in August 1932 he was asked to sign a petition supporting the nomination of William Z. Foster and James W. Ford, the Communist candidates for president and vice president[17]—but that he decided not to do so even though the most famous leftist writers were already aboard (e.g., Sherwood Anderson, John Dos Passos, Theodore Dreiser, Langston Hughes, Waldo Frank, Edmund Wilson, Countee Cullen, and Erskine Caldwell) and even though some of his best literary friends also signed and urged him to join them (e.g., Malcolm Cowley, Matthew Josephson, Slater Brown). Ever an independent thinker, ever capable of containing contraries, Burke could not help critiquing Marx almost as much as he was criticizing capitalist formulations, and his *Permanence and Change* (published right before the congress), in its appropriation of Thorstein Veblen and its support for the same "poetic orientation" that is summoned in its own way in "Revolutionary Symbolism in America," shows his independence from doctrinaire Marxism. The first editions of *Permanence and Change* and *Attitudes toward History* do indeed pitch communism, as Norman Guterman proclaimed in his April 16 review of *Permanence and Change* ("he advocates the practical action of Communism in the most noble and eloquent language"), but more at the level of culture than economics, and never uncritically. Finally Burke's own early report of the first American Writers' Congress in the *Nation* is notable (as Robert Wess has also indicated) for showing the subtle contours of Burke's relationship with communism.[18]

Burke's position at the Writers' Congress, then, was actually much more moderate than Lentricchia implies, and it was probably this moderation in

Counter-Statement, Towards a Better Life, Auscultation, and *Permanence and Change* that made some people angry with Burke, not any especially radical particulars of "Revolutionary Symbolism in Ameri̇ " In pleading for a broader definition of what might count as proletarian literature and as propaganda, in siding with Seaver and Schneider on that Saturday morning stage, Burke was indeed independent and moderate in a way that Freeman, Conroy, Gessner, and some others could not appreciate; John Chamberlain therefore blamed Burke for "pluralism" and "revolutionary free-willism" ("Literary Left," 17). Speaking pointedly against "a certain anti-intellectualist, semi-obscurantist trend among some in the strictly proletarian school," admitting his membership in his own class, "the petty bourgeoisie" (as opposed to the working class), and attempting to heal the breach between mental and physical labor so fundamental to Marxism, Burke argued that writers who "focus all their imaginative range within this orbit [of] . . . strikes, lockouts, unemployment, unsavory working conditions, organized resistance to the police, etc., . . . must produce an oversimplified and impoverished art, which would defeat its own purposes, failing even as propaganda since it did not invigorate audiences. . . . One cannot extend the doctrine of revolutionary thought among the lower middle class without using middle-class values." In constructively criticizing the rhetorical tactics of the Communists, Burke was actually in very close keeping with the policies of the Popular Front: "I believe the symbol of 'the people' makes more naturally for *propaganda by inclusion* than does the strictly proletarian symbol [of the worker], . . . which makes naturally for a *propaganda by exclusion,* a tendency to eliminate from one's work all that does not deal specifically with the realities of the workers' oppression—and which, by my thesis, cannot for this reason engage even the full allegiance of the workers themselves." And he was beginning to develop this point about inclusion and exclusion into his well-known, more general promotion of *identification* as a "master term" of rhetoric: significantly the term *identification* appears prominently in the speech, toward the end of the long passage quoted early in this chapter.

In arguing thus, Burke was clearly also identifying himself with the sentiments of several other speakers at the conference. John Dos Passos, for example, like Burke was resisting the dualistic thinking that considered all bourgeois writing as falsification and all expressions of working-class life as truth. His paper, "The Writer as Technician," not only defended aesthetic achievement and artistic originality, but also resoundingly defended artistic individuality and freedom: "A writer must never, no matter how much he is carried away by even the noblest political partisanship in the fight for social justice, allow himself to forget that his real political aim . . . is liberty. . . . A writer can be a propagandist in the most limited sense of the word, or use his abilities for partisan invective or personal vituperation, but the living material out of which his work is built must be what used to be called the humanities: the need for clean truth and sharply whittled exactitudes."[19] Waldo Frank's talk bore out his belief that socialism was primarily a cultural or "human" matter and only secondarily an economic one. While conceding resolutely that "the revolutionary worker [today] must not be a 'fellow traveler' [but one whose] art must be coordinate with, not subordinate to, the political-economic aspects of the re-creation of mankind," Frank nevertheless also emphasized that "the term 'proletarian' . . . should be a qualitative, not quantitative, term. A story of middle-class or intellectual life, or even of mythological figures, if it is alight with revolutionary vision, is more effective proletarian art . . . than a shelf-full of dull novels about stereotypical workers" (Hart, 71–76). The young editors of the new *Partisan Review*, Philip Rahv and William Phillips, coauthored a presentation that warned against overly sectarian applications of Marxist theories to writing. Matthew Josephson's report on the "Role of the Writer in the Soviet Union," a role that he had witnessed firsthand a year before, touched only tangentially on the situation of the American writer, but in a resolute presentation just before the congress he expressed frank disapproval of narrow orthodoxy in criticism: "I believe that the political duties of writers can be . . . broad enough to embrace people of various persuasions."[20] Earl Browder's speech at the general session opening the congress offered the same message of conciliation to the assembled writers: "The great majority of this Congress, being unaffiliated to the Communist Party, are interested in what it has to say because all recognize the necessity of establishing cooperative working relations, a united front. . . . We don't want to take good writers and make bad strike leaders out of them," he summarized (Hart, 68). Despite the reservations of hardcore CPUSA members, the congress was far from revolutionary; it was out to make friends—and Burke's remarks were in keeping with that goal, especially in recommending the appropriation, even speaking through, some of capitalism's key mechanisms of repression and mythmaking: Hollywood and Madison Avenue.

Actually the response to Burke's speech was very probably not all that hostile. The effects of the criticism that Burke did receive should not be understated, for it was a palpable hit that he felt for years. But Burke in his retrospective account in 1965 ("Thirty Years Later") acknowledged that his audience actually reacted warmly to his speech, with applause and encouragement. (Characteristically his talk exceeded the time limit prescribed, but he was permitted to finish by popular acclaim.) He was not drummed out of the community, as Sidney Hook had been two years earlier for other remarks critical of the Communist Party. Indeed Burke was one of seventeen people elected to the league's executive committee two days after his speech,[21] and Burke himself in his commentary in "Thirty Years Later" describes his election to the executive committee as a reconciliation of sorts with Hicks and others with whom he had been feuding. Josephson, Cowley, Gregory, James T. Farrell, and Clinton Simpson (of *Anvil* magazine) responded favorably to Burke's words at the time (as is visible in their letters) and in succeeding years;[22] and others emphasize the tolerance for critical talk at the congress.[23] Burke's own contemporary summary of the congress in the May 1935 *Nation* was anything but the record of an angry alien: the article is most respectful of the Communists who organized the meeting ("divergencies merged into unity"), it dismisses criticisms of his talk in good-humored, mock-heroic terms ("[Burke's speech] called down on him the wrath of the party's most demonic orators"), and it interprets the congress as generally friendly to his own general intellectual agenda ("every one of [the delegates] exemplif[ied] the philosophic mind"). And Burke's later, 1965 account and the one Lentricchia depended on (Yagoda) were nourished by his own tendency, inherited from his membership in modernist artistic circles, to understand himself as part of the marginalized literary avant-garde as well as by events that took place after the congress, including ideological tussles over Stalinism in the late 1930s, Burke's comparative withdrawal from politics in the 1940s and 1950s, and the emergence of McCarthyism. Burke was clearly bruised by the response he got, but it should be noted that the bruising came not directly after his speech but during a shorter and more general question-and-answer response period later in the congress; that the burly "Old Bolshevik" Joseph Freeman brushed off the incident as no big deal later in the congress and shook hands with Burke with a smile ("'Well, sorry old man' —and it was over," reported Burke in "Thirty Years Later" [508]); that other responses during the question-and-answer period were more conciliatory, especially in their published form (including Gold's);[24] and that the bruising was in part Burke's overly personal response to an overly charged situation brought about not by his speech but by the situation of radicals and semi-radicals at the meeting. In any case Joseph Freeman probably did not yell "We have a traitor amongst us!" but "We have a snob among us" (Cowley, *Dream*, 278; "Thirty Years Later," 506).[25] And other witnesses of the congress "thought that the incident that I had taken so seriously was funny [and] laughed" (507).[26]

Two points about Burke's experience at the first American Writers' Congress are worth highlighting here and become a refrain in what follows. First, most notable in Burke's "Revolutionary Symbolism in America" is his emphasis on the tactics of a Popular Front rhetoric, his understanding of literature as both persuasion and source of identification. Burke's own *Towards a Better Life* is something of an avant-garde book, an aestheticized effort to insulate the literary from the social, and a surprising number of the writers at the congress (not to mention the more conservative writers who did not attend), steeped in one version of modernist literary ideology, persisted as well in understanding literature as apart from persuasion. The explicit attention to the tactics of rhetoric and the shift in focus to identification in this speech is noteworthy therefore, especially in the light of Burke's later rhetorical, literary, and critical projects. Burke's assumption in his speech that literature was a species of rhetoric, that "the imaginative writer seeks to propagandize his cause," though in a way different from the lawyer or the ad writer, was probably yet another reason why some people resisted his message.

Second, the first Writers' Congress episode undermines the legend of Burke's marginalization at the congress, a legend that contributes to a popular misconception of him. Kenneth Burke is often depicted as some sort of inspired genius set apart from society, the brilliant but eccentric hermit of remote Andover farm who dreamed up his insights largely removed from other people. The evidence indicates a very different Burke, a highly social Burke who conceived his ideas while in conversation and congress with any number of interesting intellectual circles. The 1935 Writers' Congress incident, as Burke himself taught, had a history and a setting. It was not an isolated event but was part of the seamless stream of interconnected events called culture. And it is as part of culture that the writings of Kenneth Burke should be understood.

Burke among the "Aesthetes"

That Burke and his work were implicated in a set of conflicted, cooperating, and overlapping communities is apparent as well from an account of his other associations during April 1935. For by no means were all the prominent writers and intellectuals in Burke's circles involved in the Writers' Congress.

Why they were not involved is suggested by a cartoon published in the April 6 issue of the *New Yorker*, even as the congress was meeting. The cartoon depicts an artist who is working at his easel in his studio loft, presumably in New York. Surrounded by monumental leftist paintings prepared in the stereotypical proletarian mode that dwarf him on all sides, he is engaged in something subversive: dressed in the conventional garb of the bohemian artist who prefers beauty to politics, art to life, he has been working surreptitiously on a still-life study of fruit on a plate. So engrossed has he been in his own private creative process and in his art-for-art's-sake subject that he is obviously surprised when a looming authority figure suddenly barks to him from behind, "What's the meaning of this, Leo? Are you turning into a dirty bourgeois?" The cartoon seems to be poking fun directly at the Writers' Congress that was going on in New York as it appeared. In a comic way it implies that artists were being pressured directly or indirectly to heel to an uncompromising leftist artistic program against their better artistic impulses; artists were being forced into abandoning the claims of art-for-pure-art that had dominated the New York artistic scene only a few years before. Especially

"What's the meaning of this, Leo? Are you turning into a dirty bourgeois?"

New Yorker cartoon by Alain, April 6, 1935. © The New Yorker Collection 1935 Alain from cartoonbank.com. All rights reserved

under the signature of "Alain,"[27] the cartoon clearly sides with the hectored bohemian aesthete and lampoons the oh-so-serious imperative offered by the speaker—that art should inevitably and unconditionally serve proletarian, civic ends.

The artist in the cartoon stands in easily for any number of artists and writers who were operating in the shadow of the intellectual Left in April 1935, people who were skeptical of, distant from, or even relatively untouched by the leftist program for art in the 1930s—and who nevertheless remained on productive personal and intellectual terms with Kenneth Burke. Among the host of letters Burke received in the first days of April congratulating him for his Guggenheim award, several were from people who did not attend the first American Writers' Congress because they were politically and artistically at a remove from the People's Front. These included his close associates from his days at the *Dial* in the 1920s, Marianne Moore and J. Sibley Watson. Other friends from his old Greenwich Village Bohemia— the writer-turned-mystic Jean Toomer, the editor Gorham Munson (who had cooperated with Burke during the early 1920s in the production of the avant-garde magazine *Secession*), and Katherine Anne Porter (whose story "The Grave" appeared in *Virginia Quarterly Review* in April 1935)—also were a part of Burke's general intellectual circles. Those writers and patrons of art were certainly aware of social and intellectual developments in the early and middle 1930s, and their writing even took something of a political turn in those years. But they nevertheless retained a commitment to art that reached above politics. They favored not so much the *New Republic* or *New Masses* or *Partisan Review* as *Poetry*, *Pagany*, and *transition*. (The last explicitly espoused formalist and aesthetic artistic autonomy in a manifesto, "The Revolution of the Word," that was published in 1929 and that stood for its apolitical artistic stance well into the 1930s.) And many of them admired the piece of music criticism Burke published that month (a commentary on a performance of the American Ballet Company) more than they did his *Permanence and Change*. The friendly letters Burke traded with Toomer in April and May 1935 never even mentioned the Writers' Congress—and there were many others like them.

Aestheticism faded with the Depression, but it definitely did not die. Edwin Arlington Robinson's death on April 5, 1935, encouraged sympathetic accounts of his artistic achievements, and in Merion, Pennsylvania, near Philadelphia, Dr. Albert Barnes continued to acquire more Renoirs, bringing his total to 177; a year earlier *Hound and Horn* had reported on the recent completion of Barnes's museum near Philadelphia and on the installation there of Matisse's latest work, the fresco *La Danse*, under the supervision of the artist himself. While Edmund Wilson had repudiated pure aestheticism by pronouncing it dead in his 1931 book *Axel's Castle*, by touring the nation to cover the Depression as a journalist, and by urging writers to embrace the Left, he nevertheless gave aid and comfort to confirmed aesthetes in *Axel's Castle* by canonizing Eliot, Joyce, Proust, Pound, and Valery as committed proponents of the aesthetic life. *Vanity Fair* in April 1935 was printing Edward Steichen's photos of the American ballet (a kind of companion to Burke's review of the American Ballet Company) and promoting the view that art could be an escape from life, a retreat that might "brighten the prospect of living in these troubled times," as the *Vanity Fair* editorial writer put it (111). The *Vanity Fair* point of view implicitly gave credibility to the apolitical, escapist film and art of the period—e.g., Shirley Temple was starring in *The Little Colonel* with Bill "Bojangles" Robinson in April 1935, Fred Astaire and Ginger Rogers were just finishing *Top Hat*, and *The New Adventures of Tarzan* would be released a few months later—and it encouraged devotees of aestheticism to remain more or less true to the religion of art.

"More or less" fairly describes the vestiges of aestheticism as they persisted in the work of 1930s artists who resisted the call to the Writers' Congress.

While strict 1890s- and 1920s-style aestheticism was generally (though not completely) repudiated and discarded (so that even Dr. Barnes was being drawn to John Dewey's contention that the arts can play a pivotal role in the formation of a public), its assumptions often endured. For example William Carlos Williams's iconoclastic connection to the proletarian literary movement was in many ways akin to Burke's. Like so many of their contemporaries, both of them were wrestling with what it meant to be "modern" as artist or critic. On the one hand, Williams's experimental, frequently obscure lyric verse had taken a distinct social turn by 1935. As early as 1931 he was telling Burke (his friend and correspondent since 1921) about the "Political Poem" he had recently written (Williams to Burke, October 19, 1931); and a number of his subsequent lyrics were really one kind of "Proletarian Portrait" (a title of one of them) or another describing individuals caught in difficult social and economic circumstances. Moreover Williams wrote less poetry and more prose during the period, in keeping with the more social cast of his artistic interests. In March 1932 he published *The Knife of the Times and Other Stories*, a collection of fiction that documented to some degree working-class and ethnic life in New Jersey, and a year later he claimed that a story he had written for *Blast—Proletarian Short Stories* (not to be confused with Wyndham Lewis's *Blast* of two decades before) was "unorthodox communism" (Williams to Burke, December 6, 1933). He considered devoting to communism one of the issues of his reconstituted *Contact* (which he coedited with Nathanael West in 1932),[28] and his valedictory "Comment" in the magazine in October 1932 defended the link between poetry and communism: "Never, it may be said, has there ever been great poetry that was not born out of communist intelligence" (131; quoted in Denning, 212–13). In 1935 Williams brought out *An Early Martyr and Other Poems*, a collection of verse that is sometimes sensitive to the national economic predicament. The title poem memorializes John Coffee, who had been sent to a hospital for the criminally insane without a trial after stealing openly on behalf of the poor in an act of civil disobedience (Tashjian, 116), and other poems call attention to "The Dead Baby" or satirically claim that "To Be Hungry Is to Be Great." Williams placed some of his poems and other publications in *New Masses, Anvil*, the *New Republic, Direction*, and *Partisan Review;* he may even have attended a session or two of the Writers' Congress;[29] he joined the League of American Writers (Folsom, 329); and, as Brian Bremen has emphasized (6–8), Dr. Williams was always considered by Burke as a true "medicine man" whose works were fundamentally involved with invigorating American politics, history, and culture and whose art was out to cure.[30]

But on the other hand, Williams's prose and poetry also served as a form of private therapy, as a source of aesthetic escape and enjoyment. The stories and portraits in *The Knife of the Times* were mostly "in the same vein of his imagistic poetry"[31] in that characters were described physically, forcefully, and without comment or ornament; the panorama of characters introduced was drawn from every nook and cranny of lower- and middle-class life (prostitutes, a banjo-playing playboy, "The Colored Girls of Passenack," "Old Doc Rivers"), but they were measured as much or more by biological and instinctual characteristics as by social forces. And Williams's poems usually continued to measure off his Objectivist contentions (i.e., that art was an autonomous object, to be taken objectively more than rhetorically, impersonally more than emotionally, as, for instance, in "The Yachts" or "The Locust Tree in Flower," both from 1935).[32] Objectivism was attacked from the Left, with reason, for its detachment and for being more attentive to technique than message, but Williams's 1930s poems continued to illustrate Objectivist values. The edition of his *Collected Poems* that he published in 1934, with an introduction by Wallace Stevens (who described Williams as a stylistic virtuoso and a romantic "who still dwells in an ivory tower"), paid homage to the imagist lyric triumphs that Williams had offered in the years before the Depression—"The Attic Which Is Desire," "This Is Just to Say," "At the Faucet of June," "The Red Wheelbarrow," and so forth.

A longtime literary nationalist, Williams was finally as suspicious of Marx as he was of other Europeans: "The American tradition is completely opposed to Marxism," he would write in a 1936 *Partisan Review* symposium on Marx in America. "Marxism is a static philosophy of a hundred years ago which has not kept up—as the democratic spirit has—with the stresses of an actual trial" (qtd. in Denning, 213). In private Williams complained to Burke that only confirmed "communist shits" were getting the publications and prizes at the time of the Writers' Congress (Williams to Burke, May 7, 1935): "Hell, we act like a bunch of lost sheep. . . . Are we so impotent that we can't do anything but yell for a Lenin or else go pantsless. . . . I wish I knew how to get us together on even the most purely selfish front—barring theory or god damned economics." Goddamned economics (and politics), indeed: *An Early Martyr and Other Poems* was brought out in a lavish, elaborate, and expensive limited edition (by Alcestis Press, the publisher of Wallace Stevens's *Ideas of Order*, also in 1935)—hardly the medium of the proletarian poet.[33] Throughout the 1930s Williams remained attentive to surrealism and the methods of surrealism (e.g., automatic writing) even though surrealism was usually focused far more intently on the private than the public—and was regularly lampooned as such in *New Masses*. Above all Williams thought of himself as an artist who finally worked above and outside politics: "How can I be a Communist, being what I am," he asked while sending in a subscription to *New Masses*. "Poetry is the thing which has the hardest hold on my daily experiences. I cannot, without an impossible wrench of my understanding, turn it into a force directed toward one end, Vote the Communist Ticket, or work for world revolution" (Williams, "Letter"; quoted in Tashjian, 116). Thus in a lengthy effort to articulate his editorial position for *Blast* in 1933, Williams emphasized the primacy of artists and individuals over and above collective society. Communism and the present economic crisis, he claimed, were challenging the artist not to write "communistically" but to "retreat to the essentials" represented by poetry and the aesthetic life (Tashjian, 118). When he came to write his *Autobiography* in 1948, Williams would devote about 1 percent of its pages to the 1930s.

Marianne Moore, like Williams (the two corresponded regularly during the 1930s and sometimes gave readings together), published a collection of poems in the spring of 1935; indeed her *Selected Poems* was another notable product of that amazing April. Several of the nine new poems included in the book (all the others were written and published before 1924) indicate that Moore, like Williams, was touched by the social and economic crisis of the day. "Faced . . . with the growing weight of American misery," Robin Schulze notes, Moore began to wonder "if poetry could ever be more than selfish and opulent detachment—an avoidance of moral obligation to the world" (*Web*, 66). "The Jerboa," "Plumet Basilisk," "The Frigate Pelican," and "The Buffalo," for instance—four of Moore's animal poems—are all charged by an engagement with social concerns, particularly with the issue of America's relation to other cultures. "The Jerboa," for example, is a thinly disguised commentary on contemporary power politics: Moore defends the African/Ethiopian jerboa against the abuse of power presented by Rome/Mussolini and testifies on behalf of an art of social responsibility (as opposed to Roman irresponsibility and imperialism).

Nevertheless in general Moore was a far less politically engaged writer than Williams in April 1935, not to mention the writers gathered for the Writers' Congress. "Plumet Basilisk" may gently critique "the isolationist aesthetic that Moore found problematic" in Wallace Stevens, but the poem also pardons that aesthetic as well: the basilisk, a lizard who figures a poetic escape artist, seeks protection above all; neither fish nor mammal, it inhabits the middle world between reality and imagination. As Schulze puts it, the poem "justifies Moore's apparent evasions—her poems about persimmons or basilisks in a time of economic collapse" (83). Similarly "The Frigate Pelican" demonstrates that Moore, like the *New Yorker* cartoonist, ultimately endorsed poetic independence over political engagement in politics. The poem endorses the pelican's ability to maintain a free-flying consciousness that is apart from the world and its social imperatives. Moore's *Selected Poems* was released under the sponsorship of T. S. Eliot, whose Tory notions and repudiation of Marxist and Communist orthodoxies were giving aid and comfort to conservative writers.[34] Eliot's introduction to *Selected Poems* unfortunately but influentially cast her as the precise, meticulous, technically "intricate," emotionally "frigid" poet of descriptive "minutiae" and "minor subjects" (x–xi), and her reviewers reinforced the perception that Moore was primarily interested in the private.[35] And some of Moore's writings gave them reason to do so. Asked by *New Verse* in October 1934 whether she intended her poetry "to be useful to yourself or others," she answered tersely and emphatically, "Myself" (Schulze, 128). Having moved from Greenwich Village to Brooklyn, she committed herself to magazines such as Eliot's *Criterion* (which carried "The Frigate Pelican" and a Moore review of Pound's *XXX Cantos* in 1934), *Hound and Horn* (which published "The Jerboa" and "Plumet Basilisk"), and especially *Poetry*, which in July 1934 offered Harriet Monroe's staunch, strident, and controversial defense of aesthetic values over political art, "Art and Propaganda," and which in the early 1930s would carry "The Buffalo" and "Nine Nectarines" as well as Moore reviews of Pound, Eliot, and Yeats. When *Selected Poems* appeared that April, Moore began work on another review of Eliot that would appear in the next year and began writing about Wallace Stevens's *Ideas of Order* for *Criterion*. Her speculations on the relation of the artist to society would take final and conservative shape in her 1936 poem "The Pangolin," a fable about an armored but graceful beast (not at all unlike a person, or poet), nocturnal, isolated, independent, and stealthy, who protectively "draws away from danger unpugnaciously."

And so a response by Moore to a letter from Kenneth Burke late in 1932 epitomizes her thinking. Burke had urged her in a long letter to favor Roosevelt over Hoover (for whom Moore had written a poem) and to consider giving her political and artistic allegiance to socialism because "it attempts to consider our contemporary problems organically rather than by considering factors in isolation from one another, [i.e.,] attempts to offer remedies on the basis of a complete 'circular' explanation rather than by confining itself to specific problems wrenched from their economic contexts" (Burke to Moore, November 28, 1932; Burke enclosed a couple of Marxist pamphlets to help his cause). Moore answered by emphasizing her aesthetic priorities and by keeping her distance from the Left: "I confess to . . . writing a poem on a persimmon let us say instead of joining with our capitalist friends in handing out the local dole; and I should hate to see you interrupt your remarkable writing, for it is that, to make speeches for Norman Thomas . . . , but until we get someone who is a better target than Norman Thomas, I am subterranean" politically (Moore to Burke, November 30, 1932).

Moore, in fact, fairly stands in for a whole school of writers who were remaining committed to relative aesthetic autonomy during the 1930s—for Stevens, Katherine Anne Porter, and any number of others whose aestheticism continued to engage Burke and other writers even in the midst of the Depression. Those writers acknowledged social concerns in their 1930s art and criticism, often more than has been appreciated. But they nonetheless remained steadfast in their appreciation of aesthetic values. Stuart Davis, for example, stoutly defended abstract painting in the *New York Times* Sunday edition of April 7, 1935, as against Thomas Hart Benton's highly political "realistic nationalism." (In the first two weeks of April 1935 at New York's Ferargil Gallery Benton was exhibiting explicitly social and political paintings—the most controversial of which was entitled "Lynching.")[36] Chapter 2 in particular details Burke's engagement with this group of artists and writers as he composed *Auscultation, Creation, and Revision* in 1932 and sought to reconstruct modernism for the Depression era. The chapter dramatizes Matei Calinescu's observation that the artistic avant-garde in the twentieth century was persistently defined by the contending strains of social activism and aesthetic withdrawal: artists could try to lead society as forerunners (as those at the Writers' Congress assumed), or they could retreat into a palace of art. And some of our subsequent chapters, particularly chapter 5, which considers *The Philosophy of Literary Form*, include additional evidence of how Burke's 1930s work continued to address those whose primary interests were aesthetic.

The Agrarians and the Southern Review

Katherine Anne Porter is important to the present discussion of Kenneth Burke for several reasons. First, Porter knew Burke personally; second, she deserves to be placed in the same uneasily aesthetic camp as Moore and Williams, at least in the 1930s; and third, she points to another important group of artist-intellectuals with whom Burke was engaged during the Depression, the southerners who in April 1935 were promulgating Agrarianism and putting together the first issue of the *Southern Review*. Porter and Burke had become acquainted in the mid-to-late 1920s when she joined the edges of his circles, probably via her relationships with Dorothy Day (Burke's common-law sister-in-law) and Matthew Josephson (Burke's longtime friend, who had a brief love affair with Porter and who had encouraged her writing). Burke then wrote letters on her behalf when Porter was applying for the Guggenheim grant that would take her from Mexico to Germany in 1931, and Porter exchanged personal letters with Burke and Cowley while she was in both places. Burke brokered Porter's poem "Bouquet for October" through Williams into *Pagany* for her (Porter to Burke, September 27, 1931; Burke to Williams, October 15, 1931). Porter's first stories were quite inflected by the leftist politics she had encountered soon after arriving in Greenwich Village in 1919 (three of her earliest friends were Day, Peggy Cowley, and Genevieve Taggard). She contributed to *New Masses*, was arrested (with Mike Gold and John Dos Passos) for protesting in Boston the execution of Sacco and Vanzetti in 1927, and was a member of the League of American Writers (Folsom, 312), if not a participant in its congresses. As her

Flowering Judas and Other Stories (1930; republished with four additional stories in 1935) reveals, Porter in New York also fell in with intellectuals committed to the revolutionary cause in Mexico, including the pianist Tata Nacho and artist Adolpho Best-Maugard; she began shuttling between the revolutionary scene and New York City, became acquainted with Mexican workers' groups (Hummel, 10–12, 18), and was finally expelled from Mexico for the political subversiveness she showed while writing about the cause for the English-language sections of the newspaper *El Heraldo de Mexico* in 1920–21.

But *Flowering Judas and Other Stories* also shows that by the early 1930s Porter had grown quite disenchanted with the Left and increasingly committed to the autonomy of her art. Several stories in the collection involve artists of one kind or another who devote themselves more to love than politics (e.g., "The Martyr") or whose revolutionary politics undermine either their art or their morality or both ("That Tree"; "Flowering Judas"). From Berlin on September 27, 1931, having just completed the voyage from Mexico to Bremen, Germany (via Cuba, the Canaries, and Southampton), that would translate years later into *Ship of Fools*, Porter wrote Burke that she had rejected any notion that a writer might engage with revolutionary politics: "I believe that no great poet is a fore-runner. With the artist as prophet I disagree." Well aware of the "thoroughly disagreeable mess going on from bad to worse around her," she nonetheless held that artists in such circumstances ought to play toward unchanging, eternal truths whenever possible, and she promised a novel about Mexico that might do just that. A few months before, she had written to the same effect to Allen Tate: thoroughly disgusted when she heard of Donald Davidson's vow to give up poetry in view of the current "political and social crisis," she told Tate that people like Davidson "are being disingenuous, to say the least, to pretend they are giving up art as a grand sacrifice to revolution. . . . it is a dog-in-the-mangerish attitude to say to artists . . . that it is treason to society to work in the arts in this grand social crisis. . . . [The artist] may join in these [i.e., agitations and political controversies], but there is something beyond [that]" (Porter to Tate, January 27, 1931).[37]

Porter's intellectual connection to Tate was instrumental to the way she had come to think about art in the early 1930s. A native Texan, Porter had befriended Tate and his wife, Caroline Gordon, when they were all living in New York in 1925–27; for a time in 1927, they shared the same apartment building at 561 Hudson Street (Hummel, 16). The three met up again in Paris in 1932, though there was by now considerable tension between Porter and Gordon,[38] and Porter sealed her connection to the South (and to the *Southern Review*) when she consorted with Robert Penn Warren and submitted stories to him for the new magazine.[39] Tate, probably the most resolute believer in the need to separate the literary from the political of all among those in Burke's circles in 1935, particularly since "political" at that moment for him meant "leftist," had long since committed himself in theory to the autonomy of art. An exchange between Burke and Tate during the summer of 1933 indicates how thoroughgoing was Tate's belief that art should be sealed off from the rough-and-tumble of daily life. Raised with Davidson and Robert Penn Warren as one of the Nashville Fugitives, student of John Crowe Ransom at Vanderbilt, fervent admirer of Eliot, and fresh from an expatriate stand in Paris (where he mingled with Hemingway, Hart Crane, Fitzgerald, Stein, Ford Madox Ford, and other moderns), Tate strenuously objected to Burke's contention in *Counter-Statement* (1931) that literature was ultimately "nothing else but rhetoric" (210), ultimately "an equipment . . . for handling the complexities of living" (183). In response to Burke's attempted clarifications via the mail, he rearticulated to Burke without qualification some classic aestheticist assumptions: that "High Literature . . . is not written for the specific purpose of moving anybody"; that "a great poem is great whether anybody reads it or not"; and "that High Literature is nothing less than a complete qualitative and quantitative recreation of the Very Thing-in-Itself" (Tate to Burke, August 30, 1933). Tate's manifesto did not go without an answer,[40] but neither did that answer and the others that Burke offered to Tate in the 1930s dissuade Tate from his membership in the aesthetic camp.

Then again, Tate's own writing was anything but disengaged from politics in 1935. His poetry, fiction, and criticism were all in the service of a clear social agenda: to reinvigorate southern culture on what was known as "Agrarian" lines. That goal had motivated his biographies of Stonewall Jackson (1928) and Jefferson Davis (1929), the fiction he had begun to contemplate (*The Fathers*, 1938), his "Ode to the Confederate Dead" (written in various versions between 1925 and 1930), and the critical work that had grown out of his long-term affiliation with a group of like-minded regionalists once associated with the *Fugitive* and most recently brought together in the volume *I'll Take My Stand*, a 1930 effort to establish an Agrarian model for southern culture.

I'll Take My Stand is discussed a bit more in chapter 3 because it offers some perspective on what Burke was doing in *Permanence and Change*. Here it is enough to say that the Agrarians were as radical in their own way as the leftists who gathered for the Writers' Congress—and as contemptuous of capitalism. *I'll Take My Stand*, a challenge to what its authors regarded as hegemonic northern industrialism, promised that an "imaginatively balanced life" (xvi) could countermand the excesses of capitalist culture. In some ways Agrarians were taking consolation from the deepening Depression, as it seemed to demonstrate the flaws inherent in the northern industrial model. In other ways they were reacting defensively to standard depictions of southern cultural backwardness that prevailed in the wake of the Scopes trial and the demise of the *Fugitive* (both in 1925); what the Fugitives were fleeing, among other things, were popular stereotypes of the South like those that Quentin Compson was fighting at Harvard in Faulkner's novel *Absalom, Absalom!*, in production during 1935. They were reacting negatively as well to leftist political, cultural, and aesthetic values. Southern intellectuals, particularly Tate, began to imagine an organized defense of southern values as early as the spring of 1927, when Tate wrote to Ransom that "we must do something about Southern history and culture of the South" (qtd. in Young, *Gentleman*, 3). And so *I'll Take My Stand: The South and the Agrarian Tradition*, by "Twelve Southerners," emerged as a series of essays favoring the regional sympathies implied by its title. The idea was to renew a distinctively southern "culture of the soil" (xix) by resisting industrialism, honoring southern traditions, and reimagining the Agrarian model put forward by Jefferson. Scornful of any strong central government in Washington and even more vociferously anti-Communist—"the Communist menace is a menace indeed" (xli)—the Agrarians understood the Civil War as a mythic Lost Cause, a struggle not over slavery but between industrialism and Agrarianism, and so they glorified cultural heroes such as Robert E. Lee, Jefferson Davis, Nathan Bedford Forrest, and Stonewall Jackson. Inattentive to issues of class and social justice in the South, they testified in *I'll Take My Stand* on behalf of cultural homogeneity and an alternative way of life to the industrialism they despised.

The introductory "Statement of Principles" (drafted by Ransom, revised by several others, and agreed to by all twelve contributors), held up "the culture of the soil [as] the best and most sensitive of vocations," savaged the "evil dispensation" of industrialism (xlviii), and claimed that agrarian society provided an alternative "form of labor that if pursued with intelligence and leisure, . . . [could be] the model to which the other forms approach as they may" (xix). Ransom's "Reconstructed but Unregenerate" (chapter 1) attacked unbridled consumption, ridiculed the "gospel of Progress" and the "dehumanization" of modern industrial labor practices, and defended the principled and rewarding labor of the self-sufficient family farm. Davidson's satiric account of art in industrialized society (probably the one Porter was responding to in her January 27, 1931, letter to Burke) followed: under capitalism, Davidson predicted, art would be something that comes "later," "when we are all rich, when life has been reduced to some last pattern of efficiency. . . . Since nice, civilized people are supposed to have art, we shall [then] have art. We shall buy it, hire it, can it, or—most conclusively—manufacture it" (28). In search of a usable past, John Gould Fletcher extolled the classical education offered in the Old South as a way of attacking the vocational schools springing up in 1930. Lyle Lanier denounced "The Philosophy of Progress," especially Dewey's, being put forward by advocates for a New South. And Andrew Lytle developed an aesthetic sensibility dependent on a

right attitude toward nature and celebrated Old South yeoman farmers toil-
ing in the ways before "progressive farming": "the triumph of industry, commerce, trade," he intoned, "brings misery to those who live on the land"
(202). Reacting to social disintegration, Agrarians detested science since its
methods had destroyed the old organic way of life, paved the way for industrialism, and alienated working men and women: "the scientific mind always
plays havoc with the spiritual life," summarized one contributor (173). The
Agrarians protested that they were not trying to turn back the clock, were not
literally calling for a wholesale return to antebellum life.[41] What they did
insist upon was offering in the South an alternative culture, an antidote to the
northern industrial capitalism that it regarded as sterile and pernicious.

Tate's sympathies for Agrarianism ran very deep indeed, though his own
essay in *I'll Take My Stand*, "Remarks on the Southern Religion," was characteristically iconoclastic and combative.[42] In sympathy with the Agrarian social
project and with Eliot's Anglo-Catholicism (*Murder in a Cathedral* would first
be performed in 1935), Tate implied that Catholicism was more in keeping
with feudal agrarianism and tradition than was southern Protestantism.
Before and after a sojourn in Paris in the summer of 1932, he and Gordon
took up the agrarian lifestyle near Trenton, Kentucky, on the Tennessee border and the Cumberland River near Clarksville (and two miles from the
Cloverlands plantation that Malcolm Cowley used, at Tate's arrangement, as
a writers' retreat in 1933). When his eastern friends begged Tate to get
"Southern writers [to] intervene to protest" (Wheelwright to Tate, undated)
on behalf of striking miners and their supporters in Harlan County, Kentucky, late in 1931, Tate responded in Agrarian fashion: he did make an effort
to drum up support for miners' and writers' civil rights, but he also protested
vociferously "the use of communist propaganda in labor disputes" (Tate to
Davidson and Warren, December 10, 1931); and he offered as an ideal the
Agrarian labor practices provided by his brother in his own eastern Kentucky
mines, where there "has never been a strike" since "every miner is independent of his job [because] he is compelled, before he is given the job, to take a
cow and from one to three acres, in which he is obligated to raise his meat,
bread, and vegetables" (Tate to Wheelwright, December 4, 1931).[43]

When Tate was exchanging those letters with Burke in 1933, he was fresh
from a May reunion of Fugitives in Nashville. Two years later, in April 1935,
he was planning another Agrarian symposium (*Who Owns America? A New
Declaration of Independence*, arranged with Lytle and Lanier, including contributions by Brooks and Warren, and published—and reviewed by Burke—in
time for the election campaign of 1936); working on *The Fathers* (a dramati-
zation of the clash between Old South and New);[44] quarreling with Cowley
through the mail about the future of capitalism and Agrarianism; and finishing *Reactionary Essays on Politics and Ideas*, a 1936 broadside against capitalism

whose preface ridiculed the leftist notion of a connection between poetry and politics. Instead of mixing with the Communists at the first American Writers' Congress, Tate, on April 10 and 11, 1935, attended something of an alternative event: the Baton Rouge Conference on Literature and Reading in the South and Southwest. With him and Gordon on the roof of the Heidelberg Hotel were forty other writers, all of them white, nearly all of them southerners, and many (though hardly all) of them Agrarians, among them John Gould Fletcher, Robert Penn Warren, John Peale Bishop, Randall Jarrell, and Cleanth Brooks (Cutrer, *Parnassus*, 54); Ford Madox Ford was an honored European visitor. The conference was intended to assess the future of southern letters, but it was plagued by the same kind of dissent that would mark the Writers' Congress three weeks later. New southerners and old, Agrarians and progressives, had very different social agendas, and delegates disagreed as well about the degree to which they should tie their futures to New York publishers and literary magazines (54–56). Ford, the outsider, tried to conclude the conference on a hopeful and conciliatory note: "You in the South have the world at your feet. The North and East are exhausted, and the industrialism of the Middle West is even worse than Eastern industrialism," so the new vitality of the South offered hope that the region could become a distinctive cultural center: "your dominance of the hemisphere is as inevitable as your survival!" (58).

At the conference it was announced that a new magazine was in the works, the *Southern Review*. For in April 1935 several of the cultural critics associated with Agrarianism were gradually turning to a literary agenda—establishing New Criticism and the *Southern Review* as one of its key media outlets —that would increasingly connect with Burke personally, professionally, and intellectually as the decade wore on. The *Southern Review* came about when the president of Louisiana State decided that Huey Long's university could gain in prestige by hosting its own literary and intellectual quarterly (Brooks and Warren, *Stories*, xi). He offered financial support to two young assistant professors, Robert Penn Warren and Cleanth Brooks, and their even younger assistant, Albert Erskine, to launch a magazine designed (as Warren indicated in a letter to Burke soliciting his participation) to feature the latest and most important literary and cultural criticism, fiction, and poetry to be found (March 28, 1935). (Charles Pipkin, a senior social scientist, was listed as the magazine's editor, but from the first the three younger faculty members actually ran most of it, Brooks and Warren editorially and Erskine as de facto managing editor.) Through the *Southern Review* Burke would quickly develop a mutually stimulating relationship with Warren, another Fugitive student of Ransom's at Vanderbilt who had probably met Burke through Tate in the late 1920s (Singal, 344) and who had contributed to *I'll Take My Stand*.[45] Brooks had not contributed to *I'll Take My Stand*, but he was a Vanderbilt product, a

devotee of Ransom's, and a supporter the Agrarian project. Ransom, still at
Vanderbilt in 1935 (he moved to Kenyon in 1937), would become a central
intellectual and spiritual contributor to the new magazine.[46]

Tate, Warren, Ransom, and other Agrarian sympathizers in April 1935
were in the process of transforming that social movement into what came to
be known as the New Criticism. Tate's belief in the autonomy of art expressed
in his letters to Burke reflected values that had been promulgated by the
Fugitives in the 1920s and picked up by Eliot (and his magazine the *Criterion*)
and others in England. Ransom and Tate, convinced as Agrarians and mod-
ernists of the decadence of contemporary society and equally convinced that
literature (and the criticism of literature) offered a way of transcending that
condition, endeavored to purify art and criticism by insulating it from politics. In the tradition of Kantian art for art's sake, they railed against the
"genetic" and "receptionist" and "impressionistic" reading practices of the
1920s: the author's intention, the reader's experience, history, and the critic's
political presuppositions would hold no place in New Critical practice. And
they were not alone. As the Writers' Congress met, R. P. Blackmur was
expressing in "A Critic's Job of Work" (a chapter of his 1935 *The Double
Agent*, which collected "first-rate exegeses of a number of difficult poems"
[Hyman, 204] by Moore, Hart Crane, Stevens, Cummings, and others) central tenets of New Criticism: he disapproved of "extrinsic" kinds of criticism,
"tendentious or distorted" by dogma of one kind of another (for instance,
Santayana's reading of literature against moral philosophy, Van Wyck
Brooks's psychological approaches, and the "fanatical" Marxist "economism"
of Granville Hicks).[47] Instead Blackmur called for close attention to "form"
and "technique" and "the work itself": "criticism must be concerned, first and
last—whatever comes between—with the poem as it is." Significantly Blackmur ended his essay with a respectful critique of Burke's criticism, which he
nevertheless criticized for being "more interested in the psychological means
of meaning" for readers, and for regarding literature as a persuasive interven-
tion into politics and culture. And equally significantly several other pieces of
Blackmur's work appeared in the first issue of the *Southern Review* and frequently thereafter, often juxtaposed with something by Burke.[48]

Tate, like Blackmur, would maintain his commitment to New Critical, aestheticist values for the rest of his critical life. Ransom (whose 1941 book *The
New Criticism* would institutionalize the term) was in the process of developing from Kant and Coleridge a theory of metaphor, poetic unity, and the primacy of poetry over other verbal arts. Having initiated proto–New Criticism
as a main figure in the Fugitive group that met almost weekly in Nashville
from 1919 to 1925, and having moved from literary creation to criticism in a
way that anticipated the careers of Burke, Warren, and Tate, Ransom would
encourage New Critical close reading practices and analytical techniques

in the *Southern Review:* his "The Tense of Criticism" in the second issue (Autumn 1935), for example, emphasized distinctions between prose and poetry and urged readers to think of poems as dramatic monologues. He pushed those same values as editor of the *Kenyon Review* from late 1938 to 1959, where he published some of Burke's most important essays.

Brooks became just as fervently committed to Ransom's beliefs, and he refined, systematized, and disseminated New Critical values for decades, into the 1980s. For instance, in 1974 it was he who offered a 1,200-word condensation of New Criticism for the *Princeton Encyclopedia of Poetry and Poetics:* it separates poetic criticism from "extrinsic" concerns such as biography and politics, attends to the structure and form of the "literary object" itself, champions an "organic" criticism that frowns on the separation of form and content, practices the close reading of individual works apart from the politics recognized so centrally by leftist critics, and regards those texts (just as Ransom had recommended in the *Southern Review*) as miniature dramas organized around central "conflicts" and "tensions."[49] Brooks and Warren (and Tate—who was ubiquitous in the *Southern Review* from its inception) conceived of the *Southern Review* as a kind of successor to the *Fugitive* while they edited it between 1935 and 1942. Though appropriations for libraries were falling across the nation and though subscriptions to magazines had plunged—for information, readers were now streaming to public libraries in record numbers rather than subscribing themselves to periodicals (Cantwell), and southern periodicals such as *Virginia Quarterly Review* and *Southwest Review* were struggling (Cutrer, 59)—the subsidy provided by Louisiana State University permitted Brooks and Warren with Erskine to sustain their new periodical through 1942.

When Warren first contacted Burke about contributing to the *Southern Review* on March 26, 1935, he could therefore offer good money: "certainly . . . something better than a cent a word for prose."[50] But there was more. While acknowledging that southerners such as Ransom, Porter, Tate, and Lytle would appear in the first issues (and indeed there would come to be a heavy southern flavor in every number, as in Lytle's essay on Robert E. Lee printed next to a Burke article), Warren also promised that the *Southern Review* would "not aim at a sectional program. . . . We hope to be a real index to the most vital contemporary activities in fiction, poetry, criticism, and social thought." Therefore in April Burke proposed to Brooks and Warren "Antony in Behalf of the Play," an inventive study of political discourse that he had been trying to place for several months. When Warren expressed interest in "Antony" for fall publication, the two began to discuss additional possibilities, and on April 16 (the same day that Duke Ellington and his band, just back from Europe, were captivating a young music student named Ralph Ellison and his classmates at Tuskegee), Warren assigned Burke to do a "long

portrait review" of recent American poetry. Burke immediately and throughout the rest of April began to gather books and thoughts on that essay so that
he could submit a draft of it in mid-May (Warren to Burke, May 26, 1935).
After adding (at Warren's suggestion) a section on Mark Van Doren and
expanding the part on E. E. Cummings, Burke forwarded the finished essay
in the first days of June, in time for the first issue.

Burke's first contributions to the *Southern Review* were not exactly in a
New Critical mode, but neither were they orthodox instances of proletarian
criticism. "Antony" offers a clever rewriting of the famous speech in *Julius
Caesar*, in a way that underscores literature's function as rhetoric, "as a com-
municative relationship between writer and audience." His essay "Recent
Poetry" was a balanced aesthetic consideration of recent poems by Moore,
Archibald MacLeish, Stephen Spender, C. Day Lewis, Lola Ridge, Van
Doren, James Agee, Horace Gregory, Kenneth Fearing, Cummings, and a
variety of others of various schools. While the review was certainly not
apolitical—Burke gently ridiculed MacLeish for turning the story of a Wall
Street panic into a tragedy about bankers instead of a dirge for the victimized
masses—it could have been written by a moderate: "I most prize in our poets,
as distinct from the pamphleteer, publicist, or economist, the fact that they
are alive to the full complexities of human readjustment. . . . The important
thing for me is their clear awareness of the fact that a man's need for 'integration' or 'fusion' involves factors more complex, and closer to 'magic,' than
rationalistic oversimplifications of political necessities can reveal." Besides
"Antony" and the review essay, the *Southern Review* also published Burke's
1936 review of *Proletarian Literature in the United States*, which offered a balanced justification and critique of the Writers' Congress artists that was
clearly calculated for those beyond any leftist pale: "They become so intent
upon the emphasizing of the situation, that they overlook the humane development of character. Their characters are formed in haphazard fashion, for
the specific partisan purpose at hand, like the distortions of a political cartoonist." (The next issue nevertheless carried a rejoinder by Tate, "Mr. Burke
and the Historical Environment," which gently scolded Burke for his leftist
sympathies.)[51] And in the winter of 1936–37, the *Southern Review* printed
an anything-but-formalist excerpt from *Attitudes toward History* entitled
"Acceptance and Rejection." Later were a piece on "the folklore of capitalism" (Warren to Burke, January 5, 1938; the phrase comes from Thurman
Arnold's book by that name) called "The Virtues and Limitations of Debunking," "Semantic and Poetic Meaning," and his famous essay on Hitler's *Mein
Kampf*.[52] Indeed, as the Hitler essay suggests, the journal for the first
years was hardly limited to criticism, poetry, and fiction, but included broad-
ranging social criticism by people such as Norman Thomas (on the New
Deal), John Dewey (on William James), and Sidney Hook (on Trotsky). By

the time the decade came to a close, the *Southern Review* did indeed sponsor the creation of a critical school, as Tate advised in his 1936 contribution "The Function of a Critical Quarterly." And Burke in turn moved to a theoretical and practical criticism that involved Coleridge and close reading, a criticism expressed in essays that spoke directly to Tate, Ransom, Brooks, Blackmur, and Warren. Examples would be the famous analysis of *Mein Kampf* and "Semantic and Poetic Meaning" (1938), as well as the title essay of *The Philosophy of Literary Form*, published by Louisiana State University Press in 1941 with the help of Warren, Brooks, and Erskine.

Burke also reviewed Ransom's *The World's Body* and *The New Criticism*, advised Warren on his verse play *Proud Flesh* in 1939,[53] and drew himself into conversation, literal and literary, with I. A. Richards and William Empson, foundational British contributors to the New Criticism. Chapter 5 will account for Burke's intellectual relationship with Empson, whose *Seven Types of Ambiguity* (1930) was a key text in establishing New Critical reading procedures, whose principles were derived indirectly from Ransom via the Fugitive Laura Riding (Leitch, 36), and whose books *Some Versions of Pastoral* and *English Pastoral Poetry* Burke reviewed in 1937–38; and chapter 3 deals more particularly with I. A. Richards, whose engagement with New Criticism and with Burke was considerable. Indeed in April 1935, as his correspondence indicates, Burke was thinking hard about Richards's *On Imagination: Coleridge's Critical Theory* since he was reviewing the book for the October issue of *Poetry*.

The Chicago School(s)

Richards's early books *The Principles of Literary Criticism* (1924), *Practical Criticism* (1929), and *Science and Poetry* (1926) did indeed influence the New Critics—profoundly so. For example his emphasis on "tension" in poetry—the intricate balance of poised opposites—was central to Brooks's early appreciation of conflict; Richards's fast distinction between the "emotive" language of poetry and the referential, denotative language of science became a New Critical staple; and his demonstration of ahistorical, close reading practices in *Practical Criticism* offered an early model of critical practice that New Critics would build upon.

But Richards's interest in psychology and in the experiences of real readers in *Practical Criticism* also moved him away from New Critical assumptions and in the direction of a more pragmatic than aesthetic criticism. (His "revised and enlarged" version of *Science and Poetry*, published in 1935, was less compliant with New Critical assumptions.) And those terms *practical* and *pragmatics* bring up yet another intellectual circle that Burke was involved with in 1935, one connected with the contentious and conflicted neo-Aristotelians and pragmatists and social scientists associated with the city of

Chicago and the University of Chicago, where Burke would teach in the summer of 1938 and return many times after.

In 1935 R. S. Crane, then nearing fifty and well over a decade into a professorial appointment in the English department at the University of Chicago, was in the process of reorienting his own career as well as the discipline of literary studies as it would come to develop over the next decades at his university. Having established a reputation as a leading literary historian in the field of Restoration and eighteenth-century studies on the basis of impeccable publications such as *New Essays by Oliver Goldsmith* (1927) and *A Census of British Newspapers and Periodicals, 1620–1800* (1927), Crane was rather suddenly reconsidering his priorities. Whatever it was that had convinced the makers of the *Southern Review* to focus on "the work itself" had also gotten to Crane. For in sympathy with the New Critics—indeed, Crane's efforts would be roundly endorsed in Ransom's 1937 "Criticism, Inc."— Crane was now making the case that the business of literary study ought to be criticism and not history. Like Ransom, Brooks, and Warren, Crane hoped to influence English professors nationwide to attend to "intrinsic" criticism and to forsake "extrinsic" considerations. In an essay that has come to be regarded as "revolutionary" (Wimsatt, 50), "History versus Criticism in the University Study of Literature," published in the college edition of *English Journal* in 1935, Crane first sharply demarcated historical study from criticism—and then energetically testified for the latter at the expense of the former. Something of a companion to his "Literary Scholarship and Contemporary Criticism" of a year before, "History versus Criticism" might be seen as the opening manifesto in what came to be widely known as the Chicago School of literary criticism. Crane closed his argument with an outline of what his program in criticism would come to involve: "critical discussion of the principal classics of aesthetic theory . . . from the Greeks to our own contemporaries, [and] exercises in the reading and literary explication of literary texts, . . . the text itself . . . to be read appreciatively for its own sake" (665–66). A confrontation with "the classics of aesthetic theory," especially Aristotle's *Poetics*, would generate many of the critical principles associated now with the Chicago School.[54]

But even though it made an approving reference to a review essay that Burke had published in the *Dial* in 1925, Crane's argument, focused as it was on the conduct of college English departments, would have meant very little to Kenneth Burke in 1935—except that Burke's longtime friend Richard McKeon had by then joined Crane on the faculty at Chicago. An expert on Spinoza and on medieval philosophy (and one-time student of Dewey), the versatile, accomplished McKeon had stayed on to teach at Columbia after completing his doctorate there in 1928, until, in the fall of 1934, he accepted a visiting position at the University of Chicago at the invitation of President

Robert Maynard Hutchins. Hutchins, at the urging of Mortimer Adler, was committed to reviving the "Great Books" there as the basis of university education. Then in April 1935, McKeon accepted Hutchins's invitation to assume a permanent appointment as dean of humanities and professor of Greek (McNeill, 59, 78). (McKeon, whom Adler had befriended before leaving Columbia for Chicago himself in 1930, would later teach philosophy as well, after Hutchins reformed that department from its obsession with Dewey's pragmatism.) McKeon's commitment to Greek and other classical philosophy—he was beginning a famous edition of *The Basic Works of Aristotle* that would be published in 1941, and had already edited two volumes of *Selections from Medieval Philosophers* (from Augustine to Ockham) in 1929–30—gave a sturdy boost to Crane's faith in the study of classic texts in literary theory; and Crane and McKeon, in general cooperation with Hutchins's and Adler's educational program and by means of informal discussions and seminars with several others over the next decade, refined their approach to criticism in a neo-Aristotelian vein. They memorably and comprehensively articulated that program in *Critics and Criticism Ancient and Modern* (1952), a large volume of essays edited by Crane and containing by then multiple contributions not only by Crane and McKeon, but also by people that Crane and McKeon hired, including Elder Olson and Norman Maclean.[55] By the time *Critics and Criticism* was published, the Chicago School had defined itself fiercely against the New Critics. While both groups were devoted to reading literary works irrespective of history and biography (the Great Books admired by many of the Chicagoans and the great literature appreciated by the New Critics lived together in a kind of eternal present, beyond space and time), and while both therefore focused on the formal properties of literature apart from content, the Chicagoans had come to build their criticism on philosophical grounds established by Aristotle and Aquinas. They emphasized the mimetic and didactic ends of literature that the New Critics disputed, and attended to the interpretive methodologies and genre theories that were derivable from the *Poetics* and from Aristotle's four causes. *Critics and Criticism* was consequently polemical in tone, reviews of the book by established New Critics were even more polemical, and rivalry between the Chicagoans and New Critics would become a major spectacle in the critical debates that emerged in the 1940s and 1950s.[56] But in 1935 the Chicagoans and emerging New Critics were on very common ground indeed (Richter).

When he arrived in Chicago to team (not always easily, however) with Hutchins, Adler, and Crane, Richard McKeon had known Burke for the better part of two decades. They had become acquainted during the Great War while commuting from New Jersey together to undergraduate classes at Columbia, remained in touch during Burke's time at the *Dial* in the 1920s

(Selzer, 31, 141), and continued to consult with each other in the 1930s. When Burke stopped by Columbia to talk with McKeon in October 1934, he learned that McKeon was looking over opportunities in Chicago on a visiting appointment (Burke to McKeon, October 24, 1934), and so Burke wrote to him there about *Permanence and Change*. When McKeon returned to New York for a Christmas visit late in 1934 (while *Permanence and Change* was in press), the two had dinner together, and they stayed in touch while McKeon settled into his permanent deanship. McKeon was Burke's only direct connection with the University of Chicago in April 1935, then, but the connection would develop quickly and fully, especially after Burke accepted McKeon's invitation to teach at Chicago during the summer of 1938. That summer Burke met Crane and other members of the Chicago community, taught courses on Coleridge and literary criticism, became further drenched in Aristotelian discourses, and tried out some of the ideas he was developing for *The Philosophy of Literary Form* and *A Grammar of Motives*.

But of course there was another "Chicago School" in 1935, too; McKeon was by no means Burke's only intellectual connection to the University of Chicago that April. The prestige of McKeon, Crane, and the other critics who congregated at Chicago under Hutchins should not erase the fact that in some ways Chicago in the 1930s remained a bastion of philosophical pragmatism, a place where the traditionalism espoused by McKeon and the contentious Adler would encounter stiff resistance from entrenched progressives in the social sciences who drew their distinguished lineage from John Dewey. Three decades after Dewey left his position as professor of philosophy at the University of Chicago in 1904 to work at Columbia (where the young Richard McKeon would take his course), Chicago remained identified with and committed to the original "Chicago School"—the school of pragmatism —that Dewey and George Herbert Mead had established there.

Dewey had come to Chicago in 1894 to head the philosophy department shortly after the university was financed by John D. Rockefeller and organized by its first president, William Rainey Harper, as a model research university in the fashion of Johns Hopkins—a university whose faculty would concentrate on graduate programs and research, rather than on undergraduate studies. Attracted by the chance to work in a department broad and exploratory enough to include psychology and pedagogy, Dewey burnished his reputation as an innovator in the psychology of learning at Chicago, and he became widely celebrated as well for practical achievements in education. Committed to an empirically based theory of knowledge that was congruent with and indebted to emerging pragmatist values, Dewey in 1896 established a laboratory school as an incubator for educational research, and he was thereafter associated with the School of Education, formally overseen until 1902 by the legendary Francis W. Parker, whom Dewey himself came to regard by 1930 as "the father of the progressive education movement" ("How Much Freedom," 204). In 1899 Dewey published *School and Society*, which promoted his educational values to a large audience: intellectual growth through experience; active, participatory learning; the fostering of curiosity and reflective inquiry through problem-solving activities, at the expense of rote memorization; a cultivation of the imagination; and the promotion of democratic values through a school community that would encourage open communication and the consideration of a variety of interests.

School and Society rested implicitly on pragmatic philosophical principles that were developing contemporaneously in the writings of Charles Sanders Peirce and William James. (The term *pragmatism* was first used in a 1898 lecture and subsequent article by James, though it had been in use as a concept for at least two decades [Fisch, 283–93].) In 1903 Dewey published his own first explicit contribution to pragmatist philosophy, *Studies in Logical Theory*, which he and his coauthors dedicated to James. Drawing directly on James, whose *Pragmatism* would appear in 1907, Dewey held that philosophy should attend to human experience as it is situated in culture and nature, and he held to the pragmatist theory of truth: that knowledge is provisional and relative to social and behavioral situations. In addition Deweyan instrumentalism (as the Chicago philosophy was often called) held that philosophy could be regarded as the scientific study of human action, a notion that inspired many subsequent advances in the social sciences (Feffer, 3). Dewey recruited a cluster of pragmatic thinkers to Chicago who involved themselves in Chicago-area reform movements (even as Al Capone and Frank Nitti were carrying on their own "reform" measures in town) and who would come to animate the university's approaches to philosophy, psychology, education, sociology, political science, and economics: George Herbert Mead accompanied Dewey from Michigan as a philosopher whose theories would greatly influence sociology and political science; James Rowland Angell pioneered developments in experimental psychology; James Hayden Tufts chaired the philosophy department after Dewey left and maintained its pragmatic orientation; Addison Webster Moore extended Dewey's thinking into philosophical questions; and a number of others made contributions in a pragmatic spirit to other fields (Rucker, Morris). In 1904 William James could write with pleasure that pragmatism had indeed been established as a "school" at Chicago: "Professor John Dewey, and at least ten of his disciples, have collectively put into the world a statement . . . of a view of the world, both theoretical and practical, which is so simple, massive, and positive that . . . it deserves the title of a new system of philosophy" (1).

Although Dewey left for Columbia in that same year, 1904, possibly in a dispute over the future of the laboratory school after Parker's death (Rucker, 11; Dykhuizen 107–15), pragmatism continued as a vital intellectual force at the University of Chicago, particularly in the social sciences. Under Angell, the "new psychology" known as "functionalism" developed into its own department. The Department of Education continued to experiment with the ideas of Dewey and to promote them in Chicago schools. And pragmatism directed additional developments in theology, political science, biology, sociology, and economics. True, when Hutchins arrived in 1929, he began to bring to the university a fresh direction that owed little to pragmatism, and Adler for the next decade savaged the social scientists as unrelentingly as he had baited Dewey and his pragmatism at Columbia (McNeill, 35, 39). When Tufts retired as chair of philosophy in 1930 and Mead died in 1931, Hutchins was free to hire new philosophers who were not so beholden to pragmatism (though the ones especially favored by Adler were generally blocked: McNeill, 38). Angell had left to become president at Yale, Moore retired in 1929 and died in 1930, and outstanding scholars with a number of intellectual orientations came to Chicago in the 1920s and 1930s. But to speak of a "Chicago School" in 1935 was still to speak of pragmatism, especially in the social sciences. Mead remained an especially important contributor to social psychology and sociology even after his death because his students dominated the sociology department at Chicago (and many other universities) and because they brought out four influential volumes of his works in his honor: *The Philosophy of the Present* (1932), *Mind, Self, and Society* (1934), *Movements of Thought in the Nineteenth Century* (1936), and *The Philosophy of the Act* (1938).[57] Harvey Carr and Charles Judd developed "functionalism" in psychology along Deweyan lines for many years, the education department continued in an experimental vein as well (Rucker, 70–76), T. V. Smith and Charner Perry kept up a Deweyan presence in philosophy (McNeill, 77–78), and political scientists worked in a pragmatic spirit of experimentation for the purpose of social amelioration. Even the political economist Thorstein Veblen might be considered to have furthered some pragmatic ideals at Chicago, though he had long passed from the university by the 1930s and though the extent to which he was influenced by Dewey and pragmatism is in dispute.[58]

Kenneth Burke was certainly quite aware of Dewey's work during the 1920s and 1930s—if also quite wary of it. Burke could not have escaped Dewey's celebrity in the undergraduate year he spent at Columbia. He no doubt read Dewey's 1927 *The Public and Its Problems* not so much as pragmatic philosophy but as a cultural analysis that could be influential to his own thinking. In a 1930 review of *The Quest for Certainty* for the *New Republic* ("Intelligence as a Good"), Burke explained in elaborate detail the assumptions of pragmatism, and he testified at length to Dewey's brilliance and utility. (He also cogently pointed up shortcomings in Dewey's faith in experimentation: "How do we test the success of a value?") If in his correspondence Burke sometimes

referred to Dewey as "Doofy," and if in a 1933 letter he scored William Carlos Williams for approving Dewey uncritically (Williams to Burke, January
26, 1933), he also in another letter (to Matthew Josephson, August 7, 1930)
indicated the care, attention, and application that he brought to his reading
of *Experience and Nature* and *The Quest for Certainty:* "I have read twice
throughout his Experience and Nature, The Quest for Certainty, and his
series on the new individualism in Ye Olde Republic. I have taken a suicidal
number of notes (between eight and ten thousand words)." To this day his
heavily annotated copies of those books and others by Dewey and Mead rest
on Burke's shelves at Andover.[59] In the spring of 1934, Burke favorably (if
cautiously) reviewed *Art as Experience* for the *New Republic* ("The Esthetic
Strain"), and in a 1936 review of *Liberalism and Social Action*, he would call
Dewey "eye-opening" ("Liberalism's Family Tree"). Dewey's term *occupational psychosis*, not to mention other pragmatist notions, was picked up by
Burke in *Permanence and Change*.

In April 1935 Dewey remained in his "retirement" a formidable intellectual force for Kenneth Burke and those around him. A John Dewey Society
was taking shape in New York City. While he retained a reputation for wish-
ing to reform (not completely discard) capitalism (and thus won some ridicule
from the hard Left), and while his reformist agenda implied a belief in social
progress (and thus won him some ridicule from the Agrarians), Dewey himself remained forward thinking and independent: impatient with the New
Deal, he was advocating a radical socialist party that would remain independent of the Communists; and his *Liberalism and Social Action*, just coming off
the press, was arguing that liberalism had to adjust to contemporary realities
and undertake radical activities in order to survive. Thus, when the League
of American Writers soon after the Writers' Congress wanted Dewey's help
in pursuing its mission, Burke was commissioned by the LAW board to contact Dewey personally (Bliven to Burke, January 27, 1936). A vocal critic of
fascism, Dewey in 1937 would head up a controversial commission of inquiry
that went to Mexico City to look into the charges by Stalin against Leon
Trotsky (Farrell, "Dewey in Mexico"; Diggins, *Promise*, 267–68), and Burke
was still studying Dewey's ideas on human rights and the relationship
between the individual and society while *Attitudes toward History* was coming
off the press and while he was beginning to put together *The Philosophy of Literary Form* (Burke to Ernest Sutherland Bates, February 1938). Burke was
ultimately comfortable enough with Dewey's ideas that he would come to
accept a teaching position in 1943 at Bennington College, a new and experimental college founded in 1932 on avowedly Deweyan educational practices;
he would incorporate an extended analysis of James and Dewey into *A Grammar of Motives* (1945); his letters and other writings make it clear that he was
versed in James and Peirce as well (e.g., Burke to Guterman, June 23, 1937;

his fall 1936 review of a book on *The Thought and Character of William James;* and the opening chapter, in part on James, of *Attitudes toward History).* And thus it is more than possible that some of the most important principles that Burke developed and articulated in the 1930s—including that "language is symbolic action" and that literature is "equipment for living"—were calculated to carry pragmatic overtones.

As important or more important to Burke in 1935 than Dewey, however, was Veblen. For the Greenwich Village crowd in the years immediately before and after the Great War, including Burke and his circles, Veblen had been a reliable counterculture voice attacking Victorian propriety and contemporary business attitudes. By 1918 H. L. Mencken complained, Veblen was absolutely "dominating the American scene. . . . There were Veblenists, Veblen clubs, Veblen remedies for the sorrows of the world. There were even, in Chicago, Veblen girls—perhaps Gibson girls grown middle-aged and despairing" (qtd. in Diggins, *Bard,* 214). In the two years before Scofield Thayer purchased the *Dial* in 1920 and converted it—with Burke's considerable help—into the leading magazine for modernist art, Veblen and Dewey were both contributing editors to the infinitely more political, Chicago-based version of the magazine that Thayer would acquire and bring to New York. When Veblen died in 1929 and the stock market crashed, Veblen was adored generally as a prescient seer. His books were then reissued and readvertised— *The Engineers and the Price System,* originally published in 1921, became a best seller in 1930, and Leon Ardzrooni, a student of Veblen's, published a Veblen anthology, *Essays in Our Changing Order,* in 1934. Joseph Dorfman's fine *Thorstein Veblen and His America,* still the definitive biography, appeared in 1934, and Wesley Clair Mitchell's *What Veblen Taught* followed in 1936. That Veblen appeared prominently in John Dos Passos's novel *The Big Money* in 1936 indicates something of the degree to which he was reverenced as a social critic, as does his position in a 1938 *New Republic* poll of leading intellectuals. Asked to list the most provocative, influential thinker of their time, the intellectuals picked Veblen as the runaway winner, over Dewey, Freud, Spengler, Lenin, and Alfred North Whitehead (Diggins, *Bard,* 216).

But it was not just that Burke was reading the Chicago School social scientists in 1935. They were also reading him. When Lewis Wirth, a former student of Mead's and a member of the sociology department at Chicago, reviewed *Permanence and Change* for the *American Journal of Sociology,* it gave Burke an immediate audience in the sociology community, one that Wirth and his Chicago colleague Ernest Burgess enlarged when they asked Burke to contribute a book review to the journal in 1936 and a response to an article in 1937. As editor of the journal, Burgess later asked Burke to contribute "Freud and the Analysis of Poetry" to *AJS* as well (Burgess to Burke, October 18, 1938). Thomas D. Eliot, a Northwestern sociologist, reviewed *Permanence and Change* for the *American Sociological Review* early in 1936, and by 1938 had come to value Burke enough to throw him a party when Burke arrived to teach his University of Chicago courses. Hugh Dalziel Duncan, in the midst of pursuing an advanced degree from Chicago in sociology, would therefore sit in on one of Burke's courses, after which he prepared a comprehensive, 105-page draft of an article on Burke that he designed for a sociology journal (Duncan to Burke, November 10, 1938). Nathan Boden, another University of Chicago sociologist, would ask Burke to speak to a local institute in 1938; and Lewis Dexter, the Chicago-educated sociologist, would ask Burke to contribute to his Committee on Conceptual Integration for the American Sociological Society in 1940.

That invitation, related to an effort to root out linguistic ambiguities in the social sciences, in part grew out of the interest in semantics that Burke developed during and after his time in Chicago. Many of the assumptions behind semantics, the social-scientific study of the relation between words and things, were implicit in Ogden and Richards's 1923 book *The Meaning of Meaning*, but those assumptions gained more explicit formulation in 1933, when Alfred Korzybski's *Science and Sanity* proposed an explanation of how language shapes meaning (and creates ambiguities) within social institutions. Concerned about the distortions of advertisers and about the propaganda tactics that had accompanied the Great War and that seemed to be accompanying fascism, eager to reduce misunderstandings between different language users at a time when international trade and other forms of cooperation were increasing, and excited by recent research findings in biology and neurology, Korzybski and his followers were committed to finding more reliable means of arriving at meaning and eliminating confusion. They organized the First Congress on General Semantics, held in Ellensburg, Washington, in March 1935. Burke became interested in the efforts of Stuart Chase, whose *Tyranny of Words* in 1938 would be an important entry in the semantics movement; in the work of Irving Lee, who wrote textbooks popularizing Korzybski's models (and who reviewed *Permanence and Change* for the *Quarterly Journal of Speech*) while teaching in the Northwestern University School of Speech; and of course in Korzybski himself, who offered a seminar late in 1941 in Chicago that S. I. Hayakawa personally invited Burke to attend (Hayakawa to Burke, December 7 and 22, 1941). The seminar was a sequel to the original seminar on general semantics that was offered by Korzybski in May 1938 (Lee and Hayakawa attended as disciples) and which also met in Chicago.

Finally one last important Burkean connection with Dewey and pragmatism is worth mentioning in reference to April 1935, a connection that further embroiders Burke into the fabrics of the communities of which he was a part. While Sidney Hook was thoroughly Marxist, and while he was obviously a New Yorker and not a Chicagoan, he was also a devoted disciple of

Dewey. Hook had studied at Columbia under Dewey, completing his disser-
tation, "The Metaphysics of Pragmatism," in 1927. As a professor at New
York University beginning in 1927, he also pursued his fervent interest in
Marx—*Towards the Understanding of Karl Marx* appeared in 1933—and in a
series of articles in *Modern Quarterly* and *Modern Monthly* he began to articulate his conviction that Marx and Dewey shared a great deal. Though he
could never get Dewey himself to be terribly interested in Marx, Hook remained convinced, as he wrote in 1935, that "their [i.e., Dewey's and Marx's]
fundamental logical and metaphysical positions are the same" ("Experimental Naturalism"). For much of the rest of his long life, Hook read Marx
through Dewey, and vice versa (Cork).

Modern Quarterly and *Modern Monthly* were edited by the freethinking radical V. F. Calverton, so it should not be surprising that Hook published often
there. For while loyal to Marx in 1935, Hook had come to understand Stalin
as fundamentally un-Marxist and dangerous. Viewing the Soviet Union as a
pragmatic social experiment, having visited Moscow on a Guggenheim in the
summer of 1929, and in keeping with Dewey—who had visited the Soviet
Union himself and who had published "Why I Am Not a Communist" in
the *Modern Monthly* of April 1934—Hook began to express his reservations
about the practical utility of Stalinism. Hook participated in John Reed Club
activities and worked hard for the Foster-Ford campaign in 1932 (Dewey
endorsed Norman Thomas), but when *Towards the Understanding of Karl
Marx* displayed far more respect for Trotsky than for Stalin, Hook came
under fire from the American Communist Party. In the *Communist* of February 1933, Earl Browder rebutted Hook's views point by point and asserted
with an official flourish that Hook had "an understanding of Marxism in
conflict with that of the Communist Party" (qtd. in Phelps, 87). He was
therefore more or less blackballed from party activities, including the first
American Writers' Congress two years later. For the next several years, Hook
wrote consistently and frequently in support of Trotsky, including several
essays in the *Southern Review* (e.g., "Liberalism and the Case of Leon Trotsky," Autumn 1937), and it was he who was responsible for arranging Dewey's
participation in the mission to Mexico to inquire into Trotsky's alleged crimes
against the Soviet Union.[60]

Hook's articles, including the ones in the *Southern Review*, were frequently
combative, intemperate, and more than a little self-righteous. As John Patrick
Diggins put it,

> Hook carried on Dewey's thought and spirit but not exactly his character and
> temperament. To compare the two is to compare a saint to a street fighter.
> Where Dewey would gently correct an opponent, Hook would announce that
> he was going to prove his foe "not only wrong but demonstrably wrong."
> Hook seemed to be born for argument and disputation, and he could seldom

resist the polemicist's instinct for annihilation. Always loving a good fight, a raging rationalist at once scrappy, aggressive, and witty, Hook was the Jake LaMotta of American philosophy. (*Promise*, 395–96)

This characterization fairly describes Hook's relationship with Kenneth Burke. For a time the two got on well, and they were certainly amicable enough even in April 1935. Burke had come to know Hook as he was completing *Permanence and Change:* late in 1933, Hook noticed Burke's *Nation* article "The Nature of Art under Capitalism" and thought he had located a kindred spirit. He (rightly) interpreted Burke's piece as an explicit commitment to Marxist principles but an undogmatic, even iconoclastic one as well (not least because it quoted Dewey approvingly), and he wrote a long commendation of the piece as a "sound and much needed corrective of the Calverton-Freeman-Hicksian tendency in radical criticism" to define proletarian art in excessively narrow terms: "Now that you have 'come over' [to the Communist position]," he wrote, "I am particularly glad that you have not gone 'orthodox'" (Hook to Burke, December 8, 1933). Predictably Burke wrote back at length, commending Hook's controversial book on Marx and responding amiably enough to Hook's commentary on the place of "pure art" in a Communist state (Burke to Hook, December 27, 1933). Analytical to a fault, the two corresponded several times during 1934, and Hook offered to introduce Burke to some of his renegade leftist contacts in the Professional Workers League, such as James Burnham and C. Hartley Grattan. Burke even worried that Hook might be becoming too Stalinist for comfort—though Hook quickly reassured him on that score (Hook to Burke, November 26, 1934). Indeed Burke need not have worried at all: as the Writers' Congress approached in the spring of 1935, it was clear that Hook would be barred for continuing criticism of Stalin. Nevertheless Burke remained in touch and even lectured in Hook's philosophy class as April began (Hook to Burke, March 21, 1935). The cordiality between the two men began to chill, however, when, apparently unaware of or insensitive to the nature of Burke's Writers' Congress speech, Hook read Burke's happy summary of the Writers' Congress, published in the *Nation* in May, and scolded Burke for it in peremptory and parental tones:

> Intellectual responsibility demands that you compare not merely the politics of the C. P. with the politics of Fascist groups but with the politics of other Marxist groups. . . . As you know, not a single radical (socialist or communist) opposed to Stalinism was invited to this Congress. It seems to me that if the individual integrity you speak about had really been present, those possessing it would have had the courage . . . to protest the sectarian basis on which the sessions had been organized. And if the Congress itself was not the most auspicious place to express that protest, certainly a written account of the

proceedings should have contained it. . . . I cannot believe that you approve of this. (undated, May 1935)

Even as Burke was being roasted by the Stalinists for being insufficiently doctrinaire, then, he was taking heat from Hook for being insufficiently critical. In November 1935 Burke was again insufficiently critical in his review of Henri Barbusse's biography of Stalin for the *Book Union Bulletin*, Hook felt, particularly since Hook's own review of the biography that same month in *Saturday Review* had found both the book and its subject positively "revolting" ("Saint Stalin," 7). The following summer Hook scored Burke again, and again in patronizing tones (Hook to Burke, June 1936; July 1, 1936), this time for Burke's uncompromising review of James T. Farrell's anti-Stalinist *A Note on Literary Criticism* ("A Sour Note on Literary Criticism"), in which Burke dismissed Farrell's work as an "oversimplified" "attack [on] Left critics." And six months later, Hook would seal the feud forever by savaging Burke once and for all in an infamous review of *Attitudes toward History* that was published in *Partisan Review*. Whether it was because his philosophical bent was too analytical for him to accept Burke, or because his personality was too prickly, or because he could not brook Burke's implicit criticisms of Marx in *Permanence and Change* (especially when there was no corresponding criticism of Stalin), Hook would come to treat Burke as an intellectual enemy. Nonetheless, that was in the future. In April 1935 Sidney Hook was another force that Burke was reckoning with. And because Hook was tied to Deweyan pragmatism, to the political Left, and even to the *Southern Review*, his was a force that illustrates just how intertwined and inextricable were the threads that bound together the various intellectual communities that involved Kenneth Burke in the 1930s—and how negotiating them would be complicated indeed.

Uncomplicating all of that, or at least attending to the complications, is the job of this book. It is not that we want to reduce Kenneth Burke's intellectual reach and activity during the 1930s to the human circles that he was materially connected with in April 1935. Nor do we pretend that our account here and elsewhere in this book has exhausted the cultural and intellectual resonances that sounded in America in 1935. Far from it. Burke was a product of much more than the communities we have described, and his connections went far beyond the ones we have named and will name. After all, Burke remained forever considerate of European writers and thinkers and intellectual movements—Freud and Marx were just the most prominent of these—and his reading was voluminous, international, and catholic. In April 1935 alone, his letters allude to works by Bentham, Kafka, Marx, Hegel, Spengler, Richards, Freud, Mann, and Bertrand Russell. Nor do we wish to reduce Burke's genius to a function of those whom he was reading or to underappreciate the individuality and originality of Burke's contributions. Nevertheless our contention is that Kenneth Burke's work during the 1930s can be understood better if it is considered in relation to the groups and individuals that he was conversing with, literally and metaphorically, orally and in writing, during the turbulent 1930s.

Two   Resisting the "Rout of the Esthetes"

Auscultation, Creation, and Revision

Kenneth Burke's speech at the April 1935 American Writers' Congress was not the first time that he had recommended specific rhetorical tactics suitable for the spread of leftist ideology. As early as February 1931, Burke had published "Boring from Within," a response-with-suggestions to Edmund Wilson's landmark January 14, 1931, *New Republic* article, "An Appeal to Progressives." Wilson's essay, which galvanized New York intellectuals because it registered his conversion from liberal to radical and his invitation to others to come along, was probably the first one to suggest in print the use of Madison Avenue publicity methods "to sell the idea of Communism to Americans" (238). Having given up on the efforts of liberals and long-term Communist Party regulars to effect change (not to mention on Herbert Hoover), having turned away from the aestheticism anatomized in his yet-to-appear *Axel's Castle*, and getting encouragement from his friend John Dos Passos,[1] Wilson recommended in "An Appeal to Progressives" that American liberals and leftists should unify themselves ideologically around a commitment to "the ownership of the means of production by the government" while distancing themselves philosophically and rhetorically from outmoded American civic documents. "The Declaration of Independence and the Constitution are due to be supplanted by some new manifesto and some new bill of rights," he wrote (238). In his response in the *New Republic*, Burke registered general agreement with Wilson's political and economic goals, and (in anticipation of his Writers' Congress speech) with Wilson's desire "to take Communism away from the Communists"—that is, to develop an independent, American version of Communism and to find a "publicity method" suitable for the spread of socialist ideology in the United States. But Burke disagreed with the particular rhetorical tactics Wilson had recommended.

"Attack capitalism by the ideals of capitalism itself," he wrote in "Boring from Within" less than three weeks after Wilson's essay. The way to sell Communism in the United States, especially to a middle class whose assent would be essential, is not to repudiate American values, Burke felt: "Mr. Wilson makes the mistake that radicalism has always made in America. He would translate old world notions verbatim, without national adaptation" (327). Rather, success would come from identifying Communism intimately with popular symbols such as the Constitution, the flag, and so forth—to bore not from without but from within, in other words,[2] "to join Rotary Clubs, . . . play checkers at the Y.M.C.A., . . . [and] attend church. . . . To be immediately effective, we [writers] must promote changes which can be put into effect by utilizing the mentality already at hand" (327).

Burke left the matter thus for the remainder of 1931. As the Depression deepened that year, he attended to other pressing personal matters. In addition to managing the Andover farm, dealing with the emotional complexities incumbent upon his failing first marriage and developing second, and working full-time through June at the Bureau of Social Hygiene in New York, he spent his time and energy that spring and summer seeing *Counter-Statement* and *Towards a Better Life* through the publication process. After negotiating and signing a contract for *Counter-Statement* in April, Burke finished the final chapters and did some rewriting so the book could go into production in June and come out in September. That finished, he moved immediately to complete his novel *Towards a Better Life*, which he turned over to his publisher around Labor Day, after a feverish effort; it appeared in print in January 1932.[3]

Both books are mostly concerned with aesthetic matters, though they are certainly not inattentive to political and social issues. *Counter-Statement*, a collection of essays that record Burke's thinking during the course of the 1920s, includes analyses of modernist writers such as Mann and Flaubert and of bohemian aesthetic issues such as eloquence and form. It can easily be read alongside *Axel's Castle*, so much so that Gorham Munson could describe the work as associated with "the purest aestheticism" (*Destinations*, 153) and Granville Hicks (editor of *New Masses*) could complain in a review that Burke was "too principally concerned with eloquence" and technique at the expense of the social aspects of art (75). On the other hand, Burke had very good reason to object strenuously to Hicks's characterization[4] because *Counter-Statement* also includes essays, notably "Program" and "Lexicon Rhetoricae" but others as well, on issues close to the heart of the radical program: the artist's confrontation with industrialism, the connections between art and ethics, the material conditions that artists needed to address in 1931, and the pragmatic relations between art and society—essays, in other words, that treat art not as self-contained or as self-expression but as a socially engaged moral and civic force. The result is that *Counter-Statement* amounts to a careful, if unstable, negotiation between the competing claims of art and politics.

Towards a Better Life, pieces of which Burke had begun publishing in the *Dial* as early as 1928, is even more aesthetically oriented. The novel gradually "declaims" through a series of unsent epistles the fictional autobiography of one John Neal, a writer whose artistic approach to life increasingly poisons his personal relationships and isolates him as "a secular anchorite." Highly experimental in narrative technique, highly stylized in language and form, in some ways an autobiographical portrait of an artist, *Towards a Better Life* is the antithesis of the "proletarian realism" that Mike Gold was already espousing in *New Masses*. As Burke wrote in his preface, "[I] emphasiz[ed] the essayistic rather than the narrative, the emotional predicaments of my hero rather than the details by which he arrived at them. . . . In form the resultant chapters are somewhat like a sonnet sequence, a progression by stages, by a series of halts; or they might be compared to an old-style opera" (xii–xiii). In the final movement in the opera, John Neal's stream-of-consciousness "testamentum meum" records the narrator's disintegration and possible escapes from his predicament through "madness, travel, drugs, the Faith, [or] death by one's own hand." In short, *Towards a Better Life* is as aestheticized a novel as one might imagine; even its title points far more toward personal and private amelioration than to any kind of social improvement.[5] While John Neal's epistles are certainly not without rhetorical and social force—a good case can be made, in fact, that Neal is the symbolic embodiment of a bohemian, art-for-art's-sake artistic attitude that Burke wished to satirize and distance himself from—the appearance of *Towards a Better Life* early in 1932, a year after Wilson's "Appeal to Progressives" and in the same year as Wilson's *American Jitters*, must have seemed as anachronistic as the Symbolist poetry Wilson wrote about in *Axel's Castle*.

The politics at the center of "Boring from Within" and "Program" and the aesthetic interests that animate *Counter-Statement* and *Towards:* these, then, are the tensions at the core of Burke's next project, *Auscultation, Creation, and Revision*—indeed, at the core of all his 1930s books. Inevitably so; after finishing *Counter-Statement* and *Towards a Better Life*, Burke continued to wrestle with the same questions that were concerning others of his generation in 1932: What exactly are the responsibilities of the artist to society? What should be the function of art, especially during times of political and social crisis? Should art reflect, create, or mold life—and in what proportions? To what degree is a writer's artistic rebellion also a political one? How should writers balance the claims of art and politics, the individual and the collective? How should art be brought to a broad audience that would include the working class? Is propaganda something that organizers and other nonartists write, or is art always and necessarily propagandistic?

The "Literary Wars" of the Early 1930s

As Daniel Aaron documented four decades ago, such questions were not asked for the first time during the Depression. During the fifteen years before *Counter-Statement*, Mike Gold, Joseph Freeman, Max Eastman, and others on the left were fixtures in New York literary circles as much as were Alfred Stieglitz, Eugene O'Neill, and Marianne Moore; the famous Armory Show of 1913 that introduced Duchamp, Matisse, Cezanne, and other Continental moderns to New York occurred concurrently with John Reed's equally famous pageant in support of striking Paterson, New Jersey, textile strikers. While the aestheticism of the *Dial, Broom,* and the *Little Review* was widely appreciated during the 1920s, at the same time the *Masses,* the *Liberator,* and *New Masses* all nourished a vital leftist agenda for art and politics. While many of the moderns were expatriating themselves to Paris during the 1920s, many others, if less famously, were visiting Moscow, especially after the 1927 execution of Sacco and Vanzetti: by 1935, Gold, Eastman, Freeman, Wilson, Dos Passos, Matthew Josephson, Sidney Hook, John Dewey, Theodore Dreiser, Isidor Schneider, and E. E. Cummings had all inspected the Soviet experiment firsthand. Nor is it accurate to oppose aesthetes against leftists, since many people were managing quite well to be both: the *Masses* had of course offered a literary and artistic forum for left-leaning moderns before World War I; Dadaists at once promoted private, experimental poetry and highly politicized street theater; the committed Communist Joseph Freeman consistently turned out highly aestheticized verse; Eugene O'Neill, Waldo Frank, Jean Toomer, Sherwood Anderson, John Dos Passos, Theodore Dreiser, and others produced novels and criticism that were at once highly social and highly modern (e.g., *The Hairy Ape,* 1922; *Our America,* 1919; *City Block,* 1922; *Holiday,* 1923; *Cane,* 1922–23; *Winesburg, Ohio,* 1919; *Manhattan Transfer,* 1925; *Sister Carrie,* 1925); Objectivist poets with a leftist political agenda, such as Louis Zukofsky and Charles Reznikoff, nevertheless emphasized poetic technique above all in the "Program" they published in the February 1931 issue of *Poetry;* and a segment in Burke's "Notes on the Terminology" in *Counter-Statement* therefore exhorted artists and critics to resist walling off "art" from "life" (188–90).

But as the Depression deepened and hardened, emotions intensified in the literary wars, the arguments grew more strident, and positions solidified and polarized. Many artists in the aestheticist camp kept faith in—and were forced to defend—the staple artistic values that had been sustaining them: a commitment to novelty and experimentation, individuality and originality, impersonality and the autonomy of art; stylistic and formal refinement and finish; an elitist appeal to the artistically initiated and a proportionate scorn for the mass of unsophisticated philistines; personal satisfaction as a motive for writing, rather than commercial or rhetorical success. Allen Tate, one confirmed champion of autonomous art, objected to some of Burke's audience-centered pronouncements in *Counter-Statement* with a manifesto to Burke (August 3, 1933) that fairly summarized aesthete values left over from the 1920s:

> It is perfectly obvious that there are readers and writers, and it seems equally obvious that High Literature (which is usually mixed with certain incidental impurities) is not written for the specific purpose of moving anybody. My own doctrine [is] that High Literature is nothing less than a complete qualitative and quantitative re-creation of the Very Thing-in-Itself. If some of its properties incidentally lead us to cut throats, seduce a virgin, or give all our goods to the poor, that is our responsibility. But because this may be so, there is no reason to rest the case upon that, and conclude that the whole function of literature is persuasion. A great poem is great whether anybody reads it or not.

High modernist achievements in fiction and poetry continued to pour forth as they had during the 1920s: Virginia Woolf's *The Waves* in 1931; T. S. Eliot's *Ash-Wednesday* in 1930; William Faulkner's *Light in August* in 1932; Joyce's "Work in Progress" in little magazines throughout the decade before it was published as *Finnegans Wake* in 1939. While Burke was welcoming the publication of *Towards a Better Life*, Marianne Moore and Morton Zabel were concurrently welcoming Pound's *A Draft of XXX Cantos* and Stevens's *Harmonium* with lengthy, enthusiastic reviews in *Poetry*.

Although the *Dial* and *Little Review* had passed on by the end of the 1920s, there were plenty of other little magazines to sustain their artistic values. *Poetry* in particular retained its aestheticist commitments throughout the Depression—editor Harriet Monroe and her assistant (and then successor) Zabel were busy attacking the poetic program of *Blast, Anvil, Dynamo, New Masses,* and *Partisan Review* as early as Zabel's March 1932 mockery of leftist writers and as tardily as Monroe's 1934 essay "Art and Propaganda"; regular *Poetry* reviewers such as Tate, Blackmur, Moore, and Robert Penn Warren upheld the primacy of art over politics; and William Carlos Williams and his circle were placing their least political poems into *Poetry* (Williams once, in 1933, with the attendant footnote, "Walk on the delicate parts of necessary mechanisms [in poetry] and you will pretty soon have neither food, clothing, nor even Communism itself, Comrades. Read good poetry!"). *Pagany*, strongly endorsed by Williams, announced in its 1930 debut that it too would be devoted to "the word" and be "wary of definite alliance with any formulated standard," so by the time it failed in March 1933, it had published Yvor Winters's apolitical "Snow-Ghost" (as well as socially conscious stories by Caldwell and Farrell), prose selections by Stein and a chapter from *Towards a Better Life* (as well as selections from Williams's novel *White Mule*), chinoiserie by Witter Bynner and Katherine Anne Porter's elegant "Bouquet for October," and lots of Objectivist verse to go with more committed poetry by Harry Roskolenkier.[6] *Hound and Horn*, subtitled "A Harvard Miscellany" when it first appeared in 1927, shook off the close identification with Cambridge when the *Dial* failed, and under the editorship of R. P. Blackmur and Lincoln Kirstein published modernist poetry by Moore, Williams, Stevens, and Yvor Winters; stories by Porter, Caroline Gordon, and Joyce, and selections from *Towards a Better Life*; reviews and essays by Tate, Winters, and Blackmur; and the occasional contribution by its patron saint, T. S. Eliot, whose presence and influence fairly dominated the magazine. By 1932 *Hound and Horn* had ceased sponsoring a reactionary New Humanism and had begun acknowledging the economic and political crisis by publishing photos of New York by Walker Evans, passages from Dos Passos's *1919*, and articles and reviews on leftist magazines, Trotsky, and Marxism; but it nevertheless remained associated with "the creation of a leisure-class culture" (Hicks, "Crisis," 5). And it remained consistent to the end to the editorial and aesthetic position it articulated (anonymously) in its farewell issue in the summer of 1934: "the magazine has occupied itself entirely with problems, moral and technical, of the creative artist, dealing with political and social implications only as they are specifically involved" (583–84).[7] Eliot's own *Criterion*, meanwhile, promoted the commitment to impersonality and political disinterestedness that Eliot had been trumpeting for some time, and gave a number of people a chance to champion the eternal nobility of poetry as against particular political agendas. The magazine would present "literature as the beautiful expression of particular sensation and perception, general emotion, and impersonal ideas," Eliot had promised ("Idea," 4), and so as late as 1935 it was still offering "Style or Beauty in Literature" (by T. Sturge Moore) close by an attack on the Communists by A. L. Rowse. Eliot himself, back in the United States to lecture at Harvard from early November 1932 until the end of March 1933, continued to give many the impression that he professed faith in "an art that aspires to the timeless" (Aaron, 250). While it would be an exaggeration to claim that Eliot in those lectures (collected in *The Use of Poetry and the Use of Criticism*, 1933) lobbied on behalf of a separation between art and economics, it is nevertheless true that he wrote far more about "what is permanent or eternal in poetry" than about "what is merely the expression of the spirit of an age" (27). (Within days of Eliot's first lecture Franklin Roosevelt was elected president, and on January 30 Adolf Hitler was installed as chancellor of Germany, but neither was mentioned by Eliot.)[8] Joseph Wood

Krutch, a frequent contributor to aestheticist little magazines, summed up
the case against what was coming to be known as proletarian literature in
his 1932 book *Was Europe a Success?* He defended Eliot's artistic detachment
and "disinterestedness" (75), reasserted the fast distinction between "man
qua Artist and man qua Reformer" (61) that Burke had exploded in *Counter-
Statement,* and held that art was "essentially a form of rationalized and extended Contemplation, designed primarily to render more vivid . . . those
experiences which are capable of being enjoyed for their own sakes" (63; also
quoted in Aaron, 259).

In its first issue of 1931, *Pagany* also carried an attack by Pound on *New
Masses.* No surprise there either: Mike Gold and his comrades were then
imploring New York writers, artists, and photographers to commit themselves to persuasion instead of aestheticism, in particular to commit to the
form of what he called "proletarian realism," a genre designed to speed social
revolution by eschewing verbal acrobatics and explorations of the inner life—
and according to which "every poem, every novel and drama, must have a
social theme, or it is mere confectionary" (*New Masses,* September 1930, 4–5;
also quoted in Aaron, 208–9). Taking their cues from Marx instead of Freud,
Gold instead of Eliot, proletarian writers were committing themselves to
depicting workers' lives and the economic privation of millions, instead of to
the interior lives of bohemian individuals. "WE WANT TO PRINT," wrote Gold
as he assumed the editorship of *New Masses,*

> —Confessions—diaries—documents
> —The concrete—
> —Letters from hoboes, peddlers, small town atheists, unfrocked
>   clergymen and schoolteachers—
> —Revelations by rebel chambermaids and night club waiters—
> —The sobs of driven stenographers—
> —The poetry of steel workers—
> —The wrath of miners—the laughter of sailors—
> —Strike stories, prison stories, work stories—
> —Stories by Communist, I. W. W. and other revolutionary workers.
>   (Editorial, July 1928; quoted in Homberger, 126)

New Masses, the *New Republic,* the *Nation,* and any number of less celebrated
but equally socially committed magazines sought such writing in the service
of revolutionary aims throughout the 1930s.

Writers and critics sympathetic to the proletarian point of view attacked
their aesthete brethren with relish. While *Poetry, Pagany,* and *Hound and Horn*
were bashing proletarian magazines, those magazines were happily bashing
back. In the September 1932 *New Masses,* Waldo Frank, Granville Hicks,
Sherwood Anderson, Edmund Wilson, Mike Gold, and others explained how

they had come to their decision to give up bohemian themes and outlets and to embrace proletarian ends in their work; and the following February Hicks in the same magazine explained his theory of proletarian literature and criticism in a way that dismissed *Hound and Horn*, literature written for "the leisure class," and especially "technique" ("Crisis"). By the middle of 1933 things had reached such a state that Tate was provoked to defend technique— "Good craft does not make great poetry, but there is no great poetry without it" ("Poetry and Politics," 311)—against *New Masses* and *New Republic* attacks on technique. Both sides were demonizing the other and leaving little room for neutrality or third positions.

The newly proletcult writers acted on their beliefs as well, in very visible ways. Dreiser and Dos Passos (late in 1931) and Cowley, Frank, and Wilson (in February 1932) went to bloody Harlan County, Kentucky, to support striking miners.[9] And the Left mobilized behind the William Z. Foster–James W. Ford Communist Party ticket during the presidential election campaign of 1932: in September, more than fifty signers (among them Sherwood Anderson, Dreiser, Dos Passos, Frank, Wilson, Erskine Caldwell, Countee Cullen, Langston Hughes, and Josephson) published an open letter denouncing the two major political parties and committing themselves to the Ford-Foster lost cause, then followed up with a famous and widely distributed pamphlet entitled *Culture and the Crisis*, which called upon intellectuals and artists to take up the proletarian cause, for the choice facing them was "between serving either as the cultural lieutenants of the capitalist class or as allies and fellow travelers of the working class" (29).[10]

Kenneth Burke was caught in these fast antitheses. Hicks wrote in the *New Republic* that *Counter-Statement* was a book by an aesthete whose "emphasis is so unmistakably on technique . . . that the reader is bound to realize that it is technique alone that interests [Burke]" (101). And in his *New Masses* article on criticism, Hicks placed Burke among the defenders of leisure-class culture and charged that in *Counter-Statement* Burke had "attempt[ed] to separate literature from life" ("Crisis," 4–5). Nor by any means was Hicks the only one who felt Burke belonged to the aestheticist camp. C. Hartley Grattan in the November 1932 *Forum* placed Burke (along with Lincoln Kirstein, *Hound and Horn*, and Yvor Winters) within "the Fastidious Movement, which is attempting to make a last stand for leisure class dilettantism" (285). Burke was furious about both characterizations—he engaged in a fierce back-and-forth with Hicks and tried to publish an answer to Grattan[11]—but could not commit himself without qualification to either the aestheticist or proletarian positions. In August 1931 Burke tried to clarify his middle position in a *New Republic* article called "Redefinitions II" (included in *Counter-Statement*, 188–90), but the portion of his essay that criticized "the proletarian attitude"—"It overlooks entirely the fact that there is the pamphlet, the political tract, the soap box oration, to deal with the specific issues of the day, whereas the literature of the imagination may prepare the minds in a more general fashion" (47)—only provided more fodder for his Marxist critics. A year later Burke was still taking a "both-and" stance: his August 1932 review of Glenway Wescott's *Fear and Trembling* acknowledged that "this is the economist's day [and] the day of the poets and the novelists in that they must subtly complement [the work of economists and their soap-box allies]"—but added that at the same time "the aesthetic . . . must form the fulcrum of our thinking, the basis of our self-respect, the incentive of our new muscularity, lest we become 'a finished race, a race that changed in every way but could not sufficiently change its mind'" (313). And Burke was maintaining an independent political position in keeping with his aesthetics: his friend Matthew Josephson and other writers urged him to join them in committing to support the Foster-Ford ticket and signing on to *Culture and the Crisis*, but Burke decided not to do so. (He probably voted for Norman Thomas.)[12]

Auscultation: *Burke's Entry into the Literary Wars*

As early as October 15, 1931, therefore, Burke proclaimed to William Carlos Williams that he was planning to contribute his own "political tirade" to the literary wars. The result would eventually be *Auscultation, Creation, and Revision*, subtitled "The Rout of the Esthetes" or "Literature, Marxism, and Beyond," a tract completed a year later that would eventually satisfy neither the aesthetes nor the Left—nor Burke, for that matter. In *Auscultation* Burke announced to his astonished audience (or to an audience that would have been astonished had *Auscultation* been published) that the war they thought they had been fighting was not the real contest at all. Not only were the aesthetes and Marxists not enemies, they were on the same side; and not only had the aesthetes not been routed, they had in fact won the game for themselves and their allies. Aestheticism, argued Burke, was in danger not because it had lost but because it had won. The fight long over, aestheticism seemed to be left without a purpose; the key question for writers now ought to be not "What politics should writers adopt?" but "What does the aesthetic do next?"

The *Auscultation* "essay" (as Burke called it), about 130 pages long as it was finally published in James Chesebro's 1993 collection *Extensions of the Burkeian System*,[13] shows evidence of several layers of construction. Burke had originally imagined a book with four parts: historical, logical, hortatory, and poetical (Burke to Cowley, unsent, June 4, 1932).[14] But as the project developed, he apparently decided that the hortatory section, what is now known as *Auscultation*, could stand on its own. The other parts were abandoned.[15] The book begins with the introductory and self-sufficient "Spring during Crisis," an eloquent, autobiographical meditation dated (either by Burke or his editor) "between 1930 and 1934" but very likely composed mostly in 1932, with the rest of the book;[16] in "Spring during Crisis," in the course of describing his move to Andover that spring with his family, Burke contemplates strategies for countering economic and social inequities through the power of literature, strategies that the rest of the book develops. That rest of the book is made up of forty-five short chapters, two to four pages each, which detail Burke's thoughts on the particular strategies for radical change that are proposed by Marxist theory and criticism. The book concludes with an "Addendum" and "A Parting Glance at Sister Antithesis," concluding gestures that make explicit Burke's sense of the rhetorical situation that motivated his book: "The book is overeager. But my 'vested interests' were endangered. The movement, by and large, seemed an attempt to prove that good writing was a kind of crime against the state" (165). Unlike *Counter-Statement*, *Towards a Better Life*, and his short-story collection *The White Oxen*, *Auscultation* was not put together from previously written pieces but was composed all of a piece, mainly in a burst of energy in the summer of 1932; no parts were published separately. Consequently *Auscultation* presents an extended and coherent (for Burke) critical argument. If the issues at the center of *Auscultation* are predictable, given the time when the book was written, anything but predictable is Burke's conclusion: instead of joining the stampede to adopt proletarian attitudes toward art, Burke engages in a rearguard action designed to preserve the possibility of revolutionary social ends for avant-garde art. As he wrote to Cowley while he was marketing his manuscript to publishers, *Auscultation* was Burke's "lone, last-stand defense of the 'aesthetic'" (October 3, 1932) against the claims of vulgar Marxists.

As Burke's letters to Cowley indicate, Cowley in many ways embodied what Burke felt himself up against—the "vested interests" mentioned in the "Addendum" (165)—as he wrote *Auscultation*. While Burke was beginning to contemplate and compose *Auscultation* in earnest, in April 1932, Cowley published "The Poet and the World," a review of John Dos Passos's novel *1919* that reified and exploited a binary between what Cowley termed the "art novel" (which dramatizes, even celebrates the conflict between two antagonists, "the poet" and "the world") and the "collective novel" (which takes society as a whole as its protagonist). Cowley felt that Dos Passos's career illustrated the binary. In his most recent novel, *1919*, Dos Passos had committed himself to writing "the first American collective novel" by making "society itself" his protagonist and thereby conveying "a sense of depth, of striking through surfaces to the real forces beneath them." The result was that Dos Passos created "a landmark in American fiction" (304–5). But early in his career, as a "late-Romantic," Dos Passos had committed to the aesthete "propositions" that Cowley deemed characteristic of the art novel: "That the cultivation and expression of his own sensibility are the only justifiable ends for the poet. That originality is his principal virtue. That society is hostile, stupid and unmanageable: it is the world of the philistines, from which it is the poet's duty and privilege to remain aloof. . . . That he triumphs over the world, at moments, by mystically including it within himself: these are his moments of *ecstasy*, to be provoked by any means in his power—alcohol, drugs, madness or saintliness, venery, suicide. That art exists apart from the world; it is the poet's revenge on society" (303). And so on. Cowley further identified the aestheticist camp with the *Dial*, with a commitment to experimentalism, and with stereotypical novels "still being published, and favorably criticized":

> "Mr. Zed has written the absorbing story of a talented musician tortured by the petty atmosphere of the society in which he is forced to live. His wife, whom the author portrays with witty malice, prevents him from breaking away. After an unhappy love affair and the failure of his artistic hopes, he commits suicide. . . ." They [i.e., the experimentally disposed authors of art novels] adopt new manners, poetic, mystical, learned, witty, allusive or obfuscatory. . . . Not all their ingenuity is wasted. Sometimes they make valuable discoveries; a few of the art novels . . . are minor masterpieces . . . and a very few, like *A Portrait of the Artist as a Young Man*, are masterpieces pure and simple. (303)

"The Poet and the World" was a review of *1919*, but it was also a review of *Towards a Better Life* and a critique of Burke's position as a writer, though Burke was never explicitly mentioned. The aesthete whom Cowley lambasted in the review was as much (or more) Kenneth Burke as it was the early Dos Passos. Not only was Burke closely identified with the *Dial*, which he had served many years before receiving the Dial Award in 1929, the year of its passing, but he had just three months earlier published a book principled rather precisely according to the aesthete tenets detailed in the review. Burke's protagonist in *Towards a Better Life* would have agreed "that the cultivation and expression of his own sensibility are the only justifiable ends for the poet," "that originality is his principal virtue," "that society is hostile, stupid and unmanageable, the world of the philistines, from which it is the poet's duty and privilege to remain aloof." Not only that, John Neal's story is fairly and closely described by other things in Cowley's catalog: the hero in Cowley's art novel induces "his moments of *ecstasy*," by means of "alcohol, drugs, madness or saintliness, venery, suicide," a rather precise echo of Neal's longings for "madness, travel, drugs, the Faith, [or] death by one's own hand" at the end of *Towards a Better Life*. Cowley's Mr. Zed, to Burke, must have stood for Burke himself, especially given the parallels between Burke's own experimental "portrait of the artist" and Joyce's, between Burke's style in *Towards* and the "poetic, mystical, learned, witty, allusive or obfuscatory" style mocked by Cowley, and, perhaps most galling of all, between Burke's personal struggles at home and the matching situation shadowed in Cowley's words about a talented artist tortured by a complicated domestic situation.

Whether others recognized Burke as a target of Cowley's review is not known, but it is certain that Burke recognized himself there. No sooner had the review appeared than Burke immediately (on April 25, 1932) shot off a letter to Cowley in which he questioned Cowley's claim that *1919* represented something new in American fiction (Burke mentioned Dreiser and Frank Norris as precursors), hotly defended the art novels that Cowley had defamed, and most of all objected to Cowley's walling off the art novel from the collective. Always suspicious of binaries and upset that the social aspects of *Towards* (and *Counter-Statement*) were being slighted if not elided, still smarting from Cowley's February 1932 review of *Towards* (in which Cowley reduced Burke's novel to a reprise of *A Rebours*), Burke was resolutely unwilling to accept Cowley's fast dichotomy between the aesthetic and the political in art, and he accused Cowley of unfairly lumping together and then dismissing a diverse group of books. The only thing about which Burke and Cowley could agree was that Dos Passos's brand of political novel, and the criticism that supported it, had won the day, but Burke was not happy about it: "as one great Art Novelist to another," he wrote, "I will grant you this: for a season, at least, our former books are invalidated. This year we must write, not The Poet and The World, but The Man and His Job."[17]

Burke closed his letter with a sign-off: "I shall not plague you about all this, for herewith I have had my say." But six weeks later, during breaks from writing *Auscultation*, Burke was still arguing about the review in a series of letters to Cowley (only one of which was ever sent). The outpouring—four long letters in three days—was provoked by a letter Cowley wrote at the beginning of June explaining his own interest in Communism and voicing his concern that Burke had come to a dead end: "I've got the idea that the path in which you're engaged (emotional plus ideological, they work together) is one which has no issue except that list of refuges [madness, travel, drugs, religion, suicide] you made in the last chapter of your Declamations. I said as much when I reviewed your book. . . . You've got to get into another path, another pattern of behavior" (June 2, 1932). To be fair to Cowley, he may have been concerned for his friend, especially because of Hart Crane's suicide on April 26. (Cowley's first wife, Peggy, was on board with Crane when he jumped to his death, and Cowley was powerfully shaken by the event.) In any case Cowley's letter must have epitomized for Burke the almost willful misunderstanding of his politics and the narrow-minded anti-aestheticism that was characterizing the New York literary scene in mid-1932. In his epistolary responses, several of them quite bitter, Burke attempted to explain once again his positions on art and politics. Over and over in the four letters to Cowley, Burke repeated a commitment to Communist goals: "the amusing thing is that my Program

in Counter-Statement is based specifically, explicitly, on the idea that the con-
fiscation of wealth is an economic necessity" (June 2, 1932, unsent). And
Burke emphasized his exasperation at Cowley's image of Burke's dead-ended-
ness (as expressed in the sentence from Cowley's June 2 letter and in the portrait of Burke in Cowley's *Exile's Return*, then being serialized in the *New
Republic*).[18] And in his letter Burke used language that later showed up in *Auscultation* about the specific "vested interests" that motivated *Auscultation*: "the
cause of my own rage [about "The Poet and the World"] was obvious: my
own vested interests were [being] attacked" (June 2, 1932, unsent).

In *Auscultation*, therefore, Burke took dead aim at the fast dichotomies
sponsored by Cowley in "The Poet and the World" and at the specific "vested
interests" under attack by Cowley and his camp. The week after he wrote the
letters to Cowley, he took up *Auscultation* with renewed energy and purpose.
"There is no use going into the Art Novel squabble" [in *Auscultation*], he had
written to Cowley on June 2 (unsent); but the text of *Auscultation* still indicates that Burke was determined to show that what he called the "Wilson-
Hicks-Cowley" point of view on aestheticism was a mistake: "Primarily, I
should hold against you what I hold against Wilson," he wrote to Cowley on
June 2: "This idea that one cannot set up a good revolution without first
bumping off a couple of conscientious, but not wholly apposite, poets." Further,

> I have . . . notes on the quackery of people like Granville Hicks ("I know these
> people who frighten little girls in girls' schools by not finding battle-scarred
> labor-agitators radical enough, I know these people who attack leisure-class
> morality as they sit in the rose gardens of defunct stockbrokers, I know these
> Hickville Grannies, I mean those Granville Hicks"), but by the time I am done
> I shall probably eliminate that as being too "local." Some, it is true, I hate to
> sacrifice, as that on Wilson: "He felt that everyone should give up something
> for the Revolution, so he held on to his securities and gave up Yeats." But
> these are merely to get oneself going. (Burke to Cowley, June 2, 1932, unsent)

These remarks are mirrored in the text of *Auscultation*, which stands as stout
confirmation of Paul Jay's assertion that Burke insisted in principle "on the
aesthetic as a force for disrupting the social and cultural life of modernity"
(*Blues*, 15–16). The savage comments on Hicks were indeed deleted from the
book, but he kept the ones on Wilson, albeit in disguise: "They [i.e., Marxist
critics in general, not Wilson specifically] feel that every man should give up
something for the Revolution; and as they would not like to give up their
apartments, they have compromised by sacrificing a few gentle, conscientious, but not wholly apposite poets" (88).[19] Burke alludes directly to Wilson,
Cowley, and Hicks as adversaries on page 90 of *Auscultation*, when he turns
specifically to "one critic warning us that his old Symbolist masters were no

longer serviceable as 'guides'" (a comment on Wilson's *Axel's Castle*), to "another, who had written a lovely book of verse picturing the Poet against the World" (an unmistakable allusion to Cowley), and to "another . . . warning against leisure-class traditions while himself teaching at a university" (a reference to Hicks, who taught at Rensselaer Polytechnic). On the same page, in his discussion of the Saul-Paul reversal, Burke noted that "a cry [arises] among some New York literary men to turn against certain conscientious but not wholly apposite schools which had generally been the admirations of their youth. It was as though one could not properly start the Revolution without killing off a few poets" (90). Dos Passos's *1919* is one of the few contemporary novels mentioned in *Auscultation*, and Cowley, the only writer whose work is quoted and discussed in much detail, stood in as the prime example of the dilemma facing the aesthete-turned-Marxist.

Convinced that aestheticism was not at all a dead end and eager to intervene in the literary wars, Burke addresses in *Auscultation* "that somewhat remarkable phenomenon, the 'rout of the esthetes,'" that Cowley and his tribe had declared:

> Here was a case where an entire literary generation, as soon as the word "esthete" was leveled at them, promptly "cleared out." It was generally felt that the exigencies of the times made such a move advisable. Before "clearing out" myself, I thought I would take one last look around, to see if anybody had left anything of value in the hastiness of departure—and sure enough, I discovered lying about unclaimed, a Philosophy of History, a Psychology, an Apologia for Art, a Methodology of Art, a Theory of Criticism, some valuable archives on the trends of Modern Literature, and a number of devices for relating the whole to the contemporary scene. (61)

What he found, in short, were reasons to defend aestheticism.

Auscultation was more than a defense of aestheticism, though, and anything but an anti-Marxist broadside. In his work Burke articulates a rhetorically subtle and sophisticated understanding of how literature affects readers and, thus, how it might effect social change. He redefines aestheticism so that it might be understood not as an art-for-art's-sake movement but as a more general aesthetic attitude of protest against materialism and cultural vacuity, and so that it could no longer be equated with leisure-class dilettantism or associated with social irresponsibility. In addition *Auscultation* was designed to explain why so many aesthetes were being attracted to Marxism and to reclaim them thereby *as aesthetes*—that is, to show them that aestheticism and leftist politics were compatible since they sprang from a common source. In the process, as Timothy Crusius has also shown, Burke questions again and again the logic and efficacy of what seemed to him the heart of Marxist theory—the "search for antithesis" (*"Auscultation"*). In the course of his sustained "complaint against Antithesis" (105), Burke deconstructs five specific paired contraries that he felt underpinned the vulgar Marxist criticism of the time: the antitheses between historical periods, between bourgeois and proletarian, between poetry and propaganda, between aesthetes and literary Marxists, and between the aesthetic and practical frameworks. In place of those antitheses, especially the last one, Burke offers an antidote for either/or thinking, a proto-"comic corrective" that he would develop later in *Attitudes toward History:* "Antithesis, so clearly adapted to a state of affairs wherein people's minds were *necessarily closed*, may not be the best possible accommodation to a state of affairs wherein people's minds are being *necessarily opened again*. For just as antithesis tends to bolster one against other closed minds, so it can tend to close the minds of others" (163). In other words Burke in *Auscultation* offers a new aesthetic and critical position that was generally compatible with Marxism but that was more ecumenical and less dependent on Marxism's rather fixed oppositions.

Rejecting Marx's Historical Antithesis

Burke's attempt at a corrective to Marx's demarcation of historical periods is easy enough to see in *Auscultation*. "My book will have the Communist objectives, and the Communist tenor," Burke characteristically told Malcolm Cowley as he was writing it, "but the approach will be the approach that seems significant to me" (June 4, 1932). The approach that seemed significant to Burke at that moment involved a reassessment of Marx's theory of culture, beginning with his dialectical model of history.

Burke found Marx's dialectical approach to history "extravagant" (99), that is, unsatisfactory as a means for accounting for the progression of history. Marx of course had constructed history as a dialectical process developing through a series of conflicts between recurring antitheses, the resolution of which results in new successive historical stages. Marx was especially attentive to the recent historical tension between bourgeois and proletarian, which he predicted would lead inevitably to a new socialist society. As Burke summarizes it in his segment on "The Marxian Philosophy of History," according to Marx "we shall find antithetical 'class moralities,' . . . their differences widening. . . . Opposition must become more and more acute until it leads to conflict [and] . . . the institution of private property . . . must now give way to collectivist institutions" (108). But Burke was "only roughly in agreement" with Marx's view of history (109). "Hegel's dialectic was a vast and novel scheme for giving us a metaphysic of history. Marx attempted to use the basic concept upon which to found a 'science' of history. Yet . . . the concept of a progression from thesis to antithesis, and thence to synthesis, is unnecessary" (99).

Burke preferred to understand history as a more general and less predictable movement from a period of integration to one of disintegration or reintegration as a result of the entrance of "new matter" into the system. As he would explain more fully in *Permanence and Change* (especially when explaining the concept of "piety") and more generally in *Attitudes toward History*, a society is integrated when its social and economic practices and institutions work together consistently, "when its institutions enable one to do what they require of him, and its standards enable him to want to do what he is doing" (99). Such stability is threatened by the inevitable confrontation with new ideas, discoveries, or technologies that change people's ways of living and thinking about the world. A society will struggle to assimilate the new into its existing ideologies; too much change will inevitably throw people's desires and institutional requirements out of kilter: institutions will frustrate their own goals, and people will begin to seek things that are discouraged or outlawed by the system. The society then disintegrates or reintegrates; in the best of cases, it develops a new system of meanings, new ideologies that permit it to account for the new matter and thereby continue. Against Marx, Burke was contending that whether a society reintegrates or disintegrates, the new cultural configuration that results is merely different from and not necessarily antithetical to the old system; his "schema . . . lays the emphasis upon a Difference rather than upon an Antithesis" (100; also 103 and 171–72) because the concept of "difference" offers broader possibilities than the concept of "antithesis." More particularly, although Burke acknowledged in *Auscultation* that capitalist ideology is disintegrating, he did not acknowledge that a specifically proletarian revolution to counter the bourgeois framework was inevitable.[20] Indeed, Burke claims, Marxists "plead for it *precisely because they have no causal guarantee that it will prevail*" (118).

Burke's recent reading of Bertrand Russell's *The Analysis of Mind* (he refers to the book on page 78–79) had indicated to him that modern science was no longer prepared to make definitive claims about the nature of matter or an empirically verifiable theory of causality. Particularly dubious, according to Russell, were claims linking the physical realm to the mental; science simply did not yet have the ability to verify such connections. Burke therefore concluded that "Marx's so-called scientific theory of history is not scientific at all but involves judgments about the nature of the universe which science cannot make" (62). Working in the name of science, Marx had managed to "smuggle in some contraband optimism" (115); in other words, Marxism's great appeal was that it lent scientific authority to what was simply a hope that events would turn out the "right" way. But Burke regarded such optimism with suspicion.

"A Psychology": Collapsing the Bourgeois-Proletarian Antithesis

Burke extended his critique of Marx's historical dialectic by taking analogous aim at "economic determinism," Marx's fundamental contention that ideology is determined by people's relationship to their mode of production. The resulting bourgeois-proletarian antithesis, Burke argues, "gives a faulty explanation of human psychology, as it overstresses the changing or historic aspects of thought and neglects the 'constants' of human physiology" (63).[21] Bourgeois and proletarians share key characteristics: everyone is victimized by capitalist ideology, and all respond to the universal demands, the unshakable ideologies, of the human body.

If economic determinism were followed to its logical conclusion, Burke argues in *Auscultation*, what should develop is not a system of antithetical bourgeois and proletarian ideologies but rather a "heterogeneity of ideologies" arising in response to the varied work environments characteristic of industrial capitalism (111). The ideology of a miner, for instance, would differ from that of a store clerk even though both are "workers," and the ideology of a working chemist would overlap with that of a leisure-class chemistry student. Furthermore, Burke reasoned, the necessary cooperation between specialists within and between corporations should—according to a strict model of economic determinism—create an attitude of tolerance and not conflict, an attitude that would stand in contradiction to much vulgar Marxist criticism in which individual members of the bourgeoisie are held responsible for the suffering of workers, or in which individual writers are publicly criticized for their "irrelevant art." For Burke, conflict and cooperation both cut across class lines: industrial workers fight farmworkers; capital and labor work together in the colonial exploitation of other nations; bourgeois oppressors improve the lot of those they oppress. Hence Burke finds any number of competing interests, but few of them specific expressions of class conflict. "What simple antithesis is possible here?" he asks by way of summary (130–31).

Observations such as these led Burke to conclude that no exact correspondence exists between productive forces and ideology; economics is but one of many factors that account for a person's attitudes. If strict causation is omitted from Marxist theory, all that remains is the claim—well supported by Marx—that economic circumstances and environments influence the way people think. "But to say as much is to realize that we have no reason for supposing that there is only one way of thinking on the subject, or that people must come to think this one way" (116). Indeed any number of ideologies, each with its own proposal for ending the Depression, could be considered "economically determined" because they grew out of the economic crisis. Some form of collectivism is one possibility (and the possibility that Burke himself favored), but there were others: fascism and the possibility of a reformed capitalism, not to mention even more revolutionary schemes such as the Luddite effort to eliminate technology or the Agrarian scheme to reconstitute southern society on a plantation model.

In short, Burke was finding Marx's account of economic determinism to be neither realistic nor logically compelling. More to Burke's point in *Ausculta-tion*, the simple binaries that follow from the bourgeois-proletarian antithesis were undermining the power of Marxist critics by entangling them in hopeless projects and intellectual inconsistencies. For example, since the logic of antithesis seems to demand that bourgeois thinking should give rise to diametrically opposed thinking from the proletariat, "critics are now busy trying to help the inevitable course of history by discovering which of the thoughts of a bourgeois are bourgeois thoughts, so that they may advise the proletariat to think antithetical thoughts" (97). Antithetical thinking (of the kind that Hicks was articulating in "The Crisis in Criticism," for example, or that Cowley was offering in his review of *1919*) "completely misguides the functions of critical enquiry" by implying that revolutionary critics should search for "the proletarian opposite of a sonnet" or a workers' equivalent to a cathedral that might be something other than "a cathedral stood on its head" (104). In other words Marxist critics were naive first in assuming a necessary, even congruent connection between class and ideology and then in attempting to assign particular ideas to one group. "The task," Burke remarks dryly, "is not an easy one" (97). In addition Burke points to the inconsistency of maintaining the inevitability of the revolution while carrying out a massive propaganda program:

> While they are eager to show how a bourgeois, as the result of economic determinism, *simply cannot help* thinking bourgeois thoughts, they exhort the antithetically placed proletariat to *please think* antithetical proletarian thoughts. This discrepancy always bewilders the non-Marxian, who can never understand why the bourgeois learned his lesson so easily under the promptings of historical necessity, whereas the proletarian, who was exposed to antithetical promptings, still requires considerable coaching. (117)

This contradiction leads to all kinds of problems as critics try to sort out questions of responsibility and artists wonder what audiences to address and to what purposes. If members of the bourgeois class truly cannot help the way they think, is it fair or even useful to blame them individually for working-class suffering? If writers were born to the bourgeoisie, are they necessarily and permanently tainted? If the proletariat should inevitably develop the proper class consciousness, then who would be the audience for proletarian art?

Perhaps most important, the bourgeois-proletarian antithesis leads to what Burke calls "the dilemma of proletarian denudation," whereby in the attempt to erect a strict class opposition, all kinds of pleasures associated with the ruling elite—elegant poetry, opera, philosophy, chess, landscape gardens, all sorts of other leisure time activities—are to be shunned by workers (103).

An earlier draft of *Auscultation* contained a section entitled "A bourgeois, whatever he is, is *human;* hence, a strict proletarian antithesis would be *inhuman*" (Burke to Cowley, September 22, 1932): the title, which captures Burke's flair for withering sarcasm, ridicules Marxist criticism by pushing it to a logical extreme; and it suggests his outrage at the demand, which he was seeing as implicit in strict Communism, that workers' lives be stripped bare of the very things that define their humanity. The trick, Burke was arguing, is not to create art fit for workers but to make workers' lives fit for art. Burke envisioned a future when all people might share in the culture, the leisure, and the material goods made possible by industrialism—a future in which "people will vie with one another in difficult relaxations" (87).

Paradoxically and importantly, Burke further complicated Marxist economic antitheses by returning to a kind of determinism, a version of materialism. He offered for consideration the possibility of the existence of a second layer of productive forces—"organic productive forces"—by which he means simply the organs and limbs of the body (119). Since these organic forces have not changed much over the course of history, there should exist some relatively constant elements of ideology that derive from them. In other words and in anticipation of *Permanence and Change*, Burke posits the existence of "other human 'constants' overriding the bourgeois-proletarian dichotomy" (120)—namely "an ideology of the 'human substrate,' the patterns of thought common to all [people] insofar as the 'organic productive forces' are common to all" (123). If humans have hands, perhaps they also have "hand-thoughts"—"patterns of thinking to duplicate the hand's function of 'grasping'" (120); similarly the fist is translated into pugnacity, the eye into a love for clarity, and the palate into taste. Burke was offering his explanation more than half in jest, but he nevertheless was committing himself to the compulsions of the body.

In this way Burke arrived again at the possibility of a bourgeois-proletarian synthesis. This synthesis is crucial indeed since truly opposing ideologies would push the two classes so far apart that they could either ignore each other or live as perfect complements.[22] "We quarrel insofar as our ideologies are identical, insofar as you want to keep for yourself what I want to take from you" (119). The revolution will come when proletarian and bourgeois desires are the same, or are represented as the same. Synthesis, then, for Burke, is not something that follows revolution but is a necessary precondition for it. Indeed, in contrast to the vulgar Marxist critics, Burke observed that this synthesis was already emerging in American culture: "the very concept of 'the system' should lead rather to the realization that people were 'Victims All,' that bourgeois and proletarian alike had accommodated their thinking to the imperious demands of a profit-economy" (172). Burke's startling, not to mention unpopular, conclusion was that successful revolutionary criticism works not by widening the gap between the classes but by enabling people to identify more fully with one another.

Revolutionary rhetoric, therefore—including fiction, photography, film, and criticism—must be a rhetoric of synthesis, not antithesis. This conclusion is one that Burke would elaborate throughout the 1930s. An effective cultural critic must be able to produce common ground, to convert those who never before imagined that they might sympathize with Communism. Writers must produce literary works that raise consciousness and heal divisions. And to do so, "the first thing [a writer] must drop as totally inadequate to his purposes will be the note of *Antithesis*, so ably suited for convincing the convinced, and so thoroughly unsuited to anything else" (169). "Antithesis . . . must become very modest in its application; and the critic, instead of throwing out wide areas of literature in the name of Antithesis, must confine his bourgeois-proletarian divergencies to strictly party differences, particularities of the vote, questions of legal methods, etc., recognizing that when he moves into the broad sphere of imaginative art, insofar as both sides of the dichotomy are 'human,' their art must overlap" (122–23).

With these words Burke was back to the project of "Boring from Within," back to recommending rhetorical tactics for furthering revolutionary ends. Where Wilson had recommended that American radicals coalesce into "a genuine opposition" that would "sell the idea of Communism to the public" by replacing the Declaration of Independence and Constitution with "some new manifesto," Burke was indicating that forming such a "true opposition" would only alienate most Americans. "Zestful antagonism has been the bane of radicals in America," he noted in "Boring" (327). That radical whom Burke half-humorously asked to join Rotary Clubs and play checkers at the YMCA in order to gain persuasive access to a wide audience, in order to "over drinks and a cigar [be able to] say to our boon companions (training ourselves to forget that we would like to strangle them), . . . 'Why don't the big fellows have to part with a little more of their incomes in times like these?'" ("Boring," 328), becomes in *Auscultation* a "wheedler," a rhetorical gradualist whom he imagines chatting with the local folks about Communism as a solution to the nation's economic difficulties:

"why I begin to believe we might patch things up with a minimum of disaster by some of the changes recommended by the a—the—a—oh, by the Russians, or by the—a—the—the Communists." He will then show how much Communism there is in the modern state already, and suggest that we need a little more—grumbling perhaps that any change at all is necessary, agreeing that change is a nuisance, that there is nothing alluring about it, and suggesting that, since he shares the general dislike of change, we should confine ourselves to the fewest changes possible. Such minimum changes would seem to lie in the direction of a more Communistically distributed buying power. At this point he could appeal to the local grocer, who would certainly agree with him that a better distributed buying power would be a godsend to this here community. (169)

The wheedler puts aside fiery predictions of a new, utopian world order to be won through struggle and sacrifice. Instead, seeking converts rather than martyrs, the wheedler offers a familiar and pragmatic solution—a slight but significant shift in economic policy—that might eventually develop into something quite radical. Burke would continue to recommend analogous rhetorical strategies to his leftist comrades throughout the decade.

"An Apologia for Art": Collapsing the Poetry-Propaganda Antithesis

In critiquing Marxist dialectic, Burke in *Auscultation* was grounding his aesthetics and cultural criticism in a markedly different understanding of historical progression and the formation of ideology within culture. This foundation has important implications for any rhetorical strategy aimed at social change, for not only does Burke argue for a rhetoric of synthesis; he also insists that "the ways of influence are devious"—that is, that language works to shape actions in much more complex ways than either the Marxists or the aesthetes had been understanding (Burke to Cowley, June 2, 1932; unsent). There is no "categorical breach" between "pure" and "applied" literature, Burke insists, nor between "poetry" and "propaganda"—each is persuasive and potentially revolutionary (55). Nor is there good reason to condemn out of hand those who write "pure literature" (and for that reason Burke pauses to defend Joyce, Stein, Mann, and Eliot and critics such as I. A. Richards, William Empson, and Remy de Gourmont: 126–27, 146, 155).

What Burke chiefly objected to in Marxist criticism was its out-of-hand dismissal of "bourgeois" writing, particularly as that term could be used to condemn anything other than political pamphlets, proletarian novels, or protest poetry. Whether he came to his conclusions independently or took his cue from Marx himself (who never repudiated Shakespeare and who retained an appreciation for the aesthetic dimensions of life), Burke saw such an exclusion of anything other than explicitly "relevant" art as a harmful narrowing of the range of possibilities of expression. Literature, he argued, is never irrelevant; even the "purest" work serves fundamentally practical purposes: to exercise the analytical powers of the mind and to open people to change. The critique of capitalism requires sharp critical abilities, and reading literature—any kind of literature—is a good way to develop them: "The equipment which enables a mind to see things in accordance with [a Marxian] interpretation can only arise out of an equipment for interpretation in general" (134). Furthermore, if literature is to keep the mind open and agile, ready for change, it follows that Marxists should encourage a great diversity of literature.

Finally, because in a revolutionary period there will be a number of symbolic orders competing for allegiance, literature may lead the public to a particular choice. It may persuade. Burke flatly denied any categorical distinction between literature and what he called propaganda. Both are symbolic action, both are rhetoric:

> What is the difference between pure and applied literature, poetry and propaganda? Literature must always have its "gravitational pull," by which I mean that it must always be directed towards some worldly situation. Literature is the manipulation of a vocabulary in such a way that it provides us with images, the motions and emotions, relevant to such a situation. If there is to be a storm, poetry (pure literature) and propaganda (applied literature) will both deal with it. . . . The poet will prepare us for this storm by saying, "Beware, a storm approacheth," while the pamphleteer will handle the matter by saying, "Go thou, and buy rubbers." (55)

All texts that create effects on readers, whether they be sonnets or soapbox speeches or advertisements, do so by the same rhetorical mechanisms—they exploit the attitudes and expectations of the audience. The distinction between poetry and propaganda, Burke argues, should be based on the relationship between the work and the social context in which it is read rather than any quality inherent to the text or any author's method or ideology. A work may be considered "propaganda" if it addresses a "burning issue" of the day, poetry if it does not. Dos Passos's novel *1919* was, in 1932, propaganda not because it is a new type of fiction (as Cowley had argued) but because it plays upon attitudes foremost in the minds of Depression-weary readers. In fifty or a hundred years, in a period of prosperity and peace, *1919* will be poetry. "There is no fundamental difference," Burke writes, "in the literary tactics of [a] sex book, *Uncle Tom's Cabin*, *1919*, and the sweet floating imagery by which Shakespeare in *The Tempest* exploits our love of distant music" (136).

But sometimes—and this is perhaps Burke's most pointed objection to the Wilson-Hicks-Cowley school—"pure" literature is a better choice *rhetorically*. And the 1930s is one of those times, surprisingly enough. Marxist critics have forgotten, Burke says,

> that in a mere recital of calamities, in exposures, recommendations, and affidavits you have, in the end, but grounds for growing sick of recommendations and affidavits. The facts are not enough. Or, rather, they may be enough up to the eighth or ninth time—but what if we must rehearse them daily? Even revelations of the godhead had to be ritualized before the people could be induced to concern itself with these revelations regularly. But if the pamphleteers had

their way, they would think it enough to reveal again and again, without dance-steps. (56)

Burke would offer a serious and elaborate discussion of ritual in *Attitudes toward History*. Here he was simply noting that people are not always interested in considering matters that are clearly in their best interests to consider; people avoid what is difficult or unpleasant. "Who, working in a factory, wants to read about working in a factory?" (104). From a tactical point of view, literature may succeed where pamphlets do not simply because it clothes the unpleasant subject with imagination, humor, or grace. Literature may "fortify us in the deepest sense, by giving our resistance to contemporary corruption ceremonious, or dignified, connotations" (Burke to Cowley, June 2, 1932; unsent). Even the most fantastical or utopian work may be revolutionary if it gives readers a clearer sense of the good life, thereby sharpening the contrast between what is and what might be. The most effective propagandist may, therefore, be the poet. And the quintessential example of the propagandistic work is Milton's *Areopagitica*; although Milton had often "proved himself a master of filthy invective," he shrewdly chose to address Parliament "with a strategy of ingratiation that a man could invent, I believe, only by being first a violent man and then putting a check upon his violence" (46). The passage illustrates the process Burke refers to in his book's title, for he imagines Milton revising, if only mentally, his original, defiant impulse in favor of a more rhetorically effective strategy.[23]

"Protestant Poets All": Collapsing the Aesthete vs. Literary Marxist Antithesis

If the traditional dichotomy between poetry and propaganda was untenable for Burke, so would be, consequently, the presumed distinction between the writers of pure poetry and the writers of propaganda. Burke collapsed that dichotomy by placing it within a broader historical context: the century-long attack by those with a general "aesthetic attitude" upon those with a practical or "profit-economy" way of thinking. In this other, larger war, the aesthetes were aligned with bohemians, intellectuals, and those others who were defining the good life as something other than material success and who were together in a struggle against "the philistine-bourgeois-business man (including employer and employee alike)" (Burke to Leach, October 22, 1932). Thus in *Auscultation* Burke grouped together all kinds of writers under the general category "aesthetes" as writers of what amounted to protest literature:

> Once we consider the world of commerce, of Profit-Thinking as authoritative, once we take it as the essential factor affecting everyone and really constituting modern "royalty," we see how many rival schools become united as allies in the same protestant campaign: social satirists, dwellers in the Ivory Towers,

romantics, literary Marxists, classicists, humanists, even royalists and neo-Catholics. (156)

To the extent, then, that all these groups define themselves in opposition to the profit-thinking framework, Burke told Cowley, they "become identical"; they all use "different types of imagery for substantiating the same anti-profit-economy attitude" (October 3, 1932). There was common ground—a United Front, one might say—against the enemy among writers superficially disparate: ivory tower dwellers such as Stein, Joyce, and Moore; literary Marxists such as Dos Passos, Gold, and Hicks; humanists such as Irving Babbitt;[24] the royalist neo-Catholic Eliot (and Eliot's admirer Tate).

Burke's argument was a direct and—to those readers who were following the literary wars ongoing in the journals—clearly recognizable response to Cowley's assertion in his "The Poet and the World" review of Dos Passos that the collective or radical artist is something completely new, something other than the romantic artist.[25] Cowley's observation that Dos Passos had forsaken romanticism for the collective novel was an example of what Burke called in *Auscultation* the "Saul-Paul reversal":[26] the change of heart among bohemian writers who "are now prepared to be struck blind and then suddenly see, getting their new affirmations by negating what they had been, undoing past cohesions with one brutal rip (the method of Saul becoming Paul)" (90). Cowley, for Burke, was of course the perfect example of the Saul-Paul critic, one "who had written a lovely book of verse picturing the Poet against the World, now suavely burlesquing this whole way of seeing" (90). To Burke the difference between the "romantic" and the "radical" Dos Passos or Cowley was more superficial than substantial: aesthetes were simply exchanging their philistine-intellectual thesis for a bourgeois-proletarian antithesis without really needing to change many of their attitudes or their behaviors. That is, many aesthetes were turning so naturally to Communism because its "political pattern was practically identical with their poetic pattern. Here they could find the equivalent for their past uncompromising 'colony thinking,' the rigid 'with me or against me' attitude which had braced the intellectuals for a century. Their older fanaticism of beauty could now be translated into the terms of the 'perfect state'" (162).

Burke was finding the aesthete-Marxist dichotomy not only theoretically untenable but also a shortsighted waste of time and talent. Wounded himself in the bickering between the two sides, he describes the situation as "a kind of 'open season' for criticism. Antithesis, coupled with the pliancy of the 'escape' or 'evasion' concept, enables one to shoot arrows at random into the air with perfect confidence that, wherever he turns, he will find them sticking in the hearts of his friends" (97). Rather than fighting among themselves, Burke suggests, aesthetes and Marxists alike—as well as New

Humanists—should aim their arrows at the real target outside their ranks: "There is a job to be done. It will take a great many people, working in a great many ways, to do it. As long as the arrows are pointed in the same general direction, that's a sufficient basis for cooperation" (Burke to Cowley, November 1, 1932). Burke would express sympathy for the same general tactics and cooperative attitudes at the first American Writers' Congress, in *Permanence and Change*, and in *Attitudes toward History*.

The Practical-Aesthetic Merger: "What Does the 'Esthetic' Do Next?"

Having discarded a series of antitheses in the opening two-thirds of *Ausculta-tion*, Burke decisively exploded a final and quite fundamental one: the apparent split between the aesthetic and the "practical" was as much a mirage as the others; indeed "the 'esthetic' would seem to differ from the 'practical' not in essence but in degree" (140).

For it so happened, Burke felt, that the aesthetic critique of capitalism was at the current moment being matched by a critique founded on practical grounds, namely the economic failure of capitalism:

> An absurdity [capitalism] must finally prove itself an absurdity even in its own terms—and if the practical frame was once questioned only *from without* (as viewed from the alien esthetic frame), it is now being proved even incapable of fulfilling its own criteria; it is proved impractical precisely by its own scheme of the "good life," since it is unable to uphold the processes of com-modity-gourmandizing which it considered the "fulcrum of culture." (151)

Holders of the practical and aesthetic frameworks had both arrived at the acknowledgment that capitalism had failed. To put it another way, American people in 1932 were fundamentally "dis-integrated": a significant portion of the citizenry, empty and dissatisfied, no longer wished to do what capitalist ideology required; and economic institutions were no longer able to grow and flourish. Hence the once-antithetical frameworks had become "ideo-logical equivalents" (Burke to Cowley, October 3, 1932). And if the economic critique of capitalism had won, then according to Burke's equations, aesthe-ticism had won too: "The present so-called 'routing' of the 'esthetes,'" he wrote to Cowley, "is nothing other than their 'victory' under the wrong appellation" (October 3, 1932). Just as in the nineteenth century, when an anti-practical aesthetic prevailed in an imaginative sphere given over to a criticism of moneymaking—when "the 'esthetes' were simply the imaginative side of Marx" (Burke to Josephson, March 24, 1933), so aesthetes and practi-cal economists were coming together in 1930s America.

Under such circumstances "what does the 'esthetic' do next?" (159), Burke wondered in a query that directed the final section of his tract. What is the role of the aesthete, given the collapse of the aesthete-practical antithe-sis? It might seem at first glance that aesthetes were in a difficult position:

> If [the aesthetic] celebrates the marriage of the practical and esthetic frames
> by "conforming," it risks violating the basic patterns of character out of which
> it arose. . . . For the basic patterns of character are "protestant," arising as they
> do out of the esthete's long tradition of refusal to accept the authority of the
> profit-economy frame. On the other hand, if the esthete remains faithful to
> those character patterns, he puts himself in the position of attacking the very
> millennium for which he had pled. (157)

In other words, if aesthetes leave off protesting, they are, by definition, no
longer aesthetes. And yet if capitalism has been defeated, what is the point of
the protest? Burke's thinking about the "what next?" question suggested a
further problem attendant upon a merger of practical and aesthetic, too: if the
aesthetes have won, but no one realizes it—not even the aesthetes themselves—then they have not really won at all. In the marriage of aesthetic and
practical critiques, Burke sees the aesthetic as the partner that was potentially
giving up its name and power; it was being subsumed under the practical.
Indeed some aesthetes had surrendered their very identity as aesthetes, mis-
taking themselves for practical-minded Marxists. "The propounders of the
esthetic frame," Burke writes, "show some indications that the practical has
gone to their heads—for they would deal with nothing now but 'reality,' and
they would scorn the esthetic with fervor. It is by this process that out of the
old 'esthete' has come the Saul-Paul anti-esthete" (142).

But in response to this cultural dilemma, this rout of the aesthetes, Burke
proposed to recapture and reassert an aesthetic attitude, separate from the
practical frame, separate from the Marxist economic critique. And he did so
not just out of sheer love for the aesthetic but because he believed the Marxist revolution was not going far enough: capitalist ideology may have been
defeated, but not so the general materialism that pervaded American culture.
With the breakdown of capitalist ideology, Burke foresaw an opportunity to
shift the entire focus of society if it could only adopt an aesthetic perspective.
The ultimate goal, he suggests, is not to create a system in which everyone
has access to unlimited commodities but rather to create a system in which
people do not so crave "tinny things" (143): "Let the Marxians not persuade
either us or themselves that merely because the practical frame of reference
shows some sign of catching up with the esthetic frame, we are to suppose
that the ultimate configuration of meanings is now discovered, and that
henceforth the tentative-esthetic must rot" (150). As Greig Henderson has
noted, *Auscultation* "reveals the doublemindedness inherent in Burke's project" (178)—in other words, his wish to maintain an aesthetic attitude and to
assimilate the practical under it.

The concluding segments of *Auscultation* thus become a kind of eager call
to arms to Burke's fellow aesthetes. Perhaps the call was even "overeager"
(165), in that it amounted to scolding aesthetes for renouncing poetry and to

expressing frustration at their "treacheries to the Guild." But the opportunity was golden and the stakes were high, and by throwing their lot in with the Marxists—by maintaining Marxist antitheses, for example—aesthetes were taking the very path guaranteed not to succeed. *Auscultation*, out to reform aesthetes, assures them that there is still vital cultural work for them to do *as aesthetes*; in fact, Burke argues (using a term he would renew in *Permanence and Change*), they should think of themselves as *evangelists*. The problem with the aesthetes-as-Marxists is that they have misunderstood their role, that they are functioning like Paul when they should be imitating Jesus:

> We may say that the "Christ-function," as the "bringer of glad tidings," was that of propounding a new configuration of meanings, and making this con-figuration as appealing as possible. Accordingly, he minimized the antagonis-tic aspect of his doctrine. The Saul-Paul function (of consolidating the faithful, convincing the convinced) was not really serving the interests of "propaganda" at all. It was not a seeking of recruits—it was an exhorting of the recruited. (163)

Burke redefines the aesthetic accordingly as the bringer of a new order: "the esthetic, then—in science, in art, in philosophy, in criticism—is a process of naming, and of naming in such a way that one seeks to go beyond the points of reference which one finds already available around him" (146–47). No longer specifically and narrowly linked with art or the imaginative, the aesthetic becomes a general habit of mind that creates a new vocabulary and the new perspectives that permit a culture to move forward. And in the par-ticular moment of history in which Burke was writing, that meant creating a new ideology to unify the disintegrating society and to move it beyond its current materialism. Far from dilettantism or social irresponsibility, Burke's aesthetic plays the leading role in returning the culture to stability and health.

Burke had been approaching this position for some time, at least since he had written the "Program" chapter in *Counter-Statement*. "We must . . . alter the current 'philosophy' of ambition, work, earnings, economic glory," he had written there (116). In *Auscultation*, however, Burke began to theorize seriously the role that language plays in shaping perceptions and attitudes— that is, in maintaining as well as disrupting ideology (a role Burke most explicitly and famously articulates in his later essay "Terministic Screens"). The evangelist, or mystic, who advances a new vocabulary does so in three ways: by joining two separate concepts, by splitting a single concept into sev-eral distinct parts, and by moving concepts to "a different plane of discourse." Whatever the means, the mystic in effect reclassifies things, sorting them into different categories and creating altogether new ones. The result is that "by making new patterns, new sortings, new identifications, he is—to all practi-cal purposes—making new things" (101).

In one sense, this process anticipates the workings of what Burke in *P&C* would call "perspective by incongruity." In another sense, this effort at building a new vocabulary—reminiscent of the aesthetic and cultural projects of Williams, Pound, Stein, and Mann—is summed up in the term *translation*, a word that turns up often in Burke's letters and writings of the early 1930s. In the preface to *Auscultation*, Burke tied current critical vocabularies to nineteenth-century thought and promised that his book would offer "reasons for suspecting that these ways of thinking must be 'translated' somewhat, if we would adapt them to the conditions of our century" (63). As he would again in *P&C*, Burke describes the nineteenth century as a time of dazzling evolutionary and revolutionary philosophies, of unswerving faith in the promise of capitalism and industrialization; it was a century, he says, "of first drafts" (167). In the twentieth century, however, the economic crisis has made people sense that those drafts may need a good deal of revision—hence the final word in the title of Burke's book.

And Marxism is, for Burke, the perfect example of a theory that needed to be revised. Though Marx himself was interested in aesthetics, his writings about the subject are fragmentary, and so there was plenty of room among Marxists for debate about the proper Marxist stance toward art. As he began composing *Auscultation*, Burke wrote to Cowley, "I can only welcome Communism by converting it into my own vocabulary. I am, in the deepest sense, a translator. I go on translating, even if I must translate English into English" (June 4, 1932). Marxism must be revised in light of the theoretical differences discussed earlier; its antitheses need to be reconceived. But Marxism also needed to be Americanized, and *Auscultation*, an elaboration of Burke's "Boring from Within" response to Wilson, was an explanation of how to do that. For one thing America's productivity rendered useless Russian propaganda based on a desire for increased production of consumer goods. As Burke chided Cowley, "My main point of diversion from the Communists (in the matter of purpose) derives, as I have said before, from the fact that that particular type of spiritualization which comes of a 'Come, boys, let's build a railroad' materialism is denied us. The railroad is already here" (June 2, 1932; unsent).[27] In fact, Burke argued, American leftists were facing precisely the opposite problem: the problem of making revolutionaries out of people who (at least comparatively speaking) have been used to easy living. Burke's answer is to stand language on its head, to translate it: "If our whole vocabulary is reversed, so that we try to put the word 'leisure' in place of the word 'unemployment,' we no longer crack our brains in the outlandish attempt to 'make work,' we no longer praise Russia because it offers 'jobs for all,' but instead, we attempt the alterations of our social system which would be implicit in this shift of nomenclature" (Burke to Cowley, June 2, 1932; unsent). In addition Marxism must be translated because Russian and American societies place very different demands upon rhetors seeking supporters. "Basically, my scheme of Communist 'translation' in America has as its fulcrum the fact that, in the place of illiterate peasants, we have illiterate readers of the newspapers, a difference which means that classes in America must be courted which were outraged in Russia" (Burke to Cowley, June 2, 1932; unsent). Differences in audience and scene, then, were necessitating a translation if Marxism was going to prevail in America. Burke's ultimate hope, of course, was "that a shift in vocabulary may eventually lead to a whole new world" (101). Translation efforts might create a not-too-distant future when people would say "there is no further railroad that needs building; hence, we cannot rouse ourselves any longer to ennoblement by calling, 'Come, boys, let's build a railroad.'" It is "precisely at this point, historically the beginning of 'degeneration,' we propose to situate the springboard into a different sphere of efforts" (143).

Auscultation ends, therefore, with a vision of the central role played by the aesthetic in reintegrating American society:

> One can entertain the possibility of still broader configurations, within which Marxism and its similar economic theories must all appear fragmentary in turn. Such broader configurations, for instance, would provide a more "meaningful" account of human impulses in general, not taking contemporary desires and patterns of thought so much for granted as the economists do, placing in the category of *meanings* the aims and ambitions which are still too often regarded as *facts*. It is in the direction of this broader configuration that we must look if we would again erect a purely esthetic frame of revolution one step in advance of the present esthetic-practical merger.

And Beyond

What does the aesthetic do next, then? In a very concrete sense it does *Permanence and Change*. In that book, subtitled *An Anatomy of Purpose*, Burke supplies the "account of human impulses in general" that he had envisioned in *Auscultation*—the universal human motives that are permanent because they are grounded in the compulsions of the body. *Permanence and Change* would fulfill the call in *Auscultation* for a "broader configuration" by proposing a "humanistic" or "poetic" ideology, implicit in Marx if not in the Marxism Burke was encountering, which would account more fully for these "permanent" human motives. In addition *Permanence and Change* would propose a rhetorical method, perspective by incongruity, by which the aesthetic might carry out its process of renaming. The poetic ideology of *Permanence and Change* is the "purely esthetic frame of revolution one step in advance" of Marxism that Burke anatomizes in *Auscultation*. According to *Permanence and Change*, the antidote for social malaise "would seem necessarily to be a rationale for art—albeit not a performer's art, not a specialist's art that some produce and many consume but an art in its broadest sense, an *art of living*" (66).

Permanence and Change is indeed the answer to the question raised in *Auscultation*. It is the "beyond" in the subtitle of that work: *Literature, Marxism and Beyond.*

Perhaps that explains at least in part why *Auscultation* went unpublished for more than half a century. True, Burke made a sustained effort to publish his tract. On October 22, 1932, he queried Henry Goddard Leach at the *Forum* about the possibility of publishing his "brief statement" entitled "The Rout of the Esthetes," but Leach steered him to the *Bookman*, a magazine closely associated with humanism. Instead, as Franklin Roosevelt was being swept into office, Burke tried a magazine more to his liking, *Hound and Horn* (Burke to Bandler and Kirstein, November 7, 1932: "my interests and preferences have not seemed greatly to vary from those of your gazette"). A month later, the editors turned it down, calling it merely "excellent pamphleteering" written from a "curiously unreal" point of view. "We feel that you are really killing corpses, that you do Cowley, Josephson, Hicks, and the rest too great a flattery by annihilating them. It might be different if people like Joyce, Picasso, Eliot, or Corbusier were being corrupted by heresy, but the people who are diseased are, after all, rather insignificant, and I think it is a mistake to give them so much credit" (Kirstein to Burke, December 8, 1932). Apparently not everyone was agreeing with Burke that the aesthetes had been routed. In January 1933 Burke received a note from an agent informing him that the manuscript had been refused by Scribner's, Norton, Macrae Smith, Atlantic Monthly Press, and Knopf (Everitt to Burke, January 6, 1933).[28] After trying another lead in February, Burke concluded that he would not be able to get his book published.[29]

That Burke had trouble finding a publisher for such an argument is not surprising. The length of *Auscultation* is odd for a book and for magazines alike, and the argument's topicalities would have shortened its shelf life. Nor is it odd that Burke rather quickly gave up the idea of publishing it: as the Depression deepened with each passing month, leftists became more and more convinced that capitalism had entered a decisive third period and was on the brink of collapse; and the New Deal was developing as a means of salvaging the system. The topicalities that motivated *Auscultation* were fading into the background. Besides, by the time his options for publishing *Auscultation* were closing down, he was well on his way to completing a congruent and larger project not less rooted in the aesthetic but more in keeping with the aims and aspirations of the proletarian critics: he was finishing *Permanence and Change.*

Three   Translating Cultural History

Permanence and Change

Published in February 1935, *Permanence and Change* was actually composed mostly in 1933, especially during the summer and early autumn months, when Burke was also cleaning up domestic affairs and continuing to negotiate his relationships within the intellectual Left. Not that it was the only thing he was writing: Caught at the end of a failing marriage and beginning a new one, experimenting with two possible publishing ventures (neither of which came to fruition),[1] publishing some music criticism for the *Nation* and observing the launching of the New Deal in Washington, Burke also found time to finish a major essay, "The Nature of Art under Capitalism," published in the *Nation* late in 1933. The essay explained, under the circumstances, "why the contemporary emphasis must be placed largely upon propaganda, rather than 'pure' art" (675). The line of argument in Burke's essay, which in its interest in propaganda anticipates his Writers' Congress speech, reflects many of the sentiments in *Auscultation*. Drawing in novel ways on Veblen, Nietzsche, Bentham, and Dewey (and earning because of it the praise of Sidney Hook), Burke on the one hand gave comfort to the Communist credo as it had been articulated by W. E. B. Du Bois in 1926: "all art is propaganda and ever must be, despite the wailing of the purists" (296). Because "'pure art' . . . tends to promote a state of acceptance," Burke argued in "The Nature of Art," "it tends to become a social menace insofar as it assists us in tolerating the intolerable." And yet, on the other hand, Burke was still not convinced that "pure art" should be abandoned completely: the state of acceptance or "acquiescence" induced by it, Burke felt, nevertheless nurtures an appetite for the imaginative that is invaluable under any circumstances—especially because "much of the harsh literature now being turned out in the name of the 'proletariat' seems inadequate . . . since it shows us so little of the qualities in mankind worth saving . . . [and] since by substituting a cult of disaster for a cult of amenities it 'promotes our acquiescence' to sheer dismalness" (677).

In short Burke was embroiled still in the literary wars of the early 1930s while he was writing *Permanence and Change*. Having given up on publishing *Auscultation*, Burke turned in the early months of 1933 to a reformulation of his task in a book that Robert Wess has treated, with reason, as a revision of that nearly discarded 1932 tract (60). Yet the completed *Permanence and Change* is, as Wess has also noted, much more than a revision of *Auscultation*. As Burke bragged in a letter to Richard McKeon (October 24, 1934), *Permanence and Change* is no less than "a study in ethics, ecology, social psychology, methodology, metaphysics, therapeutics, [and] 'the meaning of meaning,'" an inquiry into the processes by which people and societies might be transformed. Divided into three sections, the book first offers Burke's diagnosis of contemporary critical and social ills (embedded as they are in the limitations of a disorienting method of interpreting the world); then suggests a means of gaining a new "perspective by incongruity" that can shock people into fresh insights and understandings; and concludes by proposing a "humanistic or poetic" orientation, grounded in a framework he calls "metabiology," that would hold the promise of a more complete accounting for human motivations and a reinvigorated "art of living" based on cooperation, criticism, and communication. Rather than addressing his complicated work of cultural criticism only to a narrow audience of Left intellectuals, Burke devised instead a more complete and elaborated argument in order to win the hearts and minds of a broad audience. That the book eventually sold well, earned Burke a Guggenheim, and brought him considerable public acclaim suggests that he succeeded. That the book is read today as a seminal statement of the function of art and criticism in creating a dynamic superstructure with the potential to transform society both culturally and economically suggests that his book is indeed "one of the classics of Western Marxism" (Denning, 102), if not one of the most important theoretical statements of the century.

In December 1933, having nearly completed his manuscript and beginning to contemplate finding a publisher for *Permanence and Change*, Burke offered (for twenty-five dollars) a slightly longer version of the first part of his book to a new magazine emerging from Woodstock, New York, known as *Plowshare: A Literary Periodical of One-Man Exhibits*. As its subtitle implied, *Plowshare* was developed around the notion of giving its monthly issues over to substantial selections by one writer (Ernest Brace to Burke, December 4, 1933; Henry Morton Robinson to Burke, December 21, 1933). Consequently "On Interpretation," the first segment of what appeared a year later as *Permanence and Change*, took up the entire inaugural issue in February 1934. Six months later, the *New Republic* carried a review of the monograph by the novelist and biographer Edgar Johnson, entitled—with an explicit nod

toward Cowley's "The Poet and the World"—"The Artist and the World."
"In the childish wrangles about art and propaganda we have been hearing in
recent years, the latest issue is the relationship of art to society," Johnson
wrote. "Mr. Kenneth Burke's essay 'On Interpretation' is extremely important because it is an adult contribution to this subject" (109); Burke's ideas
were "elaborated with a degree of insight that goes far beyond attacks on
propaganda and ivory towers [alike], and makes all such criticism appear
infantile and beside the point. No contemporary writing penetrates more
deeply into the basic connections between art and culture, and none does so
with such brilliance" (110). The same could be said of the entire book (and
indeed, Johnson said just that in his later review of *Permanence and Change* for
Saturday Review). Johnson's observation that Burke was moving beyond what
had become in 1933–34 rather predictable, polarized, and unproductive literary arguments and accusations suggests that he in *P&C* had done what
he looked forward to doing when he was writing *Auscultation:* namely developing an aesthetic framework that "went beyond" standard aesthete and
Marxist polarities. *Permanence and Change* was an effort to unstick the contemporary debate over the tensions between aesthetics and politics, to create
a habitable ground that would respect both aesthetes and literary Marxists on
the question of the conflicting demands of art and society. Operating squarely
within a public sphere created by 1930s artists and critics, Burke reconfigured
local power struggles and, more important, reconceived the philosophical
and moral grounds on which those struggles and others were founded.

Permanence and Change *and the Aesthetes*

The prominent writers and critics who were popularly known as "aesthetes"
during the mid-1930s—among them Marianne Moore, Wallace Stevens,
E. E. Cummings, Katherine Anne Porter, Gertrude Stein, and, if to a lesser
extent, the Objectivist poets, William Carlos Williams, and Allen Tate—
while hardly unaware of the central social, political, and intellectual developments of their day, nonetheless were striving for an art that reached beyond
those particular forces. In *Poetry, transition, Hound and Horn,* and other magazines,[2] they articulated doctrines that later became standard through the writings of the New Critics. In *Permanence and Change* Burke's attitudes toward
the aesthetes and their cultural project are complicated, sometimes contradic-
tory. As usual, he hoped to have it both ways: Burke was simultaneously
authorizing and invalidating the work of the aesthetes by designating art and
criticism as fundamental, even transcendent human activities that are nonetheless inseparable from particular political and rhetorical concerns.

Before detailing how Burke responds to and builds upon the aesthetes'
position in *Permanence and Change*, it must be conceded that defenders of the
autonomy of art did not speak with one voice in the 1930s. Pairs or small

groups of aesthetes did know each other well and shared their work in progress—Moore with Stevens, Williams with the Objectivists, Tate with Porter, and so forth. But they did not often make a self-conscious effort to articulate a consistent aesthetic or cultural project; they advanced few manifestos like the one the Agrarians offered in the opening pages of *I'll Take My Stand* or the one Edmund Wilson articulated in May 1932, to encourage writers and intellectuals to join the workers' cause (Wilson, *Letters*, 222–23). Williams's correspondence indicates that he felt considerable sympathy for Moore, and there are notable similarities between the ideas of Tate and Yvor Winters; but neither Tate nor Winters was enthusiastic about Moore and Williams. While Tate considered Eliot and Ransom his chief mentors, Williams and Winters both denounced Eliot's work, Williams regarding it as "classroom poetry" (*Autobiography*, 174) and Winters noting a "limp versification" in Eliot that he regarded as "inseparable from the spiritual limpness that one feels behind the poems" (*Primitivism and Decadence*, 6). Winters found much to admire in Tate's poetry and acknowledged his debt to Tate for several concepts fundamental to *Primitivism and Decadence* (1937), but Williams had no use for Winters, in part because Winters had panned *Sour Grapes* back in the 1920s (Williams to Burke, January 6, 1933). Nevertheless for all their differences it is still possible to think of these writers, as Burke did, as sharing, more or less, a commitment to certain artistic and critical values.

One, of course, was a commitment to craft and form as valuable in themselves. Even as leftists were abandoning both, aesthetes valued technique and form not as things opposed to content or meaning but as features of art that created or "embodied" meaning. Winters, for example, affirmed in his 1935 essay "The Morality of Poetry" that the problems of form are precisely what lead a writer to discover meaning: since "the creation of form is nothing more or less than the act of evaluating and shaping (that is, controlling) a given experience," it follows that form is "the decisive part" of a poem's "moral content" (*Primitivism and Decadence*, 5–6). For Winters and for other aesthetes, art (and particularly poetry) could never be reduced to its paraphrasable content; in fact, one criterion for judging art was in relation to its ineffability: the less paraphrasable the work, the better. It was therefore no accident that so many so-called aesthetes wrote poetry (like Moore, Stevens, Tate, Williams, and Winters) or highly "poetic prose" (like Stein and Joyce): poetry epitomized the essence of art because as aesthetic form it most completely exploited language's nonreferential and nonpragmatic resources. Williams for that reason could claim in *The Embodiment of Knowledge* and in other essays throughout the 1930s that poetry works fundamentally at the level of form, which is indeed the embodiment of the poem's knowledge. True, Williams appreciated substance quite highly—the great poem, he felt, is one that offers a fundamentally new perception—and he ridiculed mere exercises in form

that offered little substance; in "Caviar and Bread Again" (1930), for example, he chided young writers who were "playing tiddlywinks with the[ir] syl-
lables" (*Selected Essays*, 103). But he even more fundamentally appreciated
that "technique is itself substance, as all artists must know" (104). And so he
praised formal experimenters such as Stein and Joyce for inventing new forms
for expressing new knowledge: "writing to be of value to the intelligence is
not made up of ideas, emotions, data, but of words in configurations fresh to
our senses" (*Embodiment*, 17).[3]

A related article of faith among aesthetes was that art was somehow timeless and extrahistorical. If the meaning of a work of art was contained in
its form or created via the play among tone, denotation, rhythm, sound,
placement on the page, and so forth, then it followed that art could operate
outside particular historical and cultural circumstances (and indeed, the
"timelessness" of a work was another criterion according to which the aesthetes judged art). "The arts do live continuously," intoned Porter in her
introduction to *Flowering Judas*. "Their names and their shapes and their uses
and their basic meanings survive unchanged in all that matters through times
of interruption, diminishment, neglect; they outlive governments and creeds
and societies, even the very civilizations that produced them" (n.pag.). Aesthete poets and critics accordingly relied heavily on references to Shakespeare
and Dante; Tate and Winters, after Eliot's lead, drenched themselves in
Donne and the Metaphysicals. Because art was held to be timeless, it was
regarded as the perfect vessel for containing eternal truths of the human condition: "The task of poetry," offered Tate, is indeed nothing less than "the
constant rediscovery of the permanent nature of man" ("Poetry and Politics,"
310); and Winters held forth as well on what he called a "moralistic" or "absolutist" theory of art, according to which poets communicate (albeit sometimes imperfectly) absolute truths of human existence. To Tate art captured
"the kind of knowledge which is really essential to the world, the true content of its phenomena, that which is subject to no change, and therefore is
known with equal truth for all time" (*Reactionary Essays*, 112).[4]

Consequently aesthetes typically defined poetry as something that "is"
rather than something that "does." Archibald MacLeish would capture this
notion in his famous aphorism "A poem should not mean but be" ("Ars Poet-
ica," 1926), but most of the other aesthetes were expressing similar views.
They were defining art against the Victorian "genteel tradition," against the
pious moralizing of quasi-homiletic poetry, and scoffing at the idea that
poetry was designed to persuade or rectify. Hence Porter in the introduction
to *Flowering Judas* said that her stories were written "with intention and in
firm faith, though I had no plan for their future and no notion of what their
meaning might be to such readers as they would find" (n.pag.) It followed, of
course, that aesthetes sharply delimited the political or pragmatic aspects of

art. Remember, for instance, Tate's dictum that "poetry finds its true usefulness in its perfect inutility" (*Reactionary Essays*, 112).

This stance created some obvious difficulties for the aesthetes. How might
one validate something, such as poetry, while affirming that it had little direct
relevance to daily life? The question grew in importance as proletarian critics applied more and more pressure. How complete an autonomy should be
claimed for art? The aesthetes were divided on the question. Tate was at one
extreme in insisting on absolute autonomy; Williams, close to the other
extreme, was determined to maintain a vital social role for art: poetry was the
very embodiment of knowledge, and those bodies performed real work in the
world. "The artist is to be understood as a universal man of action," he wrote
in "Against the Weather: A Study of the Artist" (*Selected Essays*, 197); in "The
Basis of Faith in Art," he went out of his way to "insist, yes, that the purpose
of art is to be useful" (*Selected Essays*, 179)—not in some unspecified future,
either, but in the here and now: "Is anything more stupid than international
conflict? Where one wishes to bind or to murder the other—most specifically
in Europe. . . ? But how, barring the work in painting, in writing, will forms
be found to embody a better adjustment? The mind must be stepped up from
arithmetic to solid geometry, at least. If this is not done nothing can take
place. And pure writing will be the means" (*Embodiment*, 118). That tag line,
"pure writing," is crucial, though—"there is pure writing and writing which
is made to be the horse of anyone who has a burden to carry" (117)—because
it signals Williams's fundamental affiliation with the aesthetes. When he
acknowledged literature's utility, he was not really talking about proletarian
novels but trumpeting the experimental literatures that had "writing itself as
its substance" (74). He was talking about Stein and surrealism and such.

Moore and Winters were struggling to find a middle ground among the
aesthetes. Moore, in "The Jerboa," "The Buffalo," and other poems, was not
antisocial in her poetic aims, and "The Plumet Basilisk" gently critiques
Stevens's effort to isolate art from life. But the same poem also appreciates an
attitude of artistic withdrawal (figured in the title character); "The Frigate
Pelican" endorses poetic independence over political engagement; and "The
Pangolin" in 1936 would eulogize an armored beast, isolated and independent, who "draws away from danger unpugnaciously."[5] Winters, for his part,
in "Poetry, Morality, and Criticism" proposed poetry as a moral discipline
that had significant consequences for culture even as it was removed from the
quotidian scene of practical or rhetorical action. Poetry, he believed, "should
offer a means of enriching one's awareness of human experience and of so
rendering greater the possibility of intelligence in the face of future situations
involving action" (*Critique of Humanism*, 317). The rather abstract and con-
voluted nature of that sentence suggests some of the difficulty Winters was
having in explaining poetry's moral effects without describing art either as

narrowly didactic or as "one more doctrine of escape" (*Primitivism and Deca-dence*, 13). Winters was an admirer of poetic form and a student of poetic technique. But he did indeed wish to acknowledge a direct if abstract link between aesthetics and morality—"a poem makes a defensible rational state-ment about a given human experience . . . and at the same time communicates the emotion which ought to be motivated by that rational understanding of that experience" (*In Defense of Reason*, 11)—that had the potential to trans-form individuals and ultimately entire cultures.[6]

But Allen Tate was the aesthete who was in especially close communica-tion with Burke while *Permanence and Change* was under development. Tate and Burke had become friends during Tate's residency among the Greenwich Village avant-garde in the mid-1920s, when the two consorted closely with Malcolm Cowley, Matthew Josephson, Katherine Anne Porter, and so many others, and conducted a long correspondence and long-distance friendship that lasted until Tate's death in 1979. Despite their intellectual differences, the two were in many ways kindred spirits, and their letters in the early 1930s testify to their regard for each other's creative and critical work. Tate, who described Burke as "the most philosophical of my friends [and] a constant source of pleasure to my reflections" (Tate to Burke, April 9, 1931), wrote enthusiastically about his assignment from *Hound and Horn* to review *Counter-Statement*, "which it will please me (and I hope you) to write about at the great length that you deserve. I can barely hope to apply to your work the perspicuity and penetration required for its right comprehension, but I can assure you of a heart in the correct place" (Tate to Burke, November 6, 1931).[7] For his part, Burke imagined that Tate had found the "good life"—the "art of living," as Burke would come to call it—that he was seeking him-self: "I frequently think of you as one who has evolved a method, which is to say, a way of writing, and a way of living that offers the best inducement to this way of writing. You are (using a word which has much content for both of us) 'settled'—and the very incisive poetry I have seen of yours now and then in recent months leads me to think that you are getting the rewards of your position" (Burke to Tate, October 16, 1931). Throughout their letters the two discussed aesthetics, religion, philosophy, and the joys and sorrows of country living (Tate had settled his family on a farm on the Kentucky-Tennessee border in 1930); they critiqued industrial capitalism and defended the simpler, agrarian lifestyles they both appreciated.

But mainly, in their letters and in their published work, they tried to nego-tiate their common and contested ground on the question of the artist's or critic's role in culture.[8] While his poetry continued to carry forth an Agrar-ian agenda, Tate's essays and reviews in the late 1920s and early 1930s para-doxically mounted an all-out attack on what he called "pragmatic criticism" and the "poetry of the will," both of which he saw as misguided efforts to make art useful in an everyday world where it is, by Tate's account anyway, unable to function effectively. The ultimate result of such an attempt, Tate felt, would be the utter devaluation of art. Like Burke, then, he wanted to defend the aesthetic realm against strident leftist transgressions, but Tate's understanding of art and how it works—as evidenced by his loyalty to T. S. Eliot, his distinction between the imagination and the will in "Three Types of Poetry," and his critique of I. A. Richards—often put him at odds with his counterpart in New Jersey.

In his 1931 review of *Ash Wednesday* (1930) in *Hound and Horn*, for instance, Tate not only praised Eliot's new volume but also contested the contemporary critical practice of dismissing Eliot's post-conversion poetry on ideological rather than aesthetic grounds. Reviews of Eliot's recent work, Tate complained, rarely got around to discussing the poetry as poetry but focused instead on Eliot's Anglicanism. "Pragmatic critics," in which category Tate included not just Marxists but also conservatives such as the New Humanists (but not the Agrarians), were wrongly assuming that "all forms of human action, economics, politics, even poetry and certainly industry, are legitimate modes of salvation" (*Poetry Reviews*, 106); they were expecting writers to offer a useful set of values or social program and rejecting Eliot's poetry because they did not like his particular program. While conceding that in the past writers were judged on moral grounds, Tate claimed that "no critic expected the poet to give him a morality. . . . [A] poem [is] a piece of free and disinterested enjoyment for minds mature enough—that is, convinced enough of a satisfactory destiny—not to demand of every scribbler a way of life" (*Poetry Reviews*, 105). This belief in the poet's ability to perceive experience whole (and therefore to remain above politics) became the definitive element in Tate's aesthetic theory. In "Three Types of Poetry" (1934) he argued that "the power of seizing the inward meaning of experience, the power of sheer creation that I shall call here the vision of the whole of life, is strictly *a quality of the imagination*" and not a quality of science, the aim of which is "to produce a mechanical whole for the service of the practical will" (*Reactionary Essays*, 84). In their infatuation with science, people were supposing that science could provide a complete understanding of life; but, according to Tate (and later New Critics), only the imaginative vision expressed in art gives that kind of complete knowledge. Paradoxically, however, poetic knowledge cannot be directly applied to solve real-life problems; a true poem, Tate argued, "proves nothing; it creates the totality of experience in its quality; and it has no useful relation to the ordinary forms of action" (112). Poems "simply show what is. They do not tell readers what to think or feel or how to act in a given situation" (84).

What emerged from these pronouncements, then, was Tate's insistence on distinguishing between poetic or universal knowledge of the human condition and scientific knowledge. When poets try to function in the latter realm, the result is either poetry of the will—didacticism or propaganda (in short, rhetoric)—or what Tate called romantic irony.[9] Too much modern poetry, Tate thought, had given up on its own best function—to *present* experience—and was attempting instead to *explain* experience: those attempts "open [poetry] to the just contempt of the scientific mind" (*Reactionary Essays*, 103). This fear for the future of poetry accounts for the impatience Tate showed toward Burke and for the sharpness of his attacks on I. A. Richards, particularly the ideas in *Principles of Literary Criticism* (1924), *Science and Poetry* (1926), and *Practical Criticism* (1929). Like Tate, Richards distinguished between the verifiable statements of science and the "pseudo-statements" of poetry; also like Tate, Richards argued that these pseudo-statements could not hope to compete for belief with scientific statements. What disturbed Tate was Richards's insistence that poetry nevertheless played a vital role in practical life, that poetry could be judged according to its utility: "British utilitarians, a century ago, frankly condemned [the arts]. So, with less candor, does Mr. Richards: his desperate efforts to make poetry, after all, useful, consist in justly reducing its 'explanation' to nonsense, and salvaging from the wreck a mysterious agency for 'ordering our minds'" (*Reactionary Essays*, 104). "If we begin by thinking that [poetry] ought to 'explain' the human predicament," he wrote in the preface to *Reactionary Essays*, "we shall quickly see that it does not, and we shall end up thinking that therefore it has no meaning at all. That is what Mr. I. A. Richards' theory comes to at last, and it is the first assumption of criticism today. But poetry is at once more modest and, in the great poets, more profound. It is the art of apprehending and concentrating our experience in the mysterious limitations of form" (xi).[10]

The height of Tate's irritation with pragmatic criticism and poetry is registered in his August 2, 1933, *New Republic* article. Bearing the incendiary title "Poetry and Politics," Tate's essay roundly condemned writers "who drape their political notions upon the arts simply because they have not the political talent to put them into action" (308). Tate was surveying American poetry since 1900 through the eyes of the thirteenth-century French poet Thibaut-le-Grand in order to sharpen his focus on craft, timelessness, and the universality of human experience. Thibaut, Tate reported, would be puzzled or bored by the works of Masters, Sandburg, Lindsay, Robinson, Frost, and most other modern American poets (excepting Eliot, of course) because their work was overly topical and doing little more than catalog history or regional information in astonishingly "slovenly verse" (309). The great poets, claimed Tate, the ones who will survive to be read by future generations, are those "who can keep the modes pure" (310).

Burke and Tate Argue Aesthetics

The relationship between rhetoric and aesthetics—in Allen Tate's terms, the question of the "purity" of poetry—became the subject of intense epistolary debate between Burke and Tate during the summer and early fall of 1933, the very time when Burke was busy writing *Permanence and Change*. Reacting against *Counter-Statement* and *Towards a Better Life*, Tate in his August 1933 essay "Poetry and Politics" singled out Burke as a prime example of a writer needlessly poisoning himself with an aesthetics of practicality: "We do not care what truth in poetry is. We care very little about Mr. I. A. Richards, and we care just as little for Mr. Kenneth Burke, who finds the spring water so full of bacteria that, bitterly, he distills the water off and, laughing a long mad laugh, devours the bacteria alone" (308–9). Burke was stung by Tate's remark: "Some time back, to my great gloom, I read an affidavit, a public affidavit, to the effect that you did not care for me. Hastily and volubly I wrote you, to learn whether it was still too late for the damage to be undone. . . . Since then, I have recurred to the thought of your sharp metaphor more often than I should have liked to" (Burke to Tate, August 19, 1933). Burke's letter shows him to be puzzled and frustrated both by Tate's resistance to rhetoric and his representation of Burke as a traitor to the aesthetic cause (much as Burke had accused the aesthetes-turned-Marxists of treason in *Auscultation*). Burke could not understand why his aesthetic theory should seem so radical or so dangerous or so wrong to Tate. While conceding that *Towards a Better Life* was laced with madness and bitterness, Burke insisted that *Counter-Statement* explored "the fairly rational idea that books are written to produce effects on readers," effects that writers create by manipulating readers' preexisting "dispositions" (Burke to Tate, August 19, 1933). In other words writers play on the natural (for Burke, the biologic, the permanent) and/or cultural (i.e., changeable) ideologies of readers to evoke particular responses.

Furthermore in the August 19 letter Burke painstakingly outlined his beliefs, literally from A to Z (the letter was organized alphabetically!), about current American culture—his aversion to mechanization, his certainty that Communism would not solve the country's problems, his insistence that a social cure must be grounded on something universal—to convince Tate that their differences were tactical rather than strategic. Because Burke found "much at the very basis of contemporary purpose to which I cannot subscribe," he wrote to Tate, he had developed an "attitude of refusal": "the only way of *combating* this trend [the enslavement of man to machines]—if combat is possible, which I am not at all sure it is—is by the discovery and stressing of a point of reference outside the circle of values arising out of the machine." And given the strength and the inhumanity of the system they were trying to fight (Burke's point "N": "mechanical invention . . . serves in the end but to multiply a hundredfold the power of gluttons and fools"), Burke advocated the "preaching [of] alternative values in every conceivable way, madness and bitterness among them—and also, naturally, in the sane, sweet ways of an A. Tate." By the end of his alphabet, Burke had reached the point of explaining his interest in the mystics as writers who, like himself, grounded ideology in the human body, writers whose permanent truths he sought to rediscover. Clearly struck by the similarities between his goals and methods and Tate's, Burke concluded (point "Z"): "I note that in the article in which an A. Tate affidaves that he cares not for me, he holds that poetry is the *rediscovery* of truth. . . . (ampersand) I say what the hell." The letter ended, then, with Burke verbally throwing up his hands in frustration at Tate's inability or unwillingness to see that they could be allies.

Tate's reply indicates that he did see or accept the presence of common ground. But while his letter began with a concession—"the alphabet of your diagnoses and beliefs is my own alphabet" (August 30, 1933)—Tate quickly began to take issue with Burke's rhetoricized aesthetic: "what I should like to argue with you . . . is this question of the reader-writer relation. . . . If all literature is merely an effort to move some one to do something specific, . . . then there is nothing but a reader-writer relation. It is my view, however, that outside the crassest propaganda, and in the best literature, there is no such thing." Tate's borrowing of Hicks's crude accusation against Burke in "The Crisis in American Criticism"—that Burke felt literature tries to make a reader do some specific thing—must have infuriated Burke. An ardent believer in the autonomy of art, Tate was willing to concede that books sometimes do affect readers, but he insisted that such effects were incidental to, not definitive of, art and that the effects had more to do with something that went on inside a reader's head than anything in either the writer's intention or the work of art itself. People may read ideologically, Tate granted, but that is not the business (or fault) of artists or art, both of which can—and should—exist in an ideologically neutral space. "The Truth is One and Eternal, in spite of our friends Cowley and Wilson," concluded Tate. "I think, my esteemed sir, that the temper of the age has so galled you that emotionally you begin to respond with it, even in your Refusal" (August 30, 1933).

Determined to get in the last word, Burke composed a sentence-by-sentence rebuttal of Tate's letter that further illuminates Burke's argument in *Permanence and Change*. To Tate's claim that literature is not written "for the specific purpose of moving anybody," Burke, incredulous, remarked, "What! Does this lad not try to make his verse appealing? Has he not even *omitted* things which he considered significant but the significance of which he felt would not be apparent and moving to others?" (September 27, 1933). How does anyone write without intending to do or say something, without imagining how words or lines will be read? Burke pressed Tate to explain what literature of the will was "as distinct from other literature. For I grant that I worried over the same matter until I suddenly (perhaps through mental breakdown) came to the conclusion that there was no other kind"

(September 27, 1933). Burke noted, as an instance, that Joyce's stream of con-sciousness might be taken as an example either of extreme willfulness or of ex-treme lack of will. And, by implication, Tate's "autonomous" poetry might be read (as, no doubt, it *was* being read by some leftist critics) as literature *willed* to ignore current sociopolitical issues. Given Tate's use of Hicks's loaded phrase "specific pur-pose" as well as his accusation that Burke's theory described a direct causal link between art and action, Burke concluded that their disagreement might have been caused by Tate's willful misinterpretation of his position:

> Maybe Allen read the article by Hickville Grannie. Hickville Grannie said that I said that "literature should make the reader go out and do some specific thing." If Allen got his interpretation of my thesis from that source, then oh my God, for the same man who said that I said that literature should make people go out and do some specific thing also informed us in the same article that my esthetic system divorced literature from life. Even goodwill advertising does not guaranty that the reader will "go out" (Hicks actually used that stylism on me) and buy the product advertised. Even advertising but hopes to turn the reader in its favor. Trust me, please. (Burke to Tate, September 27, 1933).

Burke's letter to Tate also reveals much about his understanding of the social and ideological nature of knowledge and language. Tate believed that literature re-cre-ates "the Very Thing-in-itself," but Burke was scornful of such essentializing: "If I am a fat burgher traveling on the highway, and Robin Hood takes my purse, I know that Robin Hood is a thief. If I am humble and starving, and Robin Hood gives me money, I know that he is a benefactor. But as for what Robin Hood an-sich is—I am a little uneasy" (September 27, 1933). And even if it were possible to know something absolutely, Burke knew, it is not possible to communicate this knowl-edge absolutely. Even Tate admitted that high literature was usually mixed with "inci-dental impurities," to which Burke gleefully responded, "Yes, indeedee, but the trouble is that *English* is one of the 'incidental impurities' of Shakespeare" (Septem-ber 27, 1933). For Burke language was inevitably inherently ideological, embedded in its specific cultural location: "I invite you to refer me to any doctrine of the One and Eternal Truth which was not balanced by the qualification that *in this life* it is sym-bolized by impermanent, temporal images. We must 'translate back' from the multi-plicity of our given social texture" (Burke to Tate, September 27, 1933). Thus Burke argued that even writing that was not explicitly persuasive, writing intended (as Tate claimed of his poetry) simply to present experience or truth, was nevertheless shaped by the culture in which it was created—was, in short, rhetorical by nature: "I hold that if it were One and Eternal that two and two is four, we should proclaim this One and Eternal Truth differently if our age said two and two is five than if our age said two and two is a pumpkin" (Burke to Tate, September 27, 1933).

Burke, of course, was seldom interested in keeping anything pure, least of all art, and he said so in *Permanence and Change*. Having redefined the aesthetic in *Auscultation* as "a process of naming," he had already marked the category not as a subject matter nor type of object but as a method, one that could function in a variety of domains, in science and politics as well as art. In *Permanence and Change* Burke unabashedly remarked that he had been "deliberately indiscriminate in scrambling magical, religious, poetic, theological, philosophical, mystic, and scientific lore" (159). To Tate's complaints in "Poetry and Politics" that "a poetry composed of pragmatic abstractions does not illuminate, it conceals" (310) and in a review of *Ash Wednesday* that the rejection of Eliot's verse "witnesses the powerful modern desire to judge an art scientifically, practically, industrially; according to how it works" (*Poetry Reviews*, 107), Burke replied that judging how art works is a matter neither of science nor pragmatism but of rhetoric. And rhetoric, for Burke, was not something "other than" or outside of poetry but rather, as he explained in a letter to Cowley, within the poetic process itself. When Cowley complained that *Counter-Statement* set up effectiveness as the chief critical standard, Burke wrote, "Not *chief critical* but *basic poetic process*. A rhetoric, that is, is not a code of criticism. It is an account of poetic mechanisms. A rhetoric should explain not merely why some people liked Aeschylus, but also why some people like Abie's Irish Rose. In itself, as a statement of processes, it could make no choice between them" (Burke to Cowley, June 2, 1932; unsent).

Burke's conversation with Tate and his fellow aesthetes about the place of art within society continued throughout *Permanence and Change*. Writing to Cowley about his exchange with Tate, Burke expressed his hope that *Permanence and Change* would make his positions clear to the aesthetes: "Maybe if this present book [*Permanence and Change*] gets published, I shall have made my stand clear enough for those things not to occur so easily any more. At least, I am making myself so painfully clear that if any intelligent man misunderstands me I can know it for a wish-fathered thought" (July 31, 1933).[11] In *Permanence and Change*, Burke faced the rhetorical problem of convincing believers in autonomous art that their writing had cultural effects. It was the flip side of his argument in *Auscultation*: if the earlier book needed to show aesthetes-turned-Marxists such as Cowley and Wilson that they could still do cultural work as aesthetes, that "pure" art could simultaneously be revolutionary, then *Permanence and Change* was designed to show "reactionary" aesthetes such as Tate that using art for political purposes was not something unique to Marxists. The emphases in *Auscultation* and *Permanence and Change* were different because the audiences were different, but the fundamental message was similar: the aesthetic is inevitably and productively grounded in its specific cultural location and, thus, in specific sociopolitical practices. Given his acute awareness of his aesthete readers' almost certain resistance,

Burke took great pains to emphasize in *P&C* their common ground, to make it clear that his commitment to the aesthetic or "poetic" perspective remained undiminished even as he worked to persuade them that the idea of autonomous art was untenable. *Permanence and Change* makes common if complicated cause with the aesthetes in at least four ways.

Burke's Commitment to Aestheticism

It might seem surprising that a text that explicitly advocates communism, one typically accounted as Burke's most political work, is in so many respects steeped in an appreciation of the aesthetic. And yet such dualism is, in fact, characteristic of Burke's early work: *Counter-Statement, Towards a Better Life,* and *Auscultation* all show Burke's effort to maintain both the political and the aesthetic perspectives. In *Permanence and Change* Burke argues for communism and for a rhetoricized, socially engaged aesthetic from a position within aestheticism, a position reflected in his search for "permanence," in his proposal for a "poetic orientation," and in his identification with poets.

For although he would challenge their locating of the eternal in works of art, Burke joined the aesthetes in their attempt to discover, as he told Tate, "a point of reference outside the circle" of capitalistic, utilitarian values, a point of reference that would provide an incontrovertible—i.e., permanent—grounding for criticism. Hence Burke claimed that "one must seek definitions of human purpose whereby the whole ailing world of contingent demands can be appraised. Otherwise, one is trapped in a circle of self-perpetuating judgments, quite as with the practical politician of the Roosevelt type" who shores up the railroads to help the banks to help the insurance companies "*ad inf.* and *ad nauseam*" (285–86).[12] Burke sought not to add yet another perspective to the great store of personal prophetic visions accumulated during the eighteenth and nineteenth centuries, a period marked by repeated declarations that a new "way" had been found, but instead to discern the constants among the various visions, the "one fundamental course of human satisfaction, forever being glimpsed and lost again" (233–34). Tate's remark that "the task of poetry is the constant rediscovery of the permanent nature of man" is echoed in Burke's attempt to "disclose the 'ultimate motives' behind human conduct," a project that leads him "*to define the cosmic situation and man's place in it*" (282).[13]

Moreover, by proposing a poetic ideology to replace the technological one that was damaging contemporary culture, Burke, like the aesthetes, was placing art and aesthetics at the center of his system. Just as Tate had argued that art expressed "the vision of the whole of life," so Burke was choosing the "poetic or dramatic metaphor" as "the ultimate metaphor for discussing the universe and man's relation to it" (338).[14] *Permanence and Change* repeatedly insists that the aesthetic impulse or perspective, broadly defined, constitutes the permanent essence and meaning of life: "the devices of poetry are close to the spontaneous genius of man"; "it would surely be in the region of poetry that the 'concentration point' of human desires should be found" (92). Burke concludes his book by reasserting that the *"ultimate motive, the situation common to all, [is] the creative, assertive, synthetic act"* (332). For the aesthetes and for Burke alike, the good life is the creative life. A society is sound to the extent that it acknowledges and fosters action or making (*poesis*) as its principal value and purpose, and communism is Burke's political solution because it is "necessary to making things better for art" (Wess, 58).

For this reason, in *Permanence and Change* Burke sympathizes—even identifies—with the aesthetes' resistance to the scientific and technological orientation that was dominating contemporary culture and frustrating the human need to respond to the world symbolically. "It is possible," he writes, "that much of the anguish affecting poets in the modern world is due to the many symbolic outrages which a purely utilitarian philosophy of action requires us to commit" (96). Given the culture's dismissal of the poetic, the emotional, the impractical, poets can either attempt to repress their feelings or content themselves with doing work that will be rejected or, worse, ignored. Science, in particular, by striving to create a neutral vocabulary with which to describe natural phenomena—a vocabulary that Burke says "is designed for machines" (82)—erodes poets' ability to sustain their work: "naturally, with such an information-giving ideal as the basis of scientific effort, and with science enjoying prestige as the basic ideal of modern effort, the poet often felt his trade in jeopardy" (177). And, Burke continued, sounding very much like Allen Tate or, perhaps, describing Allen Tate, "In any event he [the poet] knew—without telling himself in so many words—that this was not *his* kind of communication. It was not his business to give information about objects" (226). Burke concludes that "such considerations may be at the bottom of the tendency, often noted in aesthetic theory, to stress a direct antithesis between artistic and practical responses. For if our speculations are correct, it would follow that the purely utilitarian attitude could be upheld only by the suppression of those very overtones to which the earnest poet most resolutely exposes himself" (97). And yet for Burke there is no antithesis at all between the aesthetic and rhetorical; those two realms are, in fact, one.

Burke's Commitment to "The Poetry of Action"

Burke begins part 2 of *Permanence and Change* with the enigmatic assertion that "one cannot long discuss the question of meaning, as applied to the field of art, without coming upon the problem of piety" (95). While the statement to this day continues to perplex many readers (who wonder what piety has to do with art—and why piety is a problem), it likely proved less startling for Burke's contemporaries. Questions about the meaning of art—how works

have meaning, how works are read or interpreted or used, what art does—
were being vigorously contested at the time Burke wrote *Permanence and
Change*, and certainly one purpose of the book was to complicate the aesthetes' (and the communists') ideas about the function of art—and to deny
the existence of an aesthetic realm distinct from the rhetorical and political.

The discussion of piety, which Burke initially defines as "loyalty to the
deepest roots of our being" (95), is his way into the argument about the
rhetorical nature of language (or symbols, more generally) and, hence, of art.
Piety amounts to a sense of conformity or appropriateness, a "*sense of what
properly goes with what*" (100). It is pious to associate hearts and flowers with
love, to make the cartoon villain ugly, to set a horror story on a dark and
stormy night. But piety is more: it is "a system-builder, a desire to round
things out, to fit experiences together into a unified whole" (100). Piety leads
people to integrate all the details of their lives into one "complex interpretative network" (100)—to eat, sleep, dress, think, talk like a poet or a drug
addict or a baseball player. Burke's choice of the quasi-religious term *piety* is
meant to suggest the deep psychological or emotional investments people
make in a dominant role or code. The term captures the impulse behind the
popular saying that someone has "made a religion out of" exercise, for
instance, or thrift. A pious person, Burke explains, may build an "altar" to a
chosen characteristic and, with single-minded devotion, sacrifice everything
to it, as when a businesswoman is so pious to her work ethic that she works
herself to death.

However, piety is not just a matter of individual attitudes and behavior, is
not a matter of adopting a "permanent" orientation; for interpretive net-
works, Burke argues in part 1, "On Interpretation," are social constructions
developed out of rhetorical exchange. That is, symbols are produced and read
within interpretive vocabularies and habits of thought developed through
social interaction; symbols come to mean within systems. "Any given situation," writes Burke, "derives its character from the entire framework of interpretation by which we judge it. . . . We discern situational patterns by means
of the particular vocabulary of the cultural group into which we are born. Our
minds, as linguistic products, are composed of concepts (verbally moulded)
which select certain relationships as meaningful" (52). Thus, when a person
tries to understand his own actions or attitudes, "he would naturally employ
the verbalizations of his group—for what are his language and thought if not
a socialized product?" He "is simply interpreting with the only vocabulary he
knows" (32–33). Piety thus has connections to the ideas of taste, common
sense, and ideology; piety can become a "schema of orientation" (102) and
explain the loyalty people feel toward that orientation.[15]

Language for Burke is intimately bound up with piety. People "do not
communicate by a neutral vocabulary. In the profoundest human sense, one

communicates by a *weighted* vocabulary in which the weightings are shared by his group as a whole" (211). That is, language works by playing on emotional responses piously held by the audience; all language is a matter of appeal. In Burke's words, "We cannot speak the mother-tongue without employing the rhetorical devices of a Roman orator" (101). Contrary to the aesthetes' beliefs, rhetorical appeal is not antithetical to style, beauty, and form but rather results from them. Style, after all, is typically nothing more than "ingratiation" (71), an effort to influence people by piously saying the right thing. Even Shakespeare—for the aesthetes, the example of the autonomous artist par excellence—was, according to Burke, in "the business of appeal" (73). Tate had claimed that Shakespeare had no opinions, but Burke demonstrates how Shakespeare is actually a highly rhetorical poet whose adept manipulation of his audiences' prejudices and desires persuades them to distrust or to identify with his characters and their values. Indeed, because artists strive to communicate their visions, they are more, not less, rhetorically motivated than others: "the artist is always an evangelist, quite as the religious reformer is. He wants others to feel as he does" (202n). In response to Tate's inflammatory assertion that great literature is inherently great regardless of whether it is even read, Burke was arguing that an artist's "symbolic justification is never completed until his work has been accepted" (202n). Burke even suggests that Art for Art's Sake and other movements championing autonomous art are writers' attempts to "change the rules of the game" when audiences failed to approve their work, to shift the justification for art from acceptance to performance (202n).

Because language is inherently value laden, Burke argues, "speech is not a *naming* at all, but a system of attitudes, of implicit exhortations. To call a man a friend or an enemy is *per se* to suggest a program of action with regard to him" (225). All texts—poems, more or less—offer not just knowledge (as the aesthetes often contended) but are, in fact, a form of action (symbolic action, to be exact) that performs real work in the world. For that reason Burke titles the final chapter of his book "The Poetry of Action," suggesting both that action is poetic (that is, action is pious) and that poetry is active and civic in its aim.

Finally, Burke argues, not only is language ideological, rhetorical, and active; it is embedded in the material. Burke maintains that "men have ever approached ultimate concerns from out the given vocabularies of their day, these vocabularies being not words alone, but the social textures, the local psychoses, the institutional structures, the purposes and practices which lie behind these words" (232). Hence all texts, including literary texts, function not just within an individual reader's psyche but also within the particular cultural, economic, and political systems in which they are written and read. Changing what or why or how people read or how they judge what they read is not a purely literary matter; art will not flourish within an ideological system that values information, strict denotation, and passivity, nor in an economic system that promotes material acquisition and competition. The fate of art, *Permanence and Change* argues, is directly tied up with the practices of everyday life, and to withdraw from that realm into an aesthetic retreat is to cede the only ground on which battles about art and "the good life" can be fought.

Poetry and Science

Having established for reluctant aesthetes that the aesthetic indeed functions in the sociopolitical realm, Burke needed to reassure them that the aesthetic can function there without being rendered risible or ineffectual by the empirical advantages of science (as Tate and Richards both feared). To that end— and this is one place where Burke is especially serious about trying to shift the direction of the literary-wars debate—he meditates in *Permanence and Change* on the supposed objectivity of science as well as on the particular ways that "poetry" indeed contributes to social change. It was a message that he would elaborate in *Attitudes toward History* and *The Philosophy of Literary Form*.

In *Science and Poetry* (1926) I. A. Richards had set out to answer the question "how is science in general, and the new outlook upon the world which it induces, already affecting poetry, and to what extent may science make obsolete the poetry of the past?" (52). Burke was addressing that same question in *P&C*. Like Burke, Richards noticed a global shift in ideology away from the "Magical View" (the period when, he suspects, poetry may have begun) to the scientific view, a process he called the "neutralization of nature" (57). (There are other similarities between *Permanence and Change* and *Science and Poetry;* both are books that can be called "cultural histories.") Analyzing the place of poetry within this new worldview and working through the new insights of logical positivism, Richards confirmed the existence of "a fundamental disparity and opposition" between the certifiable statements of science and the pseudo-statements of poetry (70) and, hence, between the functions of scientists and poets: "it will be admitted—by those who distinguish between scientific statement, whose truth is ultimately a matter of verification as this is understood in the laboratory, and emotive utterance, where 'truth' is primarily acceptability by some attitude . . . —that it is *not* the poet's business to make true statements" (67).[16] In this division of labor, science is granted sole, unlimited authority to discover and dispense knowledge. Trouble arises, however, because poetry *seems* to be making "true statements," often about the very important matters such as religion and ethics where science is least helpful, and encouraging readers to give themselves over to poetic pseudo-statements, "the kind of unqualified acceptance which belongs by right only to certified scientific statements" (73). Richards's solution to the trouble was to increase and further demarcate the separation between the scientific and the poetic realms, to "cut our pseudo-statements free from belief, and yet retain

them, in this released state, as the instruments by which we order our attitudes to one another and to the world. . . . Pseudo-statements to which we
attach no belief and statements proper such as science provides cannot conflict. It is only when we introduce illicit beliefs into poetry that danger arises.
To do so is from this point of view a profanation of poetry" (72–73). In other
words, in a world dominated by science, the only way for Richards to justify
the continued necessity, or even the possibility, of poetry was to limit its use
to exercising and organizing attitudes—what Burke dubs "mental prophylac-
tics" (324)—and to evoking responses through presentations of experience.

As much as Tate criticized Richards for positing the "practical" use of art
in ordering the mind, from Burke's point of view, Tate and Richards were
occupying the same theoretical ground. Both were building their aesthetics
on a fast distinction between the work of the imagination and the work of science, and both were granting scientists' claims to sole or primary authority in
the practical realm. Burke in *P&C* conceded that Tate and Richards were
partly right: the appeal of poetry *had* given way to the appeal of information
and strict denotation; a capitalist society shaped by the perspectives of science
will diminish the aesthetic dimension in people. But this was so not because
science is inherently true or objective, but rather because, given the prevailing technological orientation, people *think* it is. Far from "refusing" the dominant ideology, then, the aesthetes in separating science from poetry were in
fact thinking and acting in complete accordance with that ideology, granting
it absolute authority in everyday life.

In *Permanence and Change* (and in *Attitudes toward History* and *The Philosophy of Literary Form* as well), Burke was working to counter what he saw as a
false distinction between a value-laden aesthetic and an objective science.
What sometimes in *P&C* seem like digressions—sections with titles such as
"Reservations Concerning Logic," "Analogy and Proof," "Tests of Success,"
and "In Qualified Defense of Lawrence" that address questions of evidence
and grounding for scientific judgment—serve not only to call the scientific
ideology into question (although that is clearly one prime function) but also
to refute arguments used by aesthetes in the literary wars to justify autonomous art. Burke insists that the distinction between logical (scientific) and
analogical (imaginative) thinking is more apparent than real. He even suggests, to underscore the point, that scientific thinking can be viewed as its
own kind of poetry. Mechanical inventions or scientific discoveries, for instance, are often the result of metaphorical or analogical extension:

> The attempt to fix argument by analogy as a distinct kind of process, separa-
> ble from logical argument, seems increasingly futile. The most practical form
> of thought that one can think of, the invention of some new usable device, has
> been described as analogical extension, as when one makes a new machine by

conceiving of some old process, such as the treadle, the shuttle, the wheel . . . etc., carried over into some set of facts to which no one has previously felt that it belonged. The heuristic value of scientific analogies is quite like the surprise of metaphor. (127)

Since both scientists and poets are interested in discovering new knowledge, new ways of looking at things, it makes sense to Burke that they would follow similar thought processes, an observation confirmed by E. R. Jaensch's *Eidetic Imagery:* "If we examine the autobiographies of successful scientists, we find that productive thinking must have a close relation to artistic production" (qtd. in *P&C*, 274). Scientific or logical abstractions, like poetic metaphors, "discuss something in terms of something else" (137).

In addition, because scientists not only discover these new ways of looking at things but also explain them and argue for their acceptance, Burke maintains that science at its best is a rhetorical enterprise: "any new way of putting the characters or events together is an attempt to convert people, regardless of whether it go by the name of religion, psychotherapy, or science" (115). Science does not stand in an ideologically neutral space; it, too, is informed by interest:

To make us weep contentedly at the final reunion of brother and sister, the poet hangs telltale lockets about the necks of the little waifs lost in chapter one. When reading, we accept the final reunion as the logical conclusion of the telltale lockets planted in chapter one—but the order was exactly the reverse, the lockets in chapter one being the logical conclusion of the reunion in the chapter last. . . . Applying [this] reversal to our mention of metaphor in science, we should say that the "data" evolved by those who would prove that men are machines, or the sons of God, or chemical compounds, etc., are observations moulded by the informing point of view. (130–31)

The most important questions in life—values, definitions of the good life, politics—lie outside the arena of scientific testing, but, Burke continues, taking clear aim at Richards's claim (following the positivists) that science is true because it can be verified in the laboratory, "even in those areas where the tests of success are made possible by experiment, it is only by a deliberate limitation of *interests* that we can establish such a test" (134). The test and its evaluation are conducted within an ideological system, not in some neutral space. In short, science works not by statements but by pseudo-statements.[17] As if to bait Richards and Tate, Burke even draws an elaborate parallel between scientific and religious doctrine: both involve prophecy or predictions, both advocate new orientations or ways of understanding the world, both demand changes in behavior to suit the new orientation, and both hold out the promise of the good life for those who conform. Indeed the similarity between the

Greek words *hodos* and *methodos* prompts Burke to wonder if religion and science might not share a central motive of finding the path to the good life:
"Might we, noting the suspiciously close connection between the *hodical* and
the *methodical*, be once more encouraged to look for a unitary technique,
called in religious verbalizations the *way* and in scientific verbalizations the
way after?" (300). Like poetry, science can be a form of evangelism. Burke
thus rejects logical positivism (the governing assumption behind the scientific
orientation) and shifts attention instead to interpretation (hermeneutics) in
his treatise on language and communication.

Burke's Aesthetic Proposal: "An Art of Living"

If poetry has as much validity as science as a basis for practical life, then art
should assume a central role in transforming American society. Nevertheless,
despite all his talk about poetry and the rhetorical nature of art, Burke did not
envision rescue in the form of any particular body of poems. Given the prevailing scientistic ideology, poetry simply did not have the cultural capital to
create a revolution; "the poetic medium of communication itself [has been]
weakened" by the prevailing mindset (92). For that matter Burke was not a
great enthusiast for explicitly political poetry. As he wrote to Cowley, borrowing the title and theme from Tate's *New Republic* article, "Poetry and Politics," I have a thesis: Let such poets as consider themselves good politicians
go and shine in politics just as quickly as they can. Let the others stay out"
(July 31, 1933). Rescue, Burke thought, would come not through a body of
poetry but through a poetic ideology. In a significant shift in the terms of the
literary wars, Burke proposed a "*philosophy* or *psychology* of poetry"—that is,
"an art of living" (92, 93) that would promote an aesthetic orientation in
order to revitalize American culture: "If there are radical changes to be made
in the State, what metaphor can better guide us than the poetic one as to the
direction in which these changes must point?" (343). Burke's wording here is
critical. Tate claimed, remember, that poetry expresses "the vision of the
whole of life"; Winters assumed that poetry would generally uplift readers;
and Williams sought to create new poetic forms to embody new knowledge.
But for Burke, it is the poetic metaphor—the aesthetic impulse, the desire to
create and communicate, the life lived as art—and not artwork itself that must
serve as the impetus for change. In *Permanence and Change* Burke accordingly
endorses the values (imagination, community, cooperation) and the practical
policies (most notably communism) that he believes most fully support such
an aesthetic approach to life.

    Metaphor not only provides the goal for social transformation; it also pro-
vides a means: perspective by incongruity, the poetic "act of fusi[ng]" disparate
concepts (343). Burke traced his conception of perspective by incongruity not
only to Nietzsche and Bergson but also to the aesthete par excellence, Remy

de Gourmont; and he honored James Joyce, the modern master of these "linguistic gargoyles" (150), by inventing a nickname for the technique—*joycing*.[18] Burke also mentioned other notable practitioners of perspective by incongruity that the aesthetes would approve, including the Dadaists, the surrealist painters, and Baudelaire. Where Williams was arguing that "it is by the breakup of the language that the truth can be seen to exist and that it becomes operative again" (*Embodiment*, 19), Burke was noting that "any deliberate attempt at analogical extension"—that is, any new vision or perspective unavailable within the dominant orientation—"can be accomplished only by going beyond the (conventional) categories of speech" (156). Depression-era Americans who diligently and purposely were maintaining the repressive scientific and technological ideology (the workings of piety), or blindly going about their business (disoriented victims of "trained incapacity"), were in need of the "heuristic value of error"—perspective by incongruity—to help them be impious, to see new possibilities for living (160). In the fall of 1933 with *Permanence and Change* well under way, Burke gleefully announced his proposal for social change in a letter to Cowley that offers a gloss on the book: "Here will be the centre of the change: the idea of *escape* or *flight* to poetry will change to the idea of *poetry as bulwark*. Not *poetry as retreat*—but *poetry as basis of protest*. . . . Poetry as the campaign base from which to organize one's forays" (September 8, 1933). Society can flourish in a scientific and technological age only if it subordinates machines to human interests. And "where," he asked, "are human purposes best revealed in their purity? [I]n the most intensely *vocational*: madness, hypochondria at the low end, sentiment, attachment, hobbies, etc. in the center, religion, philosophy, and poetry at the high end; otherwise stated, the basis of a human revolt is in the documents of humanity. . . . *Homo poeta* is the central and most pliant concept from which to frame our concept of purpose and our use of instrumentalities" (Burke to Cowley, September 22, 1933).

This position unites two central concepts in *P&C*—that people largely create the worlds they inhabit and that this creation constitutes a form of civic action.[19] At the end of his book, Burke returns to the notion of piety near his reiteration that "in the course of living, we gradually erect a structure of relationships about us in conformity with our interests" (326). This pious universe-building "is *assertive*, it is *productive* or *creative*—hence, it is concerned with *action*" (274), and it accounts for Burke's choice of action or participation as the fundamental human motive. Since this action is guided by interests or piety, it is also always symbolic, a point Burke emphasizes by examining piety as an instance of the pathetic fallacy—that is, as an extension of a person's mental patterns into the external world. Rockefeller's financial empire is as much a symbol of his inner makeup as Milton's poetry was of his: "In this sense," Burke claims, "all action is poetic" (275), and "we are all poets.

. . . Indeed, all life has been likened to the writing of a poem, though some people write their poems on paper, and others carve theirs out of jugular veins" (102). Or, as he insisted in a letter to Matthew Josephson (March 24, 1933), "the 'esthetes' were simply the imaginative or poetic side of Marx." Burke concludes with conviction: "life, activity, cooperation, communication —they are identical" (302). The art of rhetoric and the art of living fold into each other; *Permanence and Change* theorizes the merger of rhetoric, poetics, and everyday life:

> Indeed, beginning with such a word as *composition* to designate the architectonic nature of either a poem, a social construct, or a method of practical action, we can take over the whole vocabulary of tropes (as formulated by the rhetoricians) to describe the specific patterns of human behavior. Since social life, like art, is a *problem of appeal*, the poetic metaphor would give us invaluable hints for describing modes of practical action which are too often measured by simple tests of utility and too seldom with reference to the communicative, sympathetic, *propitiatory* factors that are clearly present in the procedures of formal art and must be as truly present in those informal arts of living we do not happen to call arts. (339–40)

The result of this philosophy would be not a workers' state but a poets' state—a state that fosters participation as in a great drama, a state that might fuse diverse cultures the way a lyric fuses images, a state in which the most important business is the creative act, a state that would be as politically engaged as it would be attentive to the values of aesthetes. Throughout 1934 Burke lived such a life: he wrote music criticism and protested on behalf of striking workers at the Macauley Publishing Company; he wrote book reviews and petitioned Thomas Mann to resist the Nazis; newly wed, he lectured, read, wrote poems, tended his garden, and prepared *Permanence and Change* for publication.[20]

Still, though it sponsored an art of living, *Permanence and Change* is far from being a mere counterpart to *Auscultation*, far from articulating with a coterie of aesthetes in a way analogous to how *Auscultation* is addressed to a coterie of leftists. For there were many others whom Burke was incorporating into his synthesis—including Bentham, Darwin, Freud, Veblen, Nietzsche, and, of course, Marx.

Permanence and Change *and the Left*

Early in 1934, just as Burke's "On Interpretation" was appearing in the inaugural issue of *Plowshare*, Malcolm Cowley offered some news from home in a letter to Matthew Josephson in Paris: "Kenneth is taking his mild communism mildly but seriously. He spoke before the John Reed Club along with John Chamberlain and [Edward] Dahlberg, and of course tried to prove to them that the class struggle wasn't the most important question in modern life" (February 1, 1934). Cowley's oxymoronic description is telling: It documents Burke's active participation in the conversation of the Left; but it suggests, as well, the difficulties even Burke's leftist contemporaries felt in labeling his unorthodox stance toward Marxism and communism.[21]

Some of these difficulties derived, no doubt, from the challenge of following the subtleties of Burke's thinking and the influences on his highly eclectic ideas. But another source of the problems in defining Burke's relation to Marx and communism has always been the way people have tended to approach the issue, the questions they have asked about that relationship. As Don Paul Abbott rightly notes, it is "not so much *whether* Burke was influenced by Marx, but in *which ways* he was so influenced" (230–31), and so most students of Burke have focused on that question—a productive one, up to a point. But the question has also seemed to provoke a very similar and very general answer—that Burke has a highly personal, unorthodox take on Marx. What troubles about this answer is its implication that Burke was the only intellectual independent enough or critical enough or just plain eccentric enough to forge his own system of radical thought while everyone else marched lockstep with the Communist Party program. In fact, as James Murphy, Barbara Foley, Michael Denning, and many others have shown, orthodoxy was really not a hallmark of the 1930s; it was not at all uncommon for intellectuals to reinterpret Marx (as Sidney Hook's attempt to separate Marx from dialectical materialism illustrates) or to cobble together elements from a wide range of philosophical, political, religious, and literary sources. Moreover such non-Marxist or "Marxoid" socialism, far from being "personal," was itself part of a long tradition in American radical thought. So when Matthew Josephson accused Burke in early 1933 of suddenly reversing his position "contra Marx," Burke protested: "There is much, in Marx, of the utilitarians, of Darwinism, of Hegelianism and the Hegelian offshoot, of pragmatism, of historicism, etc. I could not be, in the lump, 'contra Marx,' for Marx is too typical of nineteenth-century thought, and I am too imbued with nineteenth-century thought, for such a simple inclusion or exclusion to be possible" (March 29, 1933). Burke's response to Josephson suggests at least three important considerations for readers of *Permanence and Change*. First, Marx is deeply embedded in Burke's thought and language throughout the book. Second, for Burke, Marx was never a single, separate entity but came along with other thinkers. What most interested Burke in Marx was not just ideas "unique" to Marx but also what Marx had in common and congruence with many others. Third, Burke's defense of nineteenth-century thought, a product of his education and his work at the *Dial*, associates him with European high culture—a culture that shared Burke's great respect for the aesthetic.

What, then, was Burke's precise relationship to the range of available left-ist positions? What could Burke gain by using or invoking Marx? What could Burke get from Marx that he could not get elsewhere, and what did Burke need to go elsewhere for? What was at stake for Burke in choosing to call himself a Marxist or not?[22] Although *Permanence and Change* bears the clear imprint of Marx, Burke also chose to distance himself from Marx and Marx-ism, aligning himself instead with broader traditions of aestheticism, mysti-cism, and spiritual socialism—traditions that helped him define and advocate the settling of a territory (to borrow the phrase from *Auscultation*) "beyond Marxism."

Or at least beyond Mike Gold, who stood for the most doctrinaire Marx-ist perspective. At the Second World Plenum held in Kharkov in 1930, the Communist Party had formulated a unified program for revolutionary cul-ture worldwide. In addition to offering a ten-point critique of the American Communists' cultural programs, Kharkov delegates emphasized above all the need for building a culture both revolutionary and proletarian in the United States. *New Masses*, having been scored for being insufficiently politicized and for reaching for too broad an audience to create a distinctive proletcult, was encouraged to reform itself around resolutely proletarian art and criticism, and so "spurred on by the Kharkov advice, Communist intellectuals took their most visible advocate of the prolet cult, Michael Gold, and put him on center stage" (Kutulas, 39). The point, as Kutulas notes, "was not to portray heroic workers who had sudden communist epiphanies, but to enable radical-ized intellectuals to bring their politics into the creative or critical process. Communist intellectuals struggled to articulate differences between what they did and what other intellectuals did so that they might give meaning to their perceived uniqueness" (37–38). As Kutulas, Foley, and Denning have indicated, proletcult was never as narrow in theory or practice as some critics have suggested, in part because it was never clearly defined. However, that very lack of definition provoked recurring discussions in *New Masses*, the *Nation, Partisan Review*, the *New Republic*, and other magazines about the middle-class intellectual's role in the revolutionary movement and about "the place of the prolet cult in a broader cultural world" (Kutulas, 42).

Foley has noted that definitions and defenses of proletarian literature were typically based on four criteria: authorship, audience, subject, or perspective (87). Proletcult, in other words, could be identified as art created *by* proletar-ians, *for* proletarians, *about* proletarians, and/or *from the perspective of* the revo-lutionary (as opposed to merely reformist) proletarian movement. Placing middle-class intellectuals within proletcult, even in these varied incarnations, could and did prove problematical for Gold and his camp because middle-class intellectuals could not write "authentically" about proletcult out of their own experiences, and their lack of knowledge or experience could easily make attempts to write for or about workers amount to little more than literary slumming. Often the only option for middle-class writers was to write to middle-class readers, with the goal of supporting a proletarian revolution. But just how did one go about doing that? And if middle-class intellectuals writing to middle-class audiences about the decadence of capitalism could constitute proletarian literature, how was that different from what these same intellectuals wrote when they were bohemians? The issues that stemmed from proletcult, and from its star, Mike Gold, then, fed into larger discussions about the relationship of art, rhetoric, and politics—discussions that were debated in the pages of *New Masses* and other magazines, and that Burke contributed to in *Permanence and Change*.

Gold was indeed the Communist Party member most readily identified with proletcult, and *New Masses* was Gold's sturdy proletarian platform. His first editorial for the magazine proposed reorganizing *New Masses* around the concept of a workers' literature. Along with Joseph Freeman, who would pen the introduction for the important anthology *Proletarian Literature in the United States* (1936), and, to a lesser extent, Granville Hicks (who joined *New Masses* as literary editor late in 1933 and edited *Proletarian Literature*), Gold worked to establish an uncompromising, truly revolutionary, American working-class culture.[23] Gold made *New Masses* into a magazine dedicated to the proletarian cause. He consistently shaped *New Masses* around Moscow and revolution, and his July 1928 editorial manifesto, "A New Program for Writers," called for "a national corps of writers" similar to the ones he encountered on a visit to the Soviet Union in 1925: "Instead of having a board of contributing editors made up of these vague, rootless people known as writers," he promised, "we will have a staff of industrial correspondents" in *New Masses* (9). Gold, Freeman, and Hicks agreed that since class struggle was the central experience of modern life, it provided, in Freeman's words, the most "interesting" and "significant" theme for contemporary art (16).

Not everyone was certain about the particulars, to be sure. "Most CP critics," writes Foley, "while not guided by anything resembling a party 'line' on aesthetic matters, were in fact uneasy with the view of literature as weaponry and repudiated the notion that proletarian literature should be written as propaganda" (37). Some resistance to Gold and Hicks was common even within the most committed leftist factions, therefore. Even Gold himself conceded that "the function of a revolutionary writer is not to suggest political platforms and theses, but to portray the life of the workers and to inspire them with solidarity and revolt" ("Notes," 23) and that "there is not a standard model that all writers must imitate" ("Proletarian Novel?," 74). Freeman remarked to the same effect: "All this the artist—if he is an artist and not an agitator—does with the specific technique of his craft. He does not repeat party theses; he communicates that experience out of which the theses arise"

(11). Neither Gold nor Freeman nor Hicks always defined proletarian art in a particularly narrow way (though Hicks's *The Great Tradition* in 1933 was certainly enthusiastic enough about defining great literature according to its effectiveness as a weapon in the class struggle); as indicated by their relationship to the first American Writers' Congress, they often if sometimes uneasily welcomed support from middle-class artists and critics. Hence, in May 1932, at the first national conference of the John Reed Clubs, Gold and Freeman, as delegates from the New York City JRC and authors of the draft conference manifesto, recommended efforts to appeal to more moderate fellow travelers. "In attracting such 'so-called Marxian critics' as Edmund Wilson and Waldo Frank ('who talk about Marxism which they don't understand very well but actively support the movement'), the JRCs were not capitulating to the intellectuals; rather, 'we are asking intellectuals to adopt our orientation to the Communist Party'" (qtd. in Aaron, 225–26). In addition Gold even complained about overly sectarian delegates and bureaucrats in the JRCs— "'persons who will perhaps never be artists or writers' but who drive away the real artists like Edmund Wilson, John Dos Passos, and Malcolm Cowley: 'they won't come to the meetings. They sense mechanization'" (qtd. in Aaron, 226). The minutes from the conference record Gold:

> Since the first day of the John Reed Club I have been in the minority in saying this club should be organized of the broad middle class intellectual workers. It should be the feeder, the contact organization between these and the Communist movement. . . . You believe in proletarian writing. Wilson believes in Proustian—I say bring him into the movement, if he is a writer of great influence and great talent. We cannot afford to have aesthetic quarrels. (qtd. in Aaron, 226)

For all his working-class radicalism, Gold did not always occupy the least compromising Left position on the issue of the middle-class intellectuals. He conceded that position to younger radicals—those writers for whom the JRCs were founded and who argued that what the clubs could not afford was to let their program or purpose be diluted by bourgeois elements. They wanted a genuine, pure proletcult—that is, art by, for, and about workers: no fellow travelers allowed.

Those fellow travelers (or "progressives") were more moderate and usually more temperate than party members Gold, Freeman, and Hicks. These intellectuals and artists—Burke's colleagues Wilson, Cowley, Josephson, Robert Cantwell, and Waldo Frank among them—believed in the party's overall goals, worked alongside members of the party, participated in some party functions (such as May Day parades and the relief expedition in support of striking miners in Harlan County, Kentucky), wrote more often for the *New Republic* than *New Masses*,[24] and likely thought of themselves generally as

Marxists. But they never officially joined the party. Kutulas concludes that Communism "captured [their] hearts but not their minds" (34). The romantic, revolutionary fervor of the progressives is expressed in Cowley's memoir *The Dream of the Golden Mountains:* "Great changes would surely take place; they *must* take place, and many of us felt . . . that it was our duty as writers to take part in them, at least by coming forward to bear witness" (x); Cowley remembers being "possessed . . . by a daydream of revolutionary brotherhood": "by surrendering [our] middle-class identities, by joining the workers in an idealized army, writers might help to overthrow 'the system' and might go marching with comrades, shoulder to shoulder, out of injustice and illogic into the golden mountains" (xii). But this daydream expressed itself in magazines more pluralistic than *New Masses,* and it sometimes faded before the realities of hardcore party life and the inhospitality of some Marxist philosophy and methods: some progressives found the theory impenetrable, while others understood the theory but found it too mechanistic or violent (Kutulas, 33–35).

Because of their sympathy with the CPUSA, progressives were generally accepting of proletcult despite the fact—or maybe because of the fact—that they often did not see such literature as revolutionary culture per se but rather as art that happened to be about workers. "Stripped of its political intent," Kutulas contends, it appeared to be "very like the naturalism popular earlier in the century. Sherwood Anderson, for example, greeted all the ballyhoo about the prolet cult with puzzlement. 'What in hell,' he wondered, 'has Dreiser been doing all his life?'" (41). As Kutulas and Denning have indicated very well, many progressive writers in fact appropriated parts of proletcult—its journalistic style, for instance, and its relatively unexplored subject matters. Nevertheless a significant number of progressives continued to harbor a somewhat stereotypical notion of the Communist Party as an intellectual straitjacket, prompting Wilson's 1931 *New Republic* "Appeal to Progressives" (to take communism away from the CPUSA), many of the moderate statements at the first American Writers' Congress, and this rather anguished comment by Matthew Josephson to Burke on the subject of the intellectual's duty to the revolutionary movement:

> Again and again I return to the proposition: Does the [development of Communism] justify devotion (perhaps immolation) of the intelligence to a strict partisanship? Or, does not the Intelligence have rights, prerogatives, needs, of its own, which must at all costs be retained in the long run and without which the capacity for backward and forward viewing, highest desideratum of Marxism itself, would be weakened and ruined? (September 15, 1935)

Josephson's complaint that working for the cause necessarily involved a loss of intellectual freedom troubled fellow travelers of all varieties.

Two other leftist groups registered very strong if very different attitudes to proletcult: a group Kutulas has dubbed "dissident Marxists" (most notably the Trotskyists)[25] and the liberals. The dissident Marxists (including Sidney Hook and V. F. Calverton, editor of *Modern Monthly*, who made the magazine a mouthpiece for dissidents) were, for the most part, American exceptionalists. That is, they hoped to recover the genuine Marx from the hopelessly distorting Stalin by both modernizing and Americanizing the theory. The group formed explicitly on such a program was the Lovestoneites, following Jay Lovestone, but many others worked to synthesize Marx with American values, an effort that included (for instance) Hook's effort to accommodate Marx with Dewey. Practically the dissidents objected to applying Soviet strategies in a country with vastly different productive capabilities, class structure, and mass culture; philosophically they objected to dialectic as, in Kenneth Rexroth's words, "Marx's half-baked materialist-hegelian hash" (qtd. in Kutulas, 64–65). Eventually—in the wake of the Popular Front, the Moscow trials, and finally the Hitler-Stalin pact in 1939—the dissidents increasingly grew in influence, but even in 1933 they were creating a disharmonious split between Stalin's supporters and anti-Stalinist Marxists.

The literary Trotskyists' argument against the JRCs and proletcult was ultimately derived from Leon Trotsky's *Literature and Revolution* (1924). As Burke well knew (e.g., note his comment on Trotsky in *Attitudes toward History*, 75), Trotsky regarded "proletarian culture [as] a contradiction in terms . . . since the proletariat, as a dispossessed class, had no culture of its own. The effort to create such a culture *ex nihilo* was an invitation to bureaucratization and authoritarian control of the arts" (Foley, 16). Accordingly Sidney Hook, on the basis of his readings of Trotsky and the early Marx, maintained (somewhat questionably) that Marx believed in "the relative autonomy of the esthetic experience" (*Towards the Understanding*, 88). From such explications, Calverton too concluded (with reason) that proletcult was a perversion that "flowed not out of Marxism, or Leninism, but Stalinism, which is Marxism corrupted and vitiated" (15). Philip Rahv, coeditor of *Partisan Review*, in 1936 and 1937 also began to condemn proletcult as nothing more than Stalinism by another name, an opinion that would come to be seconded by Burke's wary friend James T. Farrell (whose *A Note on Literary Criticism*, 1936, was one of the first fully articulated anti-Stalinist attacks on the Communist Party cultural line). The result, ironically, was that Trotskyists often separated politics and aesthetics—in other words, they established on the literary Left a position similar in effect to that established by the aesthetes on the literary Right.

Finally the liberals, the "right wing" of the intellectual Left, dismissed proletcult as "a bunch of badly written stories about tramps, union organizers, and farm laborers" (Kutulas, 41). Liberals such as Dewey and John Chamberlain (the genial representative of the *New York Times Book Review*) rejected

Stalinism and the Communist Party out of hand, except for their agreement on the need for substantial change organized around some sort of collectivity. As a result, *liberalism* was typically a dirty word in the leftist political lexicon. Like the Trotskyists, with whom they often sympathized, liberals separated the political and the aesthetic realms. Hence Lawrence Leighton, writing in *Hound and Horn* early in 1933, attacked party-line writers: because communism was distrusted by most Americans of all classes, he argued, it offers writers merely the opportunity for vigorous and violent missionary work. But this task is "hardly compatible with the more difficult task of being a good critic or a good artist" (qtd. in Aaron, 255). In other words, because it was persuasive, Marxist writing was by definition bad writing. And like many progressives, liberals worried that working for the party meant surrendering one's intellectual independence.

Burke's friends and intellectual associates, then, were scattered everywhere on the left political spectrum—everywhere, at least, to the right of Gold and Hicks. Although Wander claims that "Burke thought himself a Marxist in the early 1930s" (206), it is not clear that, in the parlance of the time, he would have thought of himself so simply as a Marxist, for that was a term he used most often to refer disparagingly to Communist Party members, to Hicks and Gold, and to their fervent followers in the John Reed Club of New York and in *New Masses*. Though he was certainly no Trotskyist, though he never published in *Modern Monthly*, and though he could never separate the aesthetic from the political, Burke's own position in *P&C* nevertheless bears most striking resemblance to that of the "dissident Marxists."[26] In the act of writing *Permanence and Change*, Burke resolutely countered what he perceived to be the reductive and arhetorical aesthetics, cultural criticisms, and sectarian politics of the CPUSA as well as the Trotskyists' views about the place of art in society.

As the point man for proletcult and as someone with a well-earned reputation for "megalomaniac sectarianism" (Buhle, 177), Mike Gold and his *New Masses* embodied for Burke all the weaknesses of the Communist Party's aesthetic theory and practice. First and foremost, Burke dismissed *New Masses* as "a highschool graduating-class sheet" (Burke to Farrell, July 18, 1934), especially as it began to struggle financially in 1933 and especially after it was reborn as a weekly, with the dogmatic Hicks as literary editor, with the first issue of 1934; and he frequently bemoaned the low and narrow standards of its resolute Communist Party criticism. Reacting to Cowley's and Josephson's unfavorable reviews of *Towards a Better Life*, for example, Burke complained: "Oaf! how I wince when youenz boys get down piously to pulling that lowest-common-denominator brand of criticism on me. (A marvelous device it is indeed, for lifting imbeciles [in the John Reed Club] to the insight-level of a Mike Gold—but unfortunately it is equally capable of lowering keen men to the insight-level of same Mike Gold.)" (Burke to Josephson, March 24, 1933). After reading an article by Sidney Hook in Calverton's *Modern Monthly*, Burke remarked to Cowley, "You do not know how soothed I feel, at the thought that these matters have now been taken out of the hands of the John Reed Club and transferred to the treatment of perceptive and well-docu- mented people. When I get to town I want to meet Hook—as he is one of the few in the business who is not cheese" (September 8, 1933). The dissident Hook thoroughly approved of the work that Burke was turning out as he wrote *P&C*.

Much of Burke's resistance to the Communist Party cultural program, as noted earlier, stemmed from his perception that the Communist Party would sanction only a narrow range of aesthetic options. For instance Burke glee- fully reported to Farrell, "When I saw Hicks last . . . , I said, Better get after Farrell; he's slipping; can't see what Marxism has to do with writing novels.' Said Hicks made a face, said, 'Damn that guy, he knows well enough what Marxism has to do with writing novels; only thing is, he wants to write two more books on Studs Lonigan, couldn't [do] them the way he's doing them if he went communist.'" Burke's dismissal: "Nerts to that" (July 8, 1934). Other letters like the one to Farrell similarly complain against the too-easy assump- tion that certain types of writing are proletarian and revolutionary while other types are bourgeois and, hence, necessarily support the status quo— and, further, that critics can easily distinguish the two types. An aesthetic the- ory based on this antithesis limited choices not only for writers but for readers as well. For Burke proletcult remained what he had called in *Auscul- tation* "proletarian denudation," the process whereby the richest cultural trea- sures were forbidden simply because they were connected with the aesthetes or the bourgeois. A revolutionary movement intended to enrich the lives of workers was instead impoverishing them. "Christ! but things did look gloomy for a while," Burke wrote Cowley, "with Business anti-cultural already, and the young bloods [in the JRCs] contributing to precisely the same points of view. That *was* to feel lonesome. But as things move along a little further, one by one they will come to praise God for the survival of a good book here and there" (September 8, 1933). Implicit in the attitudes Burke expressed in many of his letters are the knowledge that Marx himself retained an appreciation for the aesthetic and the assumption, common to progressives, Trotskyists, and liberals alike, that an overly sectarian party was dictating cultural lines and demanding strict obedience. "Communism . . . can always become Fas- cism over night," Burke wrote to Josephson, "for it is a mere technique of driving cattle, not a technique for enabling them to cease to be cattle" (June 2, 1933). Burke even offered up an outline for a proposed magazine, the *New State*, that would provide an independent forum for dissidents: "Citizens in a vast and complicated state such as ours must lay the first emphasis upon *criticism* and upon *judgment*. They must perfect a *technique of decision*. Fascism and Communism demand that the citizen have unquestioning faith in their rulers. A properly equipped citizenry will begin with doubt, questioning, vigilance, scrutinizing; and then, having scrutinized, it will have faith, and will know that its faith is erected upon a sound basis" (Burke to Abell, April 7, 1933).[27]

A Burke Spoof

Burke continued to read widely in economics during 1933, and a number of his letters evince enthusiasm for the Englishman C. H. Douglas's social credit theory, a proposal for reorganizing the banking and currency systems that enjoyed a boomlet of enthusiasm during the Depression among radicals of every kind (Weaver, 103–13; Orage; Hampden). A. R. Orage, Ezra Pound, William Carlos Williams, and Gorham Munson were all enthusiasts at various points. But rather than advancing the New State or social credit, Burke satisfied some of his reformist economic theories by writing satiric spoofs. Here, as an example, is "For Bond Money," published in the New Republic, *January 4, 1933, pages 218–19 (under the name "Ethel Howardell"). Another, "Preserving Capitalism," appeared in the* New Republic, *February 22, 1933, page 49 (under the name "Walter S. Hankel"): it proposed the creation of a "Privilege League," a "super-organization to resist any possible changes in the structure of capitalism." Burke tried to publish several others as well: one of them untitled (see Burke to Hazlitt, 1933, Burke Papers); "Principles of Wise Spending"; and "The New Prince" (the last two in folder P15, Kenneth Burke Papers).*

At least we think this is a satire:

For Bond Money
Sir:
I have lately noted, on the financial pages of our daily papers, an increasing number of references to the fact that Wall Street expects inflationary legislation at this session of Congress or next, and that it has finally become willing to see such measures tried. Could I review briefly some of the points in favor of "bond money," or negotiable, non-interest-bearing bonds issued by the government as legal tender in payment for public construction work?

The plan, in its simplicity, would not be a bare watering of the currency by the printing of more paper dollars without "backing." Instead, it would be a proposal for defining construction work as a backing for currency. For instance, suppose that a state wished to build a toll bridge costing ten million dollars. It would borrow, from the federal government, at no interest, ten million dollars in the new "bond money." It would pay for materials and construction by this "bond money," which would be legal tender. In return, it would pledge the tolls from the bridge to the federal government until the entire equivalent of the ten million had been received into the Treasury. The federal government could also, if it desired, receive the tolls for a few more years as a "service" charge for the loan of the bond money. Thereupon the deal would be closed, the bridge would have been paid for, the toll charge could be removed, and the government would have retired an amount of paper equivalent to that originally put into circulation for the construction of the bridge.

Such a plan would have several features to recommend it:

1. It would avoid the present enormous costs of bond flotation, which usually mean that ten or fifteen dollars out of every hundred have trickled away to underwriters of the bond issue before construction work begins at all. This would be a "self-floating" bond issue.

2. It would "tap new investment levels," as the new "baby bond" would be a dollar bill, quite simply, and any workman who took one in exchange for his services would automatically become an "investor."

3. It would avoid the mathematical absurdities of interest charges. (And why should a state pay interest like a private entrepreneur anyhow, when all the collective private wealth is behind its credit?)

In contrast with pure fiat-money schemes, it would provide a very real backing for every dollar of new currency issued. To the present kinds of backing (gold, government bonds, commercial paper) it would add the "realest" of all, tangible property.

As for earnings: with the elimination of interest charges, many a toll proposition that would, under the present system of bond flotation, be an impossibility, would become profitable. Every dollar in revenue above the operating costs could go to the federal Treasury to amortize the debt. Under the present system of interest charges, on the contrary, a bridge that was receiving in tolls a great deal more per year than its operating costs might still be going further into debt.

Also, while serving to finance pivotal construction work from which other activities might "radiate," it would avoid draining private investment capital into government projects. This private capital should be available for investment in any of the activities "radiating" from this "pivotal" construction work.

And as for those who object to such backing for money, how can they discredit property as backing without discrediting the entire myth of our bond structure? And again, if it did drop below par with relation to other money, it would in this respect be no different from the present government bonds which are accepted as backing for the issuance of money.

Ethel Howardell, New York City

Again and again in his conversations with leftist friends, Burke asserted his belief in the need to press beyond a rigid version of Marxism. "What you say about Communism," he wrote to Farrell, strikes me in the right place. I thought you were definitely going left seeing you under the wing of sectarian Hicks. . . . It's good to know you still retain a sense of balance. . . . Much as the pink brothers insist that communism must pervade all life, especially the artist's attitude toward his work, etc., I think they're talking through their hats. When the time comes we will be on the right side of the barricade; no one with a brain could be on the wrong, but in the fine frenzy they can't see anything further than the tips of their noses, can't see this is merely the next step, not the Second Coming or the Millennium, that there are many things that will remain forever uninfluenced by whatever boys are in the saddle, whatever system momentarily holds sway. (June 27, 1934)

To the fellow traveler Cowley he offered the same analysis: "As for Communism, insofar as it is a merely political or economic expedient, I can consider it as hardly more than social dentistry: a contribution to the 'good life' in precisely the sense that the pulling of a bad tooth would be. Only if it can be placed in some sentimental, non-rational framework does it seem to me adequately pointed. In other words: only if it really can substitute for religion" (March 30, 1934). Burke's ultimate impatience with sectarian squabbles, the inflexibility of proletcult, and the generally limited content of leftist conversations sprang from his sense that all of them were, at least in part, simply beside the point. The discussions in the leftist parlor needed a new direction. "The 'innovator,'" Burke had written in *Auscultation*, "is a man who, after a certain trend of conversation has been going on for some time, goes back a few sentences to some point that was made and partially neglected—and from this partially neglected point he develops a line of thought somewhat different from that which the subsequent course of discussion had taken" (102).

The "neglected point" in 1930s leftist conversations, according to Paul Buhle, was the rich sources of "homegrown radicalism"—"American currents of democratic aspiration: radical, universalist, utopian"—that "could appeal beyond the limits of class- and ethnicity-bound Marxism, beyond *homo economus* to a recurrently troubled national conscience and democratic discourse that Marxist theoreticians failed to comprehend" (14). Edmund Wilson and William Carlos Williams were not neglecting those sources as they sought a distinctively American radicalism, and neither was Kenneth Burke; he was reading both native and nonnative radicals carefully in 1933[28]—Veblen, Dewey, Bentham, Darwin, Nietzsche, Frazer, Freud, in addition to Marx— because he had more than a hunch that these older voices, many from the nineteenth century, had an important sense of the meanings and implications of monopolistic capitalism in the United States. And so he sought to reintroduce those voices into leftist conversations through *Permanence and Change*.

That is not to say, of course, that *Permanence and Change* turns its back on Marx and communism. On the contrary Burke was at pains, as Cowley had noted, to take communism seriously, beginning with the heading that introduces his proposed new orientation ("Communism a Humanistic, or Poetic, Rationalization") and continuing through his patient treatment of four reasons for turning to communism: the economic (or "rational"), the historic, the ethical, and the aesthetic.[29] Burke hardly needed to emphasize the first, for his audience understood very well the economic failures of capitalism. Suffice it to say that Burke was attentive to the significance of material conditions and assumed the insufficiency of capitalism's mechanisms: by saturating markets, "it finally creates conditions which hamper private initiative" in economics and in culture (215). Nor it is necessary to elaborate on how Burke's understanding of history as unfolding in successive stages is congruent with Marx's; even if he did not interpret history as merely a record of class struggle, Burke did acknowledge a broadly Marxist orientation toward history by predicting that collectivism would mark the next historical macrophase, following magic, religion, and science: "A corrective rationalization must certainly move in the direction of the anthropomorphic or humanistic or poetic, since this is the aspect of culture which the scientific criteria, with their emphasis on dominance rather than inducement, have tended to eliminate or minimize" (91). Like other communists, Burke interpreted the broad movement of history as toward collectivity.

The more novel grounds for Burke's support for communism in *P&C* were ethical and aesthetic. Burke surveys in his book a "whole ailing world" (285) of capitalism that causes psychological hardships (in addition to economic ones) because it denies people the opportunity to feel moral and act morally. Burke hypothesizes that in the early stages of capitalism, people who exploited others could still feel ethical because they were piously obeying capitalism's commandment to seek profit. The combined power of piety and profit induced people to "ethicize" their means of support—that is, their occupations. Burke indeed devotes several sections of the book to this topic: "Ethicizing the Means of Support," "Variants of the Ethicizing Tendency," and "Extending the Concept of Occupation." But there is a limit to what people will ethicize; if Americans were once able to "naturally" or piously participate in capitalistic exploitation, that time was passing:

> The cynicism that goes with many forms of work today would seem to arise from the fact that the natural tendency to ethicize the means of support is frustrated. No man is happy at the thought that he would "bite the hand that feeds him"—yet if he lives by a capitalist economy he must either do precisely this (in despising the duties that are placed upon him) or must give allegiance to a system which demands the expenditure of great effort in unsocial and antisocial ways. (261n)

Communism is necessary because "there is a fundamental relationship between *wealth* and *virtue* which no 'spiritual' scheme must be allowed to deny by fiat." Noting that *property* and *propriety* are etymologically similar, Burke, following Bentham's lead, indicated that "morals and property are integrally related"—so integrally related that "we must gravely doubt whether the communal property of morals can remain firm unless it is grounded in the communal ownership of its material counterpart" (270). Capitalism fosters competition and fragmentation rather than cooperation and communality, instability rather than stability, and it is precisely these evils that communism can remedy.

The emphasis on ethical and aesthetic approaches to communism in *Permanence and Change* foregrounds several important aspects of Burke's argument. Burke's foremost goal was the establishment of a communal, cooperative, creative way of life; communism is necessary because it is the cultural and economic system that supports this lifestyle.[30] Furthermore Burke saw more than one way to get to communism; significantly he chose to argue for communism and not Marxism per se. Hence he wrote Waldo Frank in praise of a recent publication:

> You are also to be congratulated for showing that your approach can lead to a Communistic philosophy of behavior. There is a general tendency among those in charge of Communistic propaganda to assume that anything other than economic materialism must lead to Fascism—and this tendency has caused me much uneasiness, as I could not possibly respect myself if I considered myself innately Fascist, yet I cannot accept naive materialism as an adequate account of man's relations to the universal process. And I am convinced that Communism alone points in the right direction, however faultily its advocates may verbalize their position. (May 23, 1934)[31]

This matter of leftists "faultily verbalizing their position" was, of course, no small issue for Burke. Since he understood *Permanence and Change* as a "treatise on communication," he was at pains to reform the thinking of leftist political leaders. More particularly Burke sought to install Veblen's concept of "trained incapacity," Dewey's concept of "occupational psychosis," and his own (and Nietzsche's) notion of "perspective by incongruity" into the Communist Party lexicon because communism could not supply everything in terms of vocabulary that was needed for Americans to adopt a cooperative and creatively constructive way of life. Burke's point to "those in charge of Communistic propaganda" is that an effective revolutionary rhetoric needs to be based on an accurate understanding of criticism and ideology and to be grounded in the dominant vocabulary.

The discussion of rhetoric in *Permanence and Change* begins in the book's opening pages with Burke's reconsideration of the Communists' tactic of labeling aesthetes "escapists." A holdover from *Auscultation* (it was apparently quite a sore point with Burke), it makes for a rather disconcerting start since Burke seemed to feel little need to contextualize or identify the issue except to mention "the contemporary tendency to discuss matters of orientation by reference to 'avoidance' and 'escape'" (14). The problem with "escape" as a critical label is that

> it suggested that the people to whom it was applied tended to orientate them-selves in a totally different way from the people to whom it was not applied, the former always trying to escape from life or avoid realities, while the latter faced realities. . . . In the end, the term came to be applied loosely, in literary criticism especially, to designate any writer or reader whose interests and aims did not closely coincide with those of the critic. (15–16)

Burke caustically noted that the chief act of avoidance was, rather, that these critics "avoided telling us precisely what they meant by life, avoidance, and facing reality. In this way, through escaping from the difficulties of their critical problem, they were free to accuse many writers and thinkers of escape" (16). Burke, then, implicitly establishes the project of his book as thinking through the difficulties of critical problematics, particularly the problems of persuading people to give up one ideological system for another.

It is to this end that Burke introduced the concepts of "trained incapacity" and "occupational psychosis" as alternatives to the idea of "escape" and to other unhelpful critical labels designed to signal errors in interpretation. The idea of trained incapacity is central to *P&C:* "one adopts measures in keeping with his past training—and the very soundness of this training may lead him to adopt the wrong measures" (18). An important advantage of the concept of trained incapacity is that, unlike some Marxist labels whose "high emotive value endangers their usefulness for criticism" (20), it allows critics to point out unproductive or unhealthy choices—in this case, support of capitalism and the technological orientation—without questioning people's morality or intelligence or political allegiances. Burke hoped that a less weighted term would make cultural criticism useful without making Americans defensive or hostile.

By emphasizing trained incapacity, Burke by implication was questioning the effectiveness of a strictly Marxist (or, for that matter, a strictly Freudian) perspective as a means of fully understanding people's motives. The Marxist vocabulary, like all vocabularies, is itself a trained incapacity, one that classi-fies and analyzes an individual with reference to only one quality:

> This deceptive attitude towards the whole subject of classification is at pres-ent observable in the intense critical battles over proletarian literature. A proletarian is defined, by abstraction, as a worker of a certain sort. But he is obviously many other things as well: a particular endocrine combination, for

instance, an "introvert" or "extrovert," a man who did or did not have a bad attack of measles in his childhood, etc. All such non-proletarian factors are involved in his make-up—yet critics attempt to find some rigid distinction between proletarian and non-proletarian thinking that will serve as a schema for classifying *all* his expressions. No wonder they are forever detecting in him "bourgeois" or "feudalistic" vestiges. (163)

A Marxist perspective is not wrong per se. Indeed the Marxist perspective is actually quite beneficial because it helps people see things in a new light, for any "perspective is heuristic insofar as we see close at hand the things we had formerly seen from afar, and vice versa" (163). And Marx himself was hardly a complete economic determinist: he recognized that aesthetic and other cultural factors act on the economic order, sometimes quite independently. But Burke's program of perspective by incongruity would enlarge critical vision by encouraging people to look at things from unconventional angles. The Marxist perspective creates trouble only when it is seen as the "one" or the "right" perspective: in that case it limits rather than expands critical understanding. The "poetic perspective," by contrast, is potentially more useful because it can produce multiple perspectives, metaphorical fusions: perspectives by incongruity.

But perhaps the most important factor in creating a successful revolutionary rhetoric, Burke argues, is simply to make it *rhetorical*—that is, to make it responsive to the needs and attitudes of its audience, and in particular, to the nature of the audience's interests and pieties. In the important introduction to part 2 ("Perspective by Incongruity"), Burke remarks that "the conditions of such transformation involve not merely intellectualistic problems, but also deeply emotional ones" (3rd ed., 69); that is, the conditions of transformation involve an unquestioning devotion to a way of thinking or a way of life. Piety, "a much more extensive motive than it is usually thought to be" (3rd ed., 69), explains why people do not always do what is in their best interests; why their actions (or the ideologies behind those actions) do not make sense or why their decisions are not logical; why the Depression has not been enough to awaken the whole country to the exploitative nature of capitalism. Economic systems and revolutionary tactics constructed upon the notion that humans are entirely rational beings, as Burke implies that Marxism is, seem to him fundamentally flawed in this respect. It was a point he would develop further in *Attitudes toward History:* Marxism may be considered scientific by its supporters, but nonbelievers will not be converted to the cause for purely scientific reasons (unless, of course, they have made science their "altar"). To be successful, revolutionary rhetors must also make emotional and aesthetic arguments, must appeal to nonbelievers' pieties—must, in short, be poets. Throughout *Permanence and Change*, Burke repeats his belief that "the poet is pious" (65)—that even new visions must be conveyed through traditional language and symbols: "the artist works with the general tribal equipment by bringing outlying matter within the informing pattern" of the prevailing orientation (58); "whatever the source of a writer's preoccupations, he can communicate only by manipulating the symbols common to his group" (314); "the poet can make [a cause] heroic only by identifying it with assumptions already established as to what the heroic is" (116). At one point Burke even switches to a medical metaphor and offers up homeopathic rhetoric to the same effect: "one can cure a psychosis only by appealing to some aspect of the psychosis. The cure must bear notable affinities with the disease: all effective medicines are potential poisons" (166).[32]

At this point, difficulties within Burke's revolutionary rhetoric may be apparent. An effective rhetor appeals to his audience's pieties; yet the revolutionary rhetor is inherently impious, would overturn all his audience's pieties. Burke labels this problem the "piety-impiety conflict," with Nietzsche as his primary case in point: "[Nietzsche's] subject-matter was specifically that of reorientation (transvaluation of *all* values)—yet in facing the *problematical new* he spontaneously felt as a poet that he could glorify such a concern only by utilizing the *unquestioned old*" (116). Nietzsche's struggle with this problem produced the novel solution that Burke calls "perspective by incongruity" or, more broadly, "translation."[33]

Burke employs both the term and the concept of translation in *Auscultation*. There he discusses translating nineteenth-century philosophies, including Marxism, to fit a twentieth-century American audience and scene. In *Permanence and Change*, however, translation is literally and thematically the center of the text. Translation—most often called perspective by incongruity —becomes the "vehicckle" for Burke's program of social change: it is simultaneously analytic and productive, theory and practice.

According to *OED*, the word *translate* derives from *translatus*, the past participle of the Latin verb *transferre*, to transfer. Thus the earliest meanings of *translate*—"to bear, convey or remove from one person, place, or condition to another"—signal literal movement. Further investigation in the *OED* turns up the kind of word cluster that Burke was so fond of—*translate, transfer, transport, transform, transmute*, even *convert*; although these words often have different roots, at some point in their histories, their meanings converge. What emerges from the cluster is the sense of a word or concept jumping fences, moving from field to field, or, as Burke explains it, "taking a word usually applied to one setting and transferring its use to another setting" (119). Elsewhere Burke notes that "the surest way to balk action is to choose words that draw lines at the wrong places" ("Reading While You Run," 37); such lines create identifications between words or ideas that may not belong together or, conversely, separate those that do. In the act of translating, a critic shows where lines have been drawn incorrectly or unproductively and then redraws them.

The concept of translation is what Burke would call "fertile" in its ambiguity. In a general sense people translate all the time, often without even thinking about it, for translation can be simply a rhetorically effective presentation strategy: a shrewd speaker will put forth an explanation or argument using the values and vocabulary of the audience. Burke states, "In externalizing or impersonalizing his thesis, he seeks to translate it into a system of motivations which will be cogent with his readers because these motivations belong to the general scientific *Weltanschauung* of his times" (37–38). Indeed, as Burke explained to Josephson, *Permanence and Change* itself is just such an act of translation—a translation of his novel *Towards a Better Life*, which relies on a symbolism of "individualism" that

> was in very bad repute. Call it, then, a sentence which uses a sea-metaphor when spoken to a farmer. Say that I must say the sentence differently. All right—I am trying to do so. What I believe is that I can deal with fundamentally the same problem (the Bentham-Darwin-Marx-Nietzsche-Veblen problem of the "genesis of morals"), but that this time I can "revise" my sentence, using a symbolism in better repute . . . now speaking of decerebrate dogs, or how whole centuries went, of Indian sign-language, etc. (March 29, 1933)

Perspective by incongruity—"extending the use of a term by taking it from the context in which it was habitually used and applying it to another" (119)—is also a form of translation. As is poetry:

> Nietzsche establishes his perspectives by a constant juxtaposition of incongruous words, attaching to some name a qualifying epithet which had heretofore gone with a different order of names. He writes by the same constant reordering of categories that we find in the Shakespearean metaphor. Indeed, metaphor always has about it precisely this revealing of hitherto unsuspected connectives which we may note in the progressions of a dream. It appeals by exemplifying relationships between objects which our customary rational vocabulary has ignored. (119)

"Rebirth," too, Burke finds to be synonymous with perspective by incongruity (201n). And, in fact, in his conclusion Burke produces a long list of congruent terms that hover around the idea of translation or perspective by incongruity: *piety, ethicizing the means of support, abstraction, analogical extension, style, ingratiation, conversion, metaphor, education, evangelism, ethical universe-building, socialization,* and *simplification* (337). The list indicates how thoroughly the idea of translation permeates *Permanence and Change*. Given the book's emphasis on "the process of transformation," it should not come as much of a surprise that Burke himself translated freely throughout the book: he moves the term *piety* from religion to art and, from there, to human psychology; he describes psychology itself (as well as Marxism) as a kind of religious conversion; he offers Jesus as simultaneously psychotherapist and master rhetorician, Christian Science as secularized conversion, Pavlov's research as an example of Americans' limited tolerance for translating exploitation into virtue.[34] And, in what is perhaps Burke's most stunning rhetorical move in the book, he translates communism itself (so often associated with class struggle and antithesis) into community, cooperation, communication, communicant, and poetry.

What becomes clear from all of these definitions and applications of translation is that the concept can perform two important functions. First, translation provides the means of putting together new ideas and familiar language, of resolving the piety-impiety conflict faced by revolutionary rhetoricians. "We learn to single out certain relationships in accordance with the particular linguistic texture into which we are born, though we may privately manipulate this linguistic texture to formulate still other relationships. When we do so, we invent new terms, or apply our old vocabulary in new ways, attempting to socialize our position by so manipulating the linguistic equipment of our group that our particular additions or alterations can be shown to fit into the old texture" (53). Second, since Burke notes that translation is "the transplantation of words into 'inappropriate' settings" (143), his campaign for "planned incongruity" amounts to a deliberate attempt to undermine cultural proprieties—"the language of common sense" and the thought pattern, the ideology, that maintains and is maintained by such language (144). Translation, in short, becomes a heuristic that fuels social change by productively disrupting the assumptions both of the writer/critic who suggests the translation and of the audience who responds to it. It is easy to understand, then, why Burke later claimed that perspective by incongruity was "the essence of the whole business," for this technique is simultaneously cultural physician's cure, poetry, and cultural criticism all in one (Skodnick, 10).

This leads back to Marx and the Marxists Burke was addressing, for to be "politically suasive" requires not only that the rhetor be a poet (i.e., a translator) but a philosopher as well. "A sound system of exhortation," Burke wrote to Waldo Frank, "cannot be based upon anything short of 'first causes'" (May 23, 1934). Accordingly in *Permanence and Change* Burke presents a thorough analysis of "the Bentham-Darwin-Marx-Nietzsche-Veblen problem of the 'genesis of morals'" or motives. Although Burke considers all these thinkers in some detail, he devotes most of his attention to Marx, since some form of historical materialism was figuring as the most popular "first cause" among Burke's associates.

While writing *Permanence and Change,* Burke wrote Cowley that he was seeking (and believed he had found) "a theoretical point or critical exhortation *outside* the temporal structure (outside the 'social mind' . . .). Why outside the 'social mind'? Because its criteria are circular: one gets a job to buy new shoes, one buys new shoes to hold his job. A new factor must be introduced: why the shoes and why the job? This is a nontemporal factor—in the sense that it deals with human interests which are revealed in any era" (September 22, 1933). This desire to ground his philosophy of purpose in something permanent, something outside the circle of transitory contemporary values, served as one basis for Burke's critique of Marx, as outlined in the section entitled "The Basis of Reference." A Marxian perspective, Burke argued, is only "*partially*" outside [the accepted circle of contingencies]. It is outside as regards the basic tenets of capitalistic enterprise. [But] it is inside as regards the belief in the ultimate values of industrialism"—the materialism Burke saw as the source of America's cultural disease (286). Indeed the Marxist system "specifically starts from the material, or non-biological factors, as the determinants of human conduct" (287), while Burke held that "materials may determine the *forms* our enterprise takes, but they can hardly explain the *origins* of enterprise" (288).

Burke set out in *P&C* to refute the necessary priority of material conditions in the dialectic chain set up by Marx. According to John Strachey's 1933 account of Marxism in *The Coming Struggle for Power*—Burke reports (280) that Strachey's book "has been accepted as a reliable statement of Marxian theory" (though Burke's regard for Strachey was actually not universally shared)—Marx's chain consists of a material/economic link followed by a psychological link, "a chain of action and reaction between the economic basis and the ideal structure, which has been built on that basis" (qtd. in *P&C*, 287). But Burke argues instead that starting with the material link was simply a matter of convenience on Marx's part; history could be written just as easily (and presumably more accurately) by starting with the psychological link. To support his claim, Burke cites the behavioral psychologist John Watson's study of an infant whose arms were confined; the child became angry and struggled to get free, an observation suggesting to Burke that "the human organism manifests a thriving 'cult of liberty'" from birth (289). Burke constructs an entire alternative history from the episode, according to which "we should have to describe 'the desire for freedom of movement' as a fundamental disposition of men. . . . Hence we should find that a certain organic genius exists *prior* to any particular historical texture. And we might even interpret the historic texture as an embodiment, in external forms, of this organic genius" (289). Material structures of culture would grow up around the idea of "liberalism" until it became so all encompassing that it blocked the expression of another "innate" quality suggested by Watson's experiments with infants: the need for support. And so history would spin out with each new perspective and its material embodiment developing out of psychological demands. "Such possibilities," Burke remarks, "are offered only tentatively and primarily as illustration of our thesis that no given *historical* texture need be accepted as the underlying basis of a universal causal series" (291). Burke is not denying the existence of a universal causal series (in fact, he sets up one himself in his project of "metabiology"); rather, what he was objecting to in Marxism was the fact that the system is grounded rather purely in environmental conditions. As he wrote to Waldo Frank, "The current doctrines of economic determinism are correct as far as they go—but they are prime examples of 'truncated thinking.' For our economic architecture is itself but the embodiment or externalization of prior dispositions—hence any radical concern with 'first causes' must carry us into a region that lies behind the economic forces" (May 23, 1934).

This is more than just a chicken-or-egg argument. What is at stake here, for Burke, is the place of humans and human purpose. "Above all," Burke explains in the introduction to part 3, "the search is for arguments . . . whereby *Purpose* may be restored as a primary term of motivation" (3rd ed., 168), i.e., whereby the universe may be seen as being created by a "poetic point of view" (296). Such a view of the universe as still in process would restore people's natural sense of themselves as agents. In contrast "the student of scientific causality"—the Marxist, in other words—"considers [the universe] solely as *having been created*" (278), which implies a "*vis a tergo* concept of causality (the notion that all human acts are prompted by a 'kick in the rear')" (295). Burke questions Marxism (or at least Marx's historical materialism) because it seems to him overly mechanistic or deterministic.[35]

Burke's efforts to restore purpose led him to consider where the source of human purpose might be located or how it might be grounded in something permanent—something "*outside* the temporal structure (outside the 'social mind')." In place of economic materialism and in place of Freudian explanations he offers "the most undeniable point of reference we could possibly have: the biological" (335)—hence the name for his critical project, "metabiology": that which is rooted in but also moves beyond or transcends the body. "Our calling has its roots in the biological, and our biological demands are clearly implicit in the universal texture. To live," Burke writes, "is to have a vocation" (329).[36] And what is the vocation of the human body? For Burke, it is action. Since combat, action, and participation are all part of a continuum of human motives, Burke acknowledges that he might have chosen combat as the essential purpose, as Nietzsche had. However, Burke chooses to assume that human purpose is grounded in goodness, adding that "if one says that activity is merely a neutral quality rather than a good, I should answer that inactivity is categorically an evil, since it is not possible to the biologic process" (302). Thus Burke arrives at "the approach to human motives *in terms of action* (with poetic or dramatic terminologies being prized as the paradigms of action)" (3rd ed., 168).

In his final act of translation or perspective by incongruity, then, Burke in *P&C* proposes Marx not as a revolutionary or a determinist but simply as a nineteenth-century thinker, one in a long line of brilliant nineteenth-century thinkers—Darwin, Hegel, Nietzsche, Bentham, and others—who all constructed accounts of historical change and cultural evolution. It is in this role as nineteenth-century thinker that Marx becomes one more of the things that Burke, twentieth-century thinker, defines his project against: unlike Marx and the others, Burke indeed chooses permanence over change (Wess, 66).

The philosophies of the great nineteenth-century thinkers all represent attempts to understand humankind's relation to the universe and, thus, to chart a course toward the good life. These thinkers—prophets or evangelists offering some kind of reorientation—necessarily emphasized the differences or the "newness" of their approaches, but Burke chose a perspective (by incongruity) that cut across the bias: he wondered not how each philosophy can be distinguished from the others but what they might all have in common: "Might we not assume a constancy of message throughout history precisely to the extent that the biologic purposes of the human genus have remained constant?" (300); "might we take the variations not as essential, but as contingent?" (230); or, as he puts it in a letter to Cowley, might there not be "terminological rather than basic, disputes over symbols of reference rather than over the objects of reference?" (June 4, 1933).

Burke accordingly classifies philosophies into two types:

> If we choose to emphasize the shifting particularities, we approach human problems *historically*, as in the philosophies of *becoming* which seem to have reached their flowering in nineteenth-century thought (Goethe, Hegel, Marx, Darwin, Nietzsche, and the vast horde of lesser evolutionary or revolutionary thinkers). If we choose to emphasize the underlying similarities, we return through symbolism to a philosophy of *being*. (212)

In marked contrast to Marx (whose "truncated thinking," after all, was "exactly 180 degrees short of being a completely rounded philosophy of human motivation"), Burke writes a philosophy of being, replacing the metaphor of evolution and progress (and their corollary, decay) with "the metaphor of a *norm*, the notion that at bottom the aims and genius of man have remained fundamentally the same, that temporal events may cause him to get far from his sources"—as Burke certainly felt had happened in his lifetime—"but that he repeatedly struggles to restore, under new particularities, the same basic patterns of the 'good life'" (212–13). "Might the great plethora of symbolizations lead, through the science of symbolism itself, back to a concern with 'the Way,' the old notion of Tao, the conviction that there is one fundamental course of human satisfaction, forever being glimpsed and lost again, and forever being restated in the changing terms of reference that correspond with the changes of historic texture?" he wondered (233–34).[37] Magic and religion, Marxism, Darwin's theory of natural selection, Hegelian dialectic, even the prevailing scientific orientation—all the earlier orientations ought to be understood as attempts to reach Tao. Burke's proposed poetic orientation, true to the "historic texture" of the twentieth century, also merely renames or translates a permanent means of gratification.

Burke concludes *Permanence and Change* with a moving refutation aimed at, among others, radical critics who might assume that the ahistorical philosophy of being that he advocates does little more than provide a rationale for political quietism. In fact, Burke argues, quite the opposite is true. It is the philosophies of becoming, with their emphasis on the inevitability of progress or the certainty of change, that most easily lead to passivity or resignation. A philosophy of being, by contrast, gives people "absolute values," "permanent biologic norms" (350) with which to argue for better living conditions or better culture. "I kn[o]w that 'absolute values' equip us best [for living]," he wrote Josephson, "since they afford us the maximum strength behind our movements" (March 29, 1933). Additionally, "since we insist that a point of view requires, as its material counterpart, adequate embodiment in the architecture of the State, a philosophy of being may commit one to open conflict with any persons or class of persons who would use their power to uphold the institutions serving an anti-social function" (350). The weapons in such a confrontation, however, are not to be violence but rather "education, propaganda, or suasion" and more particularly "the arts of translation and inducement" (350). Through his philosophy of being, Burke was advocating, then, not passive resistance but active, poetic, and rhetorical resistance.

Afterword: The Genre of Permanence and Change

For all its eloquence, originality, and brilliance, *Permanence and Change* is today a perplexing document, one that continues to confound readers and to frustrate summary. Many people have agreed over the years with Austin Warren's 1935 assessment that "Burke's mind [in *P&C*] is at variance with itself, pulled asunder by the attractions of its uncertain discourse" (qtd. in Rueckert, *Critical Responses*, 52). The book's vocabulary—"orientation"; "transvaluation of values"; "trained incapacity"; "perspective by incongruity"; "evangelism"; "recalcitrance"; "piety"—is as quirky as it is intriguing. Its synthesis of thinkers as disparate as Spinoza, Veblen, Marx, Mary Baker Eddy, St. Paul, Richards, Dewey, Nietzsche, and Emily Post can be disorienting. Its understanding of history as unfolding through three macrophases (magic, religion, science) seems idiosyncratic and oversimplified. The overall form of *Permanence and Change*—the relationships among its parts—appears to defy Burke's own prescription that form in a work ought to be the patient creation and fulfillment of expectations for readers.[38] Finally, like the dialogues of Plato, the financial pages of the Sunday paper, or a racing form, *Permanence and Change* can seem perplexing at first because it is written in a genre that is unfamiliar and therefore confusing to readers who are unaware of the cultural work that genre performs. But actually this last difficulty can be the key to overcoming the others: *Permanence and Change* is an instance of a largely discarded form, the cultural history, a genre that was quite popular before World War II among both aesthetes and leftists—and one that guided many of Burke's decisions about purpose, structure, style, and content.

"As recurrent patterns of language use," notes Carolyn Miller, "genres help constitute the substance of our cultural life" (163); they teach people how (i.e., in what forms and through what linguistic behaviors) to enter particular cultural conversations, and what the ends of the conversations might be. As a "typified rhetorical action," a genre and its recognizable formal features develop out of the responses people make to recurring rhetorical situations, Miller notes. Or, to use the terminology of *Permanence and Change*, "motives are shorthand terms for situations" (44); "we discern situational patterns by means of the particular vocabulary of the cultural group into which we were born" (52). When *P&C* is read as a cultural history, the book turns out to be if not quite typical then certainly not atypical as an instance of its kind. Indeed some of the features of the book that make it seem most foreign today are actually some of the most characteristic elements of the cultural history. If, as Miller notes, genres teach members of a society what is at issue, then it is certain that during the 1920s Kenneth Burke acquired a specific kind of education from cultural histories as various as Van Wyck Brooks's *Three Essays on America* (1934—a collection of three earlier books: *America's Coming-of-Age, Letters and Leadership*, and *The Literary Life of America*); Stuart Chase's *Men and Machines* (1929), *The Promise of Power* (1933), and *Technocracy: An Interpretation* (1933); John Dewey's *The Public and Its Problems* (1927); Waldo Frank's *Our America* (1919); I. A. Richards's *Science and Poetry* (1926); Lewis Mumford's *The Golden Day* (1926) and *Technics and Civilization* (1934); Vernon Parrington's *Main Currents in American Thought* (1926); Thorstein Veblen's *The Theory of the Business Enterprise* (1904) and *The Instinct of Workmanship* (1914); William Carlos Williams's *In the American Grain;* and the Southern Agrarians' *I'll Take My Stand*—among others. Cultural histories may have derived ultimately from some of those nineteenth-century thinkers Burke admired, from Nietzsche (who distinguished the superior poetic perspective from the inferior mechanistic perspective in *The Will to Power*) or from Marx's dialectical view of history or even from Auguste Comte (who theorized that human thought had evolved through three stages, the theological, the metaphysical, and the scientific); and the prestige of cultural histories unquestionably got a boost from the appearances of Frazer's *The Golden Bough* between 1911 and 1915 (which famously influenced Eliot's *The Waste Land* and less famously a host of other writers, including Yeats, Conrad, and Joyce) and Spengler's *The Decline of the West* (translated into English in 1922–23).[39] Indeed, Burke's saturation in cultural histories schooled him to pay attention to certain cultural phenomena, to interpret issues through the particular terministic screens sanctioned by cultural histories, and to look to history for antidotes to contemporary cultural quandaries.

In their simplest terms the cultural histories written in the first three decades of the twentieth century served as a form of social medicine, their explicit goal to cure an ailing patient: America. These histories often mentioned specific cultural crises that prompted them, events such as increasing industrialization, the Great War, and economic depression. Yet it was not material circumstances themselves that provided the cultural historians with their motive for writing, but rather the writers' interpretation of those events as signs of danger or evidence of the end of an era. Cultural histories written before 1929 in particular, were calculated to persuade Americans that their culture was indeed quite sick, in the face of a prevailing sense that the nation was economically prosperous and progressive in fulfilling its special destiny. After 1929, when it was easier to persuade readers that the nation was ill, the writers attended more to offering particular cures. But whether they were written before or after the beginning of the Depression, the cultural histories always offered a diagnosis for a cultural illness—and a prospective remedy.

The cultural histories that Burke read in the two decades before *Permanence and Change* all rehearsed the symptoms of American malaise. Without exception they attacked the shallow, materialistic, soulless texture of American life—the money mania that had become a governing force in many lives, the practical and mechanistic mental frames of American citizens. Images of sterility filled the writing of Van Wyck Brooks, for instance: the careers of Twain, Melville, Howells, and many others were "blighted" by American life, which was losing its vitality by the year; "American things" were becoming "old without majesty, old without mellowness, old without pathos, just shabby and bloodless and worn out"; and even young American intellectuals were seeming "pallid and wizened, little old men . . . and I said to myself, it is a barren soil these men have sprung from" (*Three Essays*, 118–19). Convinced that the creative and emotional wellsprings of life were being choked off by science and technology, cultural historians called for a restoration of values: a "transvaluation" (Mumford, Burke) or "revaluation" (Brooks) of things that were crooked or imbalanced or out of sorts. Typically the historians looked to some distant past to locate the source of American stagnation or to discover some essence that had been lost.[40] They claimed that the standard American historical storyline did not accurately represent the nation's past, and they endeavored to offer Americans a new vision of themselves and the national destiny, rewriting history to illuminate the problem and to suggest a palliative. That revisionist history was typically presented in one of two ways: as a story with three or four progressive stages, divided not according to the usual periodization accounts (classical, medieval, Renaissance, and so forth) but according to large-scale shifts in ideology or technological development; or as a story of a recurring national agon, the part of the villain played by science, consumerism, technology, or "Puritans" of one kind or another.[41] Veblen, Mumford, Spengler, Richards, and Frazer took the first approach, Veblen dividing Western civilization into savage culture, predatory culture, handicraft culture, and machine culture; Frazer into the successive stages of magic, religion, and science; and Mumford into configurations he dubbed the eotechnic, the paleotechnic, and the neotechnic. Williams and Brooks adopted the second approach, *In the American Grain* presenting American history as a struggle between freedom seekers and order seekers and Brooks's *America's Coming-of-Age* attributing the problem to a tension between highbrow idealism and lowbrow materialism that he offered to heal through the invention of a "middlebrow" synthesis.

Both accounts of history were offered by cultural historians as proof that America was poised at the dawn of a new era. Cultural historians usually placed the nation within a disorienting but critical transition phase: either an old order had crumbled but a new one had yet to emerge; or a new order had begun but a cultural lag in institutions and ideologies was motivating creative individuals to rebel, sometimes without tangible results, against entrenched but failing systems. In either case Americans were stuck in a kind of cultural limbo and suffering from what Veblen called "trained incapacity":[42] old ways of thinking were no longer working but were nevertheless so thoroughly ingrained that people lacked the wherewithal to reinvent their lives and their cultures. What America needed was something to get the culture unstuck, to reorient it, to restore its health, to make it grow and regenerate—a new vocabulary or set of symbols, a new direction or orientation. And that was precisely what the cultural histories provided: a new set of cultural heroes and values, figures from the past who embodied a new sense of what a renewed American life might be.

Often that figure was an artist, for by common definition the artist, as forerunner, had the special sensibility required to see deeply and to think outside conventional lines. Brooks, for instance, praised Whitman as the prototypical American visionary; Williams looked to Poe; and Mumford's "golden day" recalled the heyday of Hawthorne, Melville, Emerson, Thoreau, and Whitman. Or the heroes celebrated by the cultural historians were artist equivalents—explorers, inventors, and statesmen whose artistic sensibility translated itself into action, as in the case of Williams's Daniel Boone, Abraham Lincoln, and Sam Houston. Either way, the cultural historians' common goal was the depiction of lives made whole, of agonistic values brought into harmony: the pragmatic with the ideal, the emotional with the reasonable, the aesthetic with the mechanical and commercial. Though their concern with wholeness often expressed itself in a fondness for communal life, such that many cultural historians were communists or socialists, cultural histories were flexible enough to accommodate a range of ideological positions, everything from the reactionary politics of the New Humanists and Agrarians to the collectivism celebrated by Frank, Veblen, Brooks, and Mumford. All the cultural historians were angling for the souls of American intellectuals, longing for an American core on which to erect a new national foundation. What Cleanth Brooks remarked of the Agrarians could be attributed to all the cultural historians: they sought to develop "certain fundamental assumptions about the 'good life' and what it truly is and about the relations of means to ends in modern America" (qtd. in Young, *Gentleman*, 24).

Burke and his friends wrote and read a great many of these cultural histories. He had consumed Brooks's *America's Coming-of-Age* as part of his *Dial* apprenticeship[43] and no doubt had read Brooks's later cultural histories as well. He had certainly read Frank's *Our America*. He had translated segments of *The Decline of the West* for the *Dial* in 1924 (under the title "The Downfall of Western Civilization"), wrote about Spengler in *Counter-Statement*, and contributed thereby to making Spengler's book something of a national sensation. He read *The Golden Bough* thoroughly enough to build on its ideas about ritual. He could not have missed Mumford's *The Golden Day*, was on good enough terms with Mumford to ask him for a recommendation in support of his Guggenheim application (Burke Papers, 1934), and was thinking on similar lines to the ones Mumford was developing in *Technics and Civilization*. He reviewed several of Dewey's books, if not *The Public and Its Problems;* and he knew Veblen's books very well indeed. And obviously Burke was quite familiar with *I'll Take My Stand* and *In the American Grain*, both of them so dependent on agricultural metaphors of sterility and rebirth,[44] both of them dedicated to reshaping cultural practices, both of them written wholly or in part by close friends of his. Thus it is no surprise that *Permanence and Change* exploits a great many of the conventions of the genre of cultural history.

Without question Burke in *Permanence and Change* was sharing the cultural historians' mission of revitalizing American life. While he wrote many pieces of specifically literary criticism during his career, Burke also wrote more broadly cultural criticism, increasingly so as the 1920s became the 1930s,[45] and many analysts of Burke have noted a "therapeutic impulse" in his 1930s books (Jay, "Motives," 540).[46] The title of the work Burke wrote before *P&C—Auscultation, Creation, and Revision*—certainly betrays that same impulse ("auscultation" meaning the act of listening carefully, as with a stethoscope, to make a medical diagnosis), and the book he wrote after *P&C—Attitudes toward History*—is something of a cultural history as well. But *Permanence and Change*, in its appropriation of the therapeutic metaphor and subsequent turn to history, even more explicitly takes up the motives of the cultural history. Most obvious, of course, is Burke's employment of the familiar macrophase model of history that he borrowed from Veblen, Mumford, and particularly Frazer and that organizes much of the analysis of parts 1 and 3. Each phase or orientation—magic (based, Burke felt, following Frazer, on the control of natural forces), religion (fixed on the control of people), and science (the current orientation)—helped people to negotiate the difficulties of being human by providing a system of meanings, values, and behaviors with which to make sense of things; but each orientation, by overemphasizing one aspect of human experience, also made inevitable the advent of a new order, a "philosophic corrective" (85) that would compensate for the inadequacies of each prevailing perspective. Like Brooks, Veblen, Frazer, and Mumford, Burke located current contemporary culture at one of the transition points between orientations: the inadequacies of the scientific attitude (which established consumption as a primary motive and yet denied purchasing power to a great many consumers through the glorification of individual initiative and the tolerance of monopoly capitalism) were beginning to disorient people and to witness to the need for a new order (based on cooperation and collectivism).[47] The cultural ills of the scientific phase, while economic in nature and origin, were not only economic, however: the disorientations caused by the scientific perspective were also impairing communications (invalidating poetry along the way), eroding people's cooperative impulses, and denying people any sense of themselves as agents—"the sense of *acting upon something* rather than of *being acted upon by something*" (278–79). "In line with some of Bentham's later theorizing," Burke explained to Richard McKeon, "[*Permanence and Change*] tends to trace the 'original sin' back to the nature of language itself" (October 24, 1934).

Telling are direct parallels between *Permanence and Change* and the cultural histories of Veblen. The two cultural historians agreed that people tended to maintain a given perspective even when it was damaging because they were simply unable to reimagine their lives and their cultures: Veblen's idea of "trained incapacity" (and Dewey's notion of "occupational psychosis") explained the phenomenon for Burke, who listed a number of such incapacities and psychoses operating in the 1930s: the "capitalist, monetary, individualist, *laissez-faire*, free market, independent enterprise" psychosis (59); the agrarian psychosis; the investor's psychosis;[48] the worker's psychosis; the criminal psychosis; and, "in and about all of these, above them, beneath them, mainly responsible for their perplexities, . . . the technological psychosis, . . . [which] is at the center of our glories and our distress" (63). Veblen's savage critiques of the culture of materialism and mechanization in *The Theory of the Leisure Class* and in *The Theory of the Business Enterprise* were on Burke's mind as he testified to the inadequacies of the American scene. And so unlike Marx but like Veblen and Mumford[49] (Veblen is particularly notable for locating economic explanations within a larger system of cultural values), Burke focused his attack less on the materialism of American culture and more on its general scientistic, rationalistic, mechanistic ideology. The patient—America— needed "a reorientation, a direct attempt to *force* the critical structure by shifts of perspective" (215).

Who could provide this shift in perspective? In keeping with the traditions of cultural history, Burke imagined the aesthetic reorientation outlined earlier. "A corrective rationalization," he wrote, "must certainly move in the direction of the . . . humanistic or poetic, since this is the aspect of culture which the scientific criteria . . . have tended to eliminate or minimize" (91). Poetry was the most appropriate orientation, not only because it offered an antidote to scientism but also because it is *"our ultimate motive, the situation common to all, the creative, assertive, synthetic act"* (332). Thus Burke's aesthetic perspective was available to all, not just to the cultural elite; it was "an art in its widest aspects, an *art of living*" (93) that constructed all people as potential poets.[50] Further, Burke's poetic perspective, like Mumford's and Dewey's, emphasizes community: "the ultimate goal of the poetic metaphor would be a society in which the participant aspect of action attained its maximum expression. By its emphasis on the communicative, it would emphasize certain important *civic* qualities" missing in the scientific orientation (347).

In closing, several things are worth mentioning about Burke's cultural history. First, Burke was arguing that his new orientation "must be situated in a philosophy, or psychology, of poetry, rather than in a body of poetry" (92): in this way Burke distanced himself from the recommendations of Brooks, Williams, and Mumford (in *The Golden Day*), who were proposing to revitalize American culture by retrieving a more fertile literary tradition or by directing people to Whitman or some other particular forerunning poet. Second, Burke made explicit—and here he was agreeing with Williams—that the great advantage of a poetic orientation is that it affords a basis for all sorts of contingent judgments: "since poetry is essentially ethical, the poetic metaphor clearly identifies the ethical with the aesthetic, in Hellenic fashion defining the 'beautiful' life as the 'good' life" (341–42). Finally, like Williams and Mumford, Burke ultimately was linking the ethical to the body: by aligning poetry with action and then choosing action as the highest end of life, Burke was basing his choice of orientations on "the most undeniable point of reference we could possibly have: the biological. It aims less at a *metaphysic* than at a *metabiology*. And a point of view biologically rooted seems to be as near to 'rock bottom' as human thought could take us" (335). In comparison with many other cultural histories, *Permanence and Change* is limited in its use of images of fertility and rebirth, but this sentence stands as a significant corollary to Williams's and the Agrarians' concern for a grounded aesthetics.

Given that it appeared well after the onset of the Depression and given that it was written after the genre of the cultural history was well established, *Permanence and Change* appropriately gave far more emphasis to lobbying for its proposed cure than to documenting a cultural illness. Burke did not need to convince people in the mid-1930s that America was in trouble or that its technological orientation was the master psychosis at the center of its cultural malaise. Nevertheless the shape of *Permanence and Change* does suggest the particular way that Burke wanted to intervene in the discussion about how to reform his society. It would be reasonable to assume that the three major segments of *P&C* would correspond to the three major elements included in cultural histories—describing symptoms, making a diagnosis, and prescribing a cure. But in fact they do not. Instead, less interested in naming the specific ideology that had benumbed America, Burke accounted for why Americans had become trapped and how they could escape. He was "inquir[ing] into the nature of transformation itself" (3rd ed., xlvii). To put it another way, most cultural historians proposed artists or artist equivalents as the keys to America's rebirth, but (except for Dewey) they seldom explained why or how artists would be able to effect such a transformation. They posited a need for wholeness and declared that art would supply that wholeness (as did some of the aesthetes discussed earlier); or (as Winters had) they held that artists could supply a necessary moral vision. But how would they do that? How do texts influence people?

Answering questions like these, questions like the ones Williams had raised in *The Embodiment of Knowledge*, was precisely what Burke set out to do in *P&C*; it was why he originally titled his book *A Treatise on Communication*. Instead of offering evidence of a cultural illness or merely asserting the superiority of the poetic perspective, part 1 of *P&C* theorizes interpretation—how it is filtered through ideology, how motives are maintained through language. Burke was interested not in cultural heroes and their values but in what kept those heroes and values in place, namely ideologies embedded in language. It might be argued that there is not enough history in *Permanence and Change* to make it a cultural history; the historical macrophases are developed only superficially, after all. But in fact, part 1 theorizes a central assumption of all cultural histories, the notion that history can be reinvented, that it is "not some fixed thing, like a table" (38) but a linguistic construct that can be reshaped for ideological and social ends. Burke thus in *P&C* theoretically authorizes the cultural work of all cultural histories. Part 2, "Perspective by

Incongruity," remains Burke's most distinctive contribution to the genre because it offers what no other cultural history could: a method of verbal displacement that, in keeping with Burke's emphasis on the process of transformation, could spark the kind of attitudinal changes that cultural historians were seeking. By reconceiving language and how it works, Burke hoped to transform and translate a scientific and technological perspective into a poetical one, an aesthetic one, for the good of all. "I am on to Part III," Burke told Cowley in the summer of 1933. "I am writing a book about 'the good life'" (July 20, 1933).

Four Heralding the Popular Front

Attitudes toward History

That his philosophies in *Permanence and Change* would not sit well with many of his most doctrinaire leftist readers, Burke was well aware. Shortly after he finished revising the manuscript, sometime in the middle or end of May 1934, Burke wrote to Waldo Frank, who had offered to read the finished work:

> I expect resistance from the orthodox Communists primarily because I take pains to assert that the mechanistic metaphor is inadequate as an explanation of human conduct, advocating the poetic or dramatic metaphor in its stead. . . . And my reservations on positivism are much too considerable for those who feel that Communistic exhortation must be tied to positivistic thought. I do not relish being "unseasonable," but I see no other choice except silence. (Burke to Frank, July 16, 1934)

That resistance would come at the first American Writers' Congress, when, on the heels of the publication of *Permanence and Change*, Burke was roughed up by party regulars on the occasion of his "Revolutionary Symbolism in America" speech, which recommended rhetorical tactics consistent with a developing Popular Front policy.

But actually *P&C* was in the main rather well received. True, the book was rejected for publication by Harcourt, Brace (which had an option to publish it, based on the contract for *Towards a Better Life*), when Burke submitted it in May 1934, in part because the publishing industry was accepting many fewer books during the Depression. But by mid-October, the New Republic Press had agreed to publish *P&C* in its Dollar Book Series. Production went quickly: the book appeared in mid-February 1935.[1] And it sold quite briskly for a book of its kind: 250 copies were ordered in the first five days after publication; booksellers as unspecialized as Macy's offered the book to their customers; the first printing of 1,000 copies was exhausted by early June; and by

the time public interest began to wane in mid-1936, nearly 2,000 copies of
Permanence and Change had been sold (Mebane to Burke, February 19, 1935;
June 4, 1935; October 21, 1936). Burke could not claim to have produced a
best seller—but *P&C* did sell quite satisfactorily, and the book was widely
reviewed and praised as well, in *Saturday Review*, the *New York Herald*, the
New York Times, *Poetry*, the *American Review*, and elsewhere. As the "big tent"
strategy of the Popular Front began to take hold in the second half of 1935
and first half of 1936, *Permanence and Change* could be appreciated as a work
orthodox enough to satisfy most Marxist regulars and yet unorthodox enough
to give comfort to liberals and Marxist dissidents.

Another tangible outcome of the publication of *Permanence and Change*
was that Burke parlayed it into the Guggenheim Fellowship that would permit him to complete his next project. When negotiations to publish *P&C* had
reached an advanced stage in September 1934, Burke turned to the Guggenheim application, and the two-thousand-dollar proceeds from the fellowship,
secured early the following spring at least partly on the reputation of *P&C*,
were intended to speed completion of the follow-up book that Burke had
begun to contemplate as early as May 1934: *Attitudes toward History*.[2] The
book was not completed as quickly as he hoped, for Burke found himself
involved in many other projects related to his own celebrity and to the
League of American Writers: e.g., as a member of the LAW executive committee, he worked on a subcommittee to create a league magazine; he was
regularly publishing essays, reviews, and other items in *New Masses*, the *New
Republic*, the *Nation*, *Poetry*, and the *Southern Review*; and he spent part of the
summer of 1936 teaching at Syracuse University and another spell that year
teaching a course at the New School. But though Burke was as active politically and intellectually as he would ever be in his life, by the end of 1936 he
had nevertheless found the time to complete his promised sequel to *Permanence and Change*, a book that grew out of and attempted to amend his associations within the committed leftist political community. In *Attitudes*, more
than in any other work, Burke walked a Marxist walk of materialist dialectic,
outlining the stages of history that lead almost inevitably to what he calls
"emergent collectivism"; and he talked a Marxist talk of class struggle and
alienation, structure and superstructure. Building on an appreciation of Marx
as one of the greatest figures of the modern age, Burke identified himself
closely with the Popular Front cause so that his fellow Marxists and Marxist
sympathizers would read his suggestions as helpful advice given from one
insider to another.

Burke's strategy of solidarity did not quite work, as indicated from the
responses Burke got to *ATH*, for he remained as original and iconoclastic as
ever, especially by recommending Freud as a necessary ancillary to Marxist
analysis, by developing additional and sometimes perplexing ways and means
for such analysis (so perplexing that he had to append a dizzying "Dictionary

of Pivotal Terms" to the conclusion), and by suggesting many other means (Marxist and not) of ameliorating the sometimes unforgiving rhetoric associated with Communist Party orthodoxy. *ATH* would resist the "mechanistic metaphor" and honor his "reservations on positivism" as resolutely as had *P&C*. But Burke's strategy of accommodation does explain many of the arguments and emphases in *ATH*. Like *Permanence and Change* and *Auscultation*, *Attitudes* continues Burke's program for improving the means that Marxists use to understand their world and the ways that ideology is socially and psychologically constructed and disseminated; like *P&C* and *Auscultation*, *Attitudes* rejects Marxist antitheses in favor of identification, "pontification" (i.e., bridge building), and a comic, forgiving point of view. But while the emphasis in *P&C* was theoretical, especially in proposing a new vocabulary for understanding prevailing cultural attachments ("piety," "trained incapacity," "orientation") and in the approach to improved analysis that Burke was recommending (perspective by incongruity), the emphasis in *ATH* would be more practical. "*P&C* is to *ATH* as Plato's *Republic* is to his *Laws*," Burke would say in his 1953 addendum to *Counter-Statement;* "just as the *Republic* deals with an ideal state, and the *Laws* deals with a real one" (216). Indeed *ATH* is nothing if not a primer on specific rhetorical methods for locating, analyzing, and modifying symbolic attachments. As its title emphasizes, Burke's book is about *attitudes* toward history—that is, about the ways and means of studying cultural phenomena located in history. As a methodological argument, it includes an elaborate and original example of a way of approaching history, superstructure, and human relations.[3] Moreover, since human relations (as well as interpretations of those relations) are inevitably rhetorical, *Attitudes* also presents a discussion of attitudes toward audiences— in effect, a rhetorical theory. Neither his arguments against antithesis in *Auscultation* nor his suggestions about shaping ideology in his Writers' Congress speech nor his discussions of piety in *P&C* were producing much change in Marxist rhetoric, so Burke resolved to focus this time on the audience analysis and historical analysis that should precede rhetorical acts. In short if *Permanence and Change* was Burke's "coming out" book in terms of his public allegiance to communism, *Attitudes toward History* targeted Marxists even more directly and practically. It retraced much of the same theoretical ground, but it also moved beyond Burke's earlier books in its presentation (and eventual articulation) of a productive method of symbolic analysis that would develop into what is known as dramatism.

Attitudes *and the Left*

Earlier in the 1930s, Burke had recommended that radical rhetors "bore from within" to move a skeptical, even hostile middle class toward socialism—that they employ a rhetorical strategy of identification with middle-class Americans. At the first American Writers' Congress Burke had offered the same suggestion: that leftists substitute the term *the people* for *the worker* in order to better identify themselves and their messages with core American values.[4] Consequently, when he came to write *ATH*, Burke naturally enough took his own advice: faced with the difficulty of persuading orthodox Communists to redirect their efforts at persuasion, he determined as a member of the Popular Front to bore from within the ranks of the committed Left.

If in *Attitudes*, more so than in any other work, Burke set out to talk as an insider, it was because he was one. Burke's political commitments involved him heavily in the first American Writers' Congress; in the aftermath of the congress, he found himself on the executive committee of the League of American Writers. Consequently, in the second half of 1935 and during 1936, as he completed *ATH*, Burke worked hard on LAW initiatives before, during, and after the twice-a-month organizational meetings that followed in the wake of the congress. The league launched membership efforts and a speakers' bureau (Burke was a respondent at Hicks's February 3, 1936, talk on "Our Revolutionary Heritage") and asked Burke to represent LAW at a Washington, D.C., meeting at the beginning of August 1935; as late as the summer of 1936 Burke was a part of LAW executive committee efforts to plan a fall conference.[5] But the initiative that probably most involved Burke was an effort by LAW to start a quarterly magazine for Popular Front fiction, poetry, and criticism, patterned after *Seven Arts* and the *Dial*. Along with Henry Hart, Granville Hicks, Edwin Seaver, and Rolfe Humphreys, Burke explored the feasibility of such a magazine for several months, agreed with them on an editorial board (that included Burke) and a title (*Decision* won out over *The Bridge*), and announced initial plans to begin production early in 1936.[6] Though the LAW magazine actually never did get itself off the ground, with the possible exception of the appearance of *Direction* in December 1937, Burke nevertheless was able to express his enthusiasm for the Popular Front by writing a November 1935 book review of Barbusse's *Stalin* for the Book Union, another LAW-related enterprise, and by participating in and helping to plan the second American Writers' Congress (see sidebar). His many other loyalist activities included writing reviews for *New Masses* and the *New Republic*, contributing to the April 1936 *Partisan Review* symposium "What Is Americanism?" (developed while LAW was considering an affiliation with *PR*), signing on to and helping to compose a LAW protest of published accounts of the outbreak of the Spanish Civil War, and creating with Gus Peck a *New Masses* cartoon ridiculing Roosevelt's military buildup as the sending of America's unknowing poor to defend America's wealthy (see illustration).[7] As a "contributing editor" he published a portion of *ATH* in the first issue of *Science and Society: A Marxian Quarterly* (September 1936), and he was drafted twice to be the one to defend the communist position—once at a December 6, 1936, debate before a gathering of Newman Club under-

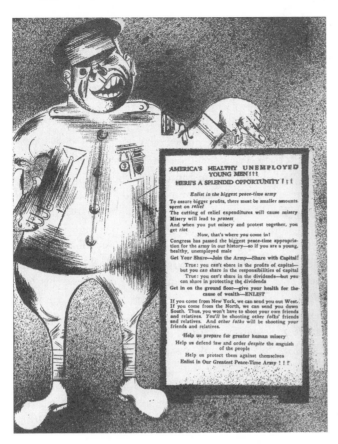

Cartoon by
Gus Peck and
Kenneth Burke.
From *New
Masses*, March 3,
1936

graduates; and again on January 16, 1937, when he answered the question
"What Is Communism?" while another speaker defined fascism (Frances
Pratt to Burke, January 7, 1937). In the summer of 1936, in the midst of completing *ATH*, he spread the gospel further by lecturing for a week at Syracuse
University to students of Leonard Brown, a Popular Front enthusiast whose
own "Dialectical Materialism and Proletarian Literature" (1937) would show
the influence of Burke's *Attitudes* and ideas.[8]

Caught up as he was in the heyday of the Popular Front, Burke was initially unfazed when news of the Moscow show trials began to issue in the
fall of 1936. A number of "old Bolsheviks" who had served in the Russian
Revolution had gone on trial in August for plotting to foment war between
Germany and Russia and to overthrow and assassinate Stalin; though the proceedings were closed, the conspirators were said to have been directed from
abroad by Trotsky, and after their conviction they were executed. At first
most American Communists defended the trials, in spite of the warnings of a
few dissidents (Cooney, 97; Wald, *New York*, 129). But when the trials were
renewed early in 1937, just as Burke had turned over the manuscript of *ATH*

to his publisher, they featured sensational new "confessions" by Soviet leaders who had "conspired" with Trotsky and who "deserved" the capital punishment they received; indeed a great many members of the general staff of the Red Army were executed for collaborating with the Nazis, as well as untold numbers of government workers and party members. The convictions all began to sound progressively implausible, particularly after Trotsky landed in Mexico in February 1937 to defend himself, and so questions about Stalin were raised more forcefully and creditably in New York (Klehr, 359; Wald, *New York*, 128–37). Over a period of a few months Trotsky was transformed from a disappointed, self-exiled oppositionist into a treacherous plotter out to destroy the Soviet Union—and then, by the publicity and by the efforts of the American Committee for the Defense of Leon Trotsky, into a brilliant and heroic intellectual who embodied (at least for some) everything opposed to what Stalin stood for. The more the trials created controversy, the more devastating they were politically not only in the Soviet Union but in the United States—not least because they divided radicals and thus undermined the Popular Front. Stalin's failure to become more materially involved in Spain when civil war broke out there in July 1936 was a cause of further distress to many of his critics, for Franco's usurpation of the Popular Front government in Madrid was a cause that mobilized people on the American left like none other before it. By June 1937, word began to leak out about Stalin-sponsored repressions of antifascist anarchists and socialists in Spain, accusations that would eventually help to persuade many people to quit the Communist Party.

But the great majority of all that criticism emerged only after *ATH* had been written. While dissident Marxists such as Hook and Farrell were stepping up their attacks on Stalin as 1936 turned into 1937, Burke's colleagues in the League of American Writers mostly were keeping the faith. Communist Party regulars Earl Browder, Corliss Lemont, and Mike Gold all defended the purges (Klehr, 360), and Malcolm Cowley and other fellow travelers supported Stalin's actions as well. Even well into 1938, diehard American Communists as prominent as Richard Wright were still defending Stalin's decision to conduct the trials. In a revealing letter that he wrote to Jack Kunitz (another of the LAW members who had written a defense of Stalin's first show trials) just as he was completing the manuscript of *ATH* (December 7, 1936), Burke vented his own thoughts. He dismissed Farrell as "too proud for [the] cooperative work" required by the Popular Front, declared himself "for the reversal of [political] splintering rather than for its intensification," and boasted that

> I make it a flat rule *not* to throw Russia to the lions—for I realize how damned easy it is for a pro-communist speaker to address a non-communist or anti-communist audience and gain asylum for his views by "sharing" with them the

attack on the Soviets. This device has become a modern convenience like steam heat or inside water closets. . . . Propaganda should be a tougher game than pingpong. And I fear that the more-communist-than-the-communists approach is usually quite different in its function from what it is in its appearance.[9]

While Burke's accommodation of Marxism and modernism was actually not unlike Trotsky's own, Burke as a Popular Front enthusiast regarded Trotskyists with suspicion and Trotskyism as merely a rhetorical convenience for some time. "I believed that Stalin was alright," Burke admitted in an interview decades later (Parker and Herenden, 97). "I didn't believe the goddam charges against Stalin at the time. I really didn't. I thought the guy was straight" (Skodnick, 16).[10] Loyal to LAW and the Popular Front, Burke worked on his manuscript and completed his arguments by the end of 1936, just before the second round of Moscow trials was announced in January 1937 and well before the most notorious of Stalin's excesses were revealed—the trials were accompanied, it turned out, by mass purges that claimed millions of lives.

Having identified himself closely with the movement, Burke consequently wrote *ATH* as a bit of helpful advice offered from one enthusiastic Marxist sympathizer to another in order to further the Popular Front causes they were all supporting and the less sectarian ideology that the Popular Front sponsored. Burke was certainly not without his customary iconoclasm, and much of *ATH* was recommending amendments to the ways Marxists and fellow travelers were seeing the world and acting within it; "the major cultural theorist of the Popular Front" (Denning, 445), he was in effect performing an identification with a Popular Front agenda throughout his book in a number of particular ways.

The Second American Writers' Congress

The second American Writers' Congress, which took place in New York from Friday, June 4 until June 6, 1937, has attracted only a fraction of the scholarly attention that the famous first congress of 1935 has received. Denning, for example, barely mentions the event, and Aaron limits his coverage to a few paragraphs, for it did not produce watershed moments or especially long-lasting critical and social contributions. Nevertheless the second congress is interesting to a study of Burke because it offers an index for measuring his loyalty to the Popular Front at the time of *Attitudes toward History*.

For the congress was, as Edwin Seaver noted in the *Daily Worker* on June 9, a thoroughly "People's Front Congress from beginning to end" (quoted in Kutulas,

"Becoming," 72).[1] If the 1935 Writers' Congress was dominated by hardline revolutionary rhetoric, by a commitment to proletarian writing, and by Communists' grudging resistance to Burke's recommendations for incipient Popular Front tactics, the 1937 event had lost its openly revolutionary tone and instead was energized by the Popular Front theme of creating a broad alliance for combating fascism, especially in Spain.

The congress was another effort of the League of American Writers, who planned and conducted the event. In its *Bulletin* for April–May 1937, the LAW issued a formal call for the congress, reprinted in other publications, that emphasized the need for concerted and committed action against "the fascist powers ... trying to impose their system on the rest of Europe and ultimately on the world. . . . If the fascists are allowed to win in Spain, then France or Czechoslovakia or the Soviet Union is likely to suffer the next attack." Against this threat the signers of the call poised not class struggle and the imperative for revolutionary change but a show of consensus among all "the forces that favor democracy." Since fascism was presenting a threat to writers—"it means censorship, it means the substitution of dogmas for the ideas that are a writer's stock in trade, ... [it] means a sharper division between social classes"—the congress would take up the challenges presented to writers by fascism at an open mass meeting at Carnegie Hall on the evening of June 4 and at closed sessions the next two days at the New School. Reflecting the broad representation that the organizers hoped to attract to the gathering (ultimately over 350 delegates attended, 83 from outside New York), the call was signed by a representative cross-section of prominent writers from across a broad Left political spectrum: Van Wyck Brooks, Erskine Caldwell, Waldo Frank, Langston Hughes, James Weldon Johnson, Robert Morss Lovett, Archibald MacLeish, Clifford Odets, Upton Sinclair, Genevieve Taggard, and a dozen others.[2]

Papers and participants at the congress took up such topics as the place of writers in the American scene historically (Newton Arvin), recently (Malcolm Cowley), regionally (B. A. Botkin), and in relation to science (Burke); the contemporary literary scene in Spain (by Martha Gellhorn), in fascist Italy and Germany (Frances Winwar), in Latin America (Carleton Beals), and in the Soviet Union (Albert Rhys Williams); and the social problems facing writers, including anti-Semitism, the Hearst press and Hollywood, and the market for books. (Burke served on the program committee that planned the events, with Joseph Freeman, Henry Hart, Malcolm Cowley, Robert Gessner, and John Howard Lawson.) The LAW, which had remained a small organization, counting slightly under 250 members, hoped to reorganize now on a broader and more national basis, so it proposed to use its event to launch the National League of American Writers ("The Second American Writers' Congress," 252). By 1939, the league would grow to more than 800 (Kutulas, "Becoming," 74).

Just how broad the Popular Front had become in June 1937, at a time when there was still hope that the Soviet Union would help win the battle for Spain and before the commission investigating Stalin's charges against Trotsky had delivered its exoneration of him, can be measured as much by the people who attended the conference as by what was discussed. Archibald MacLeish played a prominent role by presiding over the opening event and giving a paper, "Spain and the American Writer"—even though he had been openly critical of proletarian criticism and excoriated by Mike Gold. Max Bodenheim read a poem about the war in Spain, and New Deal bureaucrat Henry Alsberg was on hand to report on the Federal Writers' Project. The delegates voted for Dos Passos's *The Big Money* as the best current novel in spite of his deep ambivalence about the Communist Party, for Sandburg's *The People* as the best book of poetry, and for Brooks's *The Flowering of New England* as the best book of current criticism. For the opening general session the organizers at first hoped to secure Upton Sinclair or Albert Einstein, but when Einstein sent his regrets the organizers finally settled on Ernest Hemingway, just back from Spain, who fired an overflow crowd of more than 3,500 listeners with a personal account of the war and with selections from a visual representation of it, the Joris Ivens propaganda documentary *The Spanish Earth,* for which Hemingway (with Dos Passos and Lillian Hellman) had written the commentary. "There is only one form of government that cannot produce good writers, and that system is fascism," Hemingway said in his speech, in keeping with the theme of the congress. "A writer who cannot lie cannot live or work under fascism." Richard Wright and Ralph Ellison were on hand to hear Hemingway's keynote performance. The next morning Kyle Crichton spoke with amazement at how broad the Popular Front had become: "At Penn State College, for example, a meeting to raise money for . . . the Committee to Aid Spanish Democracy was arranged by the Rotary and Kiwanis Clubs!" ("The Second American Writers' Congress," 208).

But the breadth of the Popular Front, dedicated to protecting the Soviet Union by creating a coalition of leftists, only frustrated the dissident Marxists within the LAW (e.g., William Phillips, Philip Rahv, James T. Farrell) who were becoming increasingly critical of the Soviet Union and Stalin and who regarded the Popular Front as overly sympathetic to Stalin's tactics, and who were suspicious of CPUSA influence over the league. The more the event turned outward and trained its attention on fascism in Spain rather than on Stalin's failings and the need for anti-capitalist revolution, the more scorn it drew from the few dissidents who found their way into the event (Freeman and Farrell did not even bother to go). As Rahv wrote in his summary, sarcastically entitled "Two Years of Progress," the Communist Party at the 1937 congress had "cleverly transform[ed] its barracks ideology into the angelic diction of culture-yearning and humanist largesse [while] no attempt was made to dissociate the fight against fascism from the fight against capitalism. . . . The second Writers' Congress was . . . saturated with the once dreaded symbolism of the people [that Burke had recommended in 1935]. Within the short space of two years the 'revolutionaries' of 1935 had substituted the stars and stripes of New Deal Marxism for 'the red flag of the new materialism.'" Miffed because he was convinced that Waldo Frank had been eased out of the LAW and out of any role in the congress since on May 12, 1937, "Frank had written an unorthodox letter to The New Republic about the Moscow trials," Rahv charged that "the Stalinists, who manage and control the League of American Writers behind a façade of big-shot presidents and vice-presidents ... will not tolerate the active participation of anyone who is not ready to defend every policy of Stalin" (24–27).

The poet Harry Roskolenko thus used the congress question-and-answer periods to ask pointedly about Trotsky, who had been so completely condemned by Stalin at those trials the previous fall and winter (Hart, Writer, 234–41); but the dissidents mainly concentrated their ire in one moment. Dwight Macdonald, Mary McCarthy, and Philip Rahv coopted a working session on the writing of criticism, moderated by Granville Hicks, by offering arguments against the Popular Front and in favor of the artistic independence espoused by Trotsky. For two hours charges were supported and refuted. Roskolenko insisted on raising additional questions about the suppression of Trotsky's writing in the Soviet Union, but his objections were drowned out by testimonials about progress under Stalin ("The Second American Writers' Congress," 229). Macdonald subsequently wrote a letter of protest about the congress to the Nation, one that Hicks tried to answer ("for two hours and a quarter some fifty delegates, who had come to the session to discuss criticism, listened with almost superhuman patience to Mr. Macdonald and a handful of others and to those of us who replied to their contentions": Hicks to the Nation, June 18, 1937).[3] Macdonald, Rahv, Phillips, and others were in the process of taking over control of the Partisan Review, where they would express their reservations about Stalin and the Popular Front for the remainder of the decade—with implications for Burke.

As Hicks's words imply and as the official record of the congress indicates, anti-Stalinist dissent at the congress was otherwise muted out of deference to Popular Front solidarity: "When the tiny opposition at the Congress asked some embarrassing questions, ... the answer was that it is improper" to address those questions at this gathering (Rahv, 25). Enthusiasm for the Popular Front at the second congress, while not unanimous, was extensive and enthusiastic. Burke's own paper, "The Relation between Literature and Science," was in keeping with the sentiment and in keeping with Attitudes toward History (Wess, 89–90). The first presentation given during the closed sessions of June 5, it actually pondered not so much the relation between literature and science but the relation between literature and criticism; in so doing, it implicitly enlisted Aristotle (and refuted Augustine) in the cause of the Popular Front (160–61) and tried to reconcile the two groups gathered for the occasion, the writers and the critics, toward one end: "In Germany today, ... where the figure of Hitler completes the father pattern in political embodiment, we get an obviously inadequate structure of meanings. So I take the poetic [i.e., writerly] hypothesis to be inevitable—and I consider it the function of criticism to supply the sharp sound that awakens us" (171). Unlike Burke's famous contribution to the first American Writers' Congress, it easily generated approval and was published in the proceedings of the conference, *The Writer in a Changing World* (Henry Hart, editor), next to the essays by Hemingway, Gellhorn, Freeman, Cowley, MacLeish, and Hicks. And yet the essay also looks forward to Burke's next book, *The Philosophy of Literary Form* (it was included in that volume as well), at least in the sense that some of its phrases and distinctions (e.g., the word-for-word comparison between nominalism and realism, page 163) found their way into the title essay (page 125–26).

1. Our summary of the second American Writers' Congress draws on our inspection of LAW archives at Syracuse, the Freeman Papers, and other correspondence; on memoirs by Hicks (Part, 146–50), Folsom (chapter 8), and Josephson (*Infidel*); on accounts published contemporaneously (Rahv) and later (Aaron, 308, 359–61); on Kutulas ("Becoming" and *Long War*, 100–103); and, of course, on our inspection of the published proceedings (Hart, ed., *Writer in a Changing World*).

2. Burke, incidentally, was not one of the signers.

3. To Norbert Guterman, Burke wrote: "I hear the Congress has been vigorously maligned, by one D. Wight MacDonald. If he wanted something brilliant to be said there, why didn't he say it. The chairman asked for discussion after each paper. There was the opportunity for this perfectionist to make history" (June 23, 1937). After the congress, Burke was invited to serve on the executive council of a LAW organization working to support the loyalists in the Spanish Civil War. Burke agreed to serve, sent in a financial contribution, and got his wealthy friend J. S. Watson to contribute as well (Ellen Blake to Burke, June 8 and 14, 1937).

Most obviously Burke foregrounded his allegiance to Marx, who, as William Rueckert has indicated, "is everywhere in the book" ("Field Guide," 15). By recounting (yet again, and probably in far too much detail) in part 2 how his version of history was drawing on Marx's, Burke left no doubt that he was speaking from within the Marxist assumption that only a revolutionary socialism could provide a basis for a more just, more humane, more fulfilling society. And he proclaimed further solidarity in any number of places throughout the text, as one "Dictionary" entry, on "Perspective by Incongruity," illustrates:

We hold that a multiplicity of perspectives becomes purely gratuitous, and even anarchistic, unless it is organized about a specific point of reference. . . . And we would suggest that in the field of human relations this point of reference is provided by the social criteria of Marxism. Otherwise, you get a "calculus of individuals" whereby "identities" for the individual can be selected at random. A "calculus of individuals," without a point of reference in historical necessities, would become an embarrassment. (II, 205–6)

While in *Auscultation*, Burke had argued for moving "beyond" Marxism, and while in *Permanence and Change*, he had presented Marxism merely as a necessary first step (and not necessarily as final goal), since Marxism was retaining too many of the destructive materialistic values of industrial capitalism, in *ATH* Burke went to lengths to identify closely with a Marxist position. In *P&C* Burke typically attributed concepts to Veblen or to various nineteenth-century thinkers when he could have tied them to Marx, in order to distance himself from Communist Party orthodoxy; and in *Auscultation* he sometimes made the same move (e.g., "This doctrine is not exclusive to Marxism. It was thoroughly understood by such utilitarians as Bentham, and by the modern pragmatists": 167). But in *Attitudes*, Burke often reversed the strategy: he made Marx ubiquitous while Dewey, Bentham, Veblen, and company were relegated to the footnotes. More important, Burke was much more willing now to credit Marx for important concepts. For instance he reserved some of his highest explicit praise for Marx by defining him as a great comic thinker in a book that was defending a comic attitude as essential for moving toward a better life: "The best of Bentham, Marx, and Veblen is high comedy" (I, 53). And he tied one of his pet ideas, the dangers of a debunking frame of interpretation such as Bentham's, to Marx, who "felt this atomistic, disintegrative genius in the utilitarians' theories of motivation. . . . the approach was essentially negative, lacking the positive quality that Marx got by his concept of class solidarity" (I, 123).

Not only did Burke declare his allegiance to Marx, Marxism, and the Popular Front, but he also voiced his intention to work for the cause as a socialist propagandist—in part by writing his book. The penultimate entry in *ATH*'s "Dictionary of Pivotal Terms" ("Symbols of Authority") thus reiterated a prominent claim of the book: that his "own program, as literary critic, is to integrate technical criticism with social criticism (propaganda, the didactic) by taking the allegiance to the symbol of authority as my subject. We take this as our starting point, and 'radiate' from it. Since the symbols of authority are radically linked with property relationships, this point of departure automatically involves us in socio-economic criticism" (II, 234). That was indeed Burke's starting point and aim: while maintaining that he would still attend to "the field of technical criticism (the 'tactics' of writers)," Burke emphasized that "since the whole purpose of a 'revolutionary' critic is to contribute to a change in allegiance to the symbols of authority, we maintain our role as 'propagandist' by keeping this subject forever uppermost in our concerns" (II, 234–35). Consequently Burke committed himself to an employment of standard Marxist terminology: terms such as *class struggle, alienation, superstructure,* and *substructure* appear regularly throughout the text, a striking shift from the studious avoidance of Marxist vocabulary in *P&C*.[11] And he expressed his sympathy for the Popular Front outright in the way that he described the movement and its critics in his section on "Opportunism" (II, 200–201).

Perhaps the most significant of Burke's strategies of identification were those that indicated that he had rethought some of his positions since writing *Permanence and Change* in order to align himself more clearly with Marxism. For instance the five-act historical drama that he offered in part 2, with its stages leading almost inevitably to "collectivism," is strikingly different from the stage history he had borrowed from Frazer for *P&C*—and strikingly congruent with the Marxist historical narrative. Even more fundamentally, while he still held in *Attitudes* that human behavior is not determined solely by economic motives, Burke was willing now to assign to the economic a much larger role than he had previously—that is, he was more attentive to the theory of dialectical materialism and eager to represent *ATH* as a correction to the cultural ecumenism of *P&C:*

> While beginning this book, we tended to resist the purely "economic" interpretation of history. We felt that the rise of great imperial integers could only be explained by reference to some "spiritual" force. But as we proceeded, we found the economic emphasis inescapable. For even if you assume that there is some "spiritual" factor operating at the "core," the enterprising area from which the whole organization radiates, it still seems that the upbuilding of an empire as a whole can only be explained by economic factors. (I, 147)

In *Permanence and Change*, Burke had argued strenuously against positing the material realm as the initial causal element in history, but in *Attitudes*, what he once called "economic determinism" had become so much a part of his thinking that it is reflected in the very diction and syntax of his sentences. In the conclusion of volume 2, in which Burke summarized the book's main arguments, he therefore wrote that "the mind, being formed by language, is formed by a *public grammar.* And this public grammar involves at every turn material factors. It coaches the realm of 'values' that takes form, as a 'superstructure' to match the material 'substructure'" (II, 253). Or, again, when arguing that a critic should choose interpretative paths based on their social value, he wrote (in a passage that Lentricchia has called Burke's "meditation on some fundamental perspectives of *The German Ideology*" [120]), "A given material order of production and distribution gives rise to a corresponding set of *manners*" (II, 33–34n). Or, yet again, in his "Dictionary" entry for "'Earning' One's World," Burke wrote that "morality is basically rooted in the framework of production and distribution (deriving its 'gravitational pull' from these firm material aspects of society)" (II, 117). Even more surprising is that what Burke offered in *P&C* as the most central "material" factor— the human body—almost completely dropped out of the material matters assumed in *ATH*. There are references to the body in *ATH*, but they are infrequent and indirect—the notable exception being a hymn to "the necessities of the physical economic plant" that Burke included in his important "Dictionary" definition of the "good life" (II, 129).

Burke on Methodology

Not that Burke had reconsidered everything, or ceased trying to reform Marxism (this time from within). Indeed, when people cite Burke's description of himself as "Marxoid," they commonly refer to *ATH* because it presents a reform agenda for Marxism that is quite in keeping with his own longstanding misgivings about Marxist dogma.

First—and most famously—Burke offered a "comic approach" as an incentive for Marxists who might be seeking to broaden their understanding of human motives and, hence, to better direct their rhetoric:

> The progress of humane enlightenment can go no further than in picturing people not as *vicious*, but as *mistaken*. When you add that people are *necessarily* mistaken, that *all* people are exposed to situations in which they must act as fools, that *every* insight contains its own special kind of blindness, you complete the comic circle. (I, 51–52)

"The comic frame should enable people *to be observers of themselves, while acting*," he elaborated later, in one of the most frequently quoted passages in the book; "its ultimate would not be *passiveness*, but *maximum consciousness*" (I, 220). Playing significantly on the several senses of *acting*, Burke offered his readers several "roles"; they are cast simultaneously as potential agents, as critics, and as performers in the human drama. All three of these difficult roles are captured in the act of writing: "The comic frame of acceptance . . . considers human life as a project in 'composition,' where the poet works with the materials of social relationships. Composition, translation, also 'revision,' hence giving maximum opportunity for the resources of *criticism*" (I, 223–24). A comic corrective, or a comic attitude, is a more accurate method of understanding human interaction and symbolic action: one central purpose of *ATH* is to correct overly scientific, Marxist approaches to interpretation based on antithesis.

Because it is an advance over Marxist antitheses that he had been complaining about since *Auscultation*, the comic attitude is also an improved means of understanding human discourse, of analyzing and addressing audiences—of doing criticism and rhetoric. In a spirit of "comic ambivalence," even as he was building bridges to potential Marxist collaborators, Burke simultaneously trained his comic lens on them and their "debunking attitude" with a "maximum awareness" of the complexity of human behavior:

It is this notion of *ambivalence* that gets us to our main thesis with regard to propagandistic (didactic) strategy. We hold that it must be employed as an essentially *comic* notion, containing two-way attributes lacking in polemical, one-way approaches to social necessity. It is neither wholly euphemistic, nor wholly debunking—hence it provides the charitable attitude towards people that is required for purposes of persuasion and cooperation but at the same time maintains our shrewdness concerning the simplicities of "cashing in." (I, 213)[12]

Burke himself may have found Marx's best work "high comedy" (I, 53), but much Communist Party rhetoric, full of capitalist villains and the fervent conviction that it was presenting the one, scientific truth, was not. The comic rhetoric Burke was advocating was more balanced. It proposed a discourse between rhetors and audiences who must be neither overly naive nor overly cynical and—equally important—who would assume neither naïveté nor cynicism in the other. "The comic frame is charitable, but at the same time it is not gullible. . . . Dealing with man in society, it requires maximum awareness of the complex forensic material accumulated in sophisticated social structures" (I, 138–39). Such a comic rhetoric would be based on the most traditional foundation: whereas Marx had defined the individual as an economic entity, and whereas the church had defined an individual as "a prospective citizen of heaven" (and those in reaction to the church offered "man in nature," which quickly degenerated to "*man in the jungle*"), Burke was offering a "comic synthesis of these antithetical emphases [that] would 'transcend' them by stressing *man in society*. As such, it would come close to restoring the emphasis of Aristotle" (I, 218–19).

Realizing that his recommendation of such a comic method would be difficult for some Marxists to swallow, Burke was happy to offer concessions. "Admittedly, this business is elusive. We must ask the reader, if he can, merely to consider it as being on the track of something. We are trying to bring up an issue, rather than to persuade anyone that we can make it crystal-clear" (I, 112–13). The tentativeness and the unusual direct address to the reader suggest that Burke knew that his own performance might appear "comically" foolish. Passages such as this one[13] certainly enact the comic attitude, but they were also intended to function as training for radical readers who need to make similar admissions about their own analyses, who needed to recognize "that people are *necessarily* mistaken, . . . that *every* insight contains its own special kind of blindness" (I, 52).

In the spirit of comic forgiveness, Burke also offered his concept of "bureaucratization of the imaginative" as a means of reforming Marxist methods. As much as Burke supported the idea of socialism, his comic understanding of social complexity led him to believe that "in this 'imperfect world,' no

imaginative possibility can ever attain complete bureaucratization," complete
and perfect instantiation (II, 66). In the process of becoming reality, all ide-
alizing formulations, including communism, inevitably become ensnared "in
the realities of a social texture, in all the complexity of language and habits,
in the property relationships, the methods of government, production, and
distribution, and the developments of rituals that reinforce the same [prevail-
ing] emphasis" (II, 66). Beginning his mediation on a subject that would ultimately lead to his famous phrase "rotten with perfection," Burke therefore
warned his readers to" necessarily come upon the necessity of compromise,
since the human being is not a complete fit for *any* historic texture. A given
order must, in stressing certain emphases, neglect others. A bureaucratic
order approaches the stage of alienation in proportion as its 'unintended by-
products' become a stronger factor than the original purpose" (II, 67). Any
socialist state, once realized, will bear only an imperfect resemblance to the
original vision. Burke could not accept without compromise the Marxist
promise that history would unfold exactly as planned, from the "inevitable"
proletarian uprising to the revolution to the final withering away of the state.
Indeed Burke's description of history in *Attitudes* shows that, as Lentricchia
puts it, "historical action necessarily ends in gaping discrepancies between
intention and actualization" ("Reading History," 227). In fact, at the end of
his historic drama, Burke predicted that revolution in America would come
in a decidedly unrevolutionary way: "We prefer to be somewhat shrewd in
our notion of the way in which collectivism must emerge. Primarily, we feel
that it may enter 'by the back door,' as signalized by that highly ironic term
of modern economists, the 'socialization of losses'" (I, 206), a process he already saw at work in the bonuses granted to WWI veterans and in the wide
array of New Deal programs supporting railroads and banks, artists and
migrant workers. Burke's concept of the bureaucratization of the imaginative
was flying in the face of orthodox, less compromising beliefs, as indicated by
Sidney Hook's reaction to *ATH*, but his rhetorical motive seems less to condemn or ridicule Marxist visions than, in the spirit of comedy and the Popular Front, to give collectivism a better chance of succeeding through better
rhetorical strategies.

Such strategies would emerge, Burke promised, if Marx's insights could
be methodologically allied with Freud's. Since both Marx and Freud were
dedicated to the process of conversion, Burke proposed (as he had begun to
do in *P&C*)[14] that approaches to individual and sexual analysis could be combined productively with economic and social ones. The phenomenon of
"alienation" in particular had both material and psychological dimensions,
Burke felt, that pointed to the integration of Freudian and Marxist analysis.
As Don Abbott has explained, the basic concept in *ATH* that unites Marxist
economics and Freudian psychology is "symbols of authority" ("Marxist

Influences"): a person, or an entire community, will be able to reject established, authoritative cultural symbols insofar as that person or community becomes alienated from such symbols. Once the alienated person or community begins seeking new identifications, new symbols of authority can develop: a conversion to a new identity is possible. Collapsing the antithesis between "individual" and "environment" (II, 139), Burke explained in his section on "Identification" how new identities are created by acts of "rebirth": "Identity involves 'change of identity' insofar as any given structure of society calls forth conflicts among our 'corporate we's.' From this necessity you get . . . the various ritualizations of rebirth" (II, 147) that are detailed in the remainder of the section. This process of identification, rebirth, and reintegration around new symbols of authority is described further in *The Philosophy of Literary Form*, in *A Grammar of Motives* and *A Rhetoric of Motives*, and in the scholarship on Burke, so we will not belabor it here. But it is worth noting that the description of the process begins in *ATH* and *P&C*. And it is worth emphasizing that in seeking rapprochement between Freud and Marx, in proposing that irrational as well as rational motives might underlie social behavior, Burke was in league with a number of his contemporaries,[15] including the members of what would come to be known as the Frankfurt School.[16]

A final area of methodological blindness that Burke felt obliged to correct in *ATH* was, perhaps not surprisingly (to anyone familiar with *ACR* or *P&C*), the assumption that dialectical materialism has a firm scientific basis. Burke was not even convinced that Marxist history should be understood scientifically, as the "Dictionary" entry for "Repossess the World" indicates:

> A rationale of history is the first step whereby the dispossessed repossess the world. By organizing their interests and their characters about a purpose, as located by the rationale, they enjoy a large measure of repossession (a spiritual property that "no one can take from them") even though they are still suffering under the weight of the bureaucratic body oppressing their society. . . . By a rationale of history . . . they own a "myth" to take up the slack between what is desired and what is got. (II, 212)

By using the incendiary word *myth* here, rather than *science*, Burke was emphasizing his methodological differences with his readers. It was a theme that he would return to in "Philosophy of Literary Form," another work on methodology. But rather than chastise Marx or accuse his followers of persisting in a dangerous error, Burke this time complimented Marxist teleology for its rhetorical and psychological effectiveness. That is, he in essence excused a bit of sectarian foolishness—perhaps needed to recruit followers and maintain their morale—and hoped that it might be discarded as Marxists got closer to physically repossessing the world.

More Methodology: The Roots of Dramatism

Ultimately, however, Burke's hopeful attempt at boring from within the Left did not succeed because what Burke offered as a revision of Marxist method, including his sympathy for Freud, was too unconventional and controversial. As Wess has observed, "While there is enough economic interpretation in this history to give it its family resemblance to Marxist 'grand narrative,' this resemblance ironically proves just enough to make Burke's history a black sheep in the 1930s economistic family" (87). Burke's idiosyncratic, if not incongruous use of Marxist vocabulary—i.e., applying "alienation" as a psychological as well as economic term—made him seem like someone who had not quite gotten it right; in some passages he even appeared almost to be trying to "pass" as a Marxist, to be someone who was messing with the master's terms, terms that for the Marxist "scientists" had very precise meanings.[17] *ATH* provoked a flurry of critical reviews (and a counter-flurry of rebuttals from Burke) that reveal divisions within the Left and, more to the point, reveal the extent to which *Attitudes toward History* is, on its most fundamental level, an argument about methodology, one that was taking Burke on the path toward dramatism.

Burke was perhaps least successful at getting his readers to incorporate Freud and symbolism—that is, the nonscientific, the nonquantifiable—into their Marxist worldviews. As Michael Feehan has observed, many Marxists simply could not let go of the scientific methodology because it was one of the few remaining elements that could unify the increasingly fractured Left. It is likely too that a comic vision of Marxists as potential fools was jarring to their self-image as scientists. In any event Crane Brinton, Eliseo Vivas, and Sidney Hook all questioned Burke's conclusions and inspired responses from him on the issue of methodology.[18] But the reviews and commentaries that offer the most telling perspective on *ATH* were written by Margaret Schlauch, a linguist teaching at New York University, and V. J. McGill of Hunter College.

Schlauch and McGill were two of the four editors of the Marxian quarterly *Science and Society*, founded in mid-1936 "to publish articles . . . illustrating the manner in which Marxism integrates the various scientific disciplines and illuminates the interdependence of science and society" (Editorial statement, i). Burke was listed on the *Science and Society* masthead as a "contributing editor," and he wrote a review for the first issue, in the fall of 1936.[19] When *ATH* appeared a little more than a year later, Schlauch decided to review it herself for *Science and Society*. Then, after Burke replied ("Twelve Propositions"), Schlauch commented again (albeit superficially), and McGill articulated his own objections to Burke's ideas on methodology.

The objections of Schlauch and McGill are predictable, given the stated aim of the new magazine. Through published discussions with their opponents (of which the exchange about *Attitudes* is clearly an example), the editors "hope[d] to open up new fields for investigation and to stimulate scholars to adopt the fruitful methods of Marxism" (i). While it is common these days to think of Marxism as a philosophy of history or an economic system, the editors of *Science and Society* were foregrounding its function as a methodology for social analysis—a scientific methodology—and were eager to exemplify how that "manner" or "method" might be deployed in the service of social change. Given the perspective of the magazine, then, it is not surprising that Schlauch's review would criticize Burke's "emphasis . . . upon psychological . . . relationships at the expense of others"—notably at the expense of economic relationships more suited for "scientific" analysis; McGill's concerns were, likewise, "mostly methodological ones" (253). Burke's language simply "is *not* the language of science," McGill insisted, and scientific "method and problems are, likewise, quite different from [Burke's]" (255).

In his well-known reply to Schlauch's March 1938 review, "Twelve Propositions on the Relation between Economics and Psychology" (included in a shortened form in *The Philosophy of Literary Form*), Burke consequently elaborated on the contentions he had articulated in *ATH;* under pressure from Schlauch and other critics to justify his method of analysis,[20] Burke began his rejoinder by introducing "propositions [which] briefly state the approach exemplified in my recent work, *Attitudes Toward History.* . . . They are an attempt to codify my ideas on the relation between psychology and Marxism" (242). Foremost Burke was concerned about the limitations of science. He argued that analyses that are based on perceptions of human behavior inevitably change when viewed through different lenses, so the view through the single "scientific" lens of Marxist methodology was too narrow. Consequently it yielded a limited and distorted view of human activity and, in turn, a flawed rhetorical theory. In friendly contrast to Marx and in keeping with some of his more aestheticist friends, Burke was recommending an analytic lens that could focus on both the economic *and* the psychological attachments that humans form to symbols of authority;[21] symbolic (as opposed to merely scientific) analysis would, he promised, provide a fuller view of human action because it was calculated to understand "man in society, man in drama" (246). *Attitudes toward History,* then, is a very early entry in an intellectual debate that would rage for half a century or so among American Marxists: among, that is, those "classical Marxists," on the one hand, who championed a Marxism patterned after the natural sciences (and featuring positivist approaches based on the "laws" of historical materialism and a rigid view of economic determinism); and those "critical Marxists," on the other, who like Burke drew more from psychology (and who, critical of positivism, sponsored a more complicated and flexible account of the relationship between economics, culture, and subjectivity).

That Burke would equate man in society with man in drama was highly significant. Indeed, as Michael Feehan has noticed, "Twelve Propositions" is especially noteworthy for its eleventh: that "*Human* relations should be analyzed with respect to the leads discovered by a study of drama" (246). In the gloss to this proposition, Burke laid out some of the central assumptions that have come to be associated with dramatism, his most celebrated approach to social and symbolic analysis, and as he did so, he set them in clear opposition to the various forms of scientific, mechanistic, and behavioristic analysis that he began arguing against in *P&C* and that he continued to fight for years:

> Men enact roles. They change roles. They participate. They develop modes of social appeal. . . . People are neither animals nor machines (to be analyzed by the migration of metaphors from biology or mechanics), but actors and acters. . . . If you would avoid the antitheses of supernaturalism and naturalism, you must develop the coordinates of socialism—which gets us to cooperation, participation, man in society, man in drama. (246)

Dramatism, in short, was offering a methodology for leftists that "should make precise the nature of resistance encountered by those interested in engineering shifts in allegiance to the reigning symbols of authority" (247).[22]

It is fair to say, then, with Feehan, that Burke formally codified what would come to be known as dramatism only in the process of writing "Twelve Propositions." But *Attitudes* itself does more than simply fumble its way toward Burke's most famous methodology for doing symbolic analysis. Much of *Attitudes* is itself an *enactment* of that methodology. Part of what makes the book difficult is that Burke uses dramatism without explicitly explaining and arguing for his methodology in a sustained way, probably because he was finding his way as he wrote: "Frankly, we were not sufficiently aware of our procedure until we neared the end of the book (that is, we did not verbalize our implicit method into an explicit methodology)" (II, 182). Burke realized, in other words, that what he had jokingly referred to in a letter to Josephson as a "peach bough" method of analysis,[23] the *method* that he had built and enacted in *Attitudes*, needed to be explicitly and systematically laid out and discussed as a *methodology* of symbolic analysis (his task in "Twelve Propositions," *The Philosophy of Literary Form*, and ultimately *A Grammar of Motives*). In *Attitudes toward History* Burke was striving to build a theory of human relations, a rhetorical theory, and a complementary methodology for analysis based on a definition of humans not just as rational or economic beings or as members of certain classes, as Marxists might, but on the most inclusive definition possible, the definition of humans as symbol users.

The distinction Burke was developing between *method* and *methodology*[24] grew out of his commonsense notion that people typically perform a task —digging a garden, watching a baseball game, even raising a child or reading a poem—in a certain way, perhaps even repeating the procedure until it becomes routine, without conscious awareness or articulation of the process. What Pierre Bourdieu would later come to call *habitude* is akin to Burke's sense of *method:* method is an unconscious disposition toward routine, embodied practices that are in harmony with established regularities within a given social space. A person's *method* of gardening or child-rearing or analyzing a text thus becomes a *methodology* only when it is guided by an explicit philosophy or purpose.[25] A method, then, is just the way something happens to be done, whereas a methodology follows a deliberate plan that is grounded in some philosophy. To illustrate the point Burke claimed that the method of science is technology and the methodology of science, philosophy (II, 51): method describes the how, and methodology adds the why. Hence Burke's admission that he was not "sufficiently aware of [his] procedure," that he "did not verbalize [his] implicit method into an explicit methodology" (II, 182), indicates that in the process of writing *Attitudes*, Burke was performing a symbolic analysis of history by mere method—that his approach for understanding humans' relationships to symbols of authority was simply the way he happened to work and that near the end of his writing process and later, spurred by reviewers' attacks on his method, he developed the explicit methodology of symbolic analysis now known as dramatism. (It might even be argued that there was a certain validity to the reviewers' criticisms of Burke's method in *Attitudes* because it was just that—a method, one that must have seemed almost random and certainly ungrounded, rather than a purposeful methodology.)[26]

When Burke defined "the comic frame as a *method of study*" (I, 219),[27] he indicated that his approach to symbolic analysis (dramatism) was inextricably tied up with the comic attitude. Indeed the comic frame is what turns symbolic analysis from a mere method into a methodology; it is "the why," the guiding principle of his *methodos*—in the language of *Permanence and Change*, it is what makes his *methodos* (the way after) into a true *hodos* (or "the Way," "the Tao"). Metabiology and an art of living thus might be said to have their parallel or completion in the comic attitude: just as in *P&C*, Burke set up metabiology and the poetic orientation as an answer to the scientific or technological psychosis, so in *Attitudes*, he sets up the comic attitude and its corresponding methodology as an answer to the methodology of science and, to the extent that they overlap, of Marxism: "For technology itself has produced an analytic world—hence, no other instrument but analysis can confront it with the necessary precision. [My] analysis on the other hand, is *integrative* insofar as it gives substance to a synthesizing attitude"—i.e., the comic attitude (II, 52).

It is not especially controversial to claim that *Attitudes toward History* is one of Burke's first steps in the development of dramatism, provided that by "dramatism" is not used in this sense to mean the precise form of dramatistic analysis later described in *A Grammar of Motives* and elsewhere as "the pentad." After all, part 2 of *ATH*, "The Curve of History," explicitly presents human experience "after the analogy of a five-act play" (3rd ed., n.pag.). At this point in his career, Burke was defining dramatism fairly informally as a general methodology of social and symbolic analysis that, unlike behaviorism or other "scientific" approaches, is based on the premises that humans are actors and that aesthetic critical methods can be applied to the study of human action. To put it another way, while *Attitudes* may not *say* much about dramatism (certainly not, in comparison with *A Grammar of Motives*), the book does *perform* a kind of dramatistic analysis in Burke's presentation of "The Curve of History."

Indeed "The Curve of History" section is almost literal in presenting a dramatistic analysis. As Burke signaled a shift in his gaze from individual to communal frames of acceptance, necessarily also "shift[ing] the emphasis from the *poetic* to the *historical*" (I, 141), he launched suddenly and without explanation into the language of drama, noting that present-day historians often find that "the drama of the past must frequently be rewritten—the last act in one version may even become the first act of a later version" (I, 141). Continuing the metaphor—or frame of interpretation—Burke next explained how plays in general are structured, whether they are literal or historical ones ("In Act I of a drama we get the situation out of which the action will arise": I, 142); then he proceeded to set his own scene, finishing with the unremarkable statement that "for our Act I, we take all these resources as 'the given'" (I, 143). After some further scenic details, Burke announced simply that "Act I confronts this problem"; the curtain goes up, and the play begins (I, 145). It proceeds without interruption except for a brief note by the historian-playwright at the beginning of act 3—"Act III is our 'peripety,' with a radical turn in the arrows of the plot. Here is the act of marked transition, the 'watershed' of the historic drama" (I, 171)—and again before the final act: "Act V of one's historic drama should be left partly unfinished, that readers may be induced to participate in the writing of it. And one tries to arrange his scenario of the first four acts in such a way, so 'weighting' his material and 'pointing' his arrows, that the reader will continue in the same spirit" (I, 203–4). This final comment is followed by a brief summary of each act's content, a summary intended to show that collectivism is a logical progression from what has gone before. After a brief discussion of collectivism, the play ends; the final section of volume 1 argues for the comic corrective but not for the utility or validity of the historic drama itself.

But "The Curve of History" is not the only place where *Attitudes toward History* enacts a kind of dramatism. The previous section, "Poetic Categories," does as well, for as Burke noted, his historic drama only does on a communal, historical level what "Poetic Categories" does on an individual, literary level:

> The various poetic categories we have analyzed illustrate some major psychological devices whereby the mind equips itself to name and confront its situation. They provide in miniature the cues for us to follow when considering the broad course of Western civilization with reference to its "collective poems," the total frames of thought and action. (I, 129)

Burke introduced this section of the book by claiming that "our way of approaching the structures of symbolism might be profitably tested by the examination of various literary categories, as each of the great poetic forms stresses its own peculiar way of building the mental equipment (meanings, attitudes, character) by which one handles the significant factors of his time" (I, 42–43). As with "The Curve of History," Burke *says* very little in this introduction to explain what "our way" of approaching symbolism is; nor is he very clear about what "structures of symbolism" he means. But in this section he does apply a quasi-dramatistic method, examining the literary as a reflection of (or even a guide to) the psychic: the epic, for example, is "designed . . . under primitive conditions, to make men 'at home' in those conditions. It 'accepts' the rigors of war (the basis of the tribe's success) by magnifying the role of the warlike hero" (I, 44); and tragedy is a form that emerges whenever the success of individual entrepreneurs "sharpened the awareness of personal ambition as a motive in human acts, but the great tragic playwrights"—Shakespeare writing *Macbeth* is one of his favorite examples— "were pious, orthodox, conservative, 'reactionary' in their attitudes towards it; hence they made pride, *hubris*, the basic sin, and 'welcomed' tragic ambiguity, surrounding it with the connotations of crime" (I, 48). Through examples such as these, Burke illustrates what a dramatistic analysis might look like and the kind of rich insight into individual psychology it might afford.

Burke did take some major steps toward explaining the workings of his analytical methods, whether they are called dramatistic or not. In part 3 of *ATH*, for example, "Analysis of Symbolic Structure," he offered a rudimentary set of instructions (or a set of tips) for doing symbolic analysis. The title of the first section, "General Nature of Ritual," can be misleading in that readers do not equate "ritual" with "the analysis of symbolic structure,"[28] but that seems to be just what Burke is doing—explaining to Marxist readers overly steeped in and committed to scientific methodologies what symbols are, how they function, where they can be found, and what is involved in analyzing them. "Even in the 'best possible of worlds,'" he begins (it is particularly tempting to read the passage as directed to readers who would equate "the best possible of worlds" with the communist state), the need for symbolic tinkering would continue. One must erect a vast symbolic synthesis, a rationale of imaginative and conceptual imagery that "locates" the various aspects of experience. This symbolism guides social purpose: it provides one with "cues" as to what he should try to get, how he should try to get it, and how he should "resign himself" to a renunciation of things he can't get. (II, 1)

Symbolic structures, the stuff of ideology, are not just a mystification that will disappear when capitalism and religion have been abolished. No system can fit everyone in society perfectly; there will always be someone or some part of someone left out, and there will be always be unintended by-products from the system that work against it. And even if a social structure could account for all needs and could remain stable, Burke argues, conflicts would inevitably remain:

> To sum up: For various reasons, one has many disparate moods and attitudes. These may be called sub-identities, subpersonalities, "voices." And the poet seeks to build the symbolic superstructures that put them together into a comprehensive "super-personality." Even in the "best possible of worlds," then, there will be many factors stimulating men to the construction of symbolic mergers. Even if you remove the class issue in its acuter forms, you still have a disparate world that must be ritualistically integrated. And artist, philosopher, moralist, publicist, educator, politician, sociologist, or psychologist are all "idealistic" in the sense that they must give great attention to superstructural adjustments. (II, 8)

"General Nature of Ritual" thus launches a direct assault on "scientific" sociologies and psychologies based only on dialectical materialism—the kinds espoused by Marxists associated with *Science and Society*—as adequate approaches to human experience. Ideas or emotions and the symbols that attach to them are central parts of life, so any analytical system that fails to take them into account is fundamentally flawed.

Having established the centrality of symbols in human experience, Burke turns to illustrating the nature of symbols. In his next section, "Ambiguities of Symbolism," he uses a contemporary critical debate in Russia over Shostakovich's opera *Lady Macbeth of Mzensk* to show the social complexities involved in critical analysis. The next section, "The Tracking Down of Symbols," continues the "lesson" of the opera by reiterating in more general terms the necessity of moving beyond literal meanings; Burke was encouraging critics to look for symbols or rituals where none were thought to exist and to search for clues to their meaning in two ways: through a "functional approach," a metaphorical analysis of the author's imagery at structurally significant points; and through a "statistical approach" requiring a comparison of works sharing similar patterns of imagery. Both of these methods are ones that Burke would develop in much more detail in *The Philosophy of Literary*

Form and elsewhere.[29] Next, the sections "Synthesis and Analysis" and "Analytic Radiations" work together to illustrate the complexity of symbolic meaning and, hence, of the analysis of that meaning. Burke was cautioning the wholly programmatic critic not to oversimplify a symbol by looking for a precise, one-to-one correspondence between symbol and meaning: since a work of art synthesizes many aspects of the artist's experience, "a symbol may transcendentally fuse an author's attitude towards his parents, his friends, his State, his political party, his métier, his memories of childhood, his hopes for the future, etc." (II, 28). Furthermore "there is no 'logical progression,' like a Q.E.D., through points, 2, 3, 4, etc. Since the work of art is a synthesis, summing up a myriad of social and personal factors at once, an analysis of it necessarily radiates in all directions at once" (II, 31).

How is a critic to choose which directions to travel in, which radiations to pursue? Burke recommends in "Tests of Selectivity" that a critic should select and evaluate by "the pragmatic test of use" (II, 32).[30] "Facing a myriad of possible distinctions," Burke continues, reinforcing his most radical aesthetic pronouncements of the decade, the critic "should confine himself to those that he considers important for social reasons. . . . in the present state of the world we should group these about the 'revolutionary' emphasis, involved in the treatment of art with primary reference to symbols of authority, their acceptance and rejection" (II, 32). Echoing points that he had made earlier in "The Nature of Art under Capitalism" and "My Approach to Communism," Burke "insists" that forms of identification, alienation, purification and rebirth, bureaucratization of the imaginative, etc.,—forms that "are at the very basis of both esthetic and moralistic strategy"—should remain the focus of contemporary critics' analyses (II, 34–35). "The critic thus becomes propagandist and craftsman simultaneously," Burke declared, fulfilling his "didactic purpose" by applauding "the necessary tactics of transition" however they appear in the work of art and fulfilling his aesthetic purpose by judging the formal skill of the artist (II, 32). As Burke concluded his argument, he moved as close as he could in *Attitudes* to articulating an explicit rationale for a dramatistic analysis:

> Art is merely the dial on which fundamental psychological processes of *all* living are recorded. The "poetry exchange" is to human living as a whole what the stock exchange is to production and distribution under capitalism. A slight fluctuation in carloadings may register, on the stock exchange, as a big fluctuation in the price of securities. And similarly, the tenuous fluctuations of impulse that apply in practical life may show as wide fluctuations in the "poetry market." . . . this, to our mind, is the social function that a psychology of art should perform, as it sought to locate, on the recordings of the "poetry exchange," the processes of social commerce operating in life as a whole. (II, 35–36)

Burke's thought and language here clearly echo the arguments of *Permanence and Change:* his turn toward a "psychology of art" is taken almost verbatim from the earlier text, where he proposed a "philosophy, or psychology, of poetry" as a necessary ingredient for cultural well-being (*P&C*, 92). But the passage also shows that Burke's sense of art's role in culture had shifted (or grown) as well, for while *P&C* argues primarily for a poetic orientation, for an understanding of the function of perspectives or ideologies, and for an understanding that art, indeed all language and interpretation, is rhetorical, *Attitudes toward History* focuses more on art as reflection of or a way to get at society's psychic state. If *P&C* proposes art as social cure, *Attitudes* offers diagnostic tools for understanding art and other forms of symbolic action—so that radical rhetors might be able to subvert the "allegiance to the symbols of authority" that were compelling people in 1937. "The resources of critical analysis, whereby *we may observe ourselves*, have become very rich," Burke concludes, adding an ethical imperative for more and better analysis: "Since we have amassed the documents, it would be 'cultural vandalism' not to use them. Hence the 'moral obligation' to do as much as can be done with the resources of analysis now open to us"—resources that Burke was working to increase (II, 51; emphasis added).

A Rhetoric for the Popular Front

One purpose of *Attitudes toward History*, then, was to make Marxist sympathizers into better critics and ultimately into more persuasive rhetors—to help them see the value and the necessity of basing their rhetorical practices on the symbolic analysis of human relations in order to produce social change. Toward that end Burke concluded part 1 of his book, "Acceptance and Rejection," by emphasizing his rhetorical intentions: "We have attempted, in the foregoing pages, to illustrate some of the major factors involved in the 'strategy' of writing and thinking. We have tried to reveal the subterfuges to which the poet or thinker must resort, as he organizes the complexity of life's relationships within the limitations imposed by his perspective" (I, 137). Unlike Marxist (and non-Marxist) economic analysts, Burke assumed that people do not always act rationally—that is, in their own best material interests; there are other, less tangible but nevertheless extremely powerful motives governing human behavior that successful persuaders need to take into account. While *Permanence and Change* had begun to offer a vocabulary for talking about these powerful attachments to prevailing cultural values (*piety, orientation, trained incapacity*), *Attitudes* provided a practical method for locating and analyzing these symbolic attachments.[31] Because human nature and human symbolic action are more complicated than Marxists had been assuming, the rhetoric needed to persuade symbol users to abandon their accustomed views of the world and their place—what

Burke called "piety" in *P&C* and "allegiance to symbols of authority" in *Attitudes*—would have to be complicated as well. So in *ATH* Burke picked up where he left off in *P&C*, with practical lessons in psychology and symbolism that were designed to help Marxists understand the inevitable, widespread resistance to their attempts at persuading the unconvinced—and to help keep the peace among the committed factions in the Popular Front.

A chief difficulty for revolutionary rhetoric (i.e., rhetoric that asks people to reject their current frame of meanings) lies in the fact that people associate all kinds of thoughts and feelings with aspects of their lives—a process Burke calls "symbolic mergers." In his "Dictionary of Pivotal Terms," Burke repeated the advice that he had provided in "General Nature of Ritual": "'Metaphorical analysis' is required to get some accurate glimpse of the secret ways in which a symbol integrates." In other words, cultural critics and would-be reformers need to read a person's (or a whole culture's) psychological workings as they would read a poem. Just as in art, Burke explains, "a symbol is a vessel of much more content than is disclosed by its 'face value,'" so too "words may contain attitudes much more complex and subtle than could possibly be indicated in the efficient simplification of a 'practical' dictionary. And so with all 'symbolic mergers'" (II, 231). Those who read human motives literally or suggest that there is a single motive at work in any action have oversimplified to the point that they will never be successful persuaders. Burke reinforced his point with examples pointed to Marxist readers: "once a man has integrated his whole life about his business (interweaving it with a full texture of social relationships and personal transcendences) you will be far from knowing what is going on if you try to analyze his motives as merely the 'desire for monetary profit.' His business has become a 'vessel,' it is 'charismatic'" (II, 231); and "when an average compatriot expresses his allegiance to *capitalism*, he is not considering merely the things that make it *different* from other economic systems. The symbol also includes for him such notions as family, friendship, neighborliness, education, medicine, golf, tools, sunlight, future, and endless other such sundries. When the orator shouts, 'Down with capitalism!' the auditor often resists because he is countering in secret, 'I love the memory of the river bank where I lolled in the sun as a boy'" (I, 129–30). What one individual may symbolically connect to a job, a car, a phrase is multiplied many times over when a critic is dealing with an entire culture's ideology, for "a well-rounded frame serves as an amplifying device. Since all aspects of living tend to become tied together by its symbolic bridges, each portion involves the whole. Hence the questioning of a little becomes amplified into the questioning of a lot, until a slight deviation may look like the abandonment of all society" (I, 134). As difficult as it might be for leftist Depression-era critics to understand, capitalism for many people was remaining a "well-rounded frame." Radical and even not-so-radical leftists, Burke among them, undoubtedly felt angry and frustrated by the general resistance to "collectivism": why would so many Americans cling to a system that was abusing them, materially and psychologically? It is, perhaps, one of the central questions driving both *Permanence and Change* and *Attitudes toward History*. Burke provided an answer in his discussion of "Symbolic Mergers," an answer that explained why Marxist rhetoric was so often failing to persuade.

Not only that: When radical critics fail to analyze human behavior completely, they cut themselves off from the many potential supporters whom capitalism has *psychologically* alienated. For this reason Burke sought to broaden the working definition of alienation: "One 'owns' his social structure insofar as one can subscribe to it by wholeheartedly feeling the reasonableness of its arrangements. . . . Insofar as such allegiance is frustrated, both the materially and the spiritually dispossessed must suffer. One may not be in the mood to pity the losses of those who are not dispossessed materially; but it would be poor gauging for a critic not to take them into account when considering historical processes" (II, 233). After all, even Marx himself, who read Shakespeare, played chess, and indulged in any number of other "decadent" bourgeois activities supported by the income he received from Engels's cotton mills, "could nonetheless persist as a 'renegade'" (II, 233). "An overstressing of material possession alone," Burke continues, exactly in the spirit of the Popular Front, "may lead one to alienate men who may be his allies in the gigantic task of engineering a shift in the allegiance to the symbols of authority. . . . In fact, the peripheral class (of those spiritually alienated but still materially rewarded) can contribute insight of a sort to which the wholly dispossessed are blinded" (II, 233–34). These words describe exactly Burke's role in *Attitudes toward History:* to offer to more orthodox Marxist writers the special insight he possesses by virtue of his Popular Front allegiances. "To the wholly dispossessed, the matter may look too simple, thereby inducing them to make an over-simplified drawing of alignments. And in such over-simplification, they not only organize themselves; they also by antithesis organize the enemy—forcing into the enemy camp many who might otherwise have been with them" (II, 234).

A rhetoric based on antithesis—the result of considering only the economic motives for human action—is not only unnecessary but positively counterproductive to the agenda of the Popular Front. In his discussion of the didactic genre in "Poetic Categories," Burke pointed to the inherent weakness in Marx's psychology and, thus, in much Marxist discourse, particularly proletarian literature: "By the concept of antithesis Marx schematized the psychological issue, pitting one 'morality' against another, without analyzing the possibility that the imaginative writer tends to '*adumbrate*' *the eventual synthesis*, hence confusing the simple for-or-against attitude that prevails in a lawyer's-brief polemic" (I, 99). Because effective revolutionary rhetoric—particularly proletarian works of art—will look toward the future synthesis even as it responds to present divisiveness, it will necessarily contain a certain amount of ambivalence, an ambivalence that Marx simply did not account for. A martial rhetoric, even if it is developed for a class war, is typically written to create an us-versus-them mentality. Its symbols are strong, emotional, and unambiguous because it is developed to rally popular support and to help fighters overcome traditional cultural mores against killing. It fails to acknowledge that the enemy may be like "us"; indeed it often portrays "them" as inhuman. To bridge the gap between the old cultural frame, capitalism, and the new one, collectivism—that is, to enable members of society to negotiate the shift in their allegiances—radicals needed to base their rhetorical appeals on what the classes have in common. And the way to determine those shared values or goals is not through economic analysis but through dramatistic analysis, the analysis that most clearly reveals cultural attachments to symbols that cut across class boundaries. Thus Burke's Popular Front argument about rhetorical methods can be summed up in this appeal from "Twelve Propositions":

> It should offer a *ground in common* between propagandizer and propagandized, whereby the maximum amount of readjustment could be accomplished through the "parliamentary" (discourse, discussion). That is: it should avoid the coaching of *unnecessary* factional dispute by considering modes of response applicable to *all* men. . . . Such procedure is especially to be desired in the propagandist, since humaneness is the soundest implement of persuasion. (247)

Significantly Burke chose to end his historical drama, "The Curve of History," with a vision of human progress that was more hopeful that the one expressed in the famous concluding lines of *P&C*. Although he had begun act 5, "Emergent Collectivism," by claiming that he had deliberately left it unfinished so that his audience might "be induced to participate in the writing of it" (I, 203), Burke actually provided his own ending in the next (and final) chapter of "The Curve": "Comic Correctives," a sort of act 6 that Burke attached to his history play. There he most clearly offered his readers the opportunity and the means for curing social ills in what is certainly one of the most familiar passages of the book: "the comic frame should enable people *to be observers of themselves, while acting*. Its ultimate would not be *passiveness*, but *maximum consciousness*" (I, 220). Here Burke gives readers two specific roles to perform; they are cast simultaneously as critics and as actors. Moreover he gave his audience the ultimate dramatic role as well: they must write the script. "The comic frame of acceptance considers human life as a project in 'composition,' where the poet works with the materials of social relationships. Composition, translation, also 'revision,' hence giving maximum opportunity for the resources of *criticism*" (I, 223–24).[32] The comic corrective is an improved methodology for looking at both action and discourse, a corrective for analyzing and addressing audiences, a corrective for rhetoric—especially antithetical Marxist rhetoric.

Burke is not typically thought of as a writer of rhetoric handbooks. But in a real sense *Attitudes toward History* is just that—a manual of rhetorical strategies for social change. As Burke says in the introduction to the third edition, an updated title for the book could easily be "Manual of Terms for a Public Relations Counsel with a Heart" (n.pag.). In the original edition Burke presented his "Dictionary of Pivotal Terms" as an attempt to create a "folk criticism" to parallel the "folk art" being featured at the time: "We are considering [such terms] as a collective philosophy of motivation, arising to name the relationships, or social situations, which people have found so *pivotal* and so constantly recurring as to need names for them" (I, 223; emphasis added). As the term *folk criticism* suggests, Burke's intention in the "Dictionary" was not to create an arcane critical language but rather to take terms from "the working vocabulary of everyday relationships," especially terms that previously had no relation at all to criticism (I, 222), in order to create perspective by incongruity. So he drew his terms from religion, from vocabularies of crime, from proverbs; and he uses in his dictionary "the remarkable terms of politics and business, two terminologies which quickly chart and simplify constantly recurring relationships of our society" (I, 222–23)—familiar terms such as "Being Driven into a Corner"; "Heads I Win, Tails You Lose"; "Efficiency"; "Good Life"; "Communion"; "Discount"; and "Opportunism." (Burke used commonplaces such as "cash in on" or "move in on" or "take over" throughout the book to describe the political and/or rhetorical moves groups engaged in a power struggle were using on each other.) If "The Curve of History" shows how, when, and by whom these strategies were used in the past, the clear rhetorical point of the "Dictionary" is to foreground strategies used by those in power in the 1930s to maintain capitalist hegemony and to indicate how these strategies might be co-opted by the Left and used to disrupt that hegemony, in the interest of forming a broad and viable Popular Front.

Conclusion: Partisan Review *and Sidney Hook's Feud with Burke*

Kenneth Burke's distaste for Sidney Hook was legendary, and it is well known that it derived from Hook's notorious review of *Attitudes toward History*, published in *Partisan Review* in December 1937. Sarcastically entitled (with a snide acknowledgment that *ATH* is about methodology) "The Technique of Mystification," the review provided one long paragraph of fair summary of Burke's book and ten just-as-long and not-nearly-so-fair paragraphs of sustained, often withering criticisms. Burke wrote a response and Hook a counterresponse—but that exchange only inflamed matters further and ensured that Burke would subsequently refer to Hook only with expletives attached.

Hook's feud with Burke came to a head in that review, but it had been simmering for some time. The first contacts between the two were actually quite cordial, because Burke and Hook thought of each other at first as kindred spirits. In September 1933, having read several essays by Hook, Burke wrote to Cowley that he wanted "to meet Hook . . . when I get to town . . . as he is one of the few in the business who is not cheese" (September 8). Then in December 1933, a few months after his *Towards the Understanding of Karl Marx* had gotten him into trouble with the CPUSA (for Hook was far more sympathetic to Trotsky than to Stalin—to put it mildly), Hook wrote Burke an approving (if self-righteous) note on the basis of Burke's "The Nature of Art under Capitalism": "it is far and away the best thing on the question which I have read in English—and I have read everything." Burke's article suggested that Burke, like Hook, was a committed Marxist who was nevertheless critical of Communist Party hegemony, and so Hook was "glad that you [Burke] have not gone 'orthodox'" (December 8, 1933). That Burke had quoted Dewey approvingly was another mark in Burke's favor, for Hook's general intellectual project was to make Marxism compatible with Dewey's pragmatism. Burke soon answered Hook's letter (December 27, 1933), and during 1934, Hook and Burke wrote formally but amiably to each other several times on the issues of orthodoxy and the nature of art under Marxism; while the two were honest and frank about differences, they had obvious intellectual regard for each other. As the first American Writers' Congress was being planned in late March 1935, Burke accepted Hook's invitations to lecture twice in his philosophy classes at New York University, and Hook must have been anxious to keep Burke in the his camp.

But the Writers' Congress seeded the beginning of their discord.[33] Hook, as a dissident Marxist critical of Stalin, was effectively blackballed from the Communist Party–dominated congress and from the League of American Writers that grew out of it, and he was disappointed by Burke's decision to participate. He was even more disappointed to read Burke's favorable (and self-effacing) account of the congress published in the *Nation*. Unaware or unconcerned that Burke had himself been roasted by certain participants at the congress, Hook could only register his outrage at Burke's sunny written summary of the proceedings: "Are you seriously prepared to defend the politics of the C. P.—its theory of social-fascism, party-dictatorship instead of workers' democracy, . . . etc. etc? . . . As you are aware, not a single radical (socialist or communist) opposed to Stalinism was invited to this Congress. It seems to me that if the individual integrity you speak about had really been present, those possessing it would have had the courage . . . to protest the sectarian basis on which the sessions had been organized" (undated, May 1935). And so on.

Hook was suspicious that Burke had "gone over" once more, this time to an allegiance to the party and its tolerance for Stalin, for Hook (rightly) saw the Popular Front as part of the apparatus sustaining Stalin (and Roosevelt): anyone "who calls for the formation of a Popular Front cannot do so without in effect surrendering his socialism," he would soon write in *Partisan Review*; anyone "who supports a Popular Front government may find that as a result of its program of defense of capitalism, it may open the gates to the Fascists" ("Anatomy," 40; also quoted in Denning, 432). Burke must have felt that his own defiance of doctrinaire Stalinism was clear enough from *Permanence and Change*, but for some reason Hook did not credit Burke for the independence of that book. It is evident from Hook's letter to Burke of November 26, 1934, that Burke was making sure that Hook had a copy of *Permanence and Change*, and other allusions in the correspondence suggest that Hook even intended to write a review. But except for some general references to *P&C* in Hook's review of *ATH*, Hook remained silent about what Burke was attempting in *P&C*, even though *P&C* can fairly be considered a "dissident" contribution to Marxist ideology. Did Hook never get around to reading the book carefully? Did he find the book too difficult to comprehend?[34] Was he put off by Burke's implicit criticism of Marx's explanation of cultural development?

Whatever the case, Hook was convinced that the League of American Writers' "acceptance" of Burke and Burke's favorable account of the congress in the *Nation* together amounted to something of a group hug that he had been left out of—not that he wished to be any part of a Popular Front, anyway. And his suspicions about Burke deepened a few months later when Burke reviewed Henri Barbusse's biography of Stalin for the November 1935 Book Union newsletter. The Book Union, a sort of book-of-the-month club for the radical Left, was developed at the time of the Writers' Congress in order to publicize and to help disseminate proletarian books of all kinds (poetry, drama, fiction, history, economics), and its monthly newsletter included reviews of featured selections, which were sold to members at a discount.[35] (Barbusse's *Stalin*, normally $3.00, was available to Book Union members for $1.60.) Burke was among the fifty-five members of the Book Union Advisory Council and well acquainted with its editorial board (which at various times included Harry Block, Malcolm Cowley, Robert Dunn, Henry Hart, Granville Hicks, Corliss Lemont, Isidor Schneider, Bernard Smith, Alexander Trachtenberg, and Mary Van Kleeck), and so he apparently was willing enough to review *Stalin* for the Union, probably because the Union was closely associated with the League of American Writers, on whose board Burke was serving. (The Book Union publicized its address as 381

Fourth Avenue, the same address as the League of American Writers.) In any event, when Burke offered a purely descriptive review of *Stalin* that sounded to Hook rather appreciative—in addition to summarizing the book's content in neutral terms, Burke called the book "an engrossing record . . . written with an unmistakable fervor"—Hook became livid. He took steps to send Burke a copy of his own in-press review of Barbusse's *Stalin*, slated to appear in the November 16, 1935, *Saturday Review* under the sarcastic title "St. Stalin": the book, wrote Hook, "is the result of Barbusse's officially encouraged, if not inspired, labors. Whoever turns to it in hopes of getting some insight into Stalin . . . will be sorely disappointed. For what we have here is neither history nor biography but liturgical rhapsody . . . in which fact and fancy are hopelessly blurred." And in the margins of his review, he scratched this message:

> Dear Burke: I have just read your review of Barbusse's *Stalin* in the Book-Union circular and am wondering whether there are two different books by Barbusse on Stalin or whether your review and mine just illustrate the law of selective reference. Don't think I don't appreciate the real skill that went into the writing of your review but I am grieved that you did not dare to write a single critical line about a book which—despite your review—I know in your heart you regard as thoroughly bad. Excuse the "bad taste" of this note but you are the only "mind" whose defection to Stalinism I mourn. The rest deserve their fates. (Hook Papers, Hoover Institute)[36]

Ironically Burke's review of *Stalin* originally had indeed included remarks critical of the Soviet leader. In a letter to Cowley of April 22, 1936 (unsent), he wrote:

> I kick my pants for allowing Trachty [i.e., Trachtenberg, who produced the Book Union sales circular] to cut the article. . . . In the piece as written, I said flatly that it was written from the Stalinist angle, and also used the formulation that Wilson used in one of his recent N. R. [*New Republic*] pieces (namely, I said that Lenin contained both Stalin and Trotsky. . .).[37] I kick my pants for not trying to bargain with Trachty and find some way of leaving this observation in. Particularly because it states *exactly* my attitude toward the deplorable split [between Stalin and Trotsky], and even Trachty told me that he "saw what I meant."

Burke feared that dissident Marxists would be able to "get me" on the basis of his "sales note on the Barbusse book. Neither Hook nor Burnham[38] has answered my *tu quoque* argument; but though as private citizens they see perfectly well why I did what I did, . . . they would not be adverse to using the book-chat for purposes of political strategy." Burke's fear would prove prophetic.

Burke's Review of Henri Barbusse's *Stalin: A New World Seen through One Man* (from the *Book Union Bulletin,* November 1935)

This is not a formal biography of Stalin. Even its sub-title, "A new world seen through one man," does not quite reveal the nature of its contents. The book begins and ends with Lenin—and it contains many important sections dealing with the purely *collective* aspects of recent Russian history, seen essentially as a group enterprise rather than as background for one man. It is, to be sure, written throughout as a fervent tribute to the figure who is now, in Barbusse's words, "the heart of everything that radiates from Moscow on the surrounding world." But beyond a desire, on Barbusse's part, to make Stalin's perspective his perspective, the book spreads until the subject of the individual is merged into the history of the Communist Party, and the history of the Party is merged into the general history of Soviet Russia.

As we lay down the book, we do not carry away the sense of a personal portrait at all. "Intimate" details are few. It is the phenomena of the "political" personality that we are here concerned with—those aspects of a human character that one sees when considering him as a concentration point of historical events. The result is not a "family portrait," we might say, but a memorial statue in a park: it depicts the traits that bear most directly upon impersonal or superpersonal relationships. This emphasis upon the political rather than the intimate makes it natural and easy for the author to move, again and again, from the portrait of a man to the epic of a nation.

The word "personality" originally comes from a word referring to the role taken by an actor. In times of increasing passiveness, we have come to think of "personality" as a purely "spiritual" quality, something almost the opposite of one's public relationships. The *political* biography brings back the notion of personality closer to its origin, as it approaches character primarily from the standpoint of the role assumed by the actor in the human drama. And when such an approach is stressed, we find it natural to move, as Barbusse has done, from the man to his theories and his tactics, and thence to the historic context in which they operated.

The first chapter, "A Revolutionary Under the Tsar," depicts the rigors of that "terrible vocation," the calling of professional revolutionary, for which one must be fitted not only by reason of his convictions, but also by "iron health, at the service of indomitable energy, and an almost limitless capacity for work." Without histrionics, Barbusse impresses us with the picture, as he recounts Stalin's acceptance of his difficult role during the pre-Revolutionary days. Barbusse offers no psychological explanation of Stalin's efforts. He smiles at Emit Ludwig who asked Stalin, in an interview, "Perhaps you were ill-treated by your parents in your childhood, to have become such a revolutionary?"—and quotes Stalin's reply, "The reason that I became a revolutionary is simply because I thought the Marxists were right." In any event, Barbusse well shows that the conviction of possessing a correct philosophy fortified Stalin constantly, while he was further strengthened by the theory that the triumph of his cause was *historically inevitable*. Contemporary science has questioned the notion of historic inevitability, but it has never questioned the fact that a belief in historic inevitability may be of invaluable assistance in stimulating purpose.

The second chapter, "The Giant," depicts the master-disciple relationship between Stalin and Lenin. The stressing of this relationship is doubtless an important feature of Stalin's appeal to his countrymen. We see, in Barbusse's account, how many ingredients the public figure must unite within himself. He must symbolize not only his Party, and through his Party his people and their historic mission—he must also trace an integral connection with important features of the *past*.

Thus, it is in his role as the Perpetuator of Lenin that Stalin completes his public identity.

The third chapter describes Stalin's activities during the period of counter-revolutionary campaigns which followed the Bolshevik Revolution. This is followed by a very interesting discussion of national pluralism in Russia, the question of "homogeneousness in heterogeneousness," considering the adjustments made between the new unifying Communist framework and the separate national identities.

Barbusse next reviews the incredible difficulties of organizing the cooperative system in a state which had been but slightly industrialized to begin with, whose few industries bad been crippled by war, and where the forces of inertia and open resistance were still strong as obstacles to the new modes of production. Then, under the title of "The Parasitic War," he gives an account of the split between Stalin and Trotsky. It is told frankly as a complete partisan of Stalin would tell it.

Next comes a review of Soviet success to date, in the one country in the world blessed with an economic system rational enough for a national surplus to be a national asset. This chapter is followed by an account of the policies adopted with relation to the peasantry. In chapter nine, "What of Tomorrow," Barbusse considers Soviet Russia's equipment, both as regards internal development and as regards protection against external aggression. He next adds a chapter pleading against the belief that there is any possible intermediate position between Reaction and Revolution. And in his brief closing section, "The Man at the Wheel," he returns to the theme of Lenin-Stalin identification.

The book is written with an unmistakable fervor. And as a general picture of the vast unwieldy processes of historic adjustment, as manipulated by key figures who both make history and are made by history, it is an engrossing record.

Relations between Burke and Hook improved not a whit when Burke reviewed James T. Farrell's *A Note on Literary Criticism* in the June 24, 1936, issue of the *New Republic*. Because Farrell's book was a sustained riposte to the critical position held by Gold, Hicks, and other representatives of the strictly proletarian school sponsored by *New Masses*, it might have been approved by Burke, at least in most respects. And Burke did indeed note that "the basis of Farrell's book . . . is highly agreeable to me" (211). Farrell found fault with proletarian criticism (including the work of Malcolm Cowley) because it confused literature and propaganda, because it ignored issues of literary heritage, and because it was inattentive to the uniqueness of individual writers and works. But Burke still found *A Note on Literary Criticism* wanting because Farrell too strenuously insisted (against the grain of the party line) on a distinction between art and politics, between literature and propaganda, and because Burke thought the book oversimplified: "In the end you are left merely with the feeling that some critics, in their necessary work of simplification, have sometimes oversimplified—and you are a dumbbell if you needed a special book to tell you that" (211). The review strained relations between Farrell and Burke.[39] More to the point, Hook wrote a snide postcard to Burke on June 23 taking issue with Burke and exonerating Farrell on the grounds that he was indeed addressing a broad audience of "dumbelli." Burke tried to smooth things over the following day (after all, he was still concerned that Hook might be reviewing *Permanence and Change*) in a letter that politely but firmly reasserted his long-held belief that a literature-propaganda dichotomy could not hold, recorded his belief that he thought "of myself as a propagandist," and renewed his appeal to Hook to read his views in *Permanence and Change* and more recent essays. But Hook was not to be mollified: "it is simply untrue that Farrell hurts 'the cause' by dissociating himself from barbaric nonsense more than the Hicks tradition does," wrote Hook to Burke at the end of June. "If you had come into the movement before the exigencies of the C. P. political line led them to give a temporary Narrenfreiheit to people like you[,] that would have been your experience [too]. In fact, if I am not mistaken, in the days when you were still Saul and not Paul[,] you used to be repelled by narrow economic determinism yourself. . . . Why do you think it necessary to call yourself a propagandist? You are too good a mind (even if the role of apologist is thrust upon you) to be that or to call yourself that, for as you define the term everyone is a propagandist of sorts; the word has no intelligible opposite and by the principle of significant assertion is strictly meaningless" (Hook to Burke, June 1936).[40]

When Burke's *Attitudes toward History* appeared in the summer of 1937, therefore, Hook was ready to attack with full fury: his review took the opportunity not only to critique the book but to criticize Burke on several other extraneous shortcomings. One of his paragraphs challenged Burke's two-year-old review of *Stalin* for not pointing out Barbusse's partisanship and not being attentive to Barbusse's errors ("at least one . . . on every other page; and even some of the photographs—particularly the one showing Lenin with

Stalin's head almost on his shoulder—are obviously faked"). Another paragraph challenged Burke's use and criticism of Dewey, Hook's own patron saint. The opening paragraph made fun of Burke's writing—"obscure," "opaque," "disorganized"[41]—and the conclusion identified Burke with "relativism," "moral nihilism," and—most viciously—"weak men of minor talent [who] make a bid for acceptance to the side they think will win." The professional academic philosopher, Dr. Hook considered Burke's autodidactic scholarship "not very discriminating," his economic analysis "amateurish," and his reading "ill-digested." And he was repelled by what he called Burke's "technique of mystification"—by the methodology Burke was recommending—which Hook regarded as "home-baked objective relativism" (58). Like Schlauch and the readers of her *Science and Society*, Hook favored "the methods of science [which] are the only reliable methods by which new knowledge (and the wisdom relevant to knowledge) are won" ("Is Mr. Burke Serious?," 45).

As much as anything, Hook could not stomach Burke's failure to condemn the Moscow show trials, which had reached the height of their notoriety just as *Attitudes* was coming off the press. Charging that Burke had an "undisguised animus" against critics of Stalin and the Soviet Union (no matter that Burke was recently considered such a critic himself by Freeman and Gold), Hook refuted for a full paragraph a Burke footnote on page 153–54 (of volume 2) that blamed the trials on the Marxist habit of antithesis, which to Burke "add[ed] plausibility to the accusations laid against the 'old Bolsheviks.'" "One may persist, if he chooses, in refusing to grant the validity of the trials," wrote Burke, "but at least the accusations present no mystery as psychology." Burke's comic attitude, summed up in the phrase "bureaucratization of the imaginative," which encourages critics to see human endeavors as flawed or foolish rather than evil, Hook believed, was designed specifically to muffle criticism of Stalin: "Learn how to use the formula 'the bureaucratization of the imaginative' and you will reconcile yourself to whatever is happening in Russia" (61). Hook was convinced that against his better judgment and out of a concern for his own political comfort, Burke was making nice with the Stalinists who were in control of the CPUSA and behind the Popular Front; Burke preferred to "deliver [his] critical comments about [economic determinism and party determinism] . . . in the out-of-the-way Southern Review instead of The New Masses where it would do some good" (Hook to Burke, June 1936). Burke's "moral nihilism," the product of his insufficiently philosophical methodology, made impossible the judgments necessary to daily life, including any condemnation of Stalin.

Hook's review found an appropriate home in *Partisan Review* because the magazine was just then out to make a statement. Founded in 1934 as "a bimonthly of revolutionary literature published by the John Reed Club of New

York City" (to quote its masthead), *Partisan Review* had been carrying proletarian works by Farrell, Freeman, Dos Passos, Josephine Herbst, Tillie
Lerner, Genevieve Taggard, C. Day Lewis, Jerre Mangione, Kenneth Fearing, Muriel Rukeyser, Richard Wright, and talented others. The magazine
supported the first American Writers' Congress, and even as late as February
1936 its party loyalties were warranting an attack on Hook for his "desire to
dissociate himself from the revolutionary conclusions of dialectical materialism" (26).[42] But *PR* gradually moderated its sectarian editorial position in
accordance with the Popular Front politics endorsed by the first American
Writers' Congress, lost its sponsor when the party required the liquidation of
the John Reed Clubs, found itself the butt of *New Masses* ridicule after it published Farrell's gleeful attacks on inartistic proletarian novels, and finally was
forced to disband after the October 1936 issue. Because of the failure, *PR* was
unable to publish a segment from *ATH* in November (Alan Calmer to Burke,
November 11, 1936).

Then in mid-1937, in the wake of the show trials, Stalin's failure to support rebels in the Spanish Civil War, and the second American Writers' Congress (where Trotskyists were marginalized), *Partisan Review* was reorganized
under the resolutely anti-Stalinist, anti–Popular Front banner held by Dwight
Macdonald, Mary McCarthy, Philip Rahv, F. W. Dupee, Delmore Schwartz,
and William Phillips (the latter two were grateful former students of Hook's).
The new *Partisan Review* proclaimed its allegiance to Trotsky and Trotsky's
goal of keeping art and criticism free of cultural sectarianism.[43] Trotsky had
become the major rallying point for opposition to Stalin by the middle of
1937, particularly because he was the subject of the sensational and sympathetic hearings in Mexico presided over by John Dewey. While Mike Gold
continued to attack Trotsky as "the most horrible Judas in all history" and
Earl Browder was denouncing Trotsky as "the advance agent of fascism and
war" (Klehr, 358–59),[44] *PR* shortly began reprinting essays by and about
Trotsky. Now fiercely critical of the Communist Party, proud that it had
made "no commitments to any political party," and in general launching the
editorial cosmopolitanism that would make it so important in the two
decades after 1940, *Partisan Review* was out to make a brash declaration of
independence from the CPUSA in its first issue:[45] what better way than to
publish a bit of fiction by Farrell, an essay by Wilson, and a lengthy review
by the previously disreputed Hook, especially if that review could take a
shrill position on a leading Popular Front advocate such as Burke? Hook's
attack on *Attitudes toward History*, then, was about much more than *Attitudes
toward History*.

Partisan Review tried to make up with Burke. The editors, who had occupied the same ideological space as Burke at the first American Writers' Congress just two years before, invited Burke to make a response to Hook; but

the rebuttal ("Is Mr. Hook a Socialist?") and Hook's own counterresponse ("Is Mr. Burke Serious?"), both published in January 1938, only gave Hook another withering last word at Burke's expense: when Burke's fairly technical response established that Hook had exaggerated a very small part of *ATH* and winked at the main message, Hook ignored Burke's objections, cataloged the sins of Stalinists everywhere, and even more directly reduced Burke to a Stalinist apologist, to someone who "believe[s] in the apotheosis of Stalin to a point which makes every political cult of adoration in the past, including that of Czarism, pale in comparison"; who could "accept and defend the most monstrous frame-ups in all history—the Moscow trials"; and who could show "impatience and scorn for those . . . who affirm that socialism without democracy is not socialism."[46] Despite Burke's protest (and despite the obvious fact that Burke was arguing for his comic perspective, synonymous with collectivism, as the superior attitude—and had done so in *Permanence in Change* as well), Hook stubbornly and unfairly insisted that Burke was a committed relativist who had left no methodology for choosing among perspectives. In February the magazine tried again to make amends by publishing John Wheelwright's laudatory poem "The Word Is Deed" ("for Kenneth Burke"), excerpts of several letters defending Burke and *ATH* (including ones by Leonard Brown and R. P. Blackmur), and Rahv's respectful report of Burke's contribution to the first American Writers' Congress ("Two Years of Progress").

But the damage was done, and *Partisan Review* was still bent on criticizing Stalin and the CPUSA. Burke thenceforward committed his energies to *Direction*, which began appearing just as Hook's review came out, and not to *Partisan Review*.[47] He quietly deleted the references to the Moscow trials from subsequent editions of *ATH*. And he vowed to have no more dealings, ever, with Sidney Hook and his *Partisan Review*. He explained everything carefully in a long letter to Matthew Josephson, written as he was preparing his response to Hook's review, on November 22, 1937:

> I have actually wasted a whole week on that bastard. I had to go back and read Dewey's "Liberalism and Social Action," for instance, to see whether I had unintentionally done him wrong. There is nothing in the book of the sort Hook is talking about. . . . When Hook is discussing the "faked" photographs of Stalin and Lenin, for instance [in the review of *Stalin*], "showing Lenin with Stalin's head almost on his shoulder," I naturally assumed that there was such a picture in the book [but missed it]. . . . [But] bejeez, there is no picture "showing Lenin with Stalin's head almost on his shoulder." . . . The major political sin of my career [is] resolvable to this: Writing in a sales sheet, on a book about which I felt decidedly neutral [i.e., *Stalin*], I wrote a neutral description of its contents. Out of this the whole logic of my life has developed. . . . What I have against Hook is that I couldn't have reconstructed each

of his points without heaping up the most worthless kind of detail. Even if I proved anything to the satisfaction of anyone, I could at best be back at zero. . . . And I think he should indeed insist on the noblest, finest, highest, free-est ideals for Russia. Nothing can be too high, as counterpoise to his true self. So much for S. H. Of SH it can be said . . . etc.

Shitney Hook he would remain, to Burke, for the rest of his life.

As for an ultimate assessment of Burke's position within the leftist political conversations that took place during the 1930s, the connection with Hook offers perspective on that, too. Buffeted by some Communist Party regulars for being too dissident and too "aesthete" before mid-1935, hammered later in the decade by the dissidents and Trotskyites for his alleged blindness to Stalinism, Burke in fact promised uncritical loyalty to no group. "Concerning the matter of my 'orthodoxy,'" he had written to Hook on December 27, 1933, "having heard so much about the difficulties which many sincere and enterprising men have met with, I made peace with myself by the following formula: I would think of myself simply as anti-capitalist and pro-communist, and let all the rest go hang. Insofar as all the warring groups will accept me as an ally on that basis, I am with them."

Since they did not really accept him on that basis (and indeed, as Phelps has also noticed, at some point Hook put a large exclamation point next to Burke's words in that December 27 letter), Burke began to withdraw somewhat from political theory and practice after *ATH* appeared. Instead he warmed to the new relationships that he had been developing, with people at the *Southern Review* and in Chicago, where, as he formulated his exasperating responses to Hook, he was being invited to teach in 1938.

Five

"Thirty-Minded
Pieces"

The Philosophy of Literary Form

W hile he was in the midst of his tiff with Hook, Burke's thoughts
were actually moving elsewhere, beyond the feuding in New
York. After recounting to Matthew Josephson a three-page bill of
particular frustrations over Hook's review and his efforts to respond, Burke
also parenthetically inserted brighter news:

> My pain at seeing the way Hook reduced [my work] to the pickled embryos
> of what he thought was a formalistic contradiction was eased by the fact that
> a review of P&C has just now belatedly appeared in the American Journal of
> Sociology. It was written by one of the editors. It is a long review detailing the
> contents of the book; and it starts out, and keeps up, in the spirit of this: "This
> is a book to put some of the authors and publishers of sociological textbooks
> to shame. It contains more sound substance than any textbook on social psy-
> chology with which the reviewer is familiar." (November 22, 1937)

The review had been written by Louis Wirth, who was among the most
accomplished of many outstanding sociologists then collected at the University of Chicago, who was producing with his colleagues the *American Journal
of Sociology* (founded by John Dewey, George Herbert Mead, and Charles
Henderson in 1895), and who a month earlier, in October 1937, had asked
Burke to comment on Irene Malamud's *AJS* article "A Psychological Approach to the Study of Social Crises." (Burke eventually included his comment in the appendix of *The Philosophy of Literary Form*.) In the first month of
1938, the Hook furor persisted in public, but in private Burke was thinking
long beyond *ATH:* corresponding with Wirth, recommending *ATH* to him,
and hearing about Wirth's colleagues (Wirth to Burke, October 12, 1937;
January 28, 1938).[1] And Wirth was obviously not the only Chicagoan on
Burke's mind. Leonard Brown had invited him back to Syracuse to lecture

once again in the summer of 1938, but Burke had gotten a better offer: "It has occurred to me," wrote Richard McKeon (November 26, 1937), "that you might like to try your hand—or mind—at teaching a couple of courses in the English Department at the University of Chicago during the Summer Quarter, . . . [which] extends from June 22 to August 27." Apparently without knowing how Burke had interested Chicago social scientists, McKeon suggested that Burke lead one course in literary criticism and another on some literary figure or figures. "Needless to say, we don't want any of your later vein [i.e., *ATH*]. An unobtrusive pink is a good color for the classroom, but any deeper tinge is considered flamboyant and in bad taste. These, however, need not be considered restrictions on your freedom so much as bits of literary wisdom on the matter of rhetorical decorum." Burke felt no restrictions, and by the end of 1937 the two had agreed that for $1,300 Burke would teach, in addition to the course in literary criticism (official title: "English 306, The Psychology of Literary Form"), a class on Coleridge (English 352). By March 1938 Burke was "cramming mightily" on Coleridge in preparation for his assignment, and he eventually conducted his courses while living at 1153 East Fifty-sixth Street in Chicago with Libbie and his young son, Butchie.

Though McKeon had encouraged him to mix lots of class discussion in with his lectures, Burke felt most comfortable doing most of the talking, and so he found the work difficult and exhausting—"the business of grinding out something like 85 lectures . . . has kept me chained for months," he complained to Josephson (August 5, 1938).[2] But he also enjoyed the summer of 1938 immensely. "The whole episode has repaired my ailing ego enormously," he wrote Cowley, "through being *asked* about my theories, rather than having simply to knock at doors, and through hearing of people who actually sit down and *study* my books. . . . We gave a wind-up party for the English department the other night, to pay off our many obligations wholesale—and managed to limber them up to the point where they did kittenish ringing of doorbells on their way out at one-thirty—and Mrs. Gideouse called threatening to call the police" (August 22). Besides the people in the English department, who included R. S. Crane and David Daiches (Daiches to Burke, December 1, 1938), Burke mingled easily with a number of the social scientists: Hugh Dalziel Duncan, a sociology graduate student who nevertheless enrolled in the Coleridge class (Duncan to Burke, September 24, 1946); Ernest W. Burgess, the innovative urban ethnographer who along with Wirth was editing the *American Journal of Sociology*; Irving Lee, a linguist who was preparing for Ph.D. comprehensive exams; and Thomas Eliot, a Northwestern sociologist who corresponded with Burke after his own review of *Permanence and Change* was published in the *American Sociological Review* and who threw a party on the Burkes' arrival to introduce them around (Eliot to Burke, July 25, 1938). Best of all, Chicago brought Burke a fresh set of ideas from those new acquaintances. "The burning issue here is not between Stalinists and Trotskyites, but between Platonists and Aristotelians—and thence, to complicate the symmetry, between Aristotelians and the Social Sciences. As usual, I fell on the bias across the controversies, hence shifting tables at the Faculty Club, stoutly defending sociology when I am at the Humanities tables, and v[ice] v[ersa]" (Burke to Josephson, August 5, 1938).

Out of these controversies and new associations, in part, grew *The Philosophy of Literary Form*, particularly its Coleridge-saturated title essay but also others, including "Semantic and Poetic Meaning," "Freud—and the Analysis of Poetry" (first published in the *American Journal of Sociology*), "George Herbert Mead" (Mead's version of pragmatism was recommended to Burke in Wirth's letter of January 28, 1938), and "Semantics in Demotic," all of which (and among other essays and reviews) were written in the months after the invitation to lecture at Chicago and before the following summer of 1939, when he presented the acclaimed "The Rhetoric of Hitler's 'Battle'" at the third American Writers' Congress and then returned again to Syracuse to try out his new material. Together with the intellectual acquaintances that Burke had fallen into via the *Southern Review*, the University of Chicago circles invigorated Burke's thinking, suggested new audiences, and ultimately confirmed his decision to work toward his next intellectual project, anchored in concepts he had begun to explore in *ATH: dramatism* and *identification*. The *Philosophy of Literary Form* is indeed a backward-looking, "thirty-minded" book (as Burke called it in his prefaces to the second and third editions), one that includes several essays written at the height of Burke's engagement with the Popular Front and even before: "War, Response, and Contradiction" (1933); "The Nature of Art under Capitalism" (1933); "Reading While You Run" (1937); "Trial Translation" (1933); "The Negro's Pattern of Life" (1933); "Twelve Propositions" (1937). But the many essays and reviews in *PLF* that were written late in the decade—and published in places such as the *Southern Review*, the *Kenyon Review*, *Poetry*, and *AJS*[3]—nevertheless also point to concerns that Burke would develop in his later criticism and theory, after the tumultuous 1930s were history. Ross Wolin speaks rightly and for many, therefore, when he speaks of *The Philosophy of Literary Form* as "a critical juncture in the development of Burke's thought, a moment that simultaneously marks the culmination of one phase and the inception of another" (119).

Burke's Pragmatism

The University of Chicago's historic commitment to pragmatism, which originated with John Dewey's presence on the faculty between 1894 and 1904, began to unravel with the arrival of Robert Hutchins in 1929, the death of George Herbert Mead in 1931 (Dewey spoke at the funeral), and McKeon's arrival in 1934. McKeon and Hutchins, with intellectual support from R. S.

Crane and later Mortimer Adler, advanced an agenda grounded on the study of the ancients, especially Aristotle, although the social scientists on campus continued to build on Dewey and Mead's pragmatist, experimentalist legacy.

But Burke did not need the University of Chicago to teach him about pragmatism. He was well aware of Hook's effort to synthesize Marx and Dewey. Burke had read William James quite carefully, was generally familiar with Charles Sanders Peirce (probably through book reviews), and reviewed during the 1930s three of Dewey's books, *The Quest for Certainty*, *Art as Experience*, and *Liberalism and Social Action*. All three reviews reflect the sophistication of his knowledge of the varieties of pragmatism in general and Dewey's writing in particular.[4] (The first and the last reviews of Dewey he included in the final section of *PLF*.) While Burke had expressed strong reservations about a key element of Dewey's project in his review of *The Quest for Certainty*, namely Dewey's inability to offer through experimentation a satisfactory grounds for arriving at appropriate values, especially ethical values, his reviews are generally quite complimentary. And elsewhere Burke acknowledged "great sympathy with our indigenous philosophers of pragmatism"[5] and drew on those sympathies in *Permanence and Change* and *Attitudes toward History*.

Permanence and Change can be understood as Burke's own quest for certainty, for an "undeniable point of reference"—the biological—that seems to be "as near to rock bottom as human thought could take us" (335). And indeed the book's argument not only wrestles with the central question of Burke's review—"How do we test the success of a value?" ("Intelligence," 78)—but also borrows its language: "Tests of Success" is a section title in *P&C*. Burke's answer and the process by which he derives it reveal both the limitations and the promises of pragmatism: the review of *The Quest for Certainty* emphasizes how Dewey's reliance on "experimentalism" makes it nearly impossible for Dewey to erect an ethical system "without relying upon the existence of a prior good" (78), but Burke in *P&C* frees himself of such restraint and explicitly acknowledges his own choice to invoke the "Jamesian 'will to believe,'" assuming "that good, rather than evil lies at the roots of human purpose" (301).

Burke had appropriated another key term in *P&C*, *occupational psychosis*, directly from Dewey as well, as he acknowledged loudly any number of times (e.g., in "The Nature of Art under Capitalism," included in *PLF*). The phrase points to something more substantial: Burke's whole argument in the first section of *P&C*—his contention that interpretation and thus communication shape and in turn are shaped by "orientations," "occupational psychoses," "trained incapacities"—is an outgrowth of Peirce's sense that any understanding of reality is mediated by signs; the insight is more directly an elaboration of Dewey's acknowledgment, in *The Public and Its Problems* (1927), that frames

Kenneth Burke with wife, Libbie,
late 1930s. Courtesy of Michael
Burke and the Kenneth Burke
Literary Trust

Burke with Libbie, summer
1940. Courtesy of Michael Burke
and the Kenneth Burke Literary
Trust

Burke in the waters of
Skaneateles Lake, ca.
1937–40. By permission
of Jacqueline Mott Brown;
from the Byrd Library,
Syracuse University

of interpretation shape cultural experience. *The Public and Its Problems*, after
all, was one of the several important "cultural histories" that gave Burke a
genre for *P&C*, for Dewey's book indeed observes the conventions of the
other cultural histories of the time. First *The Public and Its Problems* addressed
a sickness within American life (actually in the American body politic) that
was robbing citizens of a sense of community, i.e., the feeling within people
that they were now powerless and clueless, "caught up in the sweep of forces
too vast to understand or master" (135). Second it assessed the source of that
cultural malaise—namely industrialism and especially the perpetuation of
"older symbols of ideal life [which] still engage thought and command loyalty" (142)—i.e., what Burke in *P&C* called piety.[6] Third *The Public and Its
Problems* offered as a cure the instantiation of a Great Community that would
be "saturated and regulated by mutual interest in shared meanings, consequences which are translated into ideas and desired objects by means of symbols" (153–54). Those new cultural symbols, Dewey predicted eight years
before *P&C*, could be created and disseminated by art, for "the function of
art has always been to break through the crust of conventionalized and routine consciousness" (183). The final chapter of *The Public and Its Problems* thus
anticipates many of the conclusions of *P&C*, including Dewey's prediction

that American life might be rejuvenated by a change in frames of interpretation and reinvigorated forms of communication: "Capacities are limited by the objects and tools at hand," wrote Dewey in a passage that could easily have appeared in *P&C*, "[and] they are still more dependent upon the prevailing habits of attention and interest which are set by tradition and institutional customs. Meanings run in the channels formed by instrumentalities of which, in the end, language, the vehicle of thought as well as of communication, is the most important" (210).[7]

In *ATH*, Burke developed additional elements of his engagement with the pragmatists. The beginning section on William James, which grew out of Burke's 1936 review of Ralph Barton Perry's *The Thought and Character of William James*, indicates that Burke had been especially attentive to "the part played by Peirce in the sharpening of James's understanding" (*ATH*, I, 10); Burke was especially complimentary toward James's use of words to shape frames of acceptance and rejection and toward James's pragmatic belief in the provisional, contingent, and social nature of knowledge. True, as Frank Lentricchia has noticed, Burke could not be enthusiastic about James's "mostly uncritical celebration of the uncontextualized individual" (4), his underwriting of the personal as against the collective.[8] But as Lentricchia has also noticed, Burke appreciated Dewey deeply and far more than most other radical leftists did: Dewey's pragmatic sensibility had a social edge, Burke saw; Dewey's portrait of experimental science in *Liberalism and Social Action* offered an image of a social cooperation that was the contrary of ruthless capitalism; and Burke took note of Dewey's emphasis in the same book that pragmatism's empirical approach to human experience must be linked with radical social action if liberalism was to survive. While he was always critical of Deweyan instrumentalism (i.e., the assumption that things ought to be judged according to what works),[9] from Hook Burke had nevertheless come to understand how pragmatism could also be understood as in broad agreement with the Marxist assumptions that ideas arise from material circumstances and that they have concrete material effects. And from Dewey Burke appropriated approvingly the fundamental distinction between education as a function of society and society as a function of education (*ATH*, II, 235), a distinction that pointed toward radical reforms in educational goals and practices (Lentricchia, 1–5; Enoch) and that Burke would expand upon later in his career. Moreover, as he emphasized in the clarifying appendix to *ATH*, "Twelve Propositions," the "pure-process thinking of pragmatism" was necessary (though not sufficient) to the new philosophical synthesis that Burke was calling for (249).[10]

Thus it is not surprising that *The Philosophy of Literary Form* also contains pragmatic moments. Most important, Burke drew on the Deweyan fundamental that the province of human inquiry ought to be the scientific study of human action—though he focused his own attention on the "symbolic action" of art, literature, and other forms of communication. Although Burke conducted no scientific study, his methods were still pragmatic enough: he proposed on his very first page to consider pragmatically "critical and imaginative works [as] answers to questions posed by the situation in which they arose." Gathering comfort from Dewey's statements in *The Public and Its Problems* and *Art as Experience* that art was the most characteristically human of human actions, Burke treated literature as a pragmatic "equipment for living," and in the *PLF* essay with that same title he offered an elaborated "statement . . . of the *sociological* criticism of literature" (293). "Poetry *is* produced for purposes of comfort," Burke had written in his title essay, "as part of the *consolatio philosophiae*. It is undertaken as *equipment for living*, as a ritualistic way of arming us to confront perplexities and risks" (61). The same might be said of criticism, "the main ideal of [which] . . . is to use all that there is to use" (23). As Burke proclaimed quite directly, his "general approach to the poem might be called 'pragmatic' in this sense: It assumes that a poem's structure is to be described most accurately by thinking always of the poem's function. It assumes that the poem is designed to 'do something' for the poet and his readers, and that we can make the most relevant observations about its design by considering the poem as an embodiment of this act" (89). Additional pragmatic inflections and emphases are visible throughout "The Philosophy of Literary Form" and other essays in *PLF.*

Moreover Dewey in *The Public and Its Problems* had also worked from another basic tenet of pragmatist, Peircian thought, the assumption that knowledge is not simply found through observation or through logic but is constructed through a process of social interchange enacted through language: "knowledge is a function of association and communication; it depends upon tradition, upon tools and methods socially transmitted, developed and sanctioned" (158). Left to themselves, that is, individuals inevitably come to flawed beliefs; but mistakes are corrected and knowledge created by means of a quest for certainty that proceeds through social intercourse. Or as George Herbert Mead would have it, at least according to the words Burke used in a review of Mead that he began writing soon after his term in Chicago concluded (and then included in *PLF*), "substitute . . . for the notion of an Absolute Self the notion of mind as a social product. . . . [Thus] the metaphor of conversation (uniting 'democratic' and 'dialectical' by the forensic element common to both) is systematically carried through" (*PLF,* 379–80). "This 'unending conversation' . . . [is] the vision at the basis of Mead's work" (111) and fundamental to the pragmatist mentality. Burke's own famous version of the metaphor of the unending conversation, therefore, though it was developed independent of Mead,[11] links Burke with pragmatists before him and to come (e.g., Richard Rorty, Stanley Fish):[12]

In equating "dramatic" with "dialectic," we automatically have also our perspective for the analysis of history, which is a "dramatic" process, involving dialectical oppositions. . . . Where does the drama get its materials? From the "unending conversation" that is going on at the point in history when we are born. Imagine that you enter a parlor. You come late. When you arrive, others have long preceded you, and they are engaged in a heated discussion, a discussion too heated for them to pause and tell you exactly what it is about. In fact, the discussion had already begun long before any of them got there, so that no one present is qualified to retrace for you all the steps that had gone before. You listen for a while, until you decide that you have caught the tenor of the argument; then you put in your oar. Someone answers; you answer him; another comes to your defense; another aligns himself against you, to either the embarrassment or gratification of your opponent, depending on the quality of your ally's assistance. However, the discussion is interminable. The hour grows late, you must depart. And you do depart, with the discussion still vigorously in progress. (109–11)

The conversation metaphor, a rather fit description of Burke's own professional life as well as an account of the processes of history and criticism, would inevitably and increasingly direct Burke in the coming years toward the pragmatic field of rhetoric.

Chicago, the Southern Review, and PLF

Burke's accommodation of pragmatic emphases and his regard for literature as "equipment for living," then, links the "thirty-minded" *The Philosophy of Literary Form* with *Permanence and Change* and *Attitudes toward History*. There are also many other ties between *PLF* and earlier works; in a way, the book looks back at the first two decades of Burke's professional career and rounds them off completely. *The Philosophy of Literary Form* continues Burke's meditations on identification, on Freud, on methodology, and on "the dramatic perspective" (69), for example, and the emphasis on form and the attention to "cluster analysis" hearken all the way back to *Counter-Statement*.[13]

And yet *The Philosophy of Literary Form* also breaks new ground, particularly in the title essay but also in the other essays, in ways that accommodated the social scientists and Aristotelians at Chicago and the proto–New Critics affiliated with the *Southern Review*. In particular some of its essays advance a theory of language that is distinctive from that of the New Critics and general semanticists; it offers a way of reading that builds on Burke's earlier notions and that speaks to the New Critics and Chicago Aristotelians; it looks past literary criticism to a broader social and cultural criticism; and it anticipates *A Grammar of Motives*, *A Rhetoric of Motives*, and *A Symbolic of Motives* in proposing a sharper means of critical reading that is based on the pentad (a concept that he outlines for the first time in a footnote to page 106) and on other critical terministic screens. When Burke told Josephson that he spent much of the summer of 1938 negotiating between Aristotelians and social scientists, that he "he fell on the bias across the controversies, . . . stoutly defending sociology when I am at the Humanities tables, and v[ice] v[ersa]," he was not just kidding. While listening to the anti-Aristotelianism of the semanticists and accommodating the pragmatic empiricism of the social scientists, he was also hearing Aristotle's defenders and their then-allies developing the New Criticism, in ways that fundamentally affected *PLF.*

Take, for example, Burke's essay "Freud—and the Analysis of Poetry." In one sense the essay may be read as an abstract of the argument of "The Philosophy of Literary Form": both essays can be understood as lessons in methodology, in how to read; people who struggle with the latter essay for good reason take consolation in the streamlined argument of "Freud"; and so the account of "The Philosophy of Literary Form" below can stand in for a discussion of much of "Freud" as well, especially the sections that discuss the concept of "dream." What is to the point here is how "Freud—and the Analysis of Poetry" was specifically concocted for social scientists, on the assumption that quasi-Freudian advice on how to read poetry will prove useful to those scientists who would read other forms of symbolic action. Composed explicitly for the *American Journal of Sociology* just after Burke left Chicago (Burke to Cowley, August 22, 1938), "Freud" recalls *Attitudes toward History* in its effort to reconcile Freud and Marx—only here Freud is foregrounded and Marx is barely mentioned (except implicitly, as for example when Burke mentions "the Freudian tendency to underrate greatly the economic factors influencing the relationships of persons" [403]). Because of his audience Burke concentrates on what he has "been commissioned" to do—"to consider the bearing of Freud's theories upon literary theory" (393),[14] particularly a comparison of the common ground and deviancies between psychoanalysis and literary criticism. Writing for the sociologists, Burke is respectful of Freud, of course, especially in viewing Freud as a sort of language theorist who articulated principles that are common to all sorts of thinking.[15] And yet Burke also gently parts ways with Freud and some of his admirers in the sociological community by proposing and employing Freud's terms for critical rather than merely psychological purposes, by appreciating Bronislaw Malinowski's emphasis on the matriarchal just as much as Freud's emphasis on the patriarchal,[16] and by preferring Freud's earlier "associational" and "proportional" approaches to his later "essentializing" ones (393–94). Freudian analysis was one useful tool for analysis, and it could be especially useful in some cases; but only one among many.

Or take Burke's essay "Semantic and Poetic Meaning." Many of the assumptions behind semantics—the socio-scientific study of the relationship between words and things—were implicit in Ogden and Richards's 1923 *The*

Meaning of Meaning, and those assumptions were formalized (and made more positivistic) when in 1933 Alfred Korzybski, an immigrant autodidact with ties to engineering, mathematics, and psychiatry, published his *Science and Sanity: An Introduction to Non-Aristotelian Systems and General Semantics.* According to Korzybski, contemporary society was quite literally going insane, and one important cause of that insanity—as evidenced by the horrors of World War I—was miscommunication. (To use one of Korzybski's favorite metaphors: language is not adequate as a map of the territory of human experience.) In the manner of the logical positivists, he consequently offered a "neuro-psycho-logical" account of how language shapes and shades meaning within social institutions and how communication breakdowns, both individual and social, might be minimized through the application of scientific principles (lxiii). Deeply concerned about the "insane" distortions offered by advertisers and propagandists and writing with the same medicinal motives as other cultural historians, Korzybski attracted the attention of budding linguists (such as Irving Lee and S. I. Hayakawa, whose 1939 book *Language in Action* was based on general semantics) and of other social scientists, including Stuart Chase and Thurman Arnold, both of whose works Burke read and reviewed, albeit not uncritically, in the late 1930s. Korzybski and his followers, accepting the invitation of Russell and Whitehead's 1910 *Principia Mathematica,* set out "to increase the efficiency of thought through an increased understanding of how language works" in particular settings (Hayakawa, 357) and through the imposition of mathematical principles on language. "The present investigation reveals that in the functioning of our nervous systems a special harmful factor is involved . . . which retards the development of sane human relations," wrote Korzybski (*Science and Sanity,* lxii); as Malinowski had found, "most people . . . still use language in the way most savages do" (Hayakawa, 354).[17] *Science and Sanity* proposed to eliminate such harmful factors over time to the benefit of social intercourse. Lee and Hayakawa (Korzybski's subsequent popularizers)[18] consequently organized the first major seminar on general semantics in Chicago in May 1938, and a month later Korzybski's Institute of General Semantics was established there as well, a few blocks from the University of Chicago campus—just as Burke was arriving in town. While semanticists fully agreed that "all terms derive their meanings . . . not from definition but from usage . . . in a larger social context" (Hayakawa, 354), their goal was nonetheless to apply the predictability of science to everyday communications in order to tame out emotional distortions from language, to seek out as an ideal a mathematical equivalence between words and meanings.

Whether Burke ever met Korzybski personally that summer is unclear. What is clear is that Burke's lengthy and somewhat technical "Semantic and Poetic Meaning" (like his briefer review of Chase's *Tyranny of Words,* "Semantics in

Demotic") is an effort to delineate Burke's relationship with the linguistic assumptions of general semantics. Written just after Burke wrapped up his summer courses at Chicago, "Semantic and Poetic Meaning" on the one hand deals sympathetically with the fundamental "semantic ideal"—clarifying meaning and using language for positive social ends. "At its best, [the semantic ideal] has an incisiveness, an accuracy of formulation, a nicety," wrote Burke (521), and it could be said that Burke's own belief that the study of language could lead to social amelioration—"ad bellum purificandum," as he would put it in *A Grammar of Motives*—was in keeping with semanticist assumptions. Burke also could readily agree that language is too often an inadequate map of the territory of human experience. But on the other hand, Burke was at elaborate pains to distance himself from the dream of a neutral language, of "evolv[ing] a vocabulary that gives the name and address [as it were] of every event in the universe" (503). Not only would the pursuit of such a vocabulary strain human resources, but the attitudes and emotional colorings that inhere in language, particularly (but not only) "poetic" language, are not only necessary but positive. Those colorings contribute to meaning, not distort it. Rather than trying like a logical positivist "to *cut away*, to *abstract*, all emotional factors that complicate the objective clarity of meaning," then, Burke advised people instead to "try to derive [a] vision from the maximum *heaping up* of all these emotional factors, playing them off against one another, inviting them to reinforce and contradict one another, and seeking to make this active participation itself a major ingredient of the vision" (508). Where Korzybski and his school saw the intricacies of language as an unfortunate flaw, Burke approached those intricacies and ambiguities as a fascinating if challenging asset.[19]

Then again, the attitudes toward language that Burke expressed in "Semantic and Poetic Meaning" were actually directed more to the *Southern Review* crowd than to the semanticists. Burke couched that essay on language theory as an argument with semanticists and logical positivists mainly because that was a gentle and indirect way of correcting—once again, as he had in *P&C*—his acquaintances from the South, who shared assumptions about language with semanticists by distinguishing sharply between poetic and scientific (i.e., "neutral") language. "Semantic and Poetic Meaning," after all, was published first in the *Southern Review*, where it was consumed by John Crowe Ransom and his mentees Allen Tate, Cleanth Brooks, Robert Penn Warren, et al. As early as his years in the Fugitive circle during the 1920s, Ransom had been at pains to distinguish sharply between the language of poetry and the language of science; for good reason Thomas Daniel Young and George Core have asserted that "no other literary critic of this century has devoted as much time and intellectual energy as John Crowe Ransom in attempting to distinguish between scientific prose and poetic discourse" (1; qtd. in Tell, 38). That distinction between scientific and poetic language, based on the Agrarian distrust of science and on the positivist assumption that science and poetry lead to two different and complementary approaches to knowledge and derived at least in part from I. A. Richards's *Science and Poetry* (1926), was fast becoming a central tenet of the nascent New Criticism, as the movement would be officially dubbed by Ransom in his 1941 book of that name. And so Burke was explicit in countering that claim in "Semantic and Poetic Meaning." Indeed, as David Tell has documented, Ransom and Burke continued to wrangle sporadically about the question of poetic and scientific language via the mail from 1939 through 1941, especially in connection with Burke's 1941 essay in Ransom's *Kenyon Review*, "Four Master Tropes." "I can't believe it," Ransom lectured Burke at one point, perhaps recalling Burke's own rather fast distinction between the scientific and poetic perspectives in *Permanence and Change*: "Scientific perspective is very different from poetic metaphor" (August 8, 1941). "I don't agree with you that a scientist's perspectivist method is like a poet's metaphor. . . . I make poetry and prose a pair of opposites, same as poetry and science" (January 4, 1941).

   The New Criticism was reviewed by Burke in 1942. So was Ransom's *The World's Body*, in the October 1939 issue of *Poetry*. That latter collection of essays includes "The Sense of Poetry" (a paean to the distinctiveness of poetry and companion to his "The Tense of Poetry," it originally appeared next to a Burke essay in the Fall 1935 *Southern Review* and expressed several dogmas of the nascent New Criticism); the early New Critical manifesto "Criticism, Inc."; and several chapters of what Burke called "close examination" (of Shakespeare's sonnets and Metaphysical poetry).[20] As "Criticism, Inc." made clear R. S. Crane was endorsed in the essay explicitly), Ransom and his followers still considered themselves in league with the Chicago Aristotelians, so much that Ransom himself was publishing essays such as "The Cathartic Principle" and "The Mimetic Principle," both of them drawing on the *Poetics*, both of them included in *The World's Body*, and both of them cited in "The Philosophy of Literary Form" (116). And Aristotelians were still thinking of themselves as "intrinsic critics" as well, especially by comparison with the Marxist analysis so current at the time. When Burke referred to Chicago Aristotelians in his letter to Josephson, then, he was probably lumping together everyone who was practicing "intrinsic" criticism at the time, whether they practiced in Baton Rouge or in Chicago.[21] Both groups, he was convinced, insufficiently appreciated the power of literature as an oppositional force in a capitalist society, and the southerners in particular were overly fascinated by aesthetic formalism; but both also had important analytical techniques to contribute to the critic and criticism.

   For Burke was also reading and/or reviewing the work of many others who would come to be closely associated with the New Critics. Speaking of ambiguity: There were two reviews of William Empson's *Some Versions of the Pastoral* (in *Poetry* in March 1937 and in the May 1938 *New Republic*): his *Seven Types of Ambiguity*, as Burke's reviews indicated, in 1930 had articulated key New Critical reading procedures because Empson was a disciple of both Ransom (via Laura Riding) and I. A. Richards.[22] (Those procedures were based on the principle that ambiguity is a virtue, as Burke reminded the semanticists, and on the primacy of irony.) Another Burke review (in the October 1935 *Poetry*) praised Richards's *On Imagination* even though Richards agreed with Ransom's distinction between the emotive language of poetry and the denotative, referential language of science, and Burke and Richards enjoyed what Burke called "three hours of sheer enjoyment" talking together when Richards stopped in New York on his way to China in early April 1937 (Burke to R. P. Warren, April 11, 1937). Burke also read Tate's essays, reviewed Blackmur's *The Double Agent* (in the October 1936 *Poetry*), and appreciated Caroline Spurgeon's *Shakespeare's Imagery* (1935). Austin Warren, having befriended Burke by writing about him for the *Sewanee Review* in 1932, called Burke's attention to his own close reading of Crashaw's poetry (slated for publication by Louisiana State University Press) in a May 27, 1938, letter; and by the fall of 1940 Warren was asking Burke to comment on a manuscript that he was developing on "Literary Criticism": "My own interest as a teacher and critic is now—and has been for two or three years —in the formal & aesthetic approach to poetry" (Austin Warren to Burke, November 23, 1940). Robert Penn Warren, having begun a lengthy correspondence with Burke in 1935 in connection with his role as managing editor of the *Southern Review*, was continuing to exchange substantial letters with Burke about possible articles, about Burke's thoughts on Agrarianism, and about their mutual current thoughts on criticism.[23]

Consequently the famous extended title essay of *PLF* is in dialogue with social scientists, New Critics, and Chicago neo-Aristotelians—and positioned as a supplement to Marxist criticism. "The Philosophy of Literary Form" is an ambitious effort to build on the assets of all three developing schools (as well as on the strengths of a Marxist orientation) while avoiding the narrow points and blind spots of each: as Burke importantly sums up in his foreword, "when discussing [words] as modes of action, we must consider *both* . . . words in themselves *and* . . . the non-verbal scenes that support their acts. I shall be happy if the reader can say of this book [*PLF*] that, while always considering words as acts upon a scene, it avoids the *excess* of environmentalist schools which are usually so eager to trace the relationships between act and scene that they neglect to trace the structure of the [symbolic] act itself" (xvii). Or, to put it another way, in offering up the concepts of dream, chart, and prayer—"to be called either 'dialectical criticism' or 'dramatic criticism methodized'" (xx)—Burke allows for the urgencies of both "purely internal relationships" and external contexts, for "the substance of the [symbolic] act within itself [and] the substance of a literary act as placed upon a scene" (xviii). He offers to "assemble in one spot some basic rules of thumb—with diffidence; and not in the forlorn hope of silencing anyone" (69).

The first rule of thumb, a methodology drawn in a manner that New Critics could approve, requires a consideration of intrinsic matters indeed—the activity Burke calls "charting." In promoting charting, Burke was advising readers to attend to tensions and conflicts within the work: the critic should note "sets of equations" that "reinforce . . . opposing principles. . . . We discover these inductively, obediently, by 'statistical' inspection of the specific work to be analyzed" (69). "The first step . . . requires us to get our equations inductively, by tracing down the interrelationships as revealed by the objective structure of the book itself" (70). That tracing involves almost a literal statistics: "The two main symbols of the charting of structural relationships would be the sign for 'equals' and some such sign as the arrow ('from ___ to ___')" (74–75), and the critic employs "objective citation" and "scissor work" to work out the equations, the "clusters." Next, or even simultaneously, the critic should take account of "the dramatic alignment," that is, "what is vs. what"; since "works embody an agon, we may be admonished to look for some underlying imagery . . . through which the agonistic trial takes place" (83). In this area he was noting the New Critical attention to conflict and Coleridge's fondness for making extremes meet, but he was looking to the sciences, too, as well as to Freud. Indeed in some respects the critic's relation to the work (and its author) is analogous to the psychoanalyst's relation to the patient (Wess, 124). "A psychology of poetry . . . is about as near to the use of objective, empirical evidence as even the physical sciences" (21), he wrote. It was all an elaboration of terms that had begun to emerge in *P&C* and *ATH: joycing* (*P&C*, 113), *statistical approach* (*ATH*, II, 19), *the charting of clusters* (*ATH*, II, 77), and *chart* itself (*ATH*, II, 155).[24]

Burke's illustration of cluster analysis and charting—his detailed discussion of "the Ancient Mariner"—was itself completely in tune with New Critics, who were fascinated by Coleridge.[25] Richards's *On Imagination* is subtitled *Coleridge's Critical Theory*, and other New Critics would be drawn to Coleridge as well, in part because of Coleridge's staunch emphasis on "unity," a key New Critical concept, as Ransom's own comments on Coleridge indicate. Robert Penn Warren, Burke notes in *PLF*, had also been working on Coleridge while Burke was writing the book (xiii). By the summer of 1939, Burke was reviewing two books on Coleridge for the *New Republic*, E. K. Chambers's *Samuel Taylor Coleridge: A Biographical Study* and Lawrence Hanson's *The Life of S. T. Coleridge: The Early Years;* had spoken on Coleridge at Cooper Union (Houston Peterson to Burke, September 7, 1938); was giving R. S. Crane advice for exam questions on Coleridge for Chicago students

(Crane to Burke, May 20, 1939); and was declaring his own identification with Coleridge's career. In the summer of 1940, with *PLF* in press, he had become informed and expert enough on Coleridge to publish a review of Arthur N. Nethercot's *The Road to Tryermaine* (a study of Coleridge's "Cristabel") as well as an essay "On Musicality in Verse" in *Poetry*, where he drew on a broad knowledge of Coleridge's poetry besides "The Rime of the Ancient Mariner." Indeed, he even planned to write a monograph on Coleridge that would be a development of Richards's book, as he explained to Josephson on August 15, 1938, just as he was finishing up his work in Chicago. Burke further spoke to New Critics and their allies in other passages of "The Philosophy of Literary Form," as in the comments on Iago and Othello and then Brutus and Caesar (76) that nod toward Caroline Spurgeon and her *Shakespeare's Imagery* (explicitly invoked on page 70, in acknowledgment of her own use of charts and "charting"). And of course the lengthy comments on Robert Penn Warren's *Night Rider* (79, 84–89) speak even more directly to the *Southern Review* circle.[26]

If the comments on Coleridge and Shakespeare were chosen for their relevance to New Critics, Burke would nevertheless not stop at charting the work itself. As his discussion of "The Rime of the Ancient Mariner" indicates, Burke would also permit into his equations "extratextual" considerations as well—the poet's wife, his wrestling with drugs, his letters and essays. "Please get me straight," he lectured Ransom, Tate, and their developing school (not to mention Spurgeon). "I am not saying we need know of Coleridge's marital troubles and sufferings from drug addiction in order to appreciate 'The Ancient Mariner.' I am saying that, in trying to understand the psychology of the poetic act, we may introduce such knowledge, where it is available" (73). "I shall go even further," he added, this time including "our current neo-Aristotelian school" as among those he was addressing "as [my opponent]." "The focus of critical analysis must be upon the structure of the given work itself; . . . it is my contention, however, that [my] proposed method of analysis is equally relevant, whether you would introduce correlations from outside the given poetic integer or confine yourself to the charting of correlations within the integer" (74).[27]

That interest in going outside the poetic integer led Burke to propose a role for the social sciences in criticism, especially in the Freudian form of "dream" and in concepts drawn from anthropology and sociology such as *scapegoat*, *fetish*, and *victimage*. As he explained in a central section of "The Philosophy of Literary Form," "The broad outlines of our position might be codified thus: 1. We have the drama and the scene of the drama. . . . 2. The description of the scene is the role of the physical sciences; the description of the drama is the role of the social sciences. 3. The physical sciences are a calculus of events; the social sciences are a calculus of acts" (114). And "by

starting from a concern with the various acts and deployments involved in ritualistic acts of membership, purification, and opposition, we can most accurately discover 'what is going on' in poetry" (124). And so, as he had with his
close reading suggestions and as he would develop in "Freud—and the Analysis of Poetry," Burke explained how concepts such as the scapegoat, purification, rebirth, and the victim played out in the dream of the author of "The
Rime of the Ancient Mariner." The point is that close analysis of the New
Critical kind could only do so much: "As for the Blackmur or [Yvor] Winters
kind of analysis," he wrote, "at least twenty years ago I made the discovery
that, by the mere use of close attention, one should be able to write a hundred lines of exegesis for every single line of the original. Each verbal act is a
miracle, and a miracle is an infinity; hence a work of art is an infinite succession of infinites. Accordingly, I felt that the analytic method must be corrected by a counter-principle" (Burke to Knickerbocker, October 28, 1941).
That counter-principle involved psychology: readers must necessarily attend
to individual subconscious burdenings, such as Coleridge's difficulties with
drugs (figured in the albatross) as well as cultural myths such as the ones presented in "Electioneering in Psychoanalysia," the satiric fable that closes
"The Philosophy of Literary Form."[28]

Having explained how *chart* and *dream* were integral parts of the reading
act, Burke turned to *prayer*. Always is there an element of audience and persuasion that the reader-critic must attend to in his or her deliberations
because every communication is directed to a reader whose situation colors
the objective recounting of facts: "every document bequeathed to us by history must be treated as a strategy for encompassing a situation. . . . we shall
be automatically warned not to consider it in isolation, but as the answer or
rejoinder to assertions current in the situation in which it arose" (109). The
writer should be understood as a "medicine man": always "the poem is
designed to 'do something' for the poet and his readers, and . . . we can make
the most relevant observations about its design by considering the poem as
the embodiment of this act" (89). Those sentences, while not as emphasized
in *PLF* as *dream* and *chart*,[29] could nonetheless be read as a prod to the
Chicago Aristotelians to read beyond structure and genre (though the *Poetics*
was always an inducement to look at effects), and to the New Critics to go
beyond a consideration of the poem as "verbal icon." For Burke, the literary
work was ever an act, never an artifact.

Of course it would be wrong to poise the social sciences (rooted in pragmatist experimentalism) too firmly against the New Critics and the Aristotelians, and all of them against Marxists, particularly during the intellectual
ferment of the late 1930s. Aristotle and neo-Aristotelians, after all, approached
the world as empirically as any pragmatist, and New Critics also had a taste for

method, objectivity, and means of validation. Aristotle understood people as fundamentally social and political, in anticipation of Marx. Burke, still resistant to antithesis, was not so much in opposition to New Critics, social scientists, Marxists, and neo-Aristotelians, then, as in dialogue with them, complementing them and offering mediating points of view. "I suppose I should dedicate [*PLF*] to mine enemies," he joked to Norbert Guterman (November 25, 1939), "since it is framed throughout to answer (explicitly or implicitly) the critical automatisms that have rankled me most (though the piece is stylized in the affirmative, rather than as a rebuttal of the negative)." The ways of reading that he was offering in *PLF* accommodated the emphases and avoided the errors of each school. A reader should chart or index key terms, and note the associations evoked by those terms (cluster analysis); should note oppositions by attending to conflicts in the work (agon analysis); should see the work as the unburdening of an author's internal tensions (psychoanalysis); and should appreciate the work as prayer by noting how its audience and occasion have shaped it (rhetorical and cultural analysis). In short Burke's "new critical" commitments and his allegiance to social ends of poetry make his heteroglossic *PLF* both a riposte and a sympathetic contribution to fervent Marxists and to uncompromising New Critics and neo-Aristotelians. It is a key instance of "Burke's desire to blend modernist aesthetics with cultural critique" (Jay, *Blues*, 16).

The Next Phase

As the summer of 1938 wound to a close, Burke began to hear intimations that he might be offered a permanent position at Chicago: "What worries me," he told Cowley (the worries developed out of the hard work of lecturing), "is that there are tentative offers in the offing—so I may . . . have to face again the decision I faced so blithely twenty years ago, when I walked out of college into Agro-Bohemianism. . . . I am quite ennobled at the thought that I have been proposed, what with my complete lack of academic badges, and my two hours of cocktail-stimulated shouting at [President] Hutchins. . . . [But] if I were a teacher by profession, my main ambition in life would be to hurry up and become 65. . . . Rights and obligations. I know that they can never be separated. . . . What I want is something like this *every once in a while*, not regularly" (August 1, 1938; see also August 8 and Burke to Josephson, August 5).[30] Not only was that summer helping Burke to think through the ideas that would land him in his next phase—dramatism and his "motives project"—but he would begin looking for a situation that ultimately delivered him to Bennington College in 1943.

Back home from Chicago, Burke took up the projects that had germinated there. In addition to several reviews, he finished "Semantic and Poetic Meaning" in September. He immediately turned to "Freud—and the Analysis of

Poetry" and then, early in 1939, to his study of Hitler's *Mein Kampf* and to other side projects, notably the third American Writers' Congress. The prospects of a book on Coleridge also continued to interest him.

The Third American Writers' Congress

The summers he spent in Chicago and Syracuse did not remove Kenneth Burke completely from his New York scenes and connections, of course. As Hitler and Mussolini moved the world closer to war, Burke continued as a loyal and active member of the League of American Writers by contributing to *Direction* and making important contributions to the third American Writers' Congress.

Direction was not the official League of American Writers publication, but the monthly was closely identified with the league and with the WPA beginning with its first appearance in December 1937. It published league and WPA business, covered the Spanish Civil War, reviewed theater, dance, and cinema, and reported on League activities and membership; with its glossy format it reached out toward a broad Popular Front audience. When *Partisan Review* reorganized late in 1937 in order to distance itself from Stalin, from *New Masses*, and from the *New Republic*, *Direction* rose to fill the void with a publication loyal to the party line that persisted, albeit on a shoestring, until the mid-1940s. At the urging of one of its editors, Tom Cochran, an New York University history professor and administrator whom Burke had befriended, Burke worked closely with *Direction*, contributing one of his best-known essays, "Literature as Equipment for Living," to the third issue, in April 1938; appropriately, in it Burke provided the fundamentals of a "sociological criticism" that denied the existence of anything like a "pure literature" and that made the essay a natural for reprinting in *PLF*. "Questions for Critics" appeared in *Direction* in May–June 1939, "Embargo" late that same year, and other items on a regular basis thereafter. Late in 1940 Burke joined the editorial board and for a time even took on the role of chief fiction editor, which he held until late the following year, when he begged off because the job was taking too much time.[1]

Direction enthusiastically publicized the third American Writers' Congress in the spring and early summer of 1939. The political situations surrounding the first and second congresses had made those meetings highly charged, even confrontational affairs, as we have indicated. But no comparable controversies animated the third. In contrast the third American Writers' Congress, Friday, June 2, to June 4, 1939, took place against a depressing and "ominous [political] background" that everyone understood all too soberly and clearly (Cowley, "Notes," 192). War seemed inevitable—the official call for the congress went "forth at a time when the world fear[ed] the outbreak of more invasions and wars"—and everywhere fascism appeared triumphant: Franco had by then secured his victory in the Spanish Civil War; Hitler, in the wake of the Munich accords of September 1938, was arming aggressively and finalizing his military alliance with Mussolini; and against this threat British Prime Minister Chamberlain still seemed impotent, his distrust of Moscow precluding any realistic chance of an alliance among Britain, France, and Russia against Hitler. (Unbeknownst to anyone, Stalin had thus opened secret negotiations with Hitler himself.) Japan was already making war in China and in other areas of the East.

In the face of this news there was comparatively little talk of world politics at the third congress, at least not after the opening public session at Carnegie Hall, when the lately deposed president of Czechoslovakia, Eduard Benes, spoke to 2,500 observers alongside LAW officers Donald Ogden Stewart and Langston Hughes. Even though a great many international delegates attended, most notably Louis Aragon, Thomas Mann (who also spoke at the first session),[2] and the host of "writers in exile" who reported on the environment that existed for writers in Spain, Italy, Czechoslovakia, and Germany, the 450 or so delegates at the private sessions mostly attended instead to practical matters associated with the writer's craft. The general theme related to keeping writers out of an ivory tower (something no one was holding out for, anyway) and reflected Stewart's Hollywood interests: "how mass audiences can most effectively be reached by existing [new] media, such as motion pictures, radio, and television" (Call). Three of the most valuable congress sessions thus involved the discussion of radio and film documentaries (in a "New Mediums in Verse" session that was organized by Genevieve Taggard),[3] the reading of a radio drama ("No Help Wanted") in which the voices of Herbert Hoover and Henry Ford were juxtaposed with voices of the needy, and a presentation of Pare Lorenz's documentary *The River*, produced in the spirit of the New Deal.[4] An inoffensive commitment to encouraging democracy seemed an appropriate subtheme under the circumstances: the Call emphasized how LAW had worked "actively in behalf of democratic culture" and promised everlasting "cooperation with all democratic and progressive forces"; and a summary of the event in *Direction* proclaimed that "democratic culture—its defense against fascism and reaction, and its development as a living heritage of the American people—was the keynote of the . . . Congress." An unsigned *New Republic* account of the event (June 14, 1939, 143) emphasized that the congress confined itself to practical, technical matters that writers would need to understand if they were to reach a mass audience—how to produce cheaper books, how to secure better translations, how to resist censorship, how to keep theater tickets reasonably priced, how to write effectively for radio, drama, and film documentaries.

Even though his second son, Michael, was born May 3 and the family had just removed for the summer to Andover, Kenneth Burke was an active presence at the third congress. Along with Cowley, Henry Hart, Lester Cohen, Joseph Freeman, Ralph Roeder, Dorothy Brewster, John Hyde Preston, and Harry Carlisle, Burke served on the committee to draft the call for the congress, and it was very much Burke's Popular Front idea to emphasize "democracy" as a nonpartisan theme

(Folsom to Burke, April 11, 1939); he played a central role in formulating the final document and was among the prominent signers. More important, Burke spoke at the final general session of the congress on June 4, again alongside Cowley and Joseph Freeman (as well as with A. B. Magil, coeditor with Freeman of *New Masses*, and journalist Vincent Sheean). Burke's memorable presentation, very much in keeping with the conference theme of democracy and the conference emphasis on how to appeal to mass audiences, was an abridged version of "The Rhetoric of Hitler's 'Battle,'" the complete version of which was later included in *PLF.*

An unabridged translation of Hitler's *Mein Kampf* was first published in English on February 28, 1939. Based on the understanding that Americans needed to see firsthand what Hitler was up to, both to arouse American opposition and to disarm fascist sympathizers in the United States, the edition was widely publicized and reviewed; the Book-of-the-Month Club even made it a featured selection. (LAW had initially resisted the publication of *Mein Kampf* in English on the grounds that it would encourage fascist movements in the United States: Folsom, 73.) Burke immediately began an analysis of the book (his self-annotated copy is still shelved at Andover), and by March 24, he had offered his essay to *Harper's,* whose editor rejected it promptly, if reluctantly, on account of its similarity to other items on Hitler and *Mein Kampf* that he had already accepted (George Leighton to Burke, March 24, 1939). Eager to place the essay while it was still timely, Burke offered it immediately to the *Southern Review,* where it appeared (without its notes, which were restored for the *PLF* reprint) in July. Two summary pages of the essay also were included in the record of the third congress, *Fighting Words* (146–48), which appeared in August—just as Hitler and Stalin, their nonaggression pact in place, were preparing to carve up Poland.[5]

Burke's prescient and timely commentary on Hitler's "Battle" was received well at the time and remains widely admired. Burke had no trouble understanding how Hitler had concocted his "Nazi magic," and while other reviewers—the "vandalistic reviewers" he places himself against in his first paragraph—were commenting on *Mein Kampf* as the ravings of a crude madman or as a prophesy of Hitler's international intentions, Burke instead sought to help Americans see through Hitler's rhetorical appeals lest Americans themselves fall for the same appeals: "A people trained in pragmatism should want to inspect this magic" (2). Huey Long had been murdered and thus silenced since Burke's first Writers' Congress speech in 1935, but Father Coughlin's right-wing language had only grown more extreme and influential with the wearing on of the decade, and he was not the only potential American demagogue to worry about in the months following Munich.

The essay remains a fine introduction to Burke's critical methodology, for it indeed "uses everything" that he was recommending. "The Rhetoric of Hitler's 'Battle'" employs the techniques of close reading that Brooks and his fellow New Critics could admire (Brooks to Burke, August 8, 1939). It appreciates that the social, reformist nature of the critic's role that Burke had emphasized in *ATH* required him to provide historical criticism attentive to Hitler's rhetorical situation. It included an analysis of Hitler's reliance on destructive antitheses. And it employed two developing concepts: identification and scapegoating. Burke uses the term *identification* several times in his discussion of Hitler (12, 17) in a way that reinforces his use of the term in "The Philosophy of Literary Form" and that anticipates the more elaborated notion of the concept expressed later in *A Rhetoric of Motives;* and he points to Hitler's employment of the scapegoat (4; 9–10, 15) in a way that builds on his use of the scapegoat in "The Philosophy of Literary Form." (On the other hand, Burke certainly did not coin the term *scapegoat,* and many others during the 1930s recognized that Hitler was using the Jews as scapegoats. Burke himself referred to Hitler's "scapegoating of Jews" and the "scapegoat mechanism" as early as March 24, 1933, in a letter to George Soule, and included the concept in *P&C,* 14.) Ralph Ellison, then twenty-five years old, was among those in attendance for Burke's session on "The Writer and Politics." Several years later he could still recall vividly the impact of Burke's presentation: "My real debt lies to you in the many things I've learned (and continue to learn) from your work. . . . That is a debt I shall never stop paying back and it begins back in the thirties when you read the rhetoric of 'Hitler's Battle' before the League of American Writers. I believe you were the only speaker out of the whole group who was concerned with writing *and politics* rather than writing as an *excuse* for politics." Ellison noted that he "was writing a novel now"—*Invisible Man*—and that "if it is worthwhile it will be my most effective means of saying thanks. Anything else seems to me inadequate" (Ellison to Burke, November 23, 1945).

While the third American Writers' Congress by all accounts was well attended and well received, the League of American Writers was becoming increasingly irrelevant. In August, even before the invasion of Poland would embarrass the remaining Stalinists once and for all, Cowley pronounced LAW dead. In a review of the conference volume, *Fighting Words* ("In Memoriam"), he expressed admiration for the "extraordinary" final congress, but he also vented his irritation that the congress and LAW had been considering the coming war as about imperialism and not about the class war. That is, the leadership of LAW was treating Great Britain and Germany as equally guilty of colonialism instead of opposing Hitler and defending the Left. Cowley consequently announced his resignation from LAW, joining what had become a general exodus. LAW continued for a time, on life support—there was even a fourth American Writers' Congress in June 1941, which emphasized peace initiatives—but that was the last time LAW was heard from. Kenneth Burke did not participate.

1. For details on Burke's connection with *Direction* we examined issues of the magazine, letters to Burke by Thomas Cochran and editor Marguerite Harris in the Kenneth Burke Papers, and Denning, 93–94.

2. After this session Burke had the chance to meet the man whose novel *Death in Venice* he had translated nearly two decades before.

3. According to Weaver (102), the session helped to inspire the documentary passages in Williams's *Paterson*.

4. *Direction*, May/June 1939. This issue of *Direction*, with a picture of a crumbling ivory tower on the cover, was given over to several special reports on the third congress. The issue also includes the congress program and official call; see also *New Republic*, May 24, 1939, 79. In addition to that issue of *Direction*, in our account of the third congress we have especially depended on the many planning documents related to the congress sent to Burke by Franklin Folsom (Kenneth Burke Papers).

5. Our summary of the circumstances around the production of the Hitler analysis largely derives from Pauley's fine but as-yet-unpublished essay. Our citations are to the version published in *PLF*. Burke's "Battle" essay also appeared that summer in a collection entitled *This Generation*. Eda Lou Walton, one of the coeditors of the collection, asked for permission to reprint it there for fifty dollars (letter to Burke May 9, 1939).

But he was also thinking about publishing what would become *The Philosophy of Literary Form*. (Pieces of that manuscript, because they included long analyses of Coleridge, ultimately precluded the possibility of a separate Coleridge book.) From late 1937 Burke had been contemplating the subject of his title essay, and he therefore conceived of his Chicago course in literary criticism under the rubric "The Psychology of Literary Form," "discussing the processes of appeal that underlie esthetic structures":

> I should begin [my course], in short, with the kind of material I consider in my Lexicon Rhetoricae (in "Counter-Statement"). But I should fill out with many concrete examples. Much stress would be placed on the internal organization of literary works. But in discussing the way in which character-recipes depend upon social values in general, I should also consider the extra-literary factors that operate in giving symbolic structures their effectiveness. I believe, in other words, that technical and sociological criticism can be shown to be all of a piece. The stress would be upon how effects are got, rather than upon what effects should be got. Ballistics, not politics. Not exhortation, but diagnosis. (Burke to McKeon, December 3, 1937)

That this description stands in well as an abstract of the finished "The Philosophy of Literary Form" indicates that Burke had conceived of his essay well before his Chicago course. By the end of August 1939, when he had returned from trying out his materials again at another Syracuse seminar organized by Leonard Brown, he was confident of his argument and ready to write in earnest: "After getting started on the Coleridge material," he reported to McKeon (who was wondering about the Coleridge book project), "I had to lay it aside in preparation for some lectures at Syracuse. And since they seemed to go well, on my return I wrote them up (borrowing the magic synecdoche, I mean title, 'Philosophy of Literary Form,' in which I not only summarized my perspective but also did a lot in the 'what to look for, how, when, where, and why' mode, on the basis of said perspective, with the whole focused on matters of literary analysis)" (Burke to McKeon, August 27, 1939). How, when, where, and why Burke's "magic synecdoche" shifted from *psychology* to *philosophy* of literary form is an intersting matter for speculation, given his repeated claims in the title essay itself that critics are able to "[discuss] the full nature" of a poetic act only insofar as they "understand the psychology of the poetic act" (*PLF*, 73).

Shirley Jackson Meets Kenneth Burke

Shirley Jackson met Stanley Edgar Hyman while they were both students at Syracuse University; the two were married in the fall of 1940. Having encountered Burke in the summer of 1939, when Burke was teaching at Syracuse in Leonard Brown's summer seminar, Hyman brought his new wife to Andover on October 19 when Burke invited them to visit (Burke to Hyman, October 9 and 16, 1940). It was the beginning of a lengthy relationship between Burke, Hyman, and Jackson, sealed when Hyman emphasized Burke in his first book of criticism *The Armed Vision* and when Burke later oiled the appointment of Hyman to the faculty at Bennington College.

On November 1, 1940, Hyman sent a thank-you letter to Burke, enclosing with it a sketch made by his wife (depicting Hyman and Jackson dizzied by their reading of Burke) and a poem by Jackson that has fun with some of Burke's critical terminology.

> Here is a man who shared the pillows
> Of a million girls and a million fillows.
> When they reproached him for being callous, he
> Said "It is just my pathetic phallus, see."
>
> Here is a man who shared the pillows
> Of a million girls and a million fillows.
> When they reproached him with being like ice,
> He sadly replied "It's a bridging device."
>
> Here is a man who shared the pillows
> Of a million girls and a million fillows.
> When they accused him of harboring lice
> He replied "It's my only salvation device."
>
> Here is a man who shared the pillows
> Of a million girls and a million fillows.

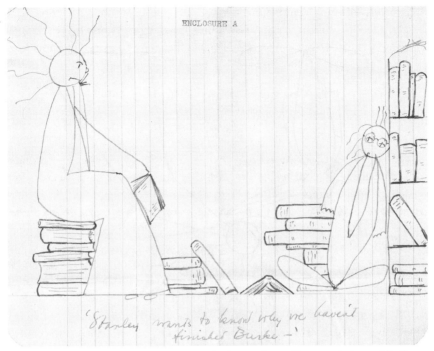

A sketch about Kenneth Burke by Shirley Jackson. By permission of Sadie Dewitt; from the Kenneth Burke Papers, Rare Books and Manuscripts, Paterno Library, Pennsylvania State University

> When they told him his balls weren't metching
> He told them "It's just casuistic stretching."
>
> Here is a man who shared the pillows
> Of a million girls and a million fillows.
> When they agreed he was very nimble
> He shrugged and told them "I'm stealing a symbol."
>
> Here is a man who shared the pillows
> Of a million girls and a million fillows.
> When they called him a catholic layer,
> He smirked "It's my method of secular prayer."

As early as April 20, 1939, Robert Penn Warren had informed Burke that Louisiana State University Press might be interested in publishing a collection of Burke's essays, so he now, with "The Philosophy of Literary Form" completed, sent a feeler to Brooks to explore options:

Recently Warren suggested that the University Press might consider publishing a collection of my essays. I asked for time, on the grounds that a friend wanted to try two publishers here. He did; they were friendly, but both called for a "unit volume." (Norton and Viking.) So I have asked myself: "Why not submit my unwieldy essay to the editors of So. Rev., with the idea that they might read it from a double standpoint, (a) the possibility of serialization in the gazette, in a cut form, and (b) the possibility of its being used as the main item in a collection." (Burke to Brooks, August 21, 1939)

Brooks and his colleagues considered the manuscript and their options and ultimately decided on plan (b). By December Burke had proposed a complete list of contents for his book (Burke to Erskine, December 1, 1939), and by March 1940 he had received a contract for *The Philosophy of Literary Form*. Then it was just a matter of details: the book went into production with Erskine keeping an eye on things (Erskine to Burke, July 17, 1940); Leonard Brown was recruited to prepare an index (Brown to Burke, November 19, 1940); page proofs were available for review by Christmas; a last-minute preface was added thereafter; and Burke received his fresh new copies of *PLF* shortly after April 15, 1941 (M. M. Wilkerson to Burke, March 31, 1941). Over a period of almost exactly a decade, Burke had published no less than five stunningly original and intriguing books: *Counter-Statement, Towards a Better Life, Permanence and Change, Attitudes toward History,* and *The Philosophy of Literary Form*.

But Burke was not looking backward. His engagement with Chicago Aristotelians and social scientists would deepen through the next two decades. While seeing *PLF* through the production process, Burke began to plan seriously yet another book that he originally saw as a kind of sequel to *P&C* and *ATH*, a notion that had occurred to him naturally as he finished *ATH*. In October 22, 1937, he was already describing a prospective book "on human relations" to William Knickerbocker, and in May 1939 he professed in a letter to Ransom (intended as a contributor's note accompanying the publication of "The Calling of the Tune" in *Kenyon Review*), that he was "now writing a book 'On Human Relations,' the third part of a critical trilogy including *Permanence and Change* and *Attitudes toward History*" (May 22, 1939). And so, in the process of publishing *PLF,* he turned seriously in the summer and fall of 1939 to

> an analysis of the stylistic strategies of constitutions (their ways of giving us [book] club offers of contradictory wishes, of presenting such contradictions pleasantly in the form of balances and complements, of smuggling in concepts of substance for the grounding of commands, etc.). [I] got into this through deciding that a representative public act would be a good theme to open the

subject of Human Relations in general—and now I maintain that few characters in modern fiction have the novelistic possibilities of the Constitution, considered as a character. "Mr. Constitution—meet an old admirer of yours, Mr. Quixote."

Now I begin to glimpse possibilities of being able to refer back, in all parts of the book, to one or another aspect of the constitutional strategy (thus using the theme not merely as an opening, but as an organizing device throughout). If I succeed, lo! I shall have written the first sociology (or characterology?) "strictly based on the Constitution." (Burke to Guterman, November 25, 1939)

The following summer, Burke explained more completely what he had in mind to the sociologist Lewis A. Dexter:[31]

In trying to organize my book "On Human Relations," [I] have found that I had to write a general introduction attempting to characterize strategies of motivation by paradigm. . . . My main regret, as regards the serviceability of your article for my particular purposes, is that you did not relate the matter back to the metaphysical theories of cause.

Again, however, it is my contention that the issue should be approached through the "dramatic" or "dialectic" perspective. I.e., perhaps via the five major terms: act, scene, agent, agency, purpose. . . . For instance, the ways in which, since the five terms overlap, philosophers of different schools will select one or another of the five and reduce them all to that. . . . The point is: since I did not "invent" the "dramatic" or "dialectic" perspective, I feel that I can force it upon people without too great a charge of self-love and coxcombry. I do believe, however, that I have come pretty close to discovering just what the damned word "dialectic" really means . . . and I believe that it has occurred to no one else (in recent years!) to sit down and ask himself what it would mean to say that "life is a drama," and just how this would be carried through all the theories of motivation. (September 2, 1940)

The book Burke planned in order to elaborate these ideas would of course become *A Grammar of Motives*; the intimations of dramatism in *ATH* and *PLF* would become the full-bodied dramatism of Burke's next phase. *The Philosophy of Literary Form*, "thirty-minded" indeed, would come to be seen as that third item in the Depression-era trilogy including *P&C* and *ATH*. And the *Grammar* would develop instead into the first book in yet another trilogy, "On Human Relations," alongside *A Rhetoric of Motives* and *A Symbolic of Motives*.

But that's a story for another book.

An Informal Chronology

What follows is an unsystematic listing of events in the life of Kenneth Burke between 1931 and 1940. The chronology derives chiefly from evidence in correspondence to and from Burke, some of it published in Jay's *Selected Correspondence* and much of it in the Kenneth Burke Papers at Penn State as well as in other collections indicated in the Works Cited. But it also makes use of biographical information scattered in Skodnick, Woodcock, Rountree, and Bak, bibliographies by Frank and Thames, and memoirs such as Josephson's *Infidel*, Cowley's *Exile's Return* and *Dream of the Golden Mountains*, Mangione's *An Ethnic at Large*, and the diary of Marya Zaturenska (at Syracuse). The chronology also includes references to certain public and publishing events that seem likely to us to have been important to Burke.

1931

Pearl Buck, *The Good Earth*.
William Faulkner, *The Hamlet*.
Virginia Woolf, *The Waves*.
Robert Frost's *Collected Poems* wins the Pulitzer Prize.
Empire State Building constructed.
Yale publishes Col. Arthur Woods's *Dangerous Drugs: The World Fight against Illicit Traffic in Narcotics*, large portions of which Burke wrote.
JANUARY 31: In the *New Republic*, Edmund Wilson's "Appeal to Progressives" recommends that writers regard the capitalist system as unfixable and endorse communism based on democracy, after the example of the Soviet Union.
FEBRUARY: Burke's essay "Boring from Within," his reply to Wilson's "Appeal to Progressives," is in the *New Republic*. *New Masses* publishes an account of the Second World Conference of the International Union of Revolutionary Writers, held in Kharkov, U.S.S.R., the previous November and discusses the conference's implications for the magazine and the John Reed Club.
MARCH: In letters to various literary friends, Burke is considering starting a new literary magazine (to be financed by Sibley Watson as a kind of successor to the *Dial*); because of internal squabbles and financial shortages, the enterprise never materializes.

APRIL: Burke signs a contract for the publication of *Counter-Statement*. He spends the next few months finishing and revising its chapters and preparing the final manuscript.

At a meeting at Theodore Dreiser's place, the National Committee for the Defense of Political Prisoners—a Communist Party writers' group—is formed.

MAY: With Malcolm Cowley, Jack Wheelwright, Robert Coates, Matthew Josephson, and Evan Shipman, Burke visits Yaddo, the artist's colony near Saratoga Springs, New York, because Cowley and Josephson have organized a gathering to hammer out a collective memoir of the 1920s. While the others enjoy themselves, Cowley continues work on what would become *Exile's Return*.

JUNE: With *Counter-Statement* in production, Burke moves to complete and publish his novel *Towards a Better Life*. *Hound and Horn* spoofs Burke's "Boring from Within."

JULY: Burke's essay "Redefinitions" (revised in *Counter-Statement* as "Applications of the Terminology") appears in the July, August, and September issues of the *New Republic*.

AUGUST: Burke is working to complete *Towards a Better Life* and is negotiating with a publisher.

SEPTEMBER: *Counter-Statement* comes off the presses, and *Towards a Better Life* is completed. Burke publishes a review of Ouspensky's *A New Model of the Universe* in the *New Republic*.

Britain abandons the gold standard, touching off more financial panic.

OCTOBER: On October 6, Burke's daughter Happy undergoes successful surgery of some kind; on October 7, Harcourt, Brace, agrees to publish *Towards a Better Life*. Burke tells William Carlos Williams on October 15 that Burke is planning to write "a political tirade"—likely a reference to what would become *Auscultation, Creation, and Revision*.

On Halloween, Burke speaks before the John Reed Club in New York. Burke's New York address is 381 Bleecker Street.

NOVEMBER: Reviews of *Counter-Statement* begin to appear. Burke writes a clarification of his 1920s dealings with Gorham Munson ("Munsoniana"), published in the *New Republic* as a corrective to parts of *Exile's Return* that Cowley has placed in the *New Republic* and as a mollification of Munson.

Under the auspices of the National Committee for the Defense of Political Prisoners, Dreiser, John Dos Passos, and other writers go to the aid of striking miners in Harlan County, Kentucky. They collect testimony from miners, published in Dos Passos's *Harlan Miners Speak* (1932).

DECEMBER: In the *New Republic* Burke publishes a "Counterblast" to Granville Hicks's review of *Counter-Statement*.

1932

John Dos Passos, *1919*.
James T. Farrell, *Young Lonigan*.
William Faulkner, *Light in August*.
Culture and Crisis (manifesto of League of Professional Groups for Foster and Ford).

Lindbergh kidnapping.

JANUARY: Reviews of *Counter-Statement* are appearing.

Gorham Munson's account of activities in the 1920s involving Burke begins appearing as "The Fledgling Years" in *Sewanee Review.*

JANUARY 28: Harcourt, Brace, Jovanovich holds a party to celebrate the publication of *Towards a Better Life.* Among the invited are Malcolm Cowley, Matthew Josephson, Jack Wheelwright, Isidor Schneider, Robert Cantwell, Robert Coates, Gilbert Seldes, Horace Gregory, William Carlos Williams, E. E. Cummings, and Slater Brown.

FEBRUARY AND MARCH: Spending the winter in New York City at 381 Bleecker Street and beginning to contemplate seriously what would become *Auscultation, Creation, and Revision,* Burke receives regular invitations to John Reed Club meetings and symposia. He attends regularly and gives a short talk at the JRC on February 28. He goes to parties at Joe Gould's Jones Street loft. Meantime, Cowley, Waldo Frank, Edmund Wilson, and other writers mount a second expedition to help striking miners in Pineville, Kentucky, near Harlan. When Frank is beaten, the episode is widely publicized, and a New York City rally is held in support.

FEBRUARY 25: Burke gives a presentation on *Towards a Better Life* for Contemporary Arts, a group that had selected *TBL* as its featured selection for February.

APRIL 26: Hart Crane commits suicide at the age of thirty-three.

LATE APRIL: Cowley publishes "The Poet and the World," a *New Republic* review of Dos Passos's *1919* that is also a commentary on *Towards a Better Life.*

MAY 1: A May Day parade in New York attracts between 35,000 and 100,000 marchers. Cowley marches with the John Reed contingent.

MAY 15: Burke and wife, Lily, return to Andover for the summer, though they retain the place on Bleecker Street (which Cantwell occupies).

LATE MAY: For two hundred dollars, Burke agrees to edit and ghostwrite some work for a recently deceased psychologist named Parker, at the invitation of his widow—the work to be completed in the following winter.

JUNE: Malcolm Cowley remarries. Burke, while reading I. A. Richards's *The Meaning of Meaning* and fixing up an Andover barn into living quarters, finishes a long review of a Glenway Wescott book for the *New Republic.* He begins formulating specific ideas and segments that would take shape in *Auscultation, Creation, and Revision.*

Hoovervilles are appearing in every city. Thousands of jobless veterans of World War I—calling themselves the Bonus Expeditionary Force—march on Washington to seek relief. At the end of July, they are routed and dispersed by federal troops led by Douglas MacArthur. Elsewhere, so many unemployed are jumping boxcars to look for work in other towns that railroads begin to add empty and open boxcars to trains so that freeloading passengers will not disturb loaded cars or fall off.

JULY 20: William Carlos Williams rejects "Trial Translation," a redoing of a scene from Shakespeare's *Twelfth Night,* which Burke had submitted to him for *Pagany.*

JULY AND AUGUST: As the economic depression deepens (e.g., with 700,000 unemployed in Chicago, the city goes bankrupt and ceases paying municipal workers), Burke continues work on *Auscultation, Creation, and Revision.* He attends regular parties and throws one for Haakon Chevalier.

SEPTEMBER: When the Burke daughters return to New York with their mother for the school year, Burke remains at Andover to complete *Auscultation* as well as several unsigned short pieces for the *New Republic*.

OCTOBER: Many writers and intellectuals on the Left (e.g., Sherwood Anderson, Erskine Caldwell, Malcolm Cowley, Countee Cullen, John Dos Passos, Theodore Dreiser, Waldo Frank, Sidney Hook, Langston Hughes, Matthew Josephson, Isidor Schneider, Edmund Wilson) endorse William Z. Foster and James W. Ford, the Communist Party candidates for president and vice president, and toward the same goal publish the pamphlet *Culture and Crisis* (subtitle: "An Open Letter to Writers, Artists, Teachers, Physicians, Engineers, Scientists, and Other Professional Workers of America"); Burke is asked to endorse Foster and Ford as well but declines (he probably preferred Norman Thomas).

Burke completes *Auscultation* and sends it out—without success—to various publishers. He returns to New York City and 381 Bleecker Street for the winter.

NOVEMBER: Franklin Roosevelt is elected president with about 23 million votes. Hoover wins 16 million votes, Thomas 1 million, and the Communists about 100,000.

Burke sends "Trial Translation" to *Virginia Quarterly Review*, where it is rejected, along with "Antony's Oration" (published two years later as "Antony in Behalf of the Play"). A book review by Burke appears in the *Nation*. Thinking *Auscultation* "muddled," Burke ponders what his next major project will be.

DECEMBER: In England, A. O. Orage accepts "Trial Translation" (through the intercession of Gorham Munson) for the February issue of his new *New English Weekly*, but *Hound and Horn* rejects *Auscultation*. Burke's review of Chevalier's *The Ironic Temper* appears in the *New Republic*.

1933

Ulysses allowed into the United States.
Ezra Pound, *Cantos*.
Granville Hicks, *The Great Tradition*.
Gertrude Stein, *Autobiography of Alice B. Toklas*.
Alfred Korzybski, *Science and Sanity*.
Reports of mass starvation in the Soviet Union.
Repeal of Prohibition.

JANUARY: Burke submits "Spring during Crisis" to *Hound and Horn* and, under the name "Ethel Howardell," a spoof entitled "For Bond Money" that is carried in the *New Republic* on January 4. (Another spoof, mocking the need for "sound money," is also submitted to the *Nation* and the *New Republic* but never published.) A review by C. K. Ogden of Bentham's *Theory of Fictions* is in the *Nation*.

JANUARY 30: Adolf Hitler is installed as chancellor of Germany.

With the editor and book promoter Franklin Spier, Burke is attempting to launch an enterprise known as "Manuscript Editions"—a scheme to publish important books that face the prospect of limited sales because of the Depression. The idea ultimately fails for lack of economic support even though Burke had spoken to Marianne Moore, William Carlos Williams, Waldo Frank, Alfred Kreymborg,

Edwin Seaver, Jack Wheelwright, and many other writers about possible contribu-
tions and received encouraging responses, including a submission from Williams.
FEBRUARY: Burke probably attends a discussion meeting between the Trotskyist Harry
Roskolenkeir and New York Stalinists. The national banking crisis deepens;
in response, Burke looks into the proposed reforms known as "Social Credit" and
conceives of his satire "Bankers Arise," written in March and published in April.
FEBRUARY 27: Reichstag burns in Berlin.
MARCH 4: Roosevelt is sworn in as president and inaugurates the New Deal—as a bank
holiday is declared. Nearly simultaneously Hitler gains dictatorial power in the
aftermath of the Reichstag burning. Thomas Mann leaves Germany.
MARCH 6: The second trial of the "Scottsboro boys" opens in Alabama.

Several letters indicate that Burke is drinking heavily and maintaining a kind of
dual marriage to Lily and Libbie: the possibility of a second marriage waxes as the
first wanes.

Burke begins conceiving of the book that becomes *Permanence and Change*.
APRIL: *Sewanee Review* carries Austin Warren's lengthy essay, "Kenneth Burke: His
Mind and Art." Burke's relationship with *Sewanee Review* has begun.

Malcolm Cowley is finishing *Exile's Return*, his memoir of the 1920s.

Burke's review of I. A. Richards's *Mencius of the Mind* appears in the *Nation*, and
he begins an essay on C. K. Ogden for the *New Republic* that is ultimately published
the following year. He is also trying to launch an idea for a magazine on economics, to be called the *New State*, but the notion fizzles.

Nelson Rockefeller refuses to permit Diego Rivera to complete his mural at the
new Rockefeller Center because it contains a portrait of Lenin.
MAY 1: The New York May Day parade attracts between 50,000 and 100,000 partici-
pants.
MAY: Burke returns to Andover with the advent of spring, but the family remains on
Bleecker Street until school is out. His "Bankers Arise" satire appears in *Americana*.

Book burnings break out in Germany; included among the interdicted works
are ones by authors that Burke had translated: Thomas Mann, Emil Ludwig, Ste-
fan Zweig.

Anvil, for the next three years a leading proletarian literary magazine, begins
publication under the editorship of Jack Conroy.
JUNE: The second installment of Warren's "Kenneth Burke: His Mind and Art"
appears in *Sewanee Review*. The National Recovery Act gives workers broad rights
to unionize. Burke has a bit of an epistolary feud with Cowley, who is writing near
Tate's farm on the Kentucky-Tennessee border.

Burke finishes "The Negro's Pattern of Life" for next month's *Saturday Review*.
He works hard on *Permanence and Change* all summer. In a letter to Cowley, he
reports that he "hammered out 46,000 words . . . between June 20 and July 16,"
and he hopes to have a draft of the book finished by Labor Day.
JULY: Burke publishes a review of Ludovici's *The Secret of Laughter* (written in May) in
Hound and Horn.
AUGUST 19–20: Burke and Lily host a large party at Andover. Soon after, Lily returns
to New York with the Burke daughters for the school year.

SEPTEMBER: Burke writes an essay on a controversy between Archibald MacLeish and Cowley, "War, Response, and Contradiction," but when the *New Republic* decides not to publish it, he turns to the *Symposium*. Another essay "on work" is also completed but never published.

OCTOBER: By now Burke has completed part 1 of *Permanence and Change* and has drafted large portions of the rest. Back in New York, at 78 Bank Street, he begins to try to publish pieces of the book.

New Masses, edited by Mike Gold since 1928, collapses. (It is reborn in 1934.) The *Nation* signs up Burke to do music criticism. His first item, on Schoenberg, appears in November. Burke reviews Roger Vercel's novel *In Sight of Eden* for Harcourt, Brace, and places "The Nature of Art under Capitalism" (a meditation on differences between pure literature and propaganda that is also known as "Combat and Service") in the *Nation*, where it is published in December; it later appears in *The Philosophy of Literary Form*. The essay gets Burke a letter from Sidney Hook and an invitation to speak at the John Reed Club on January 28, 1934. With Gregory, Joseph Freeman, and others, Burke protests at the German consulate the trial of the Communists accused of the Reichstag burning.

DECEMBER: As a favor to William Carlos Williams, Burke writes an introduction to Charles Reznikoff's *Testimony*, which appears early in 1934 from the Objectivist Press.

DECEMBER 18: Marries Elizabeth "Libbie" Batterham, having divorced Lily in November.

1934

Max Eastman, *Artists in Uniform*.
F. Scott Fitzgerald, *Tender Is the Night*.
Tess Slesinger, *The Unpossessed*.
Henry Miller, *Tropic of Cancer*.
Ezra Pound, *ABC of Reading*.
Cole Porter, *Anything Goes*.
Robert Cantwell, *Land of Plenty*.
James T. Farrell, *The Young Manhood of Studs Lonigan*.
Matthew Josephson, *The Robber Barons*.
Malcolm Cowley, *Exile's Return*.

JANUARY: Burke offers "Orpheus in New York" as music criticism for the *Nation* and reviews Thomas Mann's *Past Masters* for the *New Republic*. Hook invites Burke to join the Professional Workers' League. When *Plowshare*, a new magazine, solicits Burke for a contribution, on January 4 he offers "On Interpretation," the first section of *Permanence and Change*. New Masses is reborn as a weekly on January 2.

JANUARY 28: Burke speaks before the John Reed Club (with John Chamberlain and Edward Dahlberg; Joshua Kuntiz presiding) on the subject of "Bourgeois and Proletarian Types in World Literature." Burke's presentation is the gist of what would become his essay "My Approach to Communism."

FEBRUARY–EARLY MARCH: When Granville Hicks, the *NM* review editor, asks Burke to review a book by Dewey, Burke refuses because he is still fuming over Hicks's review of *Counter-Statement* and—more immediately—over Hicks's recent essay "The Crisis in Criticism," in which Hicks misrepresents Burke's views on the relation between art and life. To mock Hicks, Burke writes a satiric "Extra!" edition of *New Masses* that never is published. Nevertheless Burke also writes "My Approach to Communism," a commitment to the movement, for *New Masses*. His music criticism column for the *Nation* is entitled "Two Brands of Piety."

FEBRUARY: *Partisan Review* begins appearing as a publication of the John Reed Club of New York City.

FEBRUARY 16: Communist Party enthusiasts, in the sectarian belief that a united front of leftists actually amounted to "social fascism," disrupt a Socialist Party gathering at Madison Square Garden.

MARCH: At Hook's invitation, Burke lectures on criticism at New York University. He also completes "The Meaning of C. K. Ogden" for the *New Republic* and a review of Croce for *Hound and Horn*.

Mass demonstrations against the fascists break out in Madrid and Barcelona.

APRIL: As a result of "My Approach to Communism," Burke is invited to write an essay for the Allied Professional Committee to Aid Victims of German Fascism, to help the Angelo Herndon Defense Committee (a group in defense of political prisoners), and to join other leftist causes. He attends a *New Masses* party on April 21 and reviews a play called *The Strikebreaker* for *New Masses*.

Burke also publishes "The End and Origin of a Movement" and "The Art of Yielding" (music criticism for the *Nation*), as well as a *New Republic* book review of Dewey's *Art as Experience*.

MAY: *Permanence and Change* is completed and submitted to Harcourt, Brace, for publication—but Harcourt refuses it. Spring planting begins at Andover, and Burke is moving out of 78 Bank Street.

JUNE 6: At Andover, Burke begins pondering his next project. In New York, where he maintains a place at 121 Bank Street (which he will keep for several years, until April 1937), he is arrested and jailed for a night, with Sue Jenkins, Cowley, and Isidor Schneider, for their protest in support of clerical workers on strike against Macauley Publishing Company.

Hitler meets Mussolini for the first time and purges hundreds of "plotters" against him.

Having reviewed Mann's *Joseph and His Brothers* for the *New Republic*, by means of a petition Burke urges Mann to oppose the Nazis. He begins corresponding with James T. Farrell.

JULY: A review of Croce's *History of Europe in the Nineteenth Century*, finished in March, appears in *Hound and Horn*; "For Whom Do You Write" is in the inaugural issue of *New Quarterly*.

JULY 2: Burke probably attends a meeting of the "Pittsburgh Committee," sponsor of the Pittsburgh Workers' School and Bookshop in Burke's old hometown, another project associated with Sue Jenkins.

JULY 5: Two San Francisco striking longshoremen are killed and thirty are wounded by police gunfire, triggering a general strike and a Red Scare. The day becomes known as "Bloody Thursday." Other strikes develop in Toledo, Minneapolis, Portland, and elsewhere.

A band of Nazis murders Austrian Chancellor Dollfuss in an attempted putsch.

Burke puts some finishing touches on *Permanence and Change* and submits it to the New Republic Dollar Series, which agrees in mid-October to publish the book.

AUGUST: Music criticism, "The Most Faustian Art," appears in the *Nation*.

On Hindenburg's death Hitler assumes the dual roles of head of state and commander of the armed forces: his dictatorship is complete.

Burke in a letter to *Windsor Quarterly* feuds with a critic named Schachner, who has misrepresented Burke's "Art under Capitalism" in order to place Burke outside the Communist Party circle. He submits an article on aesthetic decentralization to the *Brooklyn Eagle*.

SEPTEMBER: A general strike of textile workers idles 400,000.

SEPTEMBER 8: Burke speaks at a *Partisan Review* symposium at Irving Square with Farrell and Joseph Freeman.

"Hindemith Does His Part" (music criticism) and "Gastronomy of Letters" (a review of Pound's *ABC of Reading*) appear in the *Nation*.

Edgar Johnson's review of "On Interpretation" (the piece of *Permanence and Change* that had appeared in *Plowshare*) appears in the *New Republic* as "The Artist and the World."

With *Permanence and Change* under contract and in press, Burke applies for a Guggenheim Fellowship.

OCTOBER 8: Berenice Abbott's exhibit of photos of New York City opens at the Museum of the City of New York.

NOVEMBER: Two Burke reviews appear in the *New Republic:* one of Alfred North Whitehead's *Nature and Life*, the other of Edward Dahlberg's *Those Who Perish*.

Hitler threatens the Saar region, which is under League of Nations jurisdiction.

Burke and Farrell exchange letters mocking the Legion of Decency. Burke's poem "Plea of the People" is rejected by the *Nation*.

DECEMBER: Burke finishes a piece on the Scottsboro trial, lectures on literature before the Young Men's Hebrew Association (as he would the following month), and appears before his friend Harry Slochower's class at Brooklyn College. On December 20 he hosts Richard McKeon for dinner and a discussion of *Permanence and Change*, and in the last half of the month Burke participates (with Isidor Schneider, James T. Farrell, Archibald MacLeish, and Nathan Asch) in a commission to investigate the grievances of Ohrbach's department store employees. A bit of music criticism—"A Most Useful Composition"—is published in the *Nation*.

1935

Bronislaw Malinowski, *Coral Gardens and Their Magic.*
T. S. Eliot, *Murder in the Cathedral.*
James T. Farrell, *Judgment Day.*
Sinclair Lewis, *It Can't Happen Here.*
Henry Roth, *Call It Sleep.*
Granville Hicks, Michael Gold, Isidor Schneider, et al., eds., *Proletarian Literature in the United States.*

Film: *The Thirty-Nine Steps.*
Clampdowns on Jews in Germany intensify.
Southern Review begins publication.
JANUARY 6: The first performance of Clifford Odets's *Waiting for Lefty.*
FEBRUARY: Burke's *Permanence and Change* comes off the presses at mid-month. Burke speaks at an *Anvil* magazine symposium on the proletarian short story at the John Reed Club headquarters, and on February 21 he attends a party for Henry Roth, whose new novel, *Call It Sleep*, Burke has just commented on in a letter to *New Masses* dated February 26. Other publications: "A Pleasant View of Decay" and "What Shostakovich Adds" (music criticism) in the *Nation;* and a review of Alexander Laing's *Wine and Physic* (completed in December) appears in *Poetry. Poetry* next assigns him to review I. A. Richards's *On Imagination.*
MARCH: Burke, joining the editorial board, assists in the introduction of a new magazine, *Action*, intended for the Jewish working class. His review of Waldman's *Goethe and the Jews* is published in *New Masses.* Another review, of Yarmolinsky's *Dostoevski: A Life*, appears in the *New Republic*, and the *Nation* carries another piece of music criticism: "The 'Problems' of the Ballet." Meantime Burke works on a piece on Erskine Caldwell and, on March 25 and 27, guest lectures in Sidney Hook's class at New York University.
MARCH 16: Hitler decrees rearmament in defiance of the Treaty of Versailles.
MARCH 18: Burke is invited to a meeting to plan next month's first American Writer's Congress; at the gathering he is assigned to speak at the congress on "Revolutionary Symbolism in America."
MARCH 20: Burke learns that he is the recipient of a two-thousand-dollar Guggenheim Fellowship, which is officially announced in the newspapers on April 1 and which he will use to write the book that becomes *Attitudes toward History.*
APRIL: "Caldwell: Maker of Grotesques" appears in the *New Republic.* Burke writes an article for a "Discussion Issue" of *Partisan Review* on the Writer's Congress, but the essay never appears.
APRIL 19: Burke lunches with Gorham Munson and Thomas Crowell to discuss a possible Burke book on contemporary American writers. The idea is discarded, perhaps because of Burke's commitment to the Guggenheim. (Burke later contacted Crowell about publishing *Attitudes.*) In any case, Burke is also at work on an essay on recent poetry that he will land in *Southern Review.*
    Reviews of *Permanence and Change* begin to appear. Burke goes to an *Action* board meeting on April 17, celebrates Charles Ellis's paintings at a party on April 23, and presides over the annual Boar's Head Poetry Reading at Columbia on April 25. His comments at Columbia on Horace Gregory's poetry later find their way into his review of Gregory's book in the July issue of *Poetry.*
APRIL 26–28: The first American Writer's Congress. On April 27 Burke delivers "Revolutionary Symbolism in America." At the end of the meeting he is named to the executive committee of the League of American Writers.
MAY: While maintaining the place at 121 Bank Street, Burke begins to spend weekends at Andover. He begins work on *Attitudes toward History*, promotes *Permanence and Change*, writes an account of the Writer's Congress for the *Nation*, and attends

an organizational meeting of the League of American Writers on May 16, where plans are hatched for a speakers' bureau and a quarterly journal. The quarterly is discussed again at meetings on June 12 and 17, but practical concerns are preventing its appearance.

MAY 27: The Supreme Court nullifies provisions of the National Recovery Act.

In June Burke completes his essay on recent American poetry and has his reviews of James T. Farrell's *Judgment Day* and of poems by E. E. Cummings and Kenneth Fearing appear in the *New Republic*.

JULY: The first open meeting of the League of American Writers draws more than three hundred people. The Federal Arts Project is initiated.

Cleanth Brooks and Robert Penn Warren bring out the first issue of *Southern Review*, which includes Burke's essay on poetry. Burke also submits to them an essay entitled "Antony in Behalf of the Play."

Burke reviews Gertrude Stein's *Lectures in America* and Crichton's *Redder than the Rose* for the *New Republic* and Gregory's *Chorus for Survival* for *Poetry*.

JULY 25: At the seventh Comintern meeting in Moscow (Congress of Communist Internationals), Georgi Dimitrov articulates a plan for a broad, cooperative alliance on the left—the People's Front.

AUGUST 1: Burke either represents the LAW at a Washington, D.C., meeting, or attends the regular LAW executive committee meeting.

Social Security Act passed.

Burke reviews Tugwell's *Redirecting Education* and Long's *Pittsburgh Memoranda* for August issues of the *Nation* and the *New Republic*. He offers to finish his review of Edmund Wilson's latest book for *NR*, but Cowley turns him down.

SEPTEMBER: After speaking at a *Partisan Review* symposium on Irving Square, Burke is stricken by the flu, which lands him in Memorial Hospital in Newton, New Jersey, for several days.

"Antony in Behalf of the Play" is in *Southern Review*.

John L. Lewis is founding the Congress of Industrial Organizations. The large collection called *Proletarian Literature in America*, reviewed later by Burke in the *Southern Review*, is published and featured as the first selection offered by the Book Union (a proletarian book-of-the-month club).

Nuremberg Laws deprive Jews of German citizenship and prohibit Jewish-Aryan relationships.

SEPTEMBER 10: Huey Long dies from an assassin's bullets.

OCTOBER: While continuing to work on *Attitudes toward History*, Burke reviews Fischer's *Neurotic Nightingale* for *NR*. He also reviews I. A. Richards's *On Imagination: Coleridge's Critical Theory* in *Poetry* and suggests an article for *Southern Review* that will become "What to Look For." He takes up a job for hire, to prepare the manuscript of George Antheil's *Music in America* for publication, but the task proves to be too extensive to complete.

Over the protests of England and France, Italy invades Ethiopia and moves closer to Hitler.

NOVEMBER: Burke is still pursuing with his colleagues on LAW the idea of a quarterly magazine. *Southern Review* assigns him to do a review of *Proletarian Fiction in the United States*. For the *Book Union Bulletin*, Burke reviews Henri Barbusse's *Stalin: A*

New World Seen through One Man; simultaneously Sidney Hook ridicules the book in the *Saturday Review.*

DECEMBER: After being labeled a "stooge" by a writer in *New Masses,* Burke writes "Reading While You Run" for the magazine; it is published two years later in the *New Republic.* He also completes "Recent Records," a piece of music criticism, for the *Nation,* and agrees to do a book note on E. E. Cummings for *NR.* After minor eye surgery early in the month, Burke decides he needs more time to finish *Attitudes toward History,* and so he asks for an extension of his Guggenheim award, but his appeal is later turned down.

1936

W. H. Auden, *On the Island.*
Djuna Barnes, *Nightwood.*
John Dos Passos, *The Big Money.*
William Faulkner, *Absalom, Absalom!*
Film: Charlie Chaplin's *Modern Times.*
Eugene O'Neill wins the Nobel Prize.

JANUARY: Burke is still serving on LAW committees that are hoping to get the LAW magazine going. He is reviewing James Daly's work for *Poetry* and planning another piece of economic satire. His music criticism—"A Bright Evening with Musicians"—appears in the *Nation.*

FEBRUARY: Burke reviews Muriel Rukeyser's poetry in *New Masses* and Doob's *Propaganda* for the *New Republic.* He is wrapping up the final details on *Attitudes toward History* and thinking of a publisher.

Spain installs a Popular Front government—an alliance of the Left. France follows suit in May.

FEBRUARY 6: Burke participates as a respondent in a LAW-sponsored discussion of Hicks's lecture "Our Revolutionary Heritage."

MARCH: With a daughter at Hunter College, Burke agrees to teach at Syracuse University the following summer. Still living at 121 Bank Street, he writes the copy for a political cartoon by Gus Peck that appears in *New Masses* and "that tries to claim Aristotle's zoon politikon concept for the Communists" (letter to Josephson, March 9). Burke also publishes a review of Dewey's *Liberalism and Social Action* in the *New Republic* and unsuccessfully shops his essay "Spring during Crisis," the preface of his discarded *Auscultation, Creation, and Revision,* to the *Southern Review.* He also tries unsuccessfully to place a revised version of *Auscultation* itself with a division of McGraw-Hill called Whittlesey Press.

Hitler reoccupies the Rhineland; France decides not to oppose.

APRIL: Burke learns that his Guggenheim award will not be renewed after it expires, though *Permanence and Change* goes into a second printing. He witnesses a performance of Eliot's *Murder in a Cathedral* and then lectures on it at Vassar on April 21.

Burke's review of Clifford Odets's *Paradise Lost: A Play in Three Acts* appears in the *New Republic.* "What Is Americanism?"—a symposium on American life and its likely propensity for Marxism that includes a contribution by Burke (and others by

Dreiser, Williams, Josephson, Frank, and others)—is published in *Partisan Review*. Burke is reviewing *Proletarian Literature in the United States* (published in *Southern Review* in June) and attends a tea in his honor on April 11.

MAY: Two Burke poems, "Lullaby for Oneself as an Adult Male" (written a couple of years before) and "Uneasy Thought of Peace," appear in the *New Republic*.

MAY 26: Burke is meeting with other members of the League of American Writers (including Farrell, Trachtenberg, Cowley, Gold, Hart, Taggard, and Seaver) to plan a possible LAW fall conference.

JUNE: Cowley travels to Spain for an international writers' congress amid tensions that were leading to civil war there. Burke works on an introduction to his friend Harry Slochower's *Three Ways*. Burke's review of Farrell's *A Note on Literary Criticism* in the *New Republic* contributes to a feud with Farrell—and with Farrell's sympathizer Sidney Hook.

JUNE 28: The Communist Party, meeting in Madison Square Garden, nominates Earl Browder for president and James W. Ford for vice-president. People's Front politics, however, lead to broad support on the left for Roosevelt.

JULY: The Spanish Civil War begins when Franco and other generals stage a military revolt against the established Popular Front ruling government. Italy and Germany come to Franco's aid, but Stalin mostly keeps his distance from the conflict.

Burke is asked to translate a speech by Thomas Mann (given before the Committee for Social Cooperation) for the *New Republic*. His review of the Agrarian *Who Owns America?* (edited by Herbert Agar and Allen Tate) appears in *NR* as well; and the *Nation* publishes his review of Otto Rank's *Truth and Reality* and *Will Therapy*. Burke's feud with Sidney Hook heats up via the mail.

AUGUST: During the week of August 3–7, Burke shares material from *Attitudes toward History* with students at Syracuse; Gregory and Cowley join him for lectures, for which he is paid two hundred dollars. Burke's review of Jim Daly's poetry appears in *Poetry*, he meets Allen Tate in New York, and he offers "Symbolism" or "Weeds of Symbolism" to *Southern Review*.

Olympic Games take place in Berlin.

Show trials for "disloyal" persons in the Soviet Union, many of them "Old Bolsheviks" associated with the 1917 revolution, begin to cause dissension in the American Left. When Trotsky is accused of plotting against Stalin, rifts develop.

SEPTEMBER: Now a "contributing editor" to the new *Science and Society: A Marxian Quarterly*, Burke contributes to its first issue a review of Ralph Barton Perry's *The Thought and Character of William James* that will reappear in *Attitudes toward History*. A review of John McMurray's *Reason and Emotion* appears in the *American Journal of Sociology*.

Burke is a signer of a statement that appears in *New Masses* protesting journalistic reporting of the Spanish Civil War.

Harriett Monroe, editor of *Poetry*, passes away on September 26. Morton Zabel is part of the editorial team that succeeds her.

OCTOBER: Burke's review of Blackmur's *The Double Agent* (finished in February) is in *Poetry*; for the same journal, he is now working on a review of William Empson's *Some Versions of Pastoral*.

At an October 8 meeting that includes Farrell, Cowley, Gregory, Lillian Hellman, and possibly Burke, the future of *Partisan Review* is decided: it folds for the time being.

Cowley moves to Sherman, Connecticut.

November: Burke speaks on November 19 to the Graduate History Society at Columbia. He also proposes to write a college rhetoric text; after Thanksgiving he closes Andover for the winter and returns to New York (121 Bank Street).

Roosevelt is reelected in a landslide.

December: On December 6, Burke speaks to members of twenty-two Newman Clubs about communism and finalizes arrangements to lecture at the New School in 1937. He places "Acceptance and Rejection," a large piece out of *Attitudes toward History*, into *Southern Review*, and his review of Harold Lasswell's *Politics* appears in the *New Republic*.

Burke meets with Richard McKeon, who is in New York for a visit; some of the conversation influences the ending of *Attitudes toward History*, which Burke finishes for good by the end of the year.

1937

John Dos Passos, *U.S.A.*
Zora Neale Hurston, *Their Eyes Were Watching God*.
Jean Paul Sartre, *Nausea*.
John Steinbeck, *Of Mice and Men*.
Pablo Picasso, *Guernica*.
Cowley, *After the Genteel Tradition*.
Film: *The Spanish Earth*, a documentary about the Spanish Civil War.
Orson Welles's play *Julius Caesar*.
Amelia Earhart disappears.

January: In the city for the winter, Burke attends a farewell party at Genevieve Taggard's for Isidor Schneider, who is off to visit the Soviet Union. On January 16, for fifty dollars, he speaks on "What Is Communism?" (opposite him another speaker defines fascism) for the Hartford branch of the Foreign Policy Association. He sends Cleanth Brooks the manuscript of *Attitudes* and begins work on a review of Tate's poetry.

January 29: James Anthony ("Butchie") Burke is born.

Burke's review of Hilaire Belloc's *The Restoration of Property* (completed in October) is in the *New Republic*. A review of Karl Mannheim's *Ideology and Utopia* is in the *Nation*.

February 4: Burke begins a series of Thursday evening lectures at the New School that runs until June. He also speaks at the American Writers Union meeting.

March: Burke's review of Empson's *Some Versions* is in *Poetry*, and Slochower's *Three Ways of Modern Man*, with his foreword, is out as well.

Burke attends a League of American Writers reception for Malraux. He and Libbie are busy with the new baby.

APRIL: Burke experiences "three hours of sheer enjoyment" talking with I. A. Richards, who is on his way to China, and probably meets on another occasion with R. P. Blackmur. Burke's review of Herbert Read's *Art and Society* is in the *New Republic*.

A commission of the American Committee for the Defense of Leon Trotsky, chaired by John Dewey, holds hearings in Mexico City. Late in the year, the commission declares the Moscow trials to be frame-ups.

APRIL 26: Nazi aviators bomb Guernica: more than 1,500 people die.

MAY: On his fortieth birthday, Burke is expecting *Attitudes toward History* to be out soon and is contemplating doing an essay on Shakespeare.

Burke's review of Tate's *The Mediterranean and Other Poems* is in *Poetry;* a review of Edgar Johnson's *One Mighty Torrent: The Drama of Biography* is in the *Nation*. He plans to submit "The Relation between Literature and Science" as his contribution to the second American Writers' Congress in June—and to the book that will come out of the conference, *The Writer in a Changing World.*

MEMORIAL DAY: Chicago police kill ten Republic Steel workers and wound dozens of others. Soon after the CIO capitulates to Ford and Little Steel.

JUNE: Burke works on reviews of Mortimer Clapp's poems and Herbert Grierson's book on Wordsworth and Milton. *New Masses* carries his review of Robert and Helen Lynd's *Middletown in Transition.*

JUNE 5: Burke speaks at the second American Writers' Congress. He agrees to serve on LAW's committee to oppose Franco in the Spanish Civil War. Dwight Macdonald scores the congress severely.

Attitudes toward History is out on June 28.

JULY: Two Burke reviews appear—of Clapp's *New Poems* (in *Poetry*) and of Edmund Wilson's *This Room and This Gin and These Sandwiches* (in the *Nation*).

JULY 26–30: Burke lectures (using *Attitudes toward History* material) to Leonard Brown's students at Syracuse University. He shares time with Cowley, who is just back from Spain with news of the political situation there.

AUGUST: *The Writer in a Changing World,* the volume from the second American Writers' Congress that includes Burke's "The Relation between Literature and Science," is already out. So are Burke's reviews of Stephen Spender's *Forward from Liberalism* (in the *New Republic*) and of Lord Raglan's *The Hero* (in the *Nation*). The latter once again uses the term *identity,* and Burke is beginning to use the term *identification* commonly in his letters.

SEPTEMBER: More Burke reviews are out: of Thurber's *Let Your Mind Alone!* in the *New Republic;* of Frank H. Knight's *The Ethics of Competition* in the *American Journal of Sociology*. Two more appear in October: of Jacques Barzun's *Race: A Study in Modern Superstition* in *New Masses,* and of Grierson's *Wordsworth and Milton* in *Poetry*. Burke is writing a sort of "ad" for *Attitudes* called "Maxims and Anecdotes" that is intended for he *New Republic*.

OCTOBER: A second stock market plunge—"Black Tuesday"—sends the recovering economy reeling again.

OCTOBER 20: Berenice Abbott's "Changing New York" exhibit of photos opens at the Museum of the City of New York.

OCTOBER 23: Munson visits Andover.

NOVEMBER: Back in New York for the winter (at 53 W. Eleventh Street), Burke has Melville on his mind: he is contemplating an essay on the author, and he proposes to teach a course on him at the University of Chicago. Richard McKeon is trying to arrange the course for the summer of 1938.

In the *New Republic* Burke publishes "Reading While You Run," an article written almost two years before (and accepted on January 2, 1936). He gives a talk at Sarah Lawrence on November 17.

The new *Partisan Review*, under Philip Rahv, William Phillips, and Dwight Macdonald, declares its independence from the Communist Party and the League of American Writers. Its first issue in December includes Sidney Hook's nasty review of *Attitudes toward History*. (Meantime, the League of American Writers supports its own magazine, *Direction*, which claimed editorial independence from LAW: its first issue appears, including "What Is Technology?," an article, published under the name Walter Hinkle, possibly the work of Burke.) Burke is asked to write a response to Hook's review. (He also writes a response to another *ATH* review by Eliseo Vivas for the *Nation*.) Though *Partisan Review* will reach out toward Burke in its February 1938 issue (with favorable comments by Hook and Rahv and a poem by Wheelwright for Burke called "The Word Is Deed"), Burke is never again involved with *Partisan Review*. Instead he will contribute frequently to *Direction*.

Burke's reviews of Mary Colum's *From These Roots: The Ideas That Have Made Modern Literature* and of Peter Blume's surrealist painting *The Eternal City* are in the *New Republic*, and a large piece of *Attitudes toward History*—"Acceptance and Rejection"—is in *Southern Review*. In December Burke proposes an essay on Bentham to the *New Republic*.

DECEMBER 21: Burke accepts a contract for $1,300 to teach two courses at the University of Chicago in the summer of 1938—one on Coleridge and one on literary criticism. Consequently he turns down Leonard Brown's offer to return to Syracuse in August.

1938

Thornton Wilder, *Our Town*.
Wallace Stevens, *The Man with the Blue Guitar and Other Poems*.
Hitler's *Mein Kampf* is translated into English.
Pearl Buck wins the Nobel Prize in Literature.
Cleanth Brooks and Robert Penn Warren, *Understanding Poetry*.
JANUARY: Burke's response to Hook's review ("Is Mr. Hook a Socialist?") is published in *Partisan Review*, along with Hook's counter-response ("Is Mr. Burke Serious?"). The Henry Harts throw a party for Burke in honor of *Attitudes toward History*, and he is also invited to a party by Clifford Odets. Burke also meets with Margaret Schlauch to discuss his "propositions" in *ATH* and her planned response to them in *Science and Society*. Burke's counter-response will soon be published as "Twelve Propositions" in *Science and Society*, along with Schlauch's own counter-counter-response.

Burke's review of Stuart Chase's *The Tyranny of Words* in the *New Republic* shows Burke's interest in semantics.

FEBRUARY: *Partisan Review* issue includes positive comments by Rahv on Burke's performances at writers' congresses, Jack Wheelwright's poem "for Kenneth Burke" entitled "The Word Is Deed," and defenses of Burke against the attack by Hook.

Burke describes his life as a "jumble of exacting but poor paying jobs": a review of Hilaire Belloc's *The Crisis of Civilization* is in the *New Republic;* one on Thurmond Arnold's *The Folklore of Capitalism* is in *New Masses;* an essay called "Maxims and Anecdotes" (part of *ATH*) is appearing in two issues of the *New Republic* to publicize the book. He tries to place other essays in *Southern Review* and the *New Republic,* including "The Virtues and Limits of Debunking" and "Questions for Answers" (the latter a piece on literary criticism that Cowley et al. ultimately reject for the *New Republic*—to Burke's chagrin). And he discusses "dramatism" with Richard McKeon in an exchange of letters.

MARCH 12: Hitler annexes Austria. Burke is invited to a meeting to discuss a possible response to the Moscow trials.

Burke is studying Coleridge in preparation for his summer teaching at Chicago. He is suffering from insomnia but sees the publication of two articles—"Twelve Propositions by Kenneth Burke on the Relation between Economy and Psychology" (in *Science and Society*) and the brief "A Psychological Approach to the Study of Social Crises" (in the *American Journal of Sociology*). The latter is a response to a piece by I. T. Malamud, so Malamud responds. *AJS* will publish a Burke review in August.

APRIL: "The Virtues and Limits of Debunking" is in *Southern Review,* and "Literature As Equipment for Living" is in *Direction.*

MAY: Burke's review of Empson's *English Pastoral Poetry* ("Exceptional Book") appears in the *New Republic.* Back at Andover now, he is assigned by *Poetry* to review John Crowe Ransom's *The World's Body.*

MAY 22: Hitler and Mussolini agree to a military alliance.

JUNE 20–AUGUST 27: Burke teaches for the summer at the University of Chicago, renting the place at Andover and residing at 1153 East Fifty-sixth Street in Chicago. His decision to lecture during each class costs him many hours of preparation but provides material for later essays, especially on Coleridge; he even considers doing a book on Coleridge. He meets a group of sociologists at Chicago, including Hugh Dalziel Duncan.

SUMMER AND FALL: Burke lends financial assistance to his father, who has fallen into dire economic straits in Weehawken.

AUGUST: House of Representatives Committee on Un-American Activities opens investigations of organized labor.

SEPTEMBER 15: LAW sponsors a dinner event featuring Dreiser (who is just back from Spain) in order to support an American relief ship for the Spanish Civil War.

OCTOBER 1: Nazis march into the Sudetenland a day after the area is ceded to Germany at Munich.

OCTOBER 30: Orson Welles's "War of the Worlds" radio broadcast panics Americans concerned about advancing fascism.

NOVEMBER 9–10: Kristallnacht in Germany: Jewish businesses and synagogues are looted and burned, and at least ninety-one Jews are killed.

Burke begins his correspondence with Hugh Dalziel Duncan.

Burke closes Andover for the winter and moves to 78 Christopher Street in New York. "Semantic and Poetic Meaning" (submitted in September) is published in *Southern Review*, and two poems appear in the *New Republic:* "For a Modernist Sermon" and "Offering for the Time Capsule."

1939

New York World's Fair.

James Joyce, *Finnegans Wake.*

John Steinbeck, *The Grapes of Wrath.*

Popular films: *Gone with the Wind* and *The Wizard of Oz.*

Yeats, Freud, and Ford Madox Ford die.

JANUARY 4: The Burkes throw a party for Chevalier.

JANUARY 11: WEVD radio carries a discussion of contemporary American literature with Burke, Horace Gregory, Muriel Rukeyser, and Ed Seaver. Later in the month Burke discusses "The Power of Words" at the Brooklyn Institute of Arts and Sciences.

The *American Journal of Sociology* accepts "Freud—and the Analysis of Poetry." Burke's review of *The Works of George Herbert Mead* is in the *New Republic.* A review of Kenneth Fearing's poems (*Dead Reckoning*) is in *New Masses.*

Burke offers "New Ideas for Dance" on February 5 at the American Dance Association conference at the Mecca Temple. On the last weekend of the month, he speaks on Coleridge at Cooper Union.

FEBRUARY 28: An unexpurgated translation of *Mein Kampf* appears in the United States; it is a Book-of-the-Month Club selection.

MARCH: Hitler seizes Czechoslovakia.

Harper's turns down Burke's article on "Hitler's 'Battle,'" but *Southern Review* accepts it on March 29. Burke offers a satire, "Electioneering in Psychoanalysia," to a new magazine, *Zone*, which probably never appeared. (The satire did appear in *The Philosophy of Literary Form.*)

Burke begins a correspondence with John Crowe Ransom and writes his review of Ransom's *God without Thunder.*

MARCH 7: Burke lectures for Seaver at the New School on the subject of criticism in the 1920s and 1930s.

The *New Republic* asks Burke to contribute something on Coleridge.

MARCH 28: Madrid falls to Franco, effectively ending the Spanish Civil War.

APRIL 7: Mussolini invades Albania.

Burke's review of Paul Weiss's *Reality* is in the *New Republic;* it was written the previous November.

Burke works with his colleagues at the League of American Writers on a call for the third American Writers' Congress; the final draft is approved on April 15 and appears in *Direction.*

Burke's poem "Plea of the People" is accepted by *New Masses*.

APRIL 24: Richard McKeon visits Burke.

MAY: Burke moves to Andover from 78 Christopher Street. It is a permanent move to Andover and out of New York.

Michael Burke is born on May 3.

MAY 6: Burke submits a review to *Kenyon Review* that Ransom asks him to beef up (into "The Calling of the Tune"). Burke agrees to permit his essay on Hitler, now forthcoming in *Southern Review*, to appear in a book called *This Generation*, published in 1940.

Direction prints "Questions for Critics" (possibly a revision of "Questions for Answers") in its special issue on the Writers' Congress.

Burke begins to shop the manuscript of *The Philosophy of Literary Form*.

JUNE 2–4: Burke attends the third American Writer's Congress, speaking on the subject of "Hitler's 'Battle.'" Ralph Ellison is among the listeners.

Burke's review of *Racial Proverbs* is in the *New Republic*.

Burke writes forty thousand words during this summer on "the dramatic perspective."

JULY 17–21: For two hundred dollars, Burke lectures in Leonard Brown's summer course in Syracuse; the material is from the title essay of *The Philosophy of Literary Form* and from his ideas on "cluster analysis." He meets a student in the course, Stanley Edgar Hyman, and hears about Hyman's girlfriend, Shirley Jackson. A correspondence with Hyman begins in October.

"The Rhetoric of Hitler's 'Battle'" is in *Southern Review;* "The Calling of the Tune" is in *Kenyon Review*.

AUGUST: Burke finalizes the manuscript of "The Philosophy of Literary Form" and offers the book of the same name to Louisiana State University Press, with the encouragement of Brooks and Robert Penn Warren. Warren (on a Guggenheim in Italy) is sending installments of his play "Proud Flesh" (later revised into *All the King's Men*) to Burke in installments, asking for suggestions.

SEPTEMBER 1: After signing a nonaggression pact with Stalin, Hitler invades Poland, touching off World War II; on September 17, Stalin invades Poland from the east. Writers on the left rethink their positions and their allegiance to the Communist Party. Burke generally stays put—loyal to the LAW and *Direction*.

Burke is still thinking through the concept of "identification."

Burke's review of two Coleridge books appears (after being shortened) in the *New Republic*.

OCTOBER: Burke's poem "Industrialist's Prayer" is in *New Masses*. (Burke is writing other poems as well.) The review of Ransom's *The World's Body* is in *Poetry*.

NOVEMBER: *Direction* accepts and publishes Burke's essay "Embargo"—a pro-Soviet essay that articulates similarities between Britain and Germany. His review of Neurath's *Modern Man* is in the *New Republic*, "Comments on Dr. Kilpatrick's Article" appears in *American Teacher*, and "Freud—and the Analysis of Poetry" is in *American Journal of Sociology*. (All three would be included in *The Philosophy of Literary Form*.) Burke begins thinking through what would become "The Four Master Tropes," works on "an analysis of constitutions," and sends work from the previous summer on "the dramatic perspective" to *Southern Review*.

Cowley on November 14 sponsors a *New Republic* dinner to discuss Marxism in the wake of the German-Soviet nonaggression pact, but it is postponed until December. Burke did not go anyway, perhaps because he was experiencing a possible heart ailment.

Daughter Happy writes Burke from Radcliffe.

DECEMBER: Living at Andover through the winter, Burke is still negotiating with LSU Press for *The Philosophy of Literary Form*. Two poems are published—"Plea of the People" in *New Masses* and "Dialectician's Hymn" (also known as "Dialectician's Prayer," "Metaphysician's Hymn," and "Lines on Methodology") in the *University Review*. Burke's proverbs "In the Margin" appear in the *New Republic*.

Burke is invited to a dramatic presentation of Hart Crane's poetry at Bennington College in mid-December.

Brooks comments on the Coleridge passages in an essay, "The Philosophy of Literary Form," that he has submitted to *Southern Review*. Burke and Brooks discuss in a letter the possibility of publishing it serially in *SR* or possibly in a book that might be published by LSU.

1940

Graham Greene, *The Power and the Glory*.

Ernest Hemingway, *For Whom the Bell Tolls*.

Eugene O'Neill, *Long Day's Journey into Night*.

Richard Wright, *Native Son*.

Popular films: *The Grapes of Wrath*, *The Great Dictator*, *Pinocchio*, and *Fantasia*.

JANUARY: On invitation, Burke pens "Symbolism in Waldo Frank's Work" for a book of essays honoring Frank that never appears. He is also working on "a motherlode of stuff On Human Relations," he tells Josephson.

FEBRUARY: Wintering in Andover, Burke is suffering from some sort of illness that occupies him all winter, from December until April. Is it high blood pressure? A digestion or respiration problem? He considers going to Rochester to have his friend Watson check him out, but Watson reassures him by letter.

MARCH: *The Philosophy of Literary Form* is accepted by LSU Press. Burke works on a review of a book by Mortimer Adler for *NR*, but he never completes it. He does finish thirty thousand words "On the Imputing of Motives" that involve a discussion of act, agent, agency, scene, and purpose.

APRIL: Hitler moves against Norway and Denmark.

Burke writes very little because he is feeling ill.

MAY: Churchill becomes British prime minister. On May 10 Hitler invades Belgium on the way to France.

Burke's review of *The Road to Tryermaine* (on Coleridge), assigned in January, is in the *New Republic*. Burke turns down a job working for Munson as an assistant editor at the Library of Congress for $2,900.

Cowley, who at last cannot stomach the League of American Writers' party line, resigns from the organization.

MAY 27–JUNE 4: British and French withdrawal at Dunkirk. Belgium, the Netherlands, and France have fallen to Hitler. On June 14 German troops enter Paris.

JUNE: Burke entertains McKeon at Andover and tries out his dramatism project.

Jerre Mangione and Harry Slochower (and family) are renting places from Burke at Andover; Mangione remains through September. James Sibley Watson comes for a visit.

SUMMER AND FALL: Battle of Britain. Bombing of London and Berlin.

JULY: With *The Philosophy of Literary Form* nearly finished, Burke begins serious work on his "motives book"—*A Grammar of Motives*. His friend Dr. Watson offers him a "hypnotic barbiturate" to help him sleep.

Cowley resigns publicly from the League of American Writers (he had done so privately in May).

JULY 29–AUGUST 1: Burke lectures again to Leonard Brown's students at Syracuse on material from *The Philosophy of Literary Form*, *A Grammar of Motives*, and an analysis of Richard Wright. Brown agrees to do the index to *The Philosophy of Literary Form*.

AUGUST 3–5: Soviets annex Latvia, Estonia, and Lithuania.

AUGUST 4: Burke entertains William Knickerbocker back at Andover.

AUGUST: Burke continues hard work on *A Grammar of Motives*, writes the preface to *The Philosophy of Literary Form*, and sends the completed book manuscript off for production.

AUGUST 20: Trotsky is assassinated in Mexico.

SEPTEMBER: Cowley goes to Prince Edward Island in order to write a book—in effect ending his relationship with the *New Republic*, which soon ends his salary and claims his office. In the middle of the month, John Brooks Wheelwright is killed in an automobile accident in Boston.

SEPTEMBER 23: The *New Republic* publishes "How They Are Voting"—a series of first-person testimonies concerning the coming election. Burke declares that he is undecided.

OCTOBER: "On Musicality in Verse" appears in *Poetry*.

Burke accepts a job as "chief advisory editor" (in charge of fiction selections) for *Direction*, a position that he will keep until the following spring, when it proves to be too much work.

Matthew Josephson's *The President Makers* appears.

OCTOBER 19: Burke meets Shirley Jackson for the first time; Jackson marks the occasion with a hilarious poem.

NOVEMBER: *Direction* publishes "What to Do till the Doctor Comes: Thoughts on Conscription." It also carries (without Burke's permission) a letter by Burke.

Burke writes "Surrealism" ("one of the three or four best things I have ever written") for a *New Directions* segment on the subject. The money for it helps to finance a Burke family trip to Florida for the winter—for Burke is still not feeling well.

DECEMBER: The Burkes take up winter quarters in Melbourne Beach, Florida. Burke's project is to finish "On Human Relations"—the motives project. Burke submits "The Character of Our Culture" to a *Southern Review* symposium on American culture. (Its publication is delayed until spring when other contributors are late.)

1941

Citizen Kane opens.

Duke Ellington's "Jump for Joy" revue.

JANUARY: Burke is reading page proofs for *Philosophy of Literary Form*, hoping to get New Directions to put *Counter-Statement* back into print, and doing some translating of Ludwig.

FEBRUARY: Burke's review of Ransom's *The New Criticism* and Tate's *Reason in Madness* is in *Kenyon Review; Direction* carries his "Americanism" essay.

MARCH: Still in Florida and still complaining of hypertension, Burke proposes and submits "Four Master Tropes" to Ransom for *Kenyon Review. Southern Review* carries "The Character of Our Culture." Burke is asked to sign the "call" for the next American Writers' Congress (he later refuses).

APRIL: *The Philosophy of Literary Form* appears about April 20—just about when the Burkes return to Andover.

SPRING: Philip Randolph plans a march on Washington, encouraging the development of the civil rights movement. The march, planned for July 1, is called off when FDR meets with Randolph and promises reforms.

MAY: Burke travels to Rochester to see Watson and get a complete medical checkup; he makes a follow-up visit in June. The tests show Burke to be generally very healthy, but he is still not feeling well. He has dinner with Blackmur in May; Tate visits Andover in late June.

JUNE 22: German troops pour into the Soviet Union in a surprise attack.

SEPTEMBER: "Four Master Tropes" is published in *Kenyon Review.*

OCTOBER: Burke tells friends he has "finished the first draft of my 'grammar.'" He is assigned to review a book by Marianne Moore for *Accent* and three other books for *Kenyon Review.* Tate invites him to lecture at Princeton the following spring.

NOVEMBER: Burke is doing an essay on Yeats for *Southern Review. Direction* publishes his "Where Are We Now?"; Burke complains when it appears in December, for the war has changed the situation by then.

DECEMBER 7: Japanese attack Pearl Harbor. Russians turn back Hitler near Moscow. Burke is invited by S. I. Hayakawa to a seminar in Chicago on linguistics and general semantics that features Korzybski; the idea is to bring Burke and Korzybski together, but Burke cannot attend.

DECEMBER 27: Eleanor Burke marries Richard Leacock.

Notes

Chapter 1: April 1935

1. Markey, *Adversity*. The same source indicates that in 1934, through the Relief Bureau Drama Project, 1.5 million people in New York watched 222 free performances of Shakespeare, Gilbert and Sullivan, and discontinued Broadway hits.

2. Lentricchia erroneously places the congress at Madison Square Garden and Burke's performance on April 26.

3. The story of the response to Burke's talk is also recounted in "Thirty Years Later," 506–7; Woodcock, 708–9; Klehr, 353; Wander, 204; and Cowley, *Dream*, 277–78. Stull also discusses Lentricchia's encounter with Burke (30–36)—though for very different ends than ours.

4. Friedrich Wolf, a German delegate to the congress, made precisely this charge during the congress. See Hart, 167–68.

5. Lentricchia's account of Burke's role in the congress and his well-known analysis of the speech are on pages 21–38 of *Criticism and Social Change*.

6. Lentricchia cites Yagoda and may have been influenced by Daniel Aaron's short account of the congress in his *Writers on the Left*, though Aaron for some reason strangely contends that even in 1935 "implicit in all of Burke's social and aesthetic theorizing was his belief in the autonomy of the artist" (290). Lentricchia also worked from the official proceedings of the conference, Hart's *American Writers' Congress*. In what follows we draw from the same sources as well as from the Malcolm Cowley Papers, the Matthew Josephson Papers, the Kenneth Burke Papers, the Granville Hicks Papers (including the archive of the League of American Writers in box 33), and the Joseph Freeman Papers. Our account of the congress itself is generally in keeping with Denning's brief summation (441–44). Denning also understands Burke's speech as a key formulation of People's Front values, as does Wander (202–4). See also David Cratis Williams's account of Burke and the congress, though Williams maintains the story of Burke's marginalization; Josephson, *Infidel*; Klehr, 350–53; Kutulas, *Long War*, 90–92; and Shi.

7. The course is advertised in *Partisan Review*, April–May 1934 issue. With John Chamberlain, Edward Dahlberg, and Joshua Kunitz, Burke also was part of a JRC panel on "Bourgeois and Proletarian Types in World Literature" on January 28, 1934

(Homberger, 130). For good, short accounts of the John Reed Clubs, see chapter 5 of Homberger, "Proletarian Literature and the John Reed Clubs"; Aaron, 221–30; Rideout, 144–48; and Denning, 205–12. The JRCs are documented elaborately in the Joseph Freeman Papers.

8. The People's Front was formally announced at the Seventh Comintern Conference on August 2, 1935 (Cowley, *Dream*, 290–94; and his comments in "Thirty Years Later," 497), but as we will show, it was in the air well before then.

9. As late as the spring and summer of 1934, devout Marxists—still mostly unaware that full employment and budget surpluses in the Soviet Union were being bought at the price of the deportation of peasants and the torture of resisters—were still looking at Hitler as a positive development of sorts, in that the chaos he was creating would speed the onset of the proletarian revolution. In April 1934, for example, the Comintern declared that "the Nazi dictatorship, by destroying all the democratic illusions of the masses, . . . accelerates the rate of Germany's development toward proletarian revolution." Earl Browder, secretary of the American Communist Party, echoed that assessment: "fascism hastens the exposure of all demagogic supporters of capitalism. . . . It hastens the revolutionization of the workers, destroys their democratic illusions, and therefore prepares the masses for the revolutionary struggle." (Both statements are quoted in Cowley's papers related to Eugene Lyons's *The Red Decade* in the Newberry Library.) By April 1935, such brave optimism about Hitler was gone. For an accessible short history of the highly sectarian Communist "Third Period" (1928–34), when it appeared to the Comintern that capitalism was in its last days, and of the change in policy to the Popular Front, see Wald, *Farrell*, 4–8.

10. "We believe such a Congress should create the League of American Writers, affiliated with the International Union of Revolutionary Writers" (*New Masses*, January 22, 1935).

11. Lawrence Schwartz, *Marxism and Culture*; also quoted in Wess (57).

12. Wright reported in *The God That Failed* that he was appalled in September 1934, when he heard "that the People's Front policy was now the correct vision of life and that the [John Reed] clubs could no longer exist" (Crossman, 122). He denounced the racism that he encountered at the congress itself, voted against the formation of the LAW, and scored the narrow closed-mindedness of the party line that he encountered (124–26). Whether the disillusionment that Wright expressed in *The God That Failed* was a bit of after-the-fact dramatic license is a matter for debate, however: Gayle Addison claims that Wright was actually elated by his experiences at the congress (82; see also Denning, 210, and Logie, 126).

13. The Joseph Freeman Papers contain a specific program of congress events. It indicates that Burke's paper at the Saturday morning session in the New School auditorium was sandwiched between those of hardliners: Freeman's "The Traditions of American Revolutionary Literature" and Jack Conroy's "The Worker as Writer."

14. Cowley discusses the air of controversy around the congress in *The Dream of the Golden Mountains*, 270–79, and in "Thirty Years Later," 496.

15. The controversy is summarized in Selzer, *Kenneth Burke in Greenwich Village*, 155, 249–50. See that book for a study of the tension between the aesthetic and the social as it plays out in *Counter-Statement*.

16. It is not difficult to think that Gessner's words ridiculing technique were delivered with a glance at Burke and a recollection of *Towards a Better Life*. "That's precisely what they got after me for," said Burke in "Thirty Years Later": "I said I couldn't write for the working class" (501).

17. The petition is filed under "Foster" in the 1932 files of the Kenneth Burke Papers at Penn State.

18. Burke's summation expressed strong support for the "vitality" of the Communist Party but also made it clear that he was not a party member; it expressed solidarity with the need to "consider art in relation to political necessities" but quoted, of all people, the conservative Jacques Maritain as articulating the same need; and it closed with the hope that the "broad sympathies" and "latitude" of the Popular Front would be maintained by the LAW. Sidney Hook, it should be noted, caught the reservations inherent in Burke's summation almost immediately. In a letter to Burke written in early May (undated), he said he "read [Burke's] piece in the *Nation* with a feeling of keen disappointment. Its quality suggests the attitude of 'Oh Lord, I believe, help thou my unbelief.'"

19. Dos Passos was not actually present at the congress, though he was invited. His paper did arrive for the proceedings, however, and is included in Hart (78–82). Dos Passos's words about the congress, offered to Matthew Josephson, could just as easily have been uttered by Burke: "Independent thinking is more valuable in the long run than all this copying out of manifestos. . . . With these Union Square rah rah boys, there seems to be appearing . . . a sort of Methodist-rabbinical sectarianism that rapidly becomes a racket. . . . You can stuff a red shirt just as easily as any other kind" (letter to Josephson, February 6, 1935; also quoted in part in Shi, 171).

20. Josephson's presentation was published contemporaneously with Burke's "Revolutionary Symbolism" in the *New Masses* of April 30, 1935 ("For a Literary United Front"). Both the draft of the paper (Matthew Josephson Papers, undated and untitled manuscript, 1935) and the published version suggest that Josephson was explicitly defending Burke himself: "A contemporary writer whose interests lately have been chiefly critical and philosophical came one day to the pass where he felt himself converted to faith in communism; he wrote of his convictions in his own way. . . . Another young man who was but a slightly less recent convert set to work . . . to prove that my friend (who had publicly announced himself as henceforth a champion of the communist movement) was actually an 'unconscious' Fascist!" The paper of Burke's referred to was probably "My Approach to Communism." We have been unable to identify Burke's young critic, but it is not unlikely that he was at the congress. See chapter 4, note 31.

21. Others on the executive committee were Waldo Frank, Malcolm Cowley, Joseph Freeman, Mike Gold, Henry Hart, Josephine Herbst, Granville Hicks, Matthew Josephson, Alfred Kreymborg, John Howard Lawson, Albert Maltz, Harold Clurman, Edwin Seaver, Isidor Schneider, Genevieve Taggard, and Alexander Trachtenberg.

22. Josephson, *Infidel*, 371; Gregory to Burke, May 4, 1935; Simpson to Burke, April 30, 1935. Cowley made Burke the intellectual hero of his account of the congress in *Dream* (chapter 23). Farrell's iconoclastic stance at the congress was not unlike

Burke's. Committed to the Left, he nonetheless regarded "bourgeois" and "proletarian" literature to be not cultural standards per se but categories to be investigated. His cantankerous engagement with Marxism, which soon led him to break with Stalin, was already forming (Aaron, *Writers*, 287). Farrell later, after a fallout with Burke (see chapter 5), fictionalized the incident of Burke's speech in his novel *Yet Other Waters* in a way that is rather critical of Burke—and yet that account also depicts Burke as less than devastated by the incident. Their letters to each other before and after the congress make lighthearted fun of various people and events associated with the radical Left.

And of course Burke could soon take consolation and vindication in events subsequent to the congress that in upholding the People's Front bore out the wisdom of his recommendation of the term *the people*. For example, "'Front populaire' is precisely the kind of symbol, or slogan, I had in mind for this stage in our propaganda," he wrote to Isidor Schneider on May 11, 1936 (Burke Papers; probably unsent). "And here it is in use, by the very parties (anti-Fascist parties) I had hoped to see using it. I am not silly enough to think that I had anything to do with it. But on the other hand, I am not self-effacing enough to avoid feeling gratified when I see that the policy prevails for which I was bopped. If anyone thinks that the 'symbol of the people' is necessarily Fascist, let him go after the Party, not me." Burke was responding to Schneider's sending of a review of the congress proceedings by F. D. Klingender that was published in Europe and that spoke favorably of Burke's contribution, but the later ubiquity of the term *the people* in party circles bears out his comments more broadly. Burke's speech was also acknowledged as prescient in Philip Rahv's "Two Years of Progress," published in *Partisan Review* in 1938. More evidence that Burke's suggestion about *the people* as a term was received favorably within the party is in a letter published in *New Masses* by the poet Walter Lowenfels on July 12, 1938: "May I suggest that the term 'proletarian literature' be laid on the table for a while and the term 'people's literature' be used instead?" Then again Lowenfels's echo of Burke's suggestion was opposed stubbornly by *New Masses* editor Joshua Kunitz ("In Defense of a Term").

23. Chamberlain wrote in the *Saturday Review* ("Literary Left") that the meeting "certainly showed no willingness to accept any party view"—though he was skeptical that the LAW could establish a truly "united front" without people such as Hook and Eastman. Burke's summary of the event in the *Nation* also commended the tolerance of the congress. But for a contrary view, see Wright's contribution to Crossman, ed., *The God That Failed*.

24. While taking a swipe at Burke's use of the term *myth* to describe revolutionary symbolism—"we cannot accept the idea that the class struggle is a myth, or that the working class is a myth"—Gold nonetheless conceded that "if anything has been cleared up in the last few years, it has been this point: that the revolution is a revolution led by the working class, and the lower middle classes are its allies. There is therefore room in the revolution for literature from all these groups. The viewpoint, as Edwin Seaver said, is what is important. The man with the revolutionary mind and approach can write a revolutionary book" (Hart, 166). Nevertheless Burke remained generally unsentimental about the inflexibility of Gold, Conroy, Freeman, and their

camp. "I believe, with the Communists, that the organized party nucleus should be fairly strict in its terminology," he wrote to Horace Gregory on May 21, 1935. "But not, God knows, as naively strict as the old guard rhetoricians would have it. If there were a word 'bick' to designate a shoe when worn by a communist, and a word 'boak' to designate a shoe worn by a non-communist, they would damn you for a treacherous reactionary if you suggested that, in certain kinds of discussion, both 'bicks' and 'boaks' could be classified together as shoes." The bick-boak shoe metaphor, incidentally, would occur to Burke again three years later when he came to write "Semantic and Poetic Meaning"; see *The Philosophy of Literary Form*, 166.

25. Determining exactly what Freeman said is now impossible because the official record of the congress includes not a verbatim transcript of Freeman's words but a statement that he wrote later as a representation of his remarks. All post hoc recollections of the event except one use the word *snob* as opposed to *traitor*. Aaron in *Writers on the Left* (291) accepts Freeman's published comments as the actual record of his words, but the Joseph Freeman Papers (box 25, folder 39, Hoover Institution Archives; copyright Stanford University) clearly indicate that what is published in Hart is Freeman's later construction; see J. F. Evans [Freeman's alias] to Henry Hart, May 7, 1935: "I have taken the liberty of editing the discussion freely. . . . Our stenographer butchered a number of speeches so that they sound simply stupid. As you remember, they were anything but that. In my own case, I happen to speak so rapidly that in the course of fifteen years of public speaking, I have been unable to find a single stenographer to follow me. I have my notes of the speech I made at the congress and find that the steno left out sentences, paragraphs, passages so that the entire meaning of what I said is lost. As recorded by the steno, Burke's rebuttal has none of the lucidity of the original. In his case, and in all others possible, we ought to have the speaker (if immediately available) amend [the record of] his talk." The "notes of the speech" mentioned by Freeman are still in the Freeman Papers; neither *snob* nor *traitor* appears in those notes. Freeman, past editor of *New Masses*, cofounder of *Partisan Review*, proletarian poet, and tireless worker on behalf of Marxism, was known informally as an "old Bolshevik," but he was not very old. Born in the Ukraine in the same year as Burke (1897), he immigrated to the United States in 1904 when his father, a rabbi, wished to avoid the Russo-Japanese War. After graduating in 1919 from Columbia (where he had met Burke as a fellow student), during the 1920s he worked as an expatriate writer in London and Paris, took jobs as a reporter for the *Liberator* and several newspapers, committed himself to leftist causes, and visited the Soviet Union in 1926–27. Freeman promoted John Reed Clubs on trips around the country from 1931 to 1933. For a portrait of Freeman, including the ironic news of his own blackballing by the party later in the decade, see Aaron, 68–84, 130–40, 365–75.

26. Horace Gregory in a letter to Burke (May 4, 1935) described reaction to Burke's paper this way: "My visits to the Congress were irregular, but I made a point of being there when you read your paper. It seemed to me that all the answers proved your point. And straight party members I've met (not writers) told me you were on the right track—as I knew you were. I thought Freeman was very clever to remove his objection to your essay into another context [i.e., the question-and-answer period]. The moment he did so (again proving your thesis) anything he had to say would

appear logical. In every attack they had to ignore your specific definitions of 'people' and 'myth,' which drove the argument back to where it was before you began. This blindness rises from a 'wordphobia' and the fact that people hate to think." Robert Coates's letter to Burke (undated, 1935) carries no mention of any negative reaction to "Revolutionary Symbolism." Clinton Simpson consoled Burke the following day by noting in a letter "that your point about 'the people' was not fully understood; and you were criticized for saying things you didn't say. . . . I've seen Joe Freeman and others rush to defend what they think somebody else may consider political deviations, before. It doesn't mean much, apparently, except that the party is very sensitive about its political line (as it must be), and in consequence about its slogans. . . . I suppose the blame must be laid on a certain sectarianism."

27. But this "Alain" was Daniel Brustlein Alain, not the French modernist writer associated with the *Nouvelle revue française*. Daniel Brustlein was an Alsatian-born painter who, from Paris, occasionally offered cartoons to the *New Yorker*.

28. Burke submitted his "Trial Translation" to *Contact*, but Williams rejected it on the grounds that it was too oral, that it was "a speech" that deserved hearing "in a union hall" (Williams to Burke, July 20, 1932). Since the piece is actually anything but truly oral, one wonders if the item was actually rejected because it was too little political for the new *Contact*.

29. Tashjian places Williams at the Writers' Congress on the basis of a letter from Williams to Zukofsky dated April 1935. Williams's letter to Burke of May 7, 1935, however, gives no overt indication that Williams attended—though it does refer in general to the events of the congress.

30. Burke would use the phrase "medicine man" to signify his idea of an ideal poet in *The Philosophy of Literary Form* (65); and he referred to Hitler as an evil "medicine man" in his 1939 "Rhetoric of Hitler's 'Battle.'"

31. Mariani, 47. Williams contributed to the last imagist anthology, edited by Richard Aldington, in 1930.

32. Weaver quotes George Oppen's summary as a description of Objectivism: "We were all very much concerned with poetic form. . . . 'Objectivist' meant, not an objective viewpoint, but to objectify the poem, to make the poem an object. Meant form" (55). For an authoritative account of the Objectivists, see Homberger, 170–86. As Homberger indicates, Oppen, Louis Zukofsky, Charles Reznikoff, and Carl Rakosi, like Williams, were committed to keeping subjective emotions out of poetry and were devoted instead to spare, minimalist "objectifications." In keeping with the political temper of their times, many of the Objectivists were sympathetic with left-wing politics (as is evident in Reznikoff's *Testimony*, published in 1934 with an introduction by Burke), but their poetry remained associated with imagism, with Pound, and with magazines in the more conservative aesthetic tradition of the *Dial* such as *Pagany*, *Hound and Horn*, and *Poetry*. Work by these four Jewish writers was therefore consistently marginalized by left-wing critics, editors, and publishers, and the group dispersed during the mid-1930s.

33. By contrast Burke was publishing in the inexpensive New Republic Dollar Series and in 1933 tried to organize a "Manuscript Editions" series with the publisher Franklin Spier—a venture designed to make current books available in limited

editions by cutting drastically the costs of production: "they are to be facsimile repro-
ductions, page by page, of the authors' [typed] manuscripts—thus not made by type
composition and letter press, but by photography and the litho-offset process. The
pages will be stamped together, and laid in a cardboard folder" (Burke to Williams and
many others, January 5, 1933). Williams responded enthusiastically to Burke's proposal. He offered to the series a decidedly unproletarian manuscript he called "The
Embodiment of Knowledge. . . These Are the Words," a book containing "all the
agglomerate and conglomerate bellyaches I have suffered for the past ten years—to
the one end that there is no knowledge . . . but my own" (Williams to Burke, January
6, 1933). When Burke did not like that idea, Williams offered chapters from *White
Mule*, a novel more in the proletarian mode that was finally published in 1937. But
that did not work out either, for ultimately the Manuscript Editions idea was abandoned. In 1937 Williams would find himself caught in a political quandary when he
submitted poetry to the newly independent version of *Partisan Review;* the editors of
New Masses threatened to blackball him from their magazine if Williams did not withdraw his work from *PR*, a development that the editors of *PR* proclaimed loudly in
order to prove their point that the Communist Party had grown impossibly sectarian
(Cooney, 125).

34. Eliot's place in the 1930s literary wars is discussed in Aaron's *Writers on the Left*,
chapter 8.

35. Eugene Davidson in the *Yale Review* found Moore's *Selected Poems* to be "aloof"
and "cool"; John Finch in the *Sewanee Review* described her work as "an act of isolation, of divorce from society"; and the anonymous reviewer for the *TLS* accused
Moore of Eliot's crime—an "aesthetic and intellectual revulsion from common life"
(Schulze, *Web of Friendship*, 131).

36. The argument between Davis and Benton continued one begun in 1932 when
Benton unveiled *Political Business and Intellectual Ballyhoo*, a mural destined for the
Whitney Museum that lampooned *New Masses* and the *New Republic* as "the Greenwich Village proletarian costume dancers" and the "literary playboys league of social
consciousness" (Tashjian, 122–23).

37. Porter Papers. Burke shared Porter's disdain for those who would renounce
poetry completely. In *Auscultation* (55) he would ridicule an unnamed individual who
has initiated "talk of renouncing poetry[;] . . . one striking fellow who got a prize in
Paris for a poem, forthwith came forward to make it clear that he would now turn his
mind to more serious things." We have been unable to determine with certainty to
whom Burke was referring, but it is quite possible that it was Donald Davidson, who
spoke of renouncing poetry in his contribution to *I'll Take My Stand*. But the passage
may also refer to someone else, such as Edmund Wilson. See chapter 2, note 19.

38. Hummel (27) offers evidence that Tate and Porter enjoyed a brief love affair
and that Gordon knew about it. Love letters from Porter to Josephson are in the
Josephson Papers.

39. Porter had a story, "The Circus" (a tale of a young girl's struggle to grow up),
in the first issue of the *Southern Review*. Others appeared later in the decade. She later
married Albert Erskine, the magazine's business manager, in 1938; Warren and
his wife were witnesses. She met Erskine at Tate's house in the summer of 1937

(Winchell, 144). I should add here that Porter's disillusionment with the Greenwich Village Left is also recorded in an unpublished manuscript, "Notes on a Decade," that Hummel examined in the Katherine Anne Porter Papers at the University of Maryland.

40. Burke's response is reprinted in Selzer, *Kenneth Burke in Greenwich Village*, 157–58.

41. When Cowley claimed, in keeping with other reviewers, that *I'll Take My Stand* advocated a nostalgic return to the past, Tate tried to set him straight: "If the left-wing critics were not obsessed with the dogma that we want to restore the past—that is, literally bring back some moment in history—they would at least be able to see, whether they liked it or not, that we are merely saying something like this: in the American past there was a beginning of a decent society that was overthrown by finance-capitalism; taking a *hint* from the past, we may still create a decent society" (Tate to Cowley, December 19, 1930).

42. Tate thought (rightly as it turned out) that the combative and sectionalist title of *I'll Take My Stand* would distract readers from its message; he preferred the title *Tracts against Communism* (Conkin, 71). See Tate's footnote on page 155. For a fine account of Tate's contribution to Agrarianism, see Singal, chapters 7 and 8; chapter 7 also discusses Ransom, and chapter 11 reviews the career of Robert Penn Warren. For a detailed account of the Agrarians, see Conkin.

43. Tate's role in the famous Bloody Harlan episode is preserved in his correspondence with John Brooks Wheelwright, Donald Davidson, Robert Penn Warren, and Cowley. The striking Harlan miners, as Cowley relates in chapters 6 and 7 of *The Dream of the Golden Mountains*, were supported by Dos Passos, Frank, Edmund Wilson, and Dreiser, who arranged for a delegation of writers to visit Harlan in league with the Communist Party for the purpose of gathering information and distributing food. Then in February 1932, Cowley, Mary Heaton Vorst, and Dos Passos watched as Frank was searched, beaten, and escorted out of nearby Pineville by local sheriffs; the incident was widely publicized. Tate and fellow Agrarians condemned the treatment of the writers but otherwise stayed distant from the dispute. A letter from Tate to Wheelwright (February 25, 1932) explains why in a way that clarifies the Agrarian program:

> Our position has about three points: (1) We wish to set forth the right of disinterested investigation of social affairs [by writers], and by disinterested I mean unpolitical, whether the politics be Democratic or Communistic; (2) we believe that the results of such investigation should lead to the correction of abuses from the Constitutional point of view, and not the conversion of labor to the Communist party, and certainly not the strengthening of the class war for the benefit of labor; and (3) we believe that the Kentucky situation has local features that show the real opposition to exist between industrialism and agriculture rather than between capital and labor. Our interest lies in some program that will show the Kentucky people that they must restore local autonomy, and that this can be done only by falling back on the agrarian system of the pre-coal era. Instead of furthering the class war, we should rather encourage the miners to work out their self-sufficiency on the

land, whence they originally came. . . . We should do anything in our power (we have little or none) to stir the miners to Revolution . . . if that revolution would suppress the domination of industrialism in politics, but not if it brought about increased strength for the Communism. . . . Another thing. We can't join up with the Eastern liberals because the South has some special characteristics. You have no idea what it is to live—and not merely sympathize from Boston or New York—with another race.

44. Ironically another southern writer was simultaneously writing with a different cultural memory of the antebellum South: William Faulkner's *Absalom, Absalom!*, in progress in April 1935, repudiates the southern cavalier tradition that *The Fathers* depicts far more sympathetically (though hardly mindlessly).

45. Warren's essay "The Briar Patch" addressed the issue of race relations and education. Agrarianism—and de facto segregation, it must be added (though several Agrarians still were opposed to Warren's conclusions; Singal, 346)—could be achieved satisfactorily, he concluded, only if Southern whites supported improved agricultural education for Negroes. By 1935 Warren had also studied at Oxford, Berkeley, and Yale and had contributed poetry to the *New Republic*, so he was then not so sectarian as some other Agrarians—witness his biography of John Brown (a subject matter rather opposed to that of a Confederate hero, though Warren was rather gleeful in pointing up Brown's shortcomings), his play *Proud Flesh* (which Warren sent to Burke for advice during its development in the summer of 1939), and the famous novel that grew out of *Proud Flesh, All the King's Men* (a critique of Huey Long). (He had also married Cinina Brescia, a multilingual native of Ecuador.) Warren met Brooks at Vanderbilt—he was a senior when Brooks was a freshman—and the two became good friends while studying together at Oxford in 1929–31. Brooks began teaching at LSU in the fall of 1932; Warren arrived in the fall of 1934. Incidentally Warren's biography of John Brown was part of a Depression-era vogue; see Denning, 499.

46. Burke's correspondence with Brooks dates from the founding of the *Southern Review*. Burke would come to know Ransom himself directly only after December 1938, when the two corresponded over Burke's submission to the *Kenyon Review*, another central New Critical journal that under Ransom's editorship would eventually publish some of Burke's most important essays. But indirectly the two were already acquainted through Tate and through their mutual interests. For instance on June 11, 1932, Tate wrote to Burke: "I'm forwarding your letter to Ransom: it is one of the best analyses of his book [*God without Thunder*, which included a devastating critique of science] I've seen. I agree with you in most of your objections. . . . But your belief that there is nothing wrong in science but its application in industrialism strikes me as unsound." Our summary of the history of the *Southern Review* is indebted to Winchell, Cutrer, Brooks and Warren's *Stories*, and Simpson et al., and of course to our own inspection of it. Simpson et al. includes a transcript of the Baton Rouge conference where the *Southern Review* was announced.

47. Hicks would soon have his revenge. In *The Great Tradition* he wrote that "the criticism of such men as . . . R. P. Blackmur resembles the impassioned quibbling of devotees of some game" (283).

48. Burke and Blackmur had become acquainted as early as 1929, when Blackmur was affiliated with *Hound and Horn* and publishing part of what would become Burke's *Towards a Better Life*. Especially after *Hound and Horn* failed in the early 1930s, Blackmur was a freelance critic who published in a variety of publications. Like Burke, he would have appreciated the rates paid by the *Southern Review*. And like a number of New Critics, he later outgrew some of its dogmas. Burke reviewed *The Double Agent* for *Poetry* in 1936: he approved of Blackmur's apolitical approach (and contrasted Blackmur with Granville Hicks) and called the book "one of our finest pieces of contemporary criticism."

49. This account of New Criticism—there are many others—is indebted to Leitch, chapter 2, and Core.

50. The fee was actually 1.5 cents a word (Winchell, 95).

51. Interesting, especially in view of our discussion of the first American Writers' Congress, is Joseph Freeman's lengthy introduction to *Proletarian Literature*. The original manuscript of the essay, which concerns the relationship between politics and aestheticism and which survives in the Joseph Freeman Papers under the title "Experience and Art" (box 71, folder 15, Hoover Institution Archives; copyright Stanford University), contains several references to Burke, including the following one that would have been the second paragraph: "But, as Kenneth Burke has wisely observed, the word 'science' usually does the same work among the sophisticated that Old Glory does among the naïve. We may add that the emotional value of both words varies in direct ratio to the ignorance of those mesmerised; the sophisticated are usually as illiterate in science as the naïve [are] in politics." But the references did not make it into the final version, which was substantially shortened. Burke very likely never knew of the excisions, which reveal Freeman's familiarity with and respect for Burke's work. No fiction, poetry, or criticism by Burke appeared in *Proletarian Literature*, first published in October 1935, but there is no evidence that he took offense. In fact he reviewed the book.

52. In April 1936 Brooks and Warren rejected "Spring during Crisis" (Burke to Warren, April 9, 1936), an essay that Burke had first submitted to *Hound and Horn* in January 1933. The piece was conceived late in 1932 as the preface to *Auscultation, Creation, and Revision*.

53. Warren went to Italy on a Guggenheim in the summer of 1939. As the war was breaking out, he sent Burke from Lago di Garda pieces of *Proud Flesh* to critique, in part because he hoped that Burke could help him get his Guggenheim renewed. Warren moved south to avoid the war, to Capri and then to Rome, and continued to forward sections of his play until the end of 1939. *Proud Flesh* developed into *All the King's Men*.

54. The success of the Chicago School was predicted by Ransom in "Criticism, Inc.": "At the University of Chicago, I believe that Professor Crane, with some others, is putting the revolution into effect in his own teaching, though for the time being with a modest program, mainly the application of Aristotle's critical views. . . . If the department should now systematically and intelligently build up a general school of literary criticism, I believe it would score a triumph that would be, by academic standards, spectacular. I mean that the alive and brilliant English scholars all over the

country would be saying they wanted to go there to do their work. That would place a new distinction on the university, and it would eventually and profoundly modify the practices of many other institutions" (588–89).

55. Half a century later McKeon denied that there was any such thing as a consistently principled "Chicago School of Criticism" ("Criticism and the Liberal Arts"), but he was refuted in a friendly response by Wayne Booth ("Between Two Generations"). The use of the term *Chicago School* should not assume the existence of any slavish orthodoxy among its members, nor should it assume that all English professors at Chicago belonged.

56. What might be considered the first salvo in the war between the New Critics and the Chicagoans was fired in Ransom's 1937 "Criticism, Inc." Ransom attacked those who in the tradition of Aristotle were "concerned with the effects" of literature, "reflect[ing] the view that art comes into being because the artist . . . has designs on the public, whether high moral designs or box-office ones. It is an odious view in either case, because it denies the autonomy of the artist as one who interests himself in the artistic object in its own right, and likewise the autonomy of the work itself as existing for its own sake" (597–98).

57. As we will indicate, Mead's books, reviewed together by Burke in the *New Republic* in January 1939, anticipated some of the arguments in *The Philosophy of Literary Form*. In particular Burke published his famous notion of the "unending conversation" in "The Philosophy of Literary Form" just as Mead's notion of the "unending conversation" was gaining currency through the publication of his works. Burke indicated that he came upon the notion independently (Burke to Duncan, November 15, 1938), and there is very good reason to take him at his word, since an early version of Burke's famous parlor-conversation metaphor appears in *Auscultation* (102). On the relationship between Mead's notion and Burke's, see Bushman.

58. Certainly the two men were very much aware of each other since Veblen arrived at the University of Chicago in 1892, having received his Ph.D. in philosophy in 1884, and stayed until 1906. Some commentators attentive to Dewey attribute Veblen's general outlook to Dewey, particularly his biological and scientific approach to economics, and there are general parallels between Dewey's philosophy and the social analysis that Veblen was undertaking. Veblen's sense of the inadequacy of the psychological models underlying contemporary economics may derive to a degree from Deweyan psychology. On the other hand, Dewey credited Veblen with teaching him economics, not the other way around, and with teaching him the distinction between business and industry (as Burke noted in "Liberalism's Family Tree"); Marx was obviously more important to Veblen than was Dewey; Veblen made very few references to Dewey in his work and indeed drew much of his inspiration from anthropology, not philosophy (Diggins, *Promise*, 468); and Veblen's comments on pragmatism were frequently negative (Rucker, 142–44). The book that launched Veblen's celebrity, *The Theory of the Leisure Class*, was published in 1899, before Dewey had fully established himself. It was followed by *The Theory of the Business Enterprise* in 1904 and, a decade later, by *The Instinct of Workmanship and the State of the Industrial Arts*, a book that (as University of Chicago faculty well knew—and as Burke well knew) explains business activity not in narrow economic terms but against

larger systems of cultural values, and which offers historical and anthropological perspectives on economic change.

59. Also prominent on those shelves for reasons that we will indicate: works by Veblen and Bentham, Mary Baker Eddy's *Science and Health*, Frazer's *Golden Bough*, a number of books by Dewey and Mead, and many, many books by and about Freud. Our previous paragraphs on pragmatism draw from several sources. Because the literature on the subject is voluminous and because they are especially attentive to pragmatism at Chicago and to Dewey, we particularly acknowledge the work of Dykhuizen, Diggins (*Promise*), Feffer, Morris, Rucker, and Thayer. Morris emphasizes at the end of his book his own experiences with the pragmatists at Chicago in the 1920s. Since we completed this chapter Menand has also written about the formation of the pragmatist school in Chicago (358–62).

60. Details about Hook's early career are available in his autobiography, *Out of Step*, and in Phelps. For a bibliography of Hook's writings, see Crowley. On Hook in the 1930s, see Denning, 425–34.

Chapter 2: Resisting the "Rout of the Esthetes"

1. "While [Americans] strain at a gnat of doctrine, they'll swallow an elephant of experiment—[so] the first problem is to find a new phraseology that we'll be at home with" (Dos Passos to Wilson, January 1931). Dos Passos's letter to Wilson is quoted in Homberger (143), who has a fine chapter on Wilson in the early 1930s. See also chapter 2 of Cowley, *Dream*. Wilson's independent and unpredictable brand of communism made him unwelcome at the first American Writers' Congress. When he returned from a five-month visit to the Soviet Union that began shortly after the congress, he continued to affiliate himself with renegade leftists critical of Stalin such as Hook and Farrell (Homberger, 157; Meyers, chapter 9).

2. The phrase "Boring from Within" was a commonplace when Burke invented his title early in 1931. For example it was the slogan for a strategy employed by Emily Newell Blair, a suffragist who hoped to integrate women into the daily working of the Democratic Party in the 1920s (Sharer, 176). Burke's title specifically played off the conclusion of Tate's "Remarks on Southern Religion" from *I'll Take My Stand*, which appeared late in 1930; since the southerner "cannot bore from within," concluded Tate, "he has left the sole alternative of boring from without" (175).

3. The circumstances of publication for both books and a detailed analysis of both are included in Selzer, *Kenneth Burke in Greenwich Village*, chapters 6 and 7.

4. The argument between the two, which took place in December 1931, is summarized in Selzer, *Kenneth Burke in Greenwich Village*, 249.

5. The preface to *Towards a Better Life* closes with a defense of the aesthetic in fiction that is also a bellicose rejoinder to Gold, Hicks, and other proletarians: "Why should an author spend a year or more on a single book, and end by talking as he would talk on the spur of the moment? Or why should he feel impelled to accept as the 'norm' of his elucubrations that style so admirably fitted for giving the details of a murder swiftly over the telephone and rushing them swiftly into copy in time for the next edition of the news?" (xx).

6. *Pagany* also rejected Burke's apolitical "Trial Translation," a funny rewrite of a segment from Shakespeare's *Twelfth Night:* see Williams to Burke, July 20, 1932.

7. The same issue carried Burke's review of Croce's *History of Europe in the Nineteenth Century* (704–7). In 1931 *Hound and Horn* made good-natured fun of Burke's "Boring from Within" by parodying it in a mock "Comment" on politics and literature opening the summer issue (457–60). The Comment, subtitled "All God's Chillun Got Dilemmas," stitched direct but out-of-context Burke quotations from "Boring" into a funny satire of leftist intellectual posturing that the editors of *Hound and Horn* were finding in the *New Republic*, the *Nation*, and similar magazines.

8. For a fairly contemporary sense of Burke's views on Eliot's politics, see his discussion "Didactic Transcendence in Eliot" in *Attitudes toward History*.

9. The episode is detailed in chapter 6 of Cowley's *Dream*; in Josephson's *Infidel*, 110–13; and in Meyers, 152–53.

10. With some hyperbole Denning credits *Culture and the Crisis* with providing "the origins of US Western Marxism" (98) and profiles its main author, Lewis Corey. Cowley, Hook, and Josephson also had a hand in its composition (Wald, *New York*, 58)

11. The essay by Hicks was published in February 1933, but it was given as a lecture before the John Reed Club some months before. The article infuriated Burke not only for its condemnation of leisure (which Burke did indeed defend in *Counter-Statement* and in *Auscultation*, since he could not agree that leisure was anathema to leftist politics), but also because it accused Burke of "impl[ying] that the effect of reading a book is such that the reader goes out and does some specific thing" ("Crisis," 5). The gross oversimplification rankled Burke to no end, as we will indicate further in our next chapter. He referred to it in any number of letters and was still griping about it in March 1934. After Hicks asked Burke to review a book for *New Masses* (Hicks having just recently become literary editor), Burke's icy refusal included a comment on "that atrocious misrepresentation of Counter-Statement which you gave in your Crisis in Criticism article" (Burke to Hicks, March 2, 1934). Enclosed with the refusal was a scathing mock "extra edition" of *New Masses* by Burke that ridiculed Hicks's alleged muddleheadeness and attacked him on rather personal grounds: "What can one expect, if the Communists are to get their Communist theory from an ex-divinity student, a former Unitarian, a seeker after 'revealed values,' and at present a teacher in one of those typical survivals from feudalistic stratification, a 'better' New England college?" ("New Masses Goes Revisionist. Extree! Extree" in 1934 Burke correspondence, Kenneth Burke Papers). Hicks remained unrepentant, citing an essay by George Lukacs in a forthcoming *Partisan Review* to "explain how it can be that Burke would divorce literature from life even though he does think literature aims to make people go out and do some specific thing. Lukacs, in case you are interested, is neither an ex-theological student nor a teacher at one of the better New England colleges" (Hicks to Burke, March 4, 1934). To his credit Hicks later in life did admit to muddleheadedness in some of his positions during this period of his career: see letters from Hicks to Burke written in the 1970s and Hicks's autobiography *Part of the Truth*. And he was ultimately dismissed from that New England college for his political

beliefs. (Not so much to his credit, Hicks also denounced some of his old friends during the McCarthy period; Josephson, *Infidel*, 360.)

When he read Grattan's piece, Burke immediately offered (to no avail) a segment of *Auscultation* to the *Forum* as a rejoinder to Grattan's too-easy assumption that aestheticism and social concern were mutually exclusive categories. It is easy to imagine that Grattan's article was particularly galling to Burke because Grattan praised leftist writers for goals that were not unique to them and that Burke in fact shared. Grattan claimed, for instance, that "the young writers insist that the old American world and its values had decayed . . . and that a new world and new values must be created" ("New Voices," 288), a view that Burke certainly subscribed to.

12. The 1932 election turned into a disaster for the Communists. Thomas outscored Foster impressively at the polls, in part because Foster became ill during the campaign. On Burke's likely preference for Thomas, see Burke to Moore, November 28, 1932.

13. We have not had the opportunity to inspect the original manuscript of *Auscultation*, so in this chapter we accept Chesebro's text; page numbers, typically noted in parentheses, are to this edition.

14. The final, "poetical" section was going to be a story "with a hero who approaches the world only from matters of Li Tai Po" (Burke to Cowley, June 4, 1932, unsent).

15. Also relevant to the question of Burke's original intention: "After worrying for a considerable length of time over the book of my own that I was trying to write this summer, I suddenly made the discovery that I was really trying to amalgamate three books. . . . This discovery had the signal virtue of . . . helping me realize that one of the books was already finished" (Burke to Elizabeth Parker, October 3, 1932).

16. We date "Spring during Crisis" to the second half of 1932 on the basis of references in the correspondence (especially letters to Cowley) and the fact that he submitted the essay separately to *Hound and Horn* in January 1933. Burke may have revised the piece for later occasions; for example he attempted to peddle it to the *Southern Review* in April 1936. A brief foreword also entitled "Spring during Crisis" opens *Auscultation* in the Chesebro collection even though that foreword was written years later—probably around 1983, since Burke mentions in it writing "In Retrospective Prospect" for the 1984 reissues of *Permanence and Change* and *Attitudes toward History*. Our sense that much of *Auscultation* proper was written in June, July, and August 1932, and then finished in September is drawn not just from Burke's correspondence with Cowley but from other evidence. For instance Burke entertained Haakon Chevalier in the last days of July or first days of August (Chevalier to Burke, July 28, 1932); in early October, Burke reflected on that visit in a letter to Chevalier (October 8, 1932): "I always wondered whether I owe you any apologies for our erratic reception of you. You happened in on my third day of alcoholism, and I guess the toxins were seeping pretty close to the spinal fluids. After two days of inexorable hangover . . . , I got peacefully to work and hammered out a fifty-thousand-word Credo on the relationship between our literary problems and the nature of the contemporary scene, considering Marxism at some length, [and] attempting to show that we can in general

accept the Marxian distrust of the 'profit-system' without accepting the Marxian phi-losophy of culture. The whole is now cooling its heels in a publisher's office. . . . "

17. By "our" Burke was including Cowley himself and his book of poems *Blue Juniata* (1929), which is discussed in *Auscultation*. Burke, incidentally, did not easily forget what Cowley wrote about *1919*: the paragraph in *The Philosophy of Literary Form* (1941) that begins "Mr. Q writes a novel. He has a score to settle with the world," and that mentions Cowley explicitly, probably is an allusion to this review.

18. Burke was incensed that Cowley "should find it so damned poetic to picture me walled up at seventeen" in the "Apprentice of the Arts" episode of *Exile's Return*: "So, Malcolm, who has made it his practice his whole life to bury me, who put me in a narrow house years ago, who once again sees me facing the wall, and who can imag-ine nothing prettier than a picture of me masturbating myself into extinction at the age of seventeen. . . . He bows me out when I am just beginning" (June 4, 1932). The episodes of *Exile's Return* were published as a book in 1934.

19. A full paragraph on page 55 of *Auscultation* may be a direct reference to Wil-son: a passage ridiculing an individual who has initiated "talk of renouncing poetry—one striking fellow who got a prize in Paris for a poem, [and who] forthwith came forward to make it clear that he would now turn his mind to more serious things." But the passage may also refer to someone else, such as Donald Davidson, as we indicated in chapter 1, note 37.

20. Crusius ("*Auscultation*") therefore rightly calls Burke's account of history Hege-lian more than Marxist, with special affinities to Hegel's *Speculative Reason*. Burke, notes Crusius, offers a "dialectic of continuity" (371); "opposing concepts for Burke are always polarities within a union of opposites, never reified into mutually exclusive terms" (359); "[he] wants to cast doubts on all dogma, to undermine absolutisms" (362). Wess also understands *Auscultation* as taking "Marx seriously without taking him as gospel"; "the *bete noire* throughout *ACR* is the principle of antithesis" (59, 64).

21. Burke thereby anticipates the work of later theorists—Gramsci, Bourdieu, Mouffe, for example—who have also resisted the notion that culture is part of an irre-sistible construct determined solely by material conditions.

22. Burke has in mind, for instance, the Marxist commentary that glorifies labor as opposed to bourgeois leisure. Such commentaries would seem to make work itself a goal of the proletariat, in which case there would be no need for revolution: workers could keep on working while the bourgeois enjoy their leisure and the fruits of oth-ers' labor.

23. In an afterword ("Curriculum Criticum") included in the 1954 edition of *Counter-Statement*, Burke explained that the title of *Auscultation, Creation, and Revision* refers to the three stages of a writer's creative process: "(1) the heart-conscious kind of listening or vigilance, that precedes expression; (2) the expression in its unguarded simplicity; (3) modification of the expression, in the light of more complicated after-thoughts" (213–14).

24. For an authoritative account of the fierce battle between the new humanists and literary Marxists, waged in part in the pages of the pro-humanist *Hound and Horn* and the oppositional *New Masses*, see Aaron, 235–45. Burke was mainly a bystander to

this controversy, though in 1930 he did sign an open letter in the *New Republic* against humanism and contributed an essay, "The Allies of Humanism Abroad," to Hartley Grattan's collection *A Critique of Humanism.*

25. Burke wrote to Henry Goddard Leach (editor of the *Forum*) on October 22, 1932: "Nor must we forget the fact that Communism itself stems from the early nineteenth century—and I hope that I can show [in *Auscultation*] that one reason why the esthetes, in 'clearing out,' generally went over to Communism was because, in its doctrine of Antithesis, its 'Ivory Tower' conception of the perfect state, it is simply the esthetic attitude turned into politics (as one might expect, since Marx himself was writing at a time when this aesthetic attitude ran though the entire field of specula- tion, be it the poetic-imaginative or the conceptual-critical)."

26. Not that Burke necessarily coined the term; for example, Sidney Hook (who never read *ACR*) refers to the Saul-Paul reversal in a 1936 letter to Burke.

27. "Let's Build a Railroad" is the title of Cowley's February 1932 review of *Road to Life*, the first Russian sound film to be shown in the United States. The film tells the story of a group of teenage boys left homeless by the war who form a collective to escape a miserable life on the streets. The boys work capably and enthusiastically until they run out of raw materials and grow restless. In the climactic scene their leader ral- lies them with the cry, "We need a steady supply of raw materials. Let's build a rail- road!"—which they proceed to do. In his review Cowley praises Russian films in general—because, unlike Hollywood films, they "get something done" (351)—and *Road to Life* in particular because it modeled the kind of inspiration that Americans needed.

28. Burke's contract for *Counter-Statement* gave Harcourt, Brace, first option on his next two books. Consequently Harcourt published *Towards a Better Life* and might have been approached for *Auscultation*, especially since Burke's editor, C. A. Pearce, seemed anxious for him to finish the book. There is no conclusive evidence in Burke's correspondence that he submitted the manuscript to Pearce at Harcourt. An incon- clusive note in one letter (written October 3, 1932) that he had "hammered out a fair copy [and] sent it off to the publisher this morning" (Burke to Parker) might have been a reference to Harcourt, but there is no letter from Pearce around that date. Pearce may have obtained the manuscript for Harcourt and turned it down; a letter from Pearce (April 10, 1933) suggested that Burke had hard feelings for Harcourt over something—perhaps a rejection. On February 6 Pearce suggested that Burke contact Pound (in Rapallo, Italy) for help, and Burke must have done so, because a letter from Pound (February 14, 1935) suggested one possibility, a small, academically oriented press (Edwards Brothers, in Ann Arbor, Michigan) that Burke probably did not follow up on. Burke's letter to Pound, to our knowledge, does not survive.

29. Not that he gave up trying. In March 1936, heartened by the "bright and receptive . . . young critics connected with the [new] Partisan Review," Burke "began to think of ways of trying to refurbish for publication the gloomy anti-Marxist MSS I wrote before Permanence and Change. For I was glancing through it the other day, and found to my amazement that I could still subscribe to practically all of it and find allies among the Marxists. . . . So all I have to do is shift the emphasis as follows: offer it, not as an attack upon Marxist critics, but as an attack on naïve Marxist critics, and every word of it holds. . . . It would be a great joy to me if I could salvage this book—

for it is an answer to much of Hicks's idiocy" (Burke to Josephson, March 2, 1936). A draft of a letter to William Phillips of *Partisan Review*, in folder P15 of the Kenneth Burke Papers, indicates that Burke may well have followed up on this plan, but Phillips ultimately decided not to accept Burke's proposal to have *ACR* published serially in *PR* (Phillips to Burke, March 6, 1936). Burke circulated the manuscript at least once more at that point, for on April 8, 1936, he received a reply from Clifton Simpson at Whittlesey House, a division of McGraw-Hill: "Several people here have read your book, and think that it is too limited in appeal for us to publish. As we see it, the book is concerned with differences of opinion within a literary group which itself is not very large" (Simpson to Burke, April 8, 1936). Burke also tried to place "Spring during Crisis" in the *Southern Review* at the same time (see Burke to Warren, April 9, 1936), without success.

Chapter 3: Translating Cultural History

1. Burke's marriage to Lily, which had been deteriorating for some time, concluded when she moved to New York with their children in time to begin the school year in September 1933. He moved to 78 Bank Street in Greenwich Village in October and was divorced in November. On December 18 he married Elizabeth "Libbie" Batterham, with whom he had been building a relationship for some time. In the first months of 1933, Burke toyed with the idea of starting a new magazine, *New State* (discussed below). He and Franklin Spier also took steps to found Manuscript Editions in January 1933. Frustrated by a lack of publication venues during the Depression, Burke and Spier proposed to produce (and support through subscriptions) a dozen inexpensively published books, one a month, that would normally appeal to a limited audience of 1,000–1,500 readers ("Manuscript Editions" prospectus, William Carlos Williams file, Burke Papers). Though Burke's contacts responded with enthusiasm (and submissions) to his announcement of the idea, the venture never came to pass.

2. Beginning in 1936, *New Directions* would offer the aesthetes some of the publishing opportunities that had been lost when *Pagany* folded (in the spring of 1933) and when *Hound and Horn* shut down (late in 1934).

3. *The Embodiment of Knowledge*, completed about 1930, was first published in 1974, but Burke knew its contents because he read the manuscript in January 1933, when Williams submitted it to Burke's Manuscript Editions venture. Burke apparently rejected the manuscript because it was unfinished and relied too heavily on Dewey (though Burke's rejection letter has apparently been lost); a perplexed and miffed Williams shot back, "Yes, of course. The examples are missing tho' present in my head as circus performers, net makers—anything but machines—possessors of knowledge in the flesh as opposed to a body of knowledge called science or philosophy. From knowledge possessed by a man springs poetry. From science springs the machine. . . . If I could convince myself or have anyone else convince me that I were merely following in the steps of Dewey, I'd vomit and quit" (Williams to Burke, January 26, 1933). Williams nevertheless sent two other manuscripts to Burke before the Manuscript Editions venture failed, the complete novel *White Mule* (earlier carried serially in *Pagany*) and what would appear in 1934 as *Collected Poems, 1921–1931*.

4. Williams was rather singular among the aesthetes for rejecting the notion of poetry as the expression of eternal truth, at least in *Embodiment*. "There are no 'truths'

that can be found in language," he wrote. "It is in the breakup of the language that the truth can be seen to exist and that it becomes operative again. . . . In language lodge the prejudices, the compulsions by which stupidity and ineptitude rule intelligences superior to their own" (19). Williams's understanding of the role of language in maintaining habits of stultifying thought moves him closer to Dewey and of course Burke than to Tate and Winters. Williams looked to the future rather than to the fallen past; he sought new poetic forms in order to embody new knowledge, for if language was a means to perpetuate falsehood, it was just as surely "the key to the mind's escape from bondage to the past" (19).

5. In fact, as one of us has indicated elsewhere, it is quite possible to see the pangolin as an image of Moore's view of Burke (George, *Permanence and Change*, 155). Moore had praised Burke on the occasion of his Dial Award in 1929 for maintaining a devotion to art that nevertheless did not isolate him from the world.

6. Winters's position placed him, he thought, in opposition to Burke. In "The Experimental School in American Poetry" (written in 1934, published in 1937), he launched a ferocious attack on the formal experimentation that Williams so celebrated —and he used Burke's *Counter-Statement* and *Towards a Better Life* as prime examples of the disastrous consequences of experimental modern art. Apparently unaware of Burke's recent critiques of pure aestheticism, Winters ranted against the "Laforgian double mood" that he noticed in *Towards a Better Life* and against what he saw as Burke's "relativism" in *Counter-Statement*. "As the theory [expressed in *Counter-Statement*] does not . . . admit the existence of rightness, the theory encourages shoddy writing and shoddy living. The hero of Mr. Burke's novel goes mad, for the reason that, the need of judgment having been removed by his (and Mr. Burke's) theories, the power of judgment atrophies. Yet Mr. Burke continues to preach the doctrine which brought him to this end" (*Primitivism and Decadence*, 62).

7. On June 11, 1932, however, Tate wrote that *Hound and Horn* had cancelled the review. Burke replied that he was still eager to see Tate's notes, especially the ones about Burke's "Lexicon Rhetoricae" chapter: "I should like to see just what you kicked about (rather, just *how* you kicked)—I can surmise the *what*, for do I not know how many of my own absolutist wishes I outraged?" (June 13, 1932).

8. Tate carried on a spirited correspondence with Cowley on the same issues. As that correspondence indicates, Tate and Cowley were such close friends that Cowley lived with the Tates while he was completing *Exile's Return* in the spring of 1933 (Cowley, *Exile's*, chapter 17). But that did not keep the two from arguing vociferously over the communist and agrarian approach to things, and Tate sometimes felt that Cowley was keeping him out of the pages of the *New Republic*.

9. It is tempting to compare Tate's formulation to Burke's distinction between propaganda and art in *Auscultation*. Burke based the distinction on the reader's sense of the important issues of the day, while Tate based his on the artist's will or intention. A work of propaganda, wrote Tate, is "written in the interest of social, moral, and religious ideas apart from which it has neither existence nor significance. And it is aesthetic creation at a low ebb of intensity. If the intention is innocent, the result is didacticism. If it is deliberate and systematic, and calculated to move people into some definite course of action, we get what is called in our time propaganda" (*Reactionary*

Essays, 90). Tate conceded that some didactic works can have great merit, his example being Dreiser's *An American Tragedy*.

10. For Tate the point was not simply that art is not useful. It was, rather, that art functions in a realm separate from the political, the rhetorical, the everyday world of action. "Statements in a genuine work of art," he averred, still arguing with Richards, "are neither 'certified' nor 'pseudo-'; the creative intention removes them from the domain of practicality" (*Reactionary Essays*, 109). As an index of this separateness, witness the way Tate could speak of art isolated not only from politics and practical action but also from readers—"a great poem is great whether anybody reads it or not" (Tate to Burke, August 3, 1933)—and even, in his 1938 essay "Narcissus as Narcissus," from writers: "In a manner of speaking, the poem is its own knower, neither poet nor reader knowing anything that the poem says apart from the words of the poem" (*Essays of Four Decades*, 595).

11. Burke sent a copy of part 1 of *Permanence and Change* ("On Interpretation") to Tate in June 1934. On June 22 Tate acknowledged receipt of the manuscript and promised to "peruse your opus with great interest." Yet Tate continued to tease Burke about his sources ("Any one who derives from Bentham deserves the name . . . Doctor Diabolus") and criticized his endorsement of communism. Tate did not write further to Burke about the book and in fact, after a postcard from Burke to Tate on September 19, 1934 (lamenting Tate's silence), there is a break in the correspondence until 1940.

12. Except as noted, all quotations from *Permanence and Change* are taken from the first edition. Though amended editions later appeared and though the third edition is the most widely accessible one, we have chosen to quote the edition that Burke prepared in the 1930s.

13. To Burke the people whose occupation is to discover permanence are mystics: "the mystic seeks a sounder basis of certainty than those provided by the flux of history. He seeks the ultimate motive behind our acts . . . , an ultimate situation common to all men" (283). In his letters Tate had criticized Burke for dabbling in mysticism, so Burke's linkage of poets and mystics (as groups interested in finding permanence) was not coincidental but a response to Tate.

14. By the time he wrote *A Grammar of Motives*, of course, Burke had substituted the term *dramatic* for *poetic*.

15. For Burke's meditation on his decision to use the term *orientation* rather than Marx's term *ideology* (or rather than any number of other possible synonyms), see his remarkable "Afterword: *Permanence and Change:* In Retrospective Prospect" added to the third edition (305–6). For a discussion of piety that is in keeping with ours, see Rosteck and Leff; Jack; and Hawhee, "Burke on Drugs."

16. Ogden and Richards in *The Meaning of Meaning* (1927) outline more completely the various senses of the words *meaning* and *truth*. In addition to opposing statement and pseudo-statement, Ogden and Richards distinguish between poetic and scientific uses of language: poetry works through tone, through the sounds and feel of words, while "science . . . endeavors with increasing success to bar out these factors. In its use of words poetry is just the reverse of science." Ironically Richards's analysis of the relation between science and poetry in contemporary culture begins with the

same premise that is expressed in *P&C*. Richards claims that "our thoughts are the servants of our interests" (*Science and Poetry*, 22), while Burke writes in his summary (336), "let us say that *we have been attempting to consider the many ramifications implicit in the statement that 'our thoughts and acts are affected by our interests.'*" Richards, however, as Burke implies, would exempt scientists from this rule.

17. Burke more explicitly challenges Richards's assumptions of scientific objectivity (as well as Tate's repeated criticism of Richards in his letters to Burke) by analyzing Richards's objections at the end of *Science and Poetry* to D. H. Lawrence's *Fantasia of the Unconscious*. Richards cites Lawrence's *Fantasia* as the perfect example of literature trying to do the work of science—and doing it very badly indeed, for Lawrence inverts positivistic causal order, placing human life at the center of the universe and concluding, for instance, that growing plants make the sun shine. Taken as statements, Richards implies, Lawrence's claims are nonsense; he accuses Lawrence of "ethical universe-building." But Burke is puzzled by Richards's reaction: "for the charge implies that there is some kind of universe-building which is not ethical" (321). All universes, in other words, are human creations, constructions built through the workings of piety. For more on the conversation between Burke and Richards, via Lawrence, see Wess, 70–75.

18. On Gourmont and Burke, see Selzer, *Kenneth Burke in Greenwich Village*, 140–43.

19. Burke is no radical social constructivist, however. He qualifies his understanding of how people construct their worlds with the notion of "recalcitrance": the resistance of the material world. Just as Burke grounds human purpose in the physical body, so too he argues that interpretive frameworks must be revised in light of "*the recalcitrance of the materials employed for embodying this attitude*" (328). The person who proclaims "I am a bird" and concludes that "I can safely jump from a high place" will want to revise those claims when faced with the recalcitrance of gravity, hard ground, and lack of wings. Burke's argument "does not involve us in subjectivism, or solipsism. It does not imply that the universe is merely the product of our interpretations. For the interpretations themselves must be altered as the universe displays various orders of recalcitrance to them" (*P&C*, 329).

20. On June 6, 1934, Burke was arrested and spent a night in jail for his role in the picketing on behalf of Macauley Company clerical workers (Josephson, *Infidel*, 356–57); others involved included Josephson, Cowley, Gold, Dashiell Hammett, and Tess Slessinger. In July 1934 Burke joined a New York committee (with Sue Jenkins) to raise funds in support of a "Pittsburgh Workers School and Bookshop, being organized for the purpose of disseminating radical economic lore in the mill and mining towns" (Burke to Frank, July 16, 1934). The Mann petition is discussed in a letter from Edmund Wilson to Burke, June 1934. In December 1934 Burke also served (with Isidor Schneider, James T. Farrell, Nathan Asch, and Archibald MacLeish) on a commission investigating the grievances of striking employees of the Ohrbach's department store (Schneider to Burke, December 18, 1934).

21. Just what to call or how to define Burke's relation to Marxism continues to be a problem. Burke's speech before the John Reed Club, an early version of what would become "My Approach to Communism," is discussed by Sheriff: she details Burke's uneasy relationship to Marx. Burke is typically absent (Denning is an important

exception) from intellectual histories of the American Left, making, at most, a cameo appearance in discussions of the 1935 Writers' Congress. Among Burke scholars there is agreement that Marx is an important figure in his thought, but the nature of that importance remains puzzling. Thus Aune places Burke in the tradition of American individualists such as Dewey, Emerson, James, and Veblen; Abbott describes Burke's communism as "comic" ("Marxist Influences," 228); and Burks calls Burke, after some of Burke's own self-descriptions, "the agro-bohemian Marxoid" (219).

22. We use the term *Marxism* to refer to Marxist-Leninist thought with its emphasis on historical materialism, class struggle, and proletarians as the vanguard group. We use *Communism* (or *Stalinism*) to refer to the policies and practices of the Communist Party. We use *communism* to refer to a general socioeconomic doctrine associated with a classless society and collective, socialist life. As Denning notes, people in the 1930s frequently used the term *communist* in a general sense that extended well beyond the formal limits of the Communist Party (xviii).

23. See Bloom's *Left Letters* for an excellent account of Gold's and Freeman's cultural politics. As we also indicated in chapter 2, Freeman's introduction to *Proletarian Literature* is particularly revealing to people interested in Burke. It borrows assumptions about art from the aesthetes: "The basic commonplace of criticism is that art is something different from action and something different from science. It is hard to understand why anyone should pour out bottles of ink to labor so obvious and elementary a point. No one has ever denied it, least of all the Marxists" (9). Burke, of course, was indeed denying it, at least the part about action, though in his review of *Proletarian Art* ("Symbolic War") he was as forgiving as he could be without giving up his reservations against works that too single-mindedly overstress "the situation" and consequently "overlook the *humane* development of character" (139). Burke acknowledged that Freeman's introduction, "Experience and Art," "while prolix and unnecessarily defensive," contained "many acute formulations" (147); Burke could not have known that Freeman's original, longer introduction contained approving references to Burke that had to be cut for reasons of space (see "Experience and Art" typescript, Freeman Papers).

24. The *New Republic* under George Soule remained true to its founder's belief in state planning of the national economy, and after 1932 that belief generally pointed in the direction of Marxism. But throughout the decade the magazine remained committed to an exploration of the range of available positions on the left, even as *New Masses* consistently articulated the Communist alternative.

25. Because the term *Trotskyite* was typically used as an epithet by those who despised what it stood for, we follow Denning and many others in using the more neutral term *Trotskyist.*

26. In a *Saturday Review* analysis published December 30, 1933, Bernard Smith placed Burke in an "uncommitted" position within the Left critics. Denning has treated Burke as an "independent leftist" as well. Lentricchia refers to Burke as a "deviant" Marxist (23).

27. *New State* was the brainchild of Burke and one James Abell, who was connected with Burke through Colonel Woods, Burke's employer at the Bureau for Social Hygiene in the late 1920s. The two met in the spring of 1933, and Burke wrote up a prospectus for a magazine that would instruct readers in the workings and criticism of

political organizations, the better to prepare citizens for civic participation: "Aristotle defined man as a *political* animal. The conduct of the state is man's most dignified concern—for it is only by a deep and discerning manipulation of our political machinery that we can ever hope to produce a sound, stable, and cultured way of national life. . . . Fascism and Communism seek to create organized bodies of obedient citizens who perform when the string is pulled. They seek to make people like cows, since cows are so easily driven" (Burke to Abell, April 7, 1933; Burke Papers). Burke's correspondence with Abell and *New State* effectively ended in July 1933.

28. Native radicals, according to Buhle, "had a better subjective sense of the meaning, for Americans, of the old Republic's decline and debauch at the hands of monopolistic capitalism" (58). This native tradition of radicalism in many ways reached its apex in Debsian socialism, a movement that through its "fusion of messianic hope and egalitarian political-economic promise" was able to build a previously unimaginable coalition of railroad machinists, farmers, small-town professionals, Jews, and folk cultures (82). In light of the poetic orientation Burke was offering in *P&C*, Buhle's analysis of Debs's appeal is telling: "they admired Marx's genius. . . . But without the poetic dimension, Socialism reduced itself to dry and unconvincingly rational theories. Debs was poetry come alive; he signified the birth of a movement that did not seek to reduce the symbols of Socialism but broadened them decisively" (84). When Debsian socialism was defeated, Buhle suggests, radical thought descended to an abstract economism, "sacrificing in the process the moral-utopian qualities which gave radicalism much of its currency in American tradition. The problem was not so much the uncritical embrace of Russian Revolution as the uncritical relinquishment" (117) of American socialism's "sentimental, spiritualist native vernacular" (156). In taking up the relationships between *P&C* and native radicalism, we are picking up on the observation of James Aune: "Both the neo-Marxist and post-structuralist appropriations of the thirties Burke and the eighties Burke obscure . . . Burke's continuity with the native American radical tradition, a tradition we can now begin to trace more accurately" (237).

29. These four grounds provided the organizing principle for "My Approach to Communism," Burke's long and sober more-or-less oath of solidarity published in the March 20, 1934, *New Masses*, which draws heavily from *P&C*. That *P&C* is beholden to communism has been well established; see Schiappa and Keenan. On "My Approach," see Sheriff.

30. Burke's motives, in other words, are poetic more than economic, exactly as the wording of the passage quoted previously indicates: "Communism . . . fulfills the requirements suggested by the poetic metaphor" (*P&C*, 344); communism is, for Burke, the means to an end. Communism (i.e., the policies of the CP) is also a means to an end. Burke argued for Communism, he made clear in letters to Gregory and Cowley, only because it seemed to him the best way to achieve communism. "The book, though explicitly favoring Communism, was not written as a barrister's plea. Indeed, it was not designed as an argument for Communism at all. It was written simply because, as a critic, I wished to trail down the nature of my judgments. . . . So I made the machine, and when I started it going, out came 'Communism'" (Burke to Gregory, January 28, 1935). "I embrace Communism by subterfuge—as the only system on the horizon which could conceivably drop the cult of production without

disrupting the state" (Burke to Cowley, March 30, 1934). And this halfhearted—or, better, half-headed—support may account for Cowley's comment to Josephson that Burke's communism was mild, and for Austin Warren's distinct feeling that Burke's "Communism . . . [was] a concession to the shouters of the day. . . . [T]hat it follows from your premises I, with utmost candor, am unable to see" (letter to Burke, April 24, 1935). "Your communism . . . appears, like Mumford's, to be humanistic and not doctrinairely Marxist" (letter to Burke, September 23, 1935). As Robert Wess summarizes, "Burke explicitly advocates communism in the first edition of [*P&C*]. The advocacy, however, is pitched at the level of culture and value rather than economics and power" (58).

31. That Burke worked hard to accommodate his views with Marx's but could not do so without qualification left him open to charges that his views were "fascist." For instance, in July 1934, he was infuriated when one E. A. Schachner labeled him a fascist in the *Windsor Quarterly* on the basis of "The Nature of Art under Capitalism." (Burke wrote a lengthy response to the article by Schachner that was never printed, perhaps because the *Windsor Quarterly*, a product of the proletarian Commonwealth Labor College in Mena, Arkansas, folded before it could be; Burke Papers.) Note also Burke's entry on "being driven into a corner" in the "Dictionary of Pivotal Terms" in *Attitudes toward History:* "Occasionally, when one makes a statement, his auditor will reprove him by observing that some Nazi ideologist has made a similar statement. . . . We have sometimes been grateful that no Nazi ideologist happens to have grown rhapsodic in praise of the multiplication table. Presumably, if he had, the thoroughgoing anti-Nazi would feel it necessary to condemn arithmetic" (II, 64–65). Perhaps Burke was here recalling charges that his "Revolutionary Symbolism in America" speech betrayed Nazi sentiments.

Burke was of course hardly alone in being labeled fascist on account of heterodoxy. For example in July 1933 Gold soundly denounced Archibald MacLeish's *Frescoes for Mr. Rockefeller's City*, a book that includes comments critical of those who mistook propaganda and poetry, in a *New Republic* review entitled "Out of the Fascist Unconscious." Burke contemplated entering full bore into the controversy but did so only superficially (in his September 1933 essay "War, Response, and Contradiction," which sides with MacLeish over Gold). "War, Response, and Contradiction" (included in *The Philosophy of Literary Form*) actually revolves around another controversy, this one involving Cowley and MacLeish's disagreement over a book entitled *The First World War*. Cowley discouraged Burke from entering the discussion (letters between Cowley and Burke, September 1933), but Burke wished to exploit the occasion to meditate on the relation between art and life, poetry and propaganda. Later quarrels between MacLeish and Gold are covered in Aaron, chapter 8.

32. When in a 1983 interview Burke was asked about the sources of his thinking in *P&C*, he gave a surprising answer: "This is a drastic confession. You wouldn't believe this. There's an awful lot of that book that was really secularizing what I learned as a Christian Scientist. All that psychogenic illness stuff. . . I got that from Mary Baker Eddy" (Skodnick, 18–19). There is no explicit mention of Mary Baker Eddy or Christian Science in *P&C*, but Burke's confession does highlight parallels between Christian Science and Burke's references to homeopathy and his sense of

himself as a cultural physician (which we will develop in our discussion of *P&C* as cultural history). The cornerstone of Christian Science is the effort at "mind healing," which neatly describes Burke's purpose in *P&C*. For a discussion of other parallels between *P&C* and Eddy's *Science and Health*, see Feehan, "Kenneth Burke and Mary Baker Eddy."

33. For accounts of the connections between Burke and Nietzsche that we cannot improve upon, especially with regard to *P&C*, see Hawhee, "Burke and Nietzsche," and Wess, 76–78.

34. Midway through his draft of *P&C*, Burke wrote to Cowley: "Of course, I take it that such men [Fichte, Hegel, Schelling] must be 'translated.' But many an observation which has been made about the *universe* can be seen again for the vital and accurate thing it was if one merely knows how to 'translate' it into an observation about the *human mind*" (September 22, 1933). Denning has also noticed the importance of *translation* to *P&C* (439).

35. In a note on page 330, Burke defines determinism as "a theory that the universe can make no mistakes. Not only is everything caused, but it is *accurately* caused. Alter the nature of the stimulus ever so little, and by the doctrine of determinism you get a corresponding alteration of the response. . . . Such is determinism: the picture of a vast and complex structure, acting without a single error, and without creative purpose, a machine permanently in order." The passage closely parallels, if it does not derive from, the dissenter Sidney Hook's argument in "Communism without Dogmas," collected in *The Meaning of Marx: A Symposium*, a work that Burke cites in *P&C*.

36. See Crable for an elaboration of how Burke's metabiology is a response to Marxist critics.

37. Burke's use of the phrase *science of symbolism* is a reference to Ogden and Richards's *The Meaning of Meaning*, subtitled *A Study of the Influence of Language upon Thought and of the Science of Symbolism*, a book that Burke singles out for special praise in his acknowledgments. Working from the premise that thought "is directed and organized" by symbols (9), Ogden and Richards testify to the practical importance of the study of interpretation: "All the more elaborate forms of social and intellectual life are affected by changes in our attitude towards, and use of, words" (ix–x). While it is difficult to say how much or exactly where Burke's thinking was shaped by *The Meaning of Meaning*, *P&C* clearly shares with it fundamental assumptions about language and reality, particularly ones about the constructed nature of experience. "In all thinking we are interpreting signs," maintain Ogden and Richards: "We must begin then with Interpretation" (244). Although Ogden and Richards fail to acknowledge the social or ideological dimensions within interpretation, their book often reads as something of a gloss on Burke's.

38. Burke originally intended an "introduction, giving our program in advance, covering the whole ground in a general way, so that the reader might find it easier to know where the arrows of discussion are pointing" (Burke to Frank, September 19, 1934), but "after the work was set up in type, it was found to be longer than the N. R. [New Republic Books] felt it could give its readers for $1. So I had to snip out the chunks here and there, and . . . forgo an introduction" (Burke to Gregory, January 28,

1935). Robert Coates had recommended such an introduction (letter to Burke, September 1, 1934), "for I think that your method of unfolding the argument . . . keep[s] your argument and the end it is working toward too much a secret, as the book now is."

39. For a complete account of the genre of cultural history, see George, *Permanence and Change*.

40. See Jeffrey Walker's *Bardic Ethos* for an account of some important cultural histories, particularly as they were used by Pound, Crane, Williams, and Olson to offer a Whitmanesque reconstruction of American culture.

41. As early as 1908 Brooks, in *The Wine of the Puritans*, had anatomized the Puritans as the prototype of the overly industrious, commercial, anti-artistic American, and he continued the attack in *America's Coming-of-Age* and "On Creating a Usable Past." Several cultural historians subsequently adopted "the puritans" as the enemy: Williams in *In the American Grain*, Frank in *Our America*, H. L. Mencken generally, Wilson, and so forth.

42. Where exactly Veblen used the term *trained incapacity* is no longer a mystery; see Wais.

43. Brooks was a leading intellectual in Greenwich Village when Burke moved there in 1918, an editor of *Seven Arts* and author of the famous "On Creating a 'Usable' Past." Four substantial letters from Brooks to Burke survive that were written between March 1921 and June 1923. Burke encountered Brooks quite often during this period because the *Dial* (where Burke worked) and the *Freeman* (which employed Brooks) were housed in the same building. Brooks won the Dial Award in 1925, and Burke reviewed his book on Mark Twain.

44. But there are also great differences between Williams's cultural history and the Agrarians'. Williams, for example, sought a distinctively American culture, while the Agrarians took more than a little pride in European letters and tended to identify American art with northern industrialism. Davidson, in fact, explicitly rejected Emerson's and Whitman's sponsorship of a distinctly American literature.

45. One of the first examples was Burke's 1930 *New Republic* spoof "Waste—The Future of Prosperity." Dedicated to Henry Ford, who was educating Americans "to the full realization of their function as wasters" (228), the satire mocked the notion that material prosperity could not only erect "the most prosperous civilization in the history of man" but also provide for "the spiritual welfare of society." It pictured a philosopher surrounded by the products of Fordism, "a kingdom of last year's grandeur: old-model nose straighteners, antiquated breeds of mechanical horses, mission-style electric toasters, Alpine sunlamps lacking yodel attachments, cars with a diving girl in a red bathing suit, unfinished correspondence courses, remaindered best sellers, old calendars, evening clothes without 'moderne' buttonholes, 'No Parking Here' paper weights, explosive cigars, radio-phonographico-pianos without Neo-Novo-Nevaware buffet-lunch inserts" (230). Kastely offers an excellent discussion of Burke's lifelong commitment to the "comedic and therapeutic heckling of the twin empires of capitalism and technology" (307).

46. William Rueckert has already noticed that *P&C* offers a large dose of social medication: "Having studied and diagnosed the sickly body of society, Burke is now

going to do us a detailed anatomy of human purpose so that he can suggest a cure" (*Rereading Kenneth Burke*, 243).

47. Burke built on Frazer's scheme in two ways: while Frazer in *The Golden Bough* outlined three macrophases, Burke proposed four; and while Frazer concentrated on the transition from magic to religion, Burke concentrated on the transition from science to "the next phase," poetry.

48. Within the investor's psychosis "the superstructure of credit and interest is considered basic" (60): the discussion derives from Veblen's *Theory of the Business Enterprise*, chapter 6. Burke was by no means the only intellectual who was building on Veblen in the early 1930s. As Denning indicates (172–73), Dos Passos also was "saturated in the peculiar mix of Marx and Veblen," particularly as evidenced in *1919*, and Josephson's 1934 *The Robber Barons* fused Marx and Veblen as well.

49. Mumford's *Technics and Civilization*, written concurrently with *P&C* and published in 1934, months before *P&C*, emphasizes both the limitations and promise of machine culture. Although we have uncovered no evidence that Burke and Mumford consulted with each other as they wrote their works of cultural history (Mumford finished a second draft of *Technics* in 1932 but did major revisions in 1933, while Burke was drafting *P&C*), the two traveled in the same intellectual circles, and there are startling analogies between their two books. Still seeking a usable past (as he had in *The Golden Day*) in the tradition of Brooks, Mumford contemplated a four-volume project entitled, appropriately enough for a cultural history, "The Renewal of Life." The first installment, *Technics*, analyzes how the machine mentality had developed in America, why it had been culturally disastrous, and how it might be redirected. Working, like Burke, from Veblen's suspicion of machine culture, Mumford nevertheless offers his own original history of the machine, which he felt had developed over three phases— the eotechnic (which prepared the way for social regimentation through the invention of the clock), the paleotechnic (a barbaric period characterized by Gradgrindian degradation), and the neotechnic (the present). (These three phases existed within a broader outline of the whole of human history that Mumford briefly divided into three macrophases: fantasy, magic, and technology.) Mumford considered current American culture to be transitional: in the offing, if it could be managed, was a neotechnic period of harmony between machines and people in which the darkness and disease associated with the mine and factory would give way to the light and life of machines full of "mathematical accuracy, physical economy, chemical purity, and surgical cleanliness" (247). Thus Mumford's project was to counter the Agrarians' and Veblen's out-of-hand dismissal of the machine culture and to further a communist agenda: "Whatever the politics of the country may be, the machine is a communist" (354). Mumford's plan in his final chapter for fitting machines to people rather than the reverse—for a "transvaluation" of the machine—would result in a renewed and "organic" intellectual life (highly congruent with Burke's vision of a poet's state) in which "creative activity is finally the only important business of mankind. . . . The essential task of all sound economic activity is to produce a state in which creation will be a common fact in all experience" (410).

50. Language such as this raises the issue of essentialism: to what extent did Burke see the poetic rationalization as the ultimate one? On the one hand, it is difficult to

imagine Burke as understanding anything as final, and the phase history outlined in *P&C* implies further orientations to come. On the other hand, Burke's language surrounding the aesthetic or poetic orientation is full of superlatives; e.g., "the ultimate metaphor for discussing the universe and man's relation to it must be the poetic or dramatic metaphor" (338). As Wess observes, in *Permanence and Change* Burke's constructivist impulses collide with and are ultimately contained by his "biological essentialism." Burke's historical narrative "is open-ended, moving from orientation to orientation with no final . . . place of truth at which to rest. It's a history without a telos, change without permanence" (83). But as we have indicated, the lack of a telos is precisely the reason Burke rejects Marx's materialism and the other nineteenth-century "philosophies of becoming." The search for permanence is satisfied in metabiology. For another illuminating discussion of Burke's constructivism in *P&C*, see Crable.

Chapter 4: Heralding the Popular Front

1. Burke hoped that Frank might intervene on his behalf to secure a publisher (Burke to Frank, May 23, 1934; July 16, 1934; September 19, 1934), and by September, the *New Republic* had begun considering *P&C* for its Dollar Book Series. Burke liked that series because he appreciated "the price at which the book would sell. . . . The imprint of the series would place the work clearly in the educational field, where it belongs (I have always tended to consider myself a kind of free-lance schoolteacher . . .). And the modest asking price of one dollar should make it easier to seek out those earnest indigent readers whom one would most like to think of himself as addressing" (Burke to Josephson, September 7, 1934).

2. Burke proposed "a book outlining and characterizing world outlooks that have prevailed in the past, with particular attention to the emergence and disintegration of such outlooks." By the time he accepted the Guggenheim, he had changed the description to "a book studying the effect which ideas and social values have had upon the practical and material aspects of different cultures" (Henry Allen Moe to Burke, March 20, 1935).

3. Although Burke often uses the term *attitudes* to suggest "mood" or "state of mind" (as in his proposal that critics should interpret human behavior with a "comic attitude"), he argues later that attitude, as incipient action, is always "grounded in the systematic development of method. . . . [*A Grammar of Motives*] is constructed on the belief that, whereas an *attitude* of humanistic contemplation is in itself more important by far than any *method*, only by method could it be given the body necessary for its existence even as an attitude" (*Grammar*, 318–19). In his 1955 introduction to the revised version of *ATH*, Burke indicated that what he had meant by *history* was "man's life in political communities," and that what he had meant by *attitudes* was "the characteristic responses of people in their forming and reforming of congregations" (n.pag.). In that sense *attitude* has affinities with the term *ideology*, a word that Burke may have avoided in his search for a less pejorative term (Denning, 439–40).

4. Burke formally announced *identification* as a key term in *A Rhetoric of Motives*, but he had already used the term in *Auscultation* and in "Revolutionary Symbolism." And *ATH* demonstrates that Burke was already committed to the concept as well: e.g.,

"all the issues with which we have been concerned come to a head in the problem of identity" (II, 138). In this chapter all page references are to the first edition of *ATH*. Burke made many changes (for many reasons) when he prepared later editions. For example he distanced the book somewhat from its Popular Front context, especially its references to fascism and Stalin; downplayed his role as revolutionary critic; and deleted a lengthy section on I. A. Richards (I, 239–45) and another on the sound-emotion correspondence in words (II, 82–94) that he came to regard as "too tenuous."

5. An ad for the Hicks event appears in the *New Masses* of February 4, 1936 (27). That Burke was part of the LAW executive committee at least through the summer of 1936 is evident from his signing a LAW protest that appeared in *New Masses* on September 8, 1936, and from the minutes of the executive committee meeting of May 26 (Freeman Papers). Our sense is that shortly after that time—and certainly before the second Writers' Congress in early June 1937—Burke left the executive committee, which had been growing more inactive after early 1936 until it was rekindled after the Spanish Civil War began that summer. The minutes of the May 26 meeting indicate that the LAW was exploring a reorganization of its executive committee, and Burke did not appear at subsequent executive committee meetings, though he was listed as a continuing member of the LAW. Two letters from Ellen Blake, then the LAW executive secretary, on June 8 and June 14, 1937, indicate that Burke served on the LAW-sponsored national executive council of an organization to support anti-Franco forces in the Spanish Civil War and that he had secured a major donation to the LAW from J. Sibley Watson.

6. Burke's activities in the LAW may be tracked in the LAW archives at Syracuse (including box 33 of the Granville Hicks Papers), in the Freeman Papers at Stanford, and in the Waldo Frank and James T. Farrell Papers at Penn. For a fine short history of the LAW, see Kutulas ("Becoming"). Especially instructive concerning the magazine are letters in the Freeman Papers and Burke Papers: Katherine Buckles to Freeman (June 14 and 24, 1935); Freeman to Hart (May 17, 1935); Newton Arvin to Burke (November 11, 1935), which indicates that Burke had been developing plans for a LAW magazine; Buckles to Burke (October 31, 1935), which asks Burke to report on plans for the magazine at the LAW board meeting of November 5; Wilson to Burke, November 23, 1935; Greenwood to Burke, December 28 and 30, 1935; Humphreys to Burke, January 22 and 30, 1936.

7. Among his reviews were a *New Masses* evaluation of Muriel Rukeyser's book of poems *Theory of Flight* (February 1936) and *New Republic* commentaries on Gertrude Stein's *Lectures in America* (July 3, 1935); on the "satiric propaganda" of Robert Forsythe [Kyle Crichton] (July 10, 1935); on a book critiquing Pittsburgh industrialism (August 28, 1935); on L. W. Doob's *Propaganda* (February 5, 1936); on the reluctant socialist Vardis Fisher's *The Neurotic Nightingale* (October 2, 1935); on the Agrarian "declaration of independence" *Who Owns America?*, edited by Herbert Agar and Allen Tate (July 1, 1936); on Harold Lasswell's *Politics* (December 23, 1936); and on Hilaire Belloc's *The Restoration of Property* (January 20, 1937). For the very partisan *Nation* Burke reviewed a volume on educational reform (August 1935) and, in his music criticism columns, recommended to the masses "Recent Records" of the Boston and Minneapolis symphonies (December 11, 1935) and a concert-symposium by the

New Music Society on "Music in the Crisis" (January 1, 1936). In his contribution to the "What Is Americanism?" symposium in *Partisan Review* (other contributors included Dreiser, Josephine Herbst, Arvin, Josephson, Frank, William Carlos Williams, and Joseph Freeman), Burke contended that America was distinguished from Europe only in that America offered "the almost perfect milieu for the full flowering of bourgeois-capitalist thought, in all its rigorousness," and signed himself enthusiastically "yours for the good philosophy, the philosophy of communism." The LAW protest, which appeared in *New Masses* on September 8, 1936 (page 12), and which was signed by twenty other LAW representatives, including Burke, charged "that the American press has, in the aggregate, presented an utterly false and misleading picture of the military revolt in Spain" and asserted that "the Spanish revolt is not a civil war between fascism and communism but rather an attempt by reactionaries of all sorts . . . to overthrow a democratic government elected and supported by the broad masses of people"—that is, by a Popular Front. The Gus Peck cartoon appeared in *New Masses* on March 3, 1936. That Burke composed the text is evident from the published caption below the cartoon and from a letter by Freeman to Burke (February 26, 1936).

8. Burke gave four lectures, drawing on the developing *Attitudes*, during a week at the end of July 1936, and he returned to Syracuse for the same kind of arrangement from July 26 until July 30, 1937. On both occasions he was joined by Cowley, Gregory, and other lecturers (Mumford had appeared in 1935); was paid two hundred dollars; and stayed with Brown at his summer cottage on Skaneateles Lake (see Brown's many letters to Burke of 1936 and 1937). On August 14, 1936, Brown reported that a third of the students had found Burke "over their heads" but that two-thirds followed Burke's lectures well, particularly the ones on "Acceptance and Rejection." Brown (1904–60), who was as iconoclastic as Burke in his relation to the Left and was once suspended briefly by Syracuse for explaining dialectical materialism to his English classes, also welcomed Burke in the summer of 1939, the occasion for Burke to work out ideas later published in *The Philosophy of Literary Form* (for which Brown arranged the index) and to meet Brown's students Shirley Jackson and Stanley Edgar Hyman. For more on Brown, see the Leonard Brown Papers and John Crowley's introduction to Brown's "Dialectical Materialism."

9. This letter may serve as a gloss on a passage on the "Bureaucratization of the Imaginative" entry in Burke's "Dictionary of Pivotal Terms": "The principle of the discount advises us to note that many advocates of socialism . . . can gain asylum for their views by interlarding their appeal with attacks on Russia. Thereby they can advocate an unpopular philosophy by 'sharing' with their audience the usual capitalist aversions" (II, 68–69). For the record we should add that this letter is erroneously attributed as written to John (Jack) Wheelwright in Wheelwright's papers at Brown.

10. Michael Calvin McGee has intriguingly speculated that Burke may have been somewhat stubborn in his support for Stalin because the hearings over Trotsky in Mexico were perceived as a "kangaroo trial" in that it excluded Stalinists (Kenneth Burke Discussion List correspondence, February 7, 1999). We would add only that the Stalinists worked to subvert the hearings as much as they were excluded by them, and that the Dewey commission investigated Trotsky after *ATH* had gone to press. Even Hook acknowledged that Burke wrote *ATH* before the trials in Moscow proved

to be bogus; he credited Burke for being "an apologist, not after the fact, but before the fact, of the latest piece of Stalinist brutality" (61). In a difficult-to-deny response to McGee, Scott McLemee noted that Stalin's persecution of his foes was the kind of scapegoating that Burke called attention to in *ATH* and in "Hitler's 'Battle,'" and that he might well have been more critical of Stalin than he was (February 9, 1999). Indeed several passages in *ATH* treat the show trials in a less-than-critical way: II, 169; II, 200–201. And Burke resisted condemning Stalin even after the pact with Hitler; see correspondence between Burke and Daly after September 1939; Burke to Hyman, October 1, 1940, and Burke to Josephson, May 24, 1940; articles by Burke in *Direction;* and Burke to Farrell, September 22, 1939 (Burke Papers): "I [see] Russia as attempting to save the hide of one sixth of the world, as being in a bad situation, a situation for which there is no happy solution, and doing what I would advise it if I were in their situation, looking out for #1." Burke remained in the LAW into 1941.

11. It is true that Burke uses a great deal of Marxist vocabulary in *Ausculation, Creation, and Revision*, but the terms have a different feel to them in the earlier text, as if he is using them to parody Marxism or show his audience of aesthetes how pointless or inaccurate the vocabulary is. By the time he turned to writing *Attitudes toward History*, Burke had made much Marxist vocabulary his own. For more on the Marxist aspects of *ATH*, see Abbott.

12. Burke elaborated several times on the shortcomings of debunking: e.g., "The debunking vocabulary . . . can disclose material interests with great precision. *Too* great precision, in fact, . . . [for] in lowering human dignity so greatly, it lowers us all. A comic frame of motives avoids these difficulties, showing us how an act can 'dialectically' contain both transcendental and material ingredients, both imaginative and bureaucratic embodiment, both 'service' and 'spoils'" (I, 213–14). Debunking "makes cooperation difficult, since it sees utilitarian motives everywhere. The 'debunking' frame of interpretation becomes a colossal enterprise in 'transcendence downwards' that is good for polemical, *disintegrative* purposes, but would make that man a fool who did anything but spy upon his colleagues, watching for the opportunity when he himself may 'sell out' and 'cash in'" (I, 120–21). "When the genius of pure debunking prevails, the qualifications of comic charity drop away. It is then that the invitation to 'cash in' becomes identical with the invitation to 'sell out.' And the man imbued with such a scheme of motives is as embittered when he *does* sell out as he is when he *can't.* His own *self-*indictment is implicit in the thumbs-down system of motives by which he indicts all mankind" (I, 123). Burke's debunking of the debunking attitude was not limited to comments in *Attitudes*, either. In December 1936 the *New Republic* published his review of Harold Lasswell's book *Politics: Who Gets What, When, How?* Rather like Burke's book, Lasswell's traces historical shifts in power and examines strategies whereby those in power keep their power. Burke praised Lasswell's analysis and suggested that the book made a good weapon with which to fight fascism; but, like "The Virtues and Limitations of Debunking," this review criticizes a debunking approach as being incomplete for a crisis period of transition such as the one that the U.S. faced in the 1930s: "Like all works of the purely debunking sort, the book should be serviceable for the purposes of negativisitc, disintegrative criticism" (250).

13. There are others. For example the "Dictionary" entry for "Symbols of Authority" begins, "Admittedly a vague term. Better designed for pointing-in-the-direction-

of-something than for clear demarcation of-that-in-the-direction-of-which-we-would-point" (II, 232). Here again, the tone and the exaggerated hyphenation suggest not only that Burke recognized his weaknesses but also that he was hoping readers would likewise see parts of his theorizing as foolish rather than simply wrong.

14. See especially the section of *P&C* entitled "Secular Conversions: The Fundamentals of Psychoanalysis."

15. Burke's synthesis of Freud and Marx in *ATH* may be owing in particular to an exchange with his close friend Matthew Josephson. In a letter from mid-November 1936, Burke asked Josephson for suggestions on the problem of dealing with individual and group motivations (i.e., a writer would have an individual motive for writing a book, but as a member of a particular race or class, also would have a group motive—perhaps unconsciously). When Burke wrote that he did not want to oversimplify and "dualistically grant that 'there is a little of both, sometimes together, sometimes at odds'" (November 12, 1936), Josephson replied: "If I may make only a passing suggestion here on the question you raise concerning social and individual motive, I certainly believe there is a very strong affinity between Marxian and Freudian theories of the functioning of individual consciousness. In both 'things are not what they seem.' A man says one thing, means another. I have reference chiefly to Karl Marx's analysis of ideology in political action [18th Brummiere]" (December 3, 1936). Josephson's suggestion apparently pushed Burke's thinking into high gear, for he excitedly wrote back the very next day: "In both 'things are not what they seem.' And we can only discuss the full significance of events if we 'dialectically' (to hawl in the magic word) employ the interaction of both. Thus I would justify my concerns with 'symbolism,' and adhere despite the resentment of the Old Guard. I think I have found the trick this time, if I can but get my latest elucubrations before the world" (December 4, 1936). See also a February 15, 1935, letter from Percy Winner concerning *P&C*: "To me Marx and Lenin are manifestly too limited, particularly in their understanding of 'consciousness' . . . and, hence, need the correctives suggested by Freud." Then again, Burke had already juxtaposed Freud and Marx in *P&C*, so that (with *ATH* now on his mind) he could crow in a letter to Cowley on February 27, 1936, "that P&C offers a completely adequate account of the devices whereby Marxian and psychoanalytic fields can be brought together." Cowley had recently written in the *New Republic* that "Psychoanalysis as a social theory . . . is fundamentally opposed to Marxism, and no poet or prose writer has ever succeeded in making a synthesis of the two." See also George Soule, "Psychology and Revolution," and Reuben Osborn's book *Freud and Marx*. William Reich was also trying to reconcile Marx and Freud on the Continent during the 1930s.

16. Max Horkheimer, Erich Fromm, Herbert Marcuse, and Leo Lowenthal moved the Institute for Social Research to Columbia University (with the aid of Robert Lind) during the summer of 1934; by 1938 Theodore Adorno had arrived as well. The group developed their fusion of Marxist social analysis and Freudian psychoanalysis from New York until well after World War II. In the late 1930s, however, mainly for language reasons, the group remained somewhat isolated from other New York intellectual circles. For detailed history on the Frankfurt School, see Wiggershaus and Martin Jay.

17. Burke's use of *alienation* in two senses was a particularly sore point with *Science and Society* editor V. J. McGill, who claimed that using *alienation* to denote an emotional or spiritual state "conveys, through its psychopathological associations, an unmistakable disparagement. Thus, the alienation of workers from adequate food and housing is apt to be put on a level with pathological inadequacy or autistic withdrawal. At any rate, the tendency of the language of psychopathology to identify failure of adaptation to a given status in capitalist society with plain incompetence, is something which should be remembered, I think" (253–54). McGill further suspected that Burke's use of *alienation* was suggesting a Hegelian "spiritual law of development over and above the specific methods of the sciences" (253–54).

18. On Hook's review, see below, pages 170–80. Brinton's review ("What Is History?") in the *Saturday Review of Literature* (August 1937) criticized the goals and methods of what he called the "new" historians (including Burke and other Marxists), who have given up their "hard-won gains . . . in the field of . . . scientific method" by studying knowable documents from the past (11). Instead they become pseudo-sociologists or, worse still, philosophers of history who as "prophets" "hanker after one supreme miracle—that of knowing what is going to happen" (4). Brinton might simply be dismissed as yet another reviewer who has misread Burke (Wolin, 106); yet doing so disguises the fact that he squarely addresses the fundamental question of *Attitudes:* with what methodology should critics study human behavior? Although Brinton believed, with Hook, in "sound empirical science" and "rigorous technique" (4), he agreed with Burke that scientific method should not be applied across the board: the "application [of scientific methods] to the study of man in society must at present be very tentative and limited indeed" (11). Such areas of human experience are better left, he suggests, to philosophers or poets, as Burke had indicated. Burke's response: "There was a guy in the Saturday Review, who started out stunningly, but soon thereafter fell to musing, like Antony over the corse of Caesar (and unfortunately, unlike Antony, never got back to the subjick again). So I got my picture taken with Herodotus and Thucydides, but otherwise was used as a point of depart, which must be more gratifying to a dock than an author" (Burke to Josephson, August 23, 1937).

In the December 1937 issue of the *Nation*, Eliseo Vivas was chiefly concerned that Burke's symbolic analysis "is not susceptible of verification" (723) but relies instead on intuition. Vivas indicated how much of the content of Burke's analysis he was accepting when he conceded that Burke's intuitions were often "very happy hits indeed"; he nevertheless could not sanction "the explosions of an imagination uncontrolled by a scientific governor." What he could not sanction, in other words, was Burke's methodology, which he described as "a-scientific if not unscientific" (723). Burke's reply to Vivas—"Intuitive or Scientific?"—went straight to the question of methodology by emphasizing two recurrent Burkean claims: first that "scientific" vocabularies are not suited to discussions of human action, and second that methodologies labeled "scientific" are not the neutral tools their supporters believe them to be.

Though they do not bear on disputes over Burke's methodology, two other reviews of *ATH* deserve mention, especially because they counter the common beliefs that all Marxists condemned *ATH* and that none of Burke's contemporaries understood him.

New Masses reviewer Groff Conklin praised the book as "a remarkable step forward" (26) in the study of "the symbols by which people think and act" (25) that ought to prove valuable "in the field of practical agitation" (25). And Henry Bamford Parkes, a progressive historian who contributed regularly to the *Nation* and the *New Republic*, in the Spring 1938 *Southern Review* astutely described *ATH* as "an anatomy of the nonrational factors in social change." He also scored Burke for promoting a kind of determinism via the concept of "frames of acceptance" (696). Burke's reply to Parkes, only recently published (George, ed.), provides a perspective on Burke's effort to negotiate between determinism and individual agency. For further discussion of the reviews of *ATH*, see Wolin, 105–15.

19. Burke sent in his review rather late, and so the editors were forced to cut it in order to fit it in at the last minute. Burke was quite upset at this development; perhaps that explains why he subsequently wrote very little for *Science and Society* (Samuel Sillen to Burke, September 30 and October 2, 1936).

20. Schlauch's review appeared late in 1937. On January 17, 1938, Schlauch reported to Burke that she had received Burke's rejoinder ("Twelve Propositions"), and she proposed a dinner meeting (Burke, Schlauch, McGill) to discuss how she and McGill might wish to counterrespond. The upshot was that Burke then composed his own counterreply to Schlauch's and McGill's replies—which was never published (though it survives in the Burke Papers at Penn State), probably because Burke would not agree to cut his contribution to save space. The title "Twelve Propositions" plays off James Burnham and Philip Wheelwright's "Thirteen Propositions" as well as other similar contemporary titles—"Ten Propositions," "Ten Propositions and Eight Errors," etc.—that were circulating in New York magazines that year.

21. "Burke's notion of the allegiance to symbols of authority plays a similar role to the concept of hegemony in his communist contemporary, Antonio Gramsci" (Denning, 440). We noted in earlier chapters, and we will elaborate in our next, Burke's distrust of the scientific attitude as against the poetic one, in keeping with Williams and those who would become New Critics.

22. When he responded in January 1938 to Vivas's indictment of *ATH* as unscientific ("Intuitive or Scientific?"), Burke summarized his argument: "I contend that social relations can be adequately interpreted not by physicalist or naturalistic terms but only by terms that treat experience as an 'art.' . . . I take social relations to be essentially dramatic in nature. I thus take a discussion of them to be very much like dramatic criticism" (140). The issue of Marxism's scientific basis was being debated before *ATH* ever appeared: Max Eastman had already advanced the notion that Marxism was not scientific in *The Last Stand of Dialectical Materialism* (a 1934 rejoinder to Hook's 1933 *Towards the Understanding of Karl Marx*, which defended Marxism as scientific), and he would do so again in *Marxism: Is It a Science?* (1940). See Wald, *New York*, 123–25.

23. "I exploit deposits as ruthlessly as an oil company. And I am out prospecting for more deposits. And they're not easy to find, for all I have is a peach bough. (Erase that. My methods are strickly scientific.)" (March 24, 1937).

24. Evidence that Burke's attention was drawn to questions of method and to the distinction he came to make between *method* and *methodology* abounds throughout the

text, beginning with his early discussion of William James. Although one purpose of this first section is to introduce the "frames of acceptance and rejection" and, by doing so, to set up James, Whitman, and Emerson as models of the "comic attitude," Burke is also interested in James's attitude toward empiricism and scientific method. "James," Burke notes, "was humble about his methodological laxity," as humble, perhaps as Burke is ironic about his peach bough (I, 5). Indeed Burke presents James and Ralph Barton Perry's biography of James in terms that mark clear parallels between James's situation vis-à-vis his philosophical colleagues and Burke's situation vis-à-vis literary and social critics of the 1930s. Hence Burke visits Perry's account of the influence that "made it natural for James to write a book 'too biological for the religious, too religious for the biologists'" (I, 9), a description uncannily reminiscent of the reception of *Counter-Statement* and, to a lesser degree, *Permanence and Change:* too formalist for the leftists, too socially invested for the aesthetes. Thoroughly unorthodox in his approach to human experience, James, Burke notes, took "excursions to the scientific underworld" (I, 8) and earned rebukes from Peirce for his "generous use of terms" (I, 10). Burke's quotation from one of Peirce's rebukes—"It is an indispensable requisite of science that it should have a recognized vocabulary, composed of words so unattractive that loose thinkers are not tempted to use them" (I, 10)—provides an interesting anticipation of Schlauch's serious displeasure that Burke strays into her scholarly discipline of linguistics, looking for "cues," and of her and McGill's (and Hook's) assertions that Burke is just a "loose thinker" who has not got his Marxism or his scientific method right. Finally Burke concludes his discussion of James by providing this telling explanation for James's—and, we suggest, his own—methodological subversion:

> Much of James's resistance to the procedure of his "respectable" colleagues seems to have come from his conviction that they were in danger of dealing with too restricted a world. He hated the *streng wissenschaftlich* not merely because he was too restless or too physically ill to persist in minute measurement. He also felt that too much of vital importance might, by the very nature of the method, necessarily be left out of account. Here we see James spontaneously obeying his father's injunction, striving to maintain the widest notion of *vocation*, vocation not as a *specialist*, but as a *man*. (I, 15–16)

25. Burke articulated the distinction often. For instance in his "Dictionary" entry for "Imagery," he wrote, "We shall not press the possibility that Shakespeare's choice of a master image may have sometimes been deliberate (a 'method' clarified by a 'methodology')" (II, 158). In his discussion of "casuistic stretching," he wrote that "the process of casuistic stretching must itself be subjected continually to *conscious attention*. Its own resources (for simply providing a 'higher level' of deception, a new unction) must be transcended by the explicit conversion of a method into a methodology. The difference between casuistry as a method and casuistry as a methodology is the difference between mystification and clarification, between concealing of a strategy (*ars celare artem*) and the description of a strategy (criticism as explanation)" (II, 75). See also *The Philosophy of Literary Form:* "I believe that a critic should seek to develop not only a method, but a methodology" (68). For the link between method and *habitude* we are indebted to Dana Anderson.

26. In the 1984 afterword to *ATH*, Burke used one of his most famous metaphors to describe the book's well-known and frustrating (for readers) irregularities: "I had to invent the word 'counter-gridlock,' since I was going every which way. After slapping down eight or ten pages along one line, I'd find myself trailing off. So I'd have to abandon that route and try some other, with the same damnably irritating outcome" (398).

27. To be absolutely consistent with his terms, Burke should have said a "methodology of study."

28. A passage from "Twelve Propositions" provides a gloss: "Anyone who would turn from politics to some other emphasis, or vice versa, must undergo some change of identity, which is dramatic (involving 'style' and 'ritual')" (246). See also this passage from the "Dictionary" entry on "Imagery": "Our basic principle is our contention that all symbolism can be treated as the ritualistic naming and changing of identity (whereby a man fits himself for a role in accordance with established coordinates or for a change of role in accordance with new coordinates which necessity has forced upon him)" (II, 169–70). Hence "General Nature of Ritual" as the title for the section on symbolic analysis.

29. Burke's examples, omitted from later editions of *ATH*, help clarify. The metaphorical analysis that constitutes the "functional" approach is exemplified by Malcolm Cowley's claim that images of dessication create the tone of John Dos Passos's *The Big Money*. The "statistical approach" (anticipating what Burke would later call "indexing") would compare Dos Passos's novel to other works revolving around images of dessication such as Eliot's *The Waste Land* to see if they shed light on each other (II, 18). These are clearly ideas that Burke has much more to say about. Indeed in the second edition of *Attitudes toward History*, Burke adds a note at the end of this section indicating that he later finds the whole discussion "weakened by its emergent or incipient treatment of matters that we developed in later books" (196n).

30. The fact that "Tests of Selectivity" opens with the phrase "the critic's Occam's razor" (II, 32) suggests that it may have been the section of *Attitudes* that Burke had in mind when he wrote Robert Penn Warren, editor of the *Southern Review*, to interest him in publishing a single piece of the book: "I have thought, for instance, of one chapter on 'Symbolism.' Or perhaps better, 'The Weeds of Symbolism,' wherein I should discuss the business of having a writer *do one thing* and having a critic *see something else*. I am interested in the problem of trying to tell the weeds from the posies, for this particular garden is very weedy indeed, and there seems to be no Occam's razor for us to use as a hoe. The issue rapidly branches into many side-issues: history, news, statistics, sentimentality, 'will,' etc. I should trace the relationships among these ramifications" (Burke to Warren, September 3, 1936).

31. Like Marxists, Freudians also were suffering from a too-narrow vision. "We believe that the coordinates of individual psychology invariably place a wrong emphasis upon symbolic acts. Individualistic coordinates are too non-social, whereas the basis of cure is socialization. . . . It is only by interweaving social coordinates *at every point* into the discussion of individual psychology that such faulty emphases (worse than no emphasis at all) can be rectified" (II, 174–76). Burke presented a similar critique of individualized therapy in his review ("Without Benefit of Politics") of Otto Rank's books *Truth and Reality: A Life History of the Human Will* and *Will Therapy: An*

Analysis of the Therapeutic Process in Terms of Relationship. Appearing in the July 1936 issue of the *Nation,* Burke's review criticizes both Rank's and Freud's theories in language that shows up in *Attitudes;* their work, he argues is "'infantile' in the sense that they consider human relationships in terms of non-political or pre-political coordinates (quite as the child himself does). Both lack the Aristotelian emphasis upon the forensic that must figure largely in our dealing with contemporary reality. And both deal with psychological forms at too great remove from the economic and vocational realities" stressed by Marxism (78).

32. The passage recalls the language of the final pages of *P&C:* "beginning with such a word as *composition* to designate the architectonic nature of either a poem, a social construct, or a method of practical action, we can take over the whole vocabulary of tropes (as formulated by the rhetoricians) to describe the specific patterns of human behavior" (339).

33. Actually Hook's contribution to *The Meaning of Marx,* a book that he edited for publication in 1934, indicates that he and Burke were on a philosophical collision course. In his essay in that collection, "The Meaning of Marx," first published in the April 1934 *Modern Monthly,* Hook expresses his belief in the universal applicability of the scientific method. His faith in the ability of people to bracket off their own biases (30) and in a universe that can be "empirically established" (35) especially conflicted with Burke's views in *P&C* and *ATH.*

34. In a letter to Burke (undated, June or July 1936), Hook refers to a "hasty reading of the unmanageable proofsheets of Permanence and Change [which] does not entitle me to a[n] evaluative judgment of it." In the same letter Hook mentions that he had been tapped to review *P&C* for the *Marxian Quarterly,* but no such review ever appeared. On July 1, 1936, Hook ridiculed Burke's writing ability: "I think I am one of the 17 or is it 19 people who own copies of your *Towards a Better Life.* Someone gave it to me who couldn't understand it; I read three or four chapters but abandoned it after I got lost." In an undated subsequent letter, Hook acknowledges that he still had not read *P&C.*

35. An account of the Book Union mission was printed in the April 15, 1935, *New Masses:* "Every month, the Book Union will select an important revolutionary play, a fine proletarian novel or drama, a volume of poetry or an essential work on economics. The selection will be available at reduced prices—made possible through selling in volume—to members." The union persisted for a year or two until it was put out of business by a New York Fair Price Law forbidding the selling of products at cut rates (Young, "Cowley's Politics," 172). A brochure describing the nonprofit Book Union is included in the Burke Papers; see Marian Klopfer to Burke, May 14, 1935.

36. One of us discovered Burke's review of Barbusse's *Stalin,* filed with Hook's own review of the book and his marginal comment to Burke, in the Hook Papers at Stanford. Because the papers are Hook's, it is unclear whether he actually sent his observations to Burke, but it seems likely that he did not; the manuscripts remained in Hook's possession, not in Burke's papers, where we would expect to find them if Burke had gotten them from Hook; and Burke's April 22, 1936, letter to Cowley shows ignorance of Hook's views of the Barbusse review.

37. Burke elaborated in a letter to Cowley that he did send on April 28, 1936: "Lenin could harness Trotsky for social purposes; . . . he could encompass Stalin and

Trotsky both; but . . . when [Lenin] died, the antithetical ingredients that had been 'synthesized' in him were left to affirm their oppositeness—a position, I am sorry to say, which I seem to share with Wilson—and a position which, I am even more sorry to say, was omitted by Trachty, on appeal to me, from the printed version of the book-chat."

38. William Burnham, a friend of Hook's and fellow philosophy professor at New York University, shared Hook's Trotskyist views (Wald, *New York*, 178). He published the *Symposium*, "an organ of Marxian sociology" (Josephson, *Infidel*, 108). In 1937 he published a pamphlet entitled *The Popular Front: A New Betrayal.*

39. For more of what bothered Burke about the Farrell book, see his December 7, 1936, letter to *New Masses* and Communist Party loyalist Joshua Kunitz: "As for [Farrell's] book on literary criticism: it frankly made me sore because he had blundered bluntly on things that I think I said much more sharply in Counter-Statement several years before. I could hardly salute them as 'discoveries.' But though I reviewed the book adversely (and even, au fond, vindictively), I left his character unsullied." Elsewhere in the letter, however, Burke did not leave Farrell's character so unsullied—e.g., "I believe that he [Farrell] is very proud, too proud for cooperative work in any group. . . . [The] 'splintering' tendency in him derives in large part from his failure as yet to 'transcend' the mere negation of catholicism." Four days earlier, Burke had repeated to Kunitz the words of a "satiric ditty" that he had written about Farrell "when he was at the height of his good favor among the orthodox," about the time of the first Writers' Congress: "Sets boldly forth to startle the town / By being a mick turned upside down. / The simple think that Farrell's a red, / But he's really a mick turned ass over head." According to Kathleen Farrell (personal conversation), who first directed our attention to Burke's letters to Kunitz, Farrell got word of the letters and responded with fury; Burke and Farrell's friendship was over. The change in the Burke-Farrell relationship is evident in the difference in tone between Burke's negative review of *A Note* and his sympathetic review of Farrell's novel *Judgment Day*, published in the *New Republic* on June 19, 1935.

As for Farrell's point of view, it is documented in his Diary Notes (University of Pennsylvania, box 68, F). In late May 1936 he sensed that Burke's attitude toward him had cooled: "Kenneth Burke acted strange toward me [at the League of American Writers' meeting of May 26]. He sat near me. He never looked at me. It was quite different from what he usually does. He was most uncordial. I know why. I am sure he has written a piece about me of the kind that conditioned his acting this way. It amuses me. Because he wrote me a letter, hinting not so subtly that I should read him and refer to him in my book on criticism." A month later, but still before he had encountered Burke's review, Farrell was referring to Burke as someone "who seems to have his head always in the intellectual ether, but—but—but he always knows who are the right people to praise. . . . Kenneth Burke's stale bread is buttered with adulterated oleomargarine."

40. For more on the furor in Left circles over Farrell's book, see Cooney, 83–86; Kathleen Farrell, chapter 6; Kutulas, *Long War*, 73–74; and Aaron, 301–3. Burke and Hook exchanged other subsequent letters based on their disagreement on Farrell's book. Burke's letters have not survived, but Hook continued to press his beliefs in several lengthy counterstatements, one on July 1, 1936, and another, undated, soon after.

In fairness to Hook, the letters are generally evenhanded if patronizing in tone. Here is a sample: "I haven't finished Permanence and Change because I was called off to answer half a dozen critical attacks on my From Hegel to Marx, and I had to meet some previously contracted writing commitments. But I have read enough to be impressed with your genuinely philosophical insights. If your technique was worthy of your vision, you would belong to the guild. But for the reader who likes a straightforward exposition, you write with a little too much preciosity and there are too many lacunae in the structure of the argument proper" (undated, June or July 1936). Also in fairness we note in the same letter rebuking Burke's review of Farrell, Hook's invitation to Burke to contribute to the short-lived *Marxian Quarterly*, which Hook regarded as "a real united front cultural magazine . . . , Socialist, Lovestonite, and Trotskyite," but shunned by the Communist Party. (Burke instead contributed to the first issue of *Science and Society*, which Hook described, with reason, as "a quarterly for nice people only," i.e., for Stalinists; undated, June 1936).

41. Hook was not the only person who found Burke's organization perplexing. When he first read the manuscript of *ATH*, Cowley said that, while "good, damned good," it nevertheless reverted in places to Burke's "old vice, which is that of the very keen-nosed but under-trained hound dog—he starts out a-helling after a rabbit, almost tracks it down, but gets turned aside by the strong scent of a fox, runs into a place where the fox scared up a partridge, hunts for the partridge, feels hungry and digs for a field mouse" (letter to Burke, October 30, 1936).

42. That Burke was on good terms with the original *PR* is underscored by the fact that Kenneth Fearing invited Burke to speak (along with Farrell and Freeman) at a *PR* fund-raising symposium at Irving Square on September 8, 1934 (Fearing to Burke, undated, 1934). Burke also composed a thousand-word statement on Marxian criticism, a plea for tolerance and broad-mindedness, for the *Partisan Review* issue devoted to previewing the first American Writers' Congress in April 1935. For some reason, perhaps because Burke missed the deadline (Rahv to Burke, March 22, 1935), it never appeared with the other contributions. Burke later offered to revise parts of *Auscultation* for *PR* in March 1936 (see chapter 2, note 28). Ironically (given Hook's review), Burke and William Philips nearly reached an agreement to serialize portions of *Attitudes* in *PR* early in 1936 (Phillips to Burke, February 24 and March 6, 1936). And Burke on April 28, 1936, was still finding *PR* "camplike" enough to write the following to Cowley (who was looking for a way to defend himself against an attack by Felix Morrow): "Why not ask Phillips and Rahv to have lunch with us Thursday, to plot something? The one doubt I have . . . is that my way of handling the matter may not be wholly orthodox [enough for *PR*]. . . . As holder of the unofficial chair in Chronic Disorders of the Superstructure, I have been led to the development of devices that seem not wholly satisfactory to any camp."

43. For more on Hook's relationship with *PR*, see Phelps, 166–69, and Shi, 221. On *Partisan Review* more generally during this period, see Cooney, 47–145, and Aaron, 297–303.

44. Malcolm Cowley also wrote that Trotsky was probably guilty of conspiracy (Aaron, 343–44). Hook published an acidic response in the *New Republic*, June 7, 1937. See also Felix Morrow's attack on Cowley ("Malcolm Cowley: Portrait of a Stalinist

Intellectual") in the *New Militant* of April 18, 1936; James T. Farrell's ridicule of Cowley's criticism in his *Note on Literary Criticism* (157–74); and Eugene Lyons's "Malcolm Cowley: 1938" in *Modern Monthly*, June 1938. All of these attacks on Burke's friend Cowley bear on Burke's attitudes and loyalties in 1937.

45. Their success in doing so can be measured by the vituperation *PR* received from Gold and Hicks in the December 7, 1937, *New Masses* and from Cowley in the *New Republic*, who complained that *PR* "independence" boiled down to "attacks on the Soviet Union, on literature and art in the Soviet Union, on politics in the Soviet Union, [and] on American friends of the Soviet Union" ("Red," 22).

46. Burke did not choose the title "Is Mr. Hook a Socialist?" but submitted his rejoinder as a letter to the editor. (A carbon copy of the original is in the Burke Papers. The original is somewhat longer than the printed version, and the printed version thus begins rather precipitously.) And he interpreted the editors' choice of title as further foul play by *PR:* "What they did do, as they could within the limits of my stipulations, was to give my article a title after I had seen the proofs and O.K.'d them (I not giving it a title because I thought of it as a letter). Hence they did what they could to help out Sid by giving a title that featured a 'party line' attitude on Hook, thereby strengthening Hook's sentences on that point. It wasn't much; it is almost too subtle to verbalize; one could do nothing but let it drop; but it was enough to show how thorough they are in the determination to go on naming their number" (Burke to Cowley, October 14, 1938).

47. Burke was invited to contribute to *PR* (in the form of a discussion of the current situation in American writing) in the summer of 1939 but declined (Macdonald to Burke, May 20, 1939). He was also invited to review Kafka's *In the Penal Colony* for *PR* (Dupee to Burke, October 14, 1939) but refused, still complaining of the "systematic misrepresentations" in Hook's review. A *PR* review by James Burnham in June 1938 (of a book by Morton Zabel) identified Burke as "Stalinist."

Chapter 5: "Thirty-Minded Pieces"

1. Wirth wrote again on June 15, 1938, regretting that a research trip would keep him from meeting Burke that summer and directing him instead to his colleague Ernest W. Burgess, who would later ask Burke to compose "Freud—and the Analysis of Poetry" for the *AJS*.

2. "I used to consider *one* lecture an event. When I came back from four at Syracuse, I acted as though I were returning from the wars. And here I run into *85*. The cognoscenti, of course, have all sorts of devices for shunting the burden from oneself to the students—but these tricks have to be learned, and I didn't know how to stop long enough to learn them. As a result I have done exactly 100% of the work done in the courses—and again as a result, there were days when the going was tough" (Burke to Josephson, August 15, 1938).

3. *PLF* is organized curiously: according to the principle of length. The long title essay, composed originally for the occasion of the book in the summer of 1939, initiates the collection. Then come progressively shorter items, all of them previously published: six "Long Essays," all but one from 1938–39; nine "Shorter Essays," three written after 1938; and an appendix made up of various reviews, letters, and a poem,

all but three published after 1936. For the convenience of readers, in this chapter we quote from the third edition of *PLF* (1967), not the first.

4. Soon enough, in the chapter on "Agency and Purpose" in *A Grammar of Motives*, Burke would demonstrate once again his sophistication with pragmatism (and with Peirce, James, and Dewey). Burke once indicated to Isidor Schneider that he had also drawn on Dewey in the "Lexicon" section of *Counter-Statement* for the terms *situation* and *adjustment* (Burke to Schneider, December 15, 1931). Burke in his review of *The Quest for Certainty* ("Intelligence as a Good") indicates that he had read Dewey's 1925 *Experience in Nature* as well, and indeed a copy of *Experience in Nature* as we write is still shelved next to *Art As Experience* and *The Quest for Certainty* at Burke's home in Andover. Note too the passing reference in *PLF* (5) to the work of Rudolf Carnap, who is himself associated with pragmatism.

5. Burke to the unnamed editors of *Windsor Quarterly*, July 10, 1934 (Burke Papers). Burke's complaint in "Intelligence as a Good" that Dewey's instrumentalism left no stable criteria for how values are to be judged was repeated in "The Virtues and Limits of Debunking" (*PLF,* 184). The complaint recalls if not echoes Randolph Bourne's similar complaint (in "Twilight of the Idols"), published in the famous *Seven Arts* in 1917 (Menand, 404). Burke almost certainly had read that essay when it first appeared. He first wrote himself about Dewey's inability to locate value satisfactorily in experience in his 1922 review of Paul Elmer More's *The Religion of Plato* ("Fides Querens Intellectum"), wherein he asserts that he "dislikes the pragmatist attitude" for that same reason. For calling our attention to the More review, we thank Steven Mailloux; see his "Rhetorical Paths."

6. Especially striking, for students of Burke and *P&C*, about the way Dewey articulated the problem of cultural lag is his focus on symbols and communication: "Symbols control sentiment and thought, and the new age has no symbols consonant with its activities. . . . Till the Great Society is converted into a Great Community, The Public will remain in eclipse. Communication can alone create a great community. Our Babel is not one of tongues but of the signs and symbols without which shared experience is impossible" (142). In this section we emphasize the intertextuality between Dewey's *The Public and Its Problems* and *P&C*, but we must also note that Paul Jay has brilliantly tied *P&C* to *Art and Experience:* Dewey's book ends with an acknowledgment of the "relation between permanence and change"; and Burke developed *P&C* in part as a corrective to Dewey's failure to find a productive space for avantgarde forms (*Blues,* 15). Finally we should note, concerning the phrase *occupational psychosis*, that Dewey never actually put the two words together in that combination —though Burke got the idea right. (Dewey's interest in "hunting" and "agricultural" psychoses derives from a 1902 essay, "Interpretation of Savage Mind," reprinted in the 1931 collection *Philosophy and Civilization;* Feffer, personal correspondence.)

7. See further Burke to George Soule (August 28, 1934): "I do not feel that I am unduly stretching the concept of 'communication' [in *P&C*] when I use it to cover not merely the symbolic intercourse of speech but also the operations and relationships which supply the content of speech (communication as in scientific or poetic symbolism, and communication as with 'communicating vessels'). Dewey also has observed that there is more than a mere etymological connection between *communication,*

communion, and *community.*" Then again, Burke's notion of a "public" is somewhat different from Dewey's.

8. Most 1930s radicals, for that matter, regarded the pragmatists as insufficiently critical of social institutions: Waldo Frank for that reason once complained to Burke that "everywhere I find the blight of Dewey" (Frank to Burke, May 26, 1934). And yet Dewey himself was in fact anything but conformist. For example he voted several times for Norman Thomas since FDR was insufficiently radical for him.

9. What Burke meant by "instrumentalism" and a sense of his familiarity with the pragmatists is suggested in a letter he wrote to Norbert Guterman (June 23, 1937): "Peirce . . . wanted to distinguish his notion of truth from James's (foreseeing that the pragmatic notion of truth as 'that which works' would lead to Dewey's instrumentalism and its counterpart in business instrumentalism)—and tried desperately to save the day by simply adding another syllable, thereby getting 'pragmaticism,' which is syllabically unfit. . . . There are two kinds of 'that-which-works,' one for in-and-out traders, the other for long-pull investment. Pragmatism without the *ic* led logically to the in-and-out trader's notion of efficacy. . . . With the *ic* [that Peirce came to prefer], it meant long-pull criteria of efficacy, without the need of plastic surgery as an after-thought, after the thinker beheld his creation and noted that it had an ugly mug. 'Efficiency' vs. 'ecology.'" The passage serves as a gloss on the distinction between Peirce and James (and on yet another complaint about Dewey's instrumentalism) that Burke put into "The Virtues and Limits of Debunking" (*PLF,* 183–84). Burke also complained about Dewey's alleged instrumentalism in "The Philosophy of Literary Form" (55). See Menand, especially chapter 13, for accessible explanations of the varieties of pragmatism. Crusius in *Kenneth Burke* details many of Burke's engagements with philosophy, but he deals only superficially with Burke and the pragmatists. Our account of Burke's articulation with pragmatism owes to conversations and informal communications with Andrew Feffer, including ones over a draft manuscript that he generously shared.

10. "I question whether readers of *Science and Society* are willing to admit that the history of human speculation stops with the 'process thinking' of John Dewey's instrumentalism, fruitful as his philosophy unquestionably is," Burke wrote in "Twelve Propositions." The passage was deleted from the version of "Twelve Propositions" published in *PLF.* See also *ATH,* I, 88. For more on Burke's engagement with pragmatism in *ATH,* especially with respect to the comic frame, see Blakesley and McGowan, "Kenneth Burke." McGowan in "Equipment" and *Democracy's Children* (chapter 6) considers Burke and pragmatism more broadly. Blakesley outlines Burke's relation to pragmatism in *A Grammar of Motives.* Gunn also points to a persistent pragmatist strain in Burke.

11. We indicated in chapter 1 that the conversation metaphor was first articulated by Burke in *ACR.* In a letter to Richard McKeon (October 15, 1938), Burke wrote that he had "finally got around to reading the Mead books" after returning to Andover from his summer in Chicago. "[I] was disgusted to find that he had already, in his own way, ridden considerably my slogan about the 'unending conversation,'" he continued. A month later, writing to Hugh Dalziel Duncan (and including a copy of his finished review of Mead), Burke said he was "both chagrined and delighted to discover, on digging into Mead, that he had already done a great deal with the notion of the

'unending conversation.' Had I known of this when deposing in class, I should have called attention to its use in Mead" (November 15, 1938, Duncan Papers).

12. On this point see Blakesley, "Kenneth Burke's Pragmatism."

13. Burke mentions clusters in *Counter-Statement* on pages 23 and 217. The concept of literature as "equipment for living" is also in *C-S* (183). "Frame" and "chart" and "prayer" are also found in *ATH*.

14. Burke had promised the essay to Ernest W. Burgess, an editor of *AJS*, during his summer in Chicago. On October 18, 1938, Burgess sent a follow-up inquiry, in response to which Burke asked for more time. Burgess agreed to the revised schedule (Burgess to Burke, November 17, 1938) and accepted Burke's completed essay on January 27, 1939.

15. As Ellen Quandahl summarizes so well in an essay on Burke's various readings of Freud, "Burke shows [in "Freud—and the Analysis of Poetry"] that, as a *rhetoric*, what Freud's methods teach is not how to *psychoanalyze* but rather how to understand the resources of linguistic transformation" (634).

16. Malinowski was not alone, of course, in emphasizing the matriarchal. Maud Bodkin, for instance, had emphasized Jung in her 1934 *Archetypal Patterns in Poetry*. We have found no evidence of Burke's use of Bodkin, however, before the publication of *PLF*.

17. Malinowski had contributed a supplement to *The Meaning of Meaning*. (In that essay Malinowski uses the term *symbolic action*, as well as a cluster of associated terms—*context of culture, context of situation*—that Burke would appropriate for *PLF* and deliberate on for the rest of his career; see *PLF*, 111, and Skodnick, 30. For this point we are grateful to Richard Coe.) We quote here not from *Language in Action* (which Burke once planned to review, along with *Science and Sanity:* Hayakawa to Burke, December 22, 1941) but from Hayakawa's "The Meaning of Semantics," published in August 1939, because it is especially instructive for students of Burke since it was addressed to readers of *Partisan Review*. Even though Burke owned a copy of the first edition of *Science and Sanity*, which is still on the shelves at Andover, we quote from the third edition of that book because it is more generally available; it also contains the original 1933 preface. Ironically the "special factor" in language use that deludes people and that needs to be excised is something that Korzybski terms "identification": "[Identification] involves deeply rooted 'principles' which are invariably false to facts . . . [so that] our orientations based on them cannot lead to adjustment and sanity" (lxii). Burke contrasted his notion of identification with Korzybski's in a passage in "The Calling of the Tune" (276–77). (Korzybski also employed another term, *indexing*, that Burke would use in a very different way.) General semantics still has a following, and many books (some of them with little to do with language) have been published in its name. We also acknowledge Jodie Nicotra's as-yet-unpublished essay on Burke and general semantics for orienting us to the topic.

18. In 1941 Hayakawa and Lee tried to interest Burke in accepting a teaching position at Illinois Institute of Technology, where they both worked. They also tried to get him to attend a Korzybski seminar in Chicago early in 1942. See Hayakawa to Burke, December 7 and December 22, 1941.

19. In *A Grammar of Motives* Burke famously claimed that "what we want is *not terms that avoid ambiguity*, but *terms that clearly reveal the strategic spots which ambiguities*

necessarily arise" (xviii). He continues: "instead of considering it our task to 'dispose of' any ambiguity by merely disclosing the fact that it is an ambiguity, we rather consider it our task to study and clarify the *resources* of ambiguity. For . . . it is in the areas of ambiguity that transformations take place," transformations such as the purification of war (xix).

20. Burke's review of *The World's Body* rehearsed some of the objections to Ransom's opposition of "poetic" and "scientific" language that he would bring to *PLF* and challenged Ransom to go beyond intrinsic criticism to include the sociological. Ransom would respond to Burke's reviews with a review of his own, of *Philosophy of Literary Form:* see "Address."

21. Ransom in "Humanism at Chicago," a 1952 review of the Chicago School manifesto *Critics and Criticism*, explained his own familiarity with and allegiance to Aristotle in the late 1930s. As the 1940s developed, Burke's own engagement with Aristotle and with the New Critics deepened.

22. Empson is also mentioned in *Auscultation, Creation, and Revision.*

23. As we explained in chapter 1, Burke had published "Antony in Behalf of the Play" and an essay on American poetry in *SR* in 1935, and a review of *Proletarian Literature* along with Tate's spirited response to it in 1936. "Acceptance and Rejection" (an excerpt from *ATH*), "The Virtues and Limitations of Debunking" (a review of Thurman Arnold's *The Folklore of Capitalism*), "Semantic—and Poetic Meaning," and his famous essay on Hitler followed in *SR* in 1938 and 1939. As the elaborate Robert Penn Warren–Burke and Alfred Erskine–Burke correspondences indicate, Burke also proposed several other ideas and items for publication in *SR* that were rejected, and he was an avid reader of the journal.

24. An important section in Burke's discussion of clusters in *ATH* is entitled "The Tracking Down of Symbols"—a phrase that suggests that "the tracing down of interrelationships" (*PLF*, 70) is a typographical error.

25. Chicago Aristotelians, on the other hand, would later conclude that Coleridge was responsible for many of the evils that they later ascribed to the New Critics (Winchell, 207).

26. The *Southern Review*, before it failed, had become the most important venue for the development and propagation of New Critical dogma, but it was not the only place touting an explicitly "less political" agenda that Burke could identify with as the Popular Front and Stalinism waned. As early as 1936, James Laughlin was launching *New Directions*, an annual dedicated to "the pure writer" and "experiment," to "technique" and "serious artistic writing" (as Laughlin expressed in the preface to the 1937 volume). Laughlin was committed to publishing writers more from the aesthete camp, such as E. E. Cummings, Katherine Anne Porter, Wallace Stevens, Marianne Moore, Gertrude Stein, James Joyce, and Franz Kafka. On June 11, 1938, Laughlin wrote Burke to accept an essay for that year's *New Directions*, but it never materialized in print for some reason. In 1940 Laughlin enlisted Burke to contribute to a *New Directions* segment on surrealism that included "A Third Surrealist Manifesto," a surrealist mini-anthology, and Burke's own critical essay "Surrealism" (which offers Coleridge as its inventor, especially in "Kubla Khan"). In 1941 Laughlin proposed reprinting portions of *Counter-Statement*, but the idea fell through when Harcourt asked for compensation for the reprint.

27. The use of the term *structure* in that passage has tempted some to align Burke with structuralism (e.g., Lentricchia, 69). But while he was appreciative of structure and form—of the genre imperatives increasingly emphasized by McKeon and other Chicago neo-Aristotelians as the Chicago School developed—Burke always thought of structure as but one of many elements to consider. On the relation of Burke to the New Critics, see also his letter to Brooks of January 6, 1936 (misdated by Burke January 6, 1935; *Southern Review* files): "The Southern Review is a literary man's paradise. Hence, I read it greedily. I admit to a basic difference of approach. When your writers discuss poetry, for instance, they tend to begin . . . by reference to some outstanding line of poetry; I see certain advantages, on the other hand, in beginning . . . in the way a dog scratches at his fleas. The weakness of my method is that when I finally get to the outstanding line, it may look too much like the scratching of fleas. The weakness of your method lies in its proneness to make *esthetic* legislation. . . ."

28. "Electioneering" was originally promised to a new magazine edited by Richard Johns, entitled *Zone*—which never appeared (Johns to Burke, March 23, 1939).

29. "I stressed [in *PLF*] more what is going on in the poem and its author than in the reader because of my attempt to feature the 'scissor work' motif. And it is hard to establish by scissor work what is going on in the reader. . . . Perhaps one reason why Aristotle's poetics could proceed as it did [i.e., without great consideration of the reader] was because the little Athenian village was, after all, a quite homogeneous audience as compared with any typical audience today—hence writer and audience could be eliminated as factors, in that they were relatively constants" (Burke to Knickerbocker, October 28, 1941).

30. "I know all about the ambivalence of rights and obligations now—I know that one pays enormously for a berth, and that, when wrenched free of check-bringing, papers-to-be-marked-bringing bureaucracy, there really are very many moments when unemployment does equal the most respectable kind of leisure. Teaching, as undertaken as anything but a fling, a flyer, is really another way of life. To undertake it, I should have to go through the whole business of dying and resprouting all over again" (Burke to Cowley, August 22, 1938).

31. Dexter, on behalf of his Committee on Conceptual Integration, had solicited Burke's views on definition (drawn from *ATH*) for his committee newsletter; he planned to reprint comments on definition by Korzybski and Richards as well. We have not located a copy of that newsletter, but it is likely from Dexter's letter of August 30, 1940, that Burke contributed a piece to it. Dexter had sent Burke an article of his own, from the journal *Philosophy of Science*. Nathan Boden of the Department of Sociology at Chicago had asked on behalf of the Society for Social Research to publish an abstract of a paper Burke had offered in the summer of 1938. Burke's talk at that SSR institute was entitled "Some Aspects of Motivation." Burke accurately recalled the chronology leading up to the *Grammar* in a letter to Cowley of May 3, 1950 (included in part in Jay, 292).

Works Cited and Consulted

Manuscript Collections

Djuna Barnes Papers, Hornbake Library, University of Maryland

Ben Belitt Papers, Rare Book and Manuscript Library, Butler Library, Columbia University

Berg Collection, New York Public Library

R. P. Blackmur Papers, Princeton University Library

Peter Blume Papers, Archives of American Art, Smithsonian Institute

Leonard Brown Papers, Bird Library, Syracuse University

Kenneth Burke Letters, Rare Book and Manuscript Library, Butler Library, Columbia University

Kenneth Burke Papers, Rare Books and Manuscripts, Paterno Library, Pennsylvania State University

Malcolm Cowley Papers, Newberry Library, Chicago

Hugh Dalziel Duncan Papers, Special Collections, Southern Illinois University Library

James T. Farrell Collection, Van Pelt Library, University of Pennsylvania

Waldo Frank Collection, Van Pelt Library, University of Pennsylvania

Joseph Freeman Papers, Hoover Institute, Stanford University

Horace Gregory Papers, Bird Library, Syracuse University

Norbert Guterman Papers, Rare Book and Manuscript Library, Butler Library, Columbia University

Granville Hicks Papers, Bird Library, Syracuse University

Sidney Hook Papers, Hoover Institute, Stanford University

Stanley Edgar Hyman Papers, Library of Congress

Shirley Jackson Papers, Library of Congress

Matthew Josephson Papers, Beinecke Rare Book and Manuscript Library, Yale University

William Knickerbocker Papers, Rare Book and Manuscript Library, Butler Library, Columbia University

Joshua Kunitz Papers, Rare Book and Manuscript Library, Butler Library, Columbia University

Richard McKeon Papers, Joseph Regenstein Library, University of Chicago

Marianne Moore Archive, Rosenbach Museum and Library, Philadelphia

Poetry Magazine Papers, Joseph Regenstein Library, University of Chicago

Katherine Anne Porter Papers, Hornbake Library, University of Maryland

John Crowe Ransom Papers, Olin Library, Kenyon College

Henry Robinson Papers, Rare Book and Manuscript Library, Butler Library, Columbia University

Isidor Schneider Papers, Rare Book and Manuscript Library, Butler Library, Columbia University

Southern Review Files, Beinecke Rare Book and Manuscript Library, Yale University

Allen Tate Papers, Princeton University Library

Robert Penn Warren Papers, Beinecke Rare Book and Manuscript Library, Yale University

John Brooks Wheelwright Papers, John Hay Library, Brown University

Morton Dauwen Zabel Papers, Joseph Regenstein Library, University of Chicago

Marya Zaturenska Papers, Bird Library, Syracuse University

Collections of Letters

East, James, ed. *The Humane Particulars: The Collected Letters of William Carlos Williams and Kenneth Burke.* Columbia: University of South Carolina Press, 2003.

Jay, Paul, ed. *The Selected Correspondence of Kenneth Burke and Malcolm Cowley, 1915–1981.* New York: Viking, 1988.

Rueckert, William, ed. *Letters from Kenneth Burke to William Rueckert, 1959–1987.* West Lafayette, Ind.: Parlor Press, 2003.

Bibliographies

Frank, Armin Paul, and Mechthild Frank. "The Writings of Kenneth Burke." In *Critical Responses to Kenneth Burke,* edited by William Rueckert, 495–523. Minneapolis: University of Minnesota Press, 1969.

Thames, Richard. "The Writings of Kenneth Burke, 1968–96." In *The Legacy of Kenneth Burke,* edited by Herbert Simons and Trevor Melia, 297–315. Madison: University of Wisconsin Press, 1989.

Works by Kenneth Burke

BOOKS

Attitudes toward History. 2 vols. New York: New Republic, 1937. 3rd ed. Berkeley: University of California Press, 1984.

Auscultation, Creation, and Revision: The Rout of the Esthetes, or, Literature, Marxism, and Beyond. In *Extensions of the Burkeian System,* edited by James W. Chesebro, 43–172. Tuscaloosa: University of Alabama Press, 1993.

Counter-Statement. New York: Harcourt, Brace, 1931. 2nd ed. Berkeley: University of California Press, 1968.

A Grammar of Motives. New York: Prentice-Hall, 1945. Berkeley: University of California Press, 1969.

Permanence and Change: An Anatomy of Purpose. New York: New Republic Books, 1935. 3rd ed. Berkeley: University of California Press, 1984.

The Philosophy of Literary Form: Studies in Symbolic Action. Baton Rouge: Louisiana State University Press, 1941. 3rd ed. Berkeley: University of California Press, 1973.

A Rhetoric of Motives. New York: Prentice-Hall, 1950. Berkeley: University of California Press, 1969.

Towards a Better Life. New York: Harcourt, Brace, 1932. Berkeley: University of California Press, 1966.

The White Oxen, and Other Stories. New York: A. & C. Boni, 1924. Berkeley: University of California Press, 1968.

POEMS (in chronological order of publication)

"Buildings Should Not Be Tall." *New Republic* 78 (April 8, 1934): 271.

"Lullaby—for Oneself as Adult Male." *New Republic* 87 (May 27, 1936): 71.

"Uneasy Thought of Peace." *New Republic* 87 (May 27, 1936): 71.

"For a Modernist Sermon." *New Republic* 97 (December 7, 1938): 125.

"Offering for the Time Capsule." *New Republic* 97 (December 28, 1938): 226.

"Industrialist's Prayer." *New Masses* 33 (October 17, 1939): 5.

"In the Margin." *New Republic* 101 (December 20, 1939): 257.

"Plea of the People." *New Masses* 33 (December 26, 1939): 9.

"Dialectician's Hymn." *University Review* 6 (December 1939): 133–35.

MUSIC CRITICISM (in chronological order of publication)

"Schönberg." *Nation* 137 (November 29, 1933): 633–43.

"Orpheus in New York." *Nation* 138 (January 10, 1934): 52–54.

"Two Brands of Piety." *Nation* 138 (February 28, 1934): 256–58.

"The End and the Origin of a Movement." *Nation* 138 (April 11, 1934): 422–24.

"The Art of Yielding." Rev. of *Stephen Foster, America's Troubadour*, by John Tasker Howard, and *They All Sang; From Tony Paster to Rudy Vallee*, by Edward B. Marks. *Nation* 138 (April 25, 1934): 484–86.

"The Most Faustian Art." *Nation* 139 (August 1, 1934): 138–40.

"Hindemith Does His Part." *Nation* 139 (October 24, 1934): 487–88.

"A Most Useful Composition." *Nation* 140 (December 19, 1934): 719–20.

"A Pleasant View of Decay." Rev. of *Music Ho! A Study of Music in Decline*, by Constant Lambert. *Nation* 140 (February 13, 1935): 200–201.

"What Shostakovich Adds." *Nation* 140 (February 20, 1935): 230–31.

"The 'Problems' of the Ballet." *Nation* 140 (March 20, 1935): 343–44.

"Recent Records." *Nation* 141 (December 11, 1935): 692–93.

"A Bright Evening, with Musicians." *Nation* 142 (January 1, 1936): 27.

ESSAYS (in chronological order of publication)

"The Allies of Humanism Abroad." In *A Critique of Humanism: A Symposium*, edited by C. Hartley Grattan, 169–92. New York: Brewer & Warren, 1930.

"Three Frenchmen's Churches." *New Republic* 63 (May 21, 1930): 10–14.

"Thomas Mann and André Gide." *Bookman* 73 (June 1930): 257–64.

"Waste—The Future of Prosperity." *New Republic* 63 (July 16, 1930): 228–31.

"Boring from Within." *New Republic* 65 (February 4, 1931): 326–29.

"Redefinitions." *New Republic* 67 (July 29, 1931): 286–87; 68 (August 26, 1931): 46–47; 68 (September 2, 1931): 74–75.

"Munsoniana." *New Republic* 69 (November 25, 1931): 46.

"Counterblasts on *Counter-Statement*." *New Republic* 69 (December 9, 1931): 101.

"For Bond Money." *New Republic* 73 (January 4, 1933): 218–19 (under the name Ethel Howardell).

"Preserving Capitalism." *New Republic* 74 (February 22, 1933): 49 (under the name Walter S. Hankel).

"The New Prince." Unpublished manuscript. Folder P15, Kenneth Burke Papers. Ca. 1933.

"Principles of Wise Spending." Unpublished manuscript. Folder P15, Kenneth Burke Papers. Ca. 1933.

"Trial Translation (from *Twelfth Night*)." *New English Weekly* 2 (February 1933): 373–74.

"Banker's Arise." *Americana, Satire and Humor* (May 1933): 4.

"Negro's Pattern of Life." *Saturday Review of Literature* 10 (July 29, 1933): 13–14.

"War, Response, and Contradiction." *Symposium* 4 (October 1933): 458–82.

"The Nature of Art under Capitalism." *Nation* 137 (December 13, 1933): 675–77.

"On Interpretation." *Plowshare: A Literary Periodical of One-Man Exhibits* 10 (February 1934): 3–79.

"My Approach to Communism." *New Masses* 10 (March 20, 1934): 16, 18–20.

"The Meaning of C. K. Ogden." *New Republic* 78 (May 2, 1934): 328–31.

"Caldwell: Maker of Grotesques." *New Republic* 82 (April 10, 1935): 232–35.

"For Whom Do You Write?" *New Quarterly* 1 (Summer 1934): 8.

"The Writers' Congress." *Nation* 140 (May 15, 1935): 571.

"Revolutionary Symbolism in America." Speech to American Writers' Congress, April 16, 1935. In *The First American Writers' Congress*, edited by Henry Hart, 87–94. New York: International Publishers, 1935.

"Antony in Behalf of the Play." *Southern Review* 1 (Autumn 1935): 308–19.

"What Is Americanism? A Symposium on Marxism and the American Tradition." *Partisan Review and Anvil* 3 (April 1936): 9–11.

"The Relation between Literature and Science." Speech to American Writers' Congress, June 5, 1937. In *The Writer in a Changing World*, edited by Henry Hart, 158–71. New York: Equinox Cooperative Press, 1937.

Foreword to *Three Ways of Modern Man*, by Harry Slochower, 11–16. New York: International Publishers, 1937.

"Reading While You Run: An Exercise in Translation from English into English." *New Republic* 93 (November 17, 1937): 36–37.

"Acceptance and Rejection." *Southern Review* 2 (Winter 1937): 600–632.

"Growth among the Ruins." *New Republic* 93 (December 15, 1937): 165–66.

"Intuitive or Scientific?" *Nation* 146 (January 20, 1938): 139–40.

"Is Mr. Hook a Socialist?" *Partisan Review* 4 (January 1938): 40–44.

"Maxims and Anecdotes." *New Republic* 94 (February 23, 1938): 69–70; (March 16, 1938): 159–60.

"A Psychological Approach to the Study of Social Crises." *American Journal of Sociology* 43 (March 1938): 799–803.

"Twelve Propositions by Kenneth Burke on the Relation between Economics and Psychology." *Science and Society* 2 (1938): 242–49.

"'On Must' and 'Take Care'" (undated, 1938). "Kenneth Burke's 'On Must' and 'Take Care'": An Edition of His Reply to Parkes's Review of *Attitudes toward History*." Edited by Ann George. *Rhetoric Society Quarterly* 29 (Fall 1999): 21–39.

"Literature as Equipment for Living." *Direction* 1 (April 1938): 10–13.

"The Virtues and Limitations of Debunking." *Southern Review* 3 (Spring 1938): 640–56.

"Semantic and Poetic Meaning." *Southern Review* 4 (Winter 1938): 501–23.

"Questions for Critics." *Direction* 2 (May–June 1939): 12–13.

"The Rhetoric of Hitler's 'Battle.'" *Southern Review* 5 (Summer 1939): 1–21.

"Freud—and the Analysis of Poetry." *American Journal of Sociology* 45 (November 1939): 391–417.

"Embargo." *Direction* 2 (November 1939): 2.

"Comments on Dr. [Wm. Heard] Kilpatrick's Article." *American Teacher* 24 (November 1939): 26–27.

"The Calling of the Tune." *Kenyon Review* 1 (Winter 1939): 272–82.

"Surrealism." *New Directions in Prose and Poetry* 5 (1940): 563–79.

"On Musicality in Verse." *Poetry* 62 (October 1940): 31–40.

"What to Do till the Doctor Comes: Thoughts on Conscription." *Direction* 3 (November 1940): 7, 24.

Letter in "Your Letters" section. *Direction* 3 (November 1940): 21.

"Americanism." *Direction* 4 (February 1941): 2, 3.

"Character of Our Culture." *Southern Review* 6 (Winter/Spring 1941): 675–94.

"Four Master Tropes." *Kenyon Review* 3 (Autumn 1941): 421–38.

REVIEWS (in chronological order of publication)

"Intelligence as a Good." Rev. of *The Quest for Certainty*, by John Dewey. *New Republic* 64 (September 3, 1930): 77–79.

"In Quest of the Way." Rev. of *A New Model of the Universe*, by P. D. Ouspensky. *New Republic* 68 (September 9, 1931): 104–6.

"The Poet and the Passwords." Rev. of *Fear and Trembling*, by Glenway Wescott. *New Republic* 71 (August 3, 1932): 310–13.

"Belief and Art." Rev. of *Experience and Art*, by Joseph Wood Krutch. *Nation* 135 (November 30, 1932): 536–37.

"Mainsprings of Character." Rev. of *The Ironic Temper: Anatole France and His Time*, by Haakon M. Chevalier. *New Republic* 73 (December 7, 1932): 103–4.

"Poets All." Rev. of *Bentham's Theory of Fictions*, by C. K. Ogden. *Nation* 136 (January 18, 1933): 70.

"The Technique of Listening." Rev. of *Mencius on the Mind: Experiments in Multiple Definition*, by I. A. Richards. *Nation* (April 12, 1933): 416.

"Hyperglasticism Exposed." Rev. of *The Secret of Laughter*, by A. M. Ludovici. *Hound & Horn* 6 (July–September 1933): 732–36.

"Fraught with Freight." Rev. of *Past Masters*, by Thomas Mann. *New Republic* 77 (January 10, 1934): 257.

"Rugged Portraiture." Rev. of *Rubicon or The Strikebreaker*, author not given. *New Masses* 11 (April 3, 1934): 46.

"The Esthetic Strain." Rev. of *Art as Experience*, by John Dewey. *New Republic* 78 (April 25, 1934): 315–16.

"*Permanence and Change*." Rev. of *Joseph and His Brothers*, by Thomas Mann. *New Republic* 79 (June 27, 1934): 186–87.

"In Vague Praise of Liberty." Rev. of *History of Europe in the Nineteenth Century*, by Benedetto Croce. *Hound & Horn* 7 (July–September 1934): 704–7.

"Gastronomy of Letters." Rev. of *ABC of Reading*, by Ezra Pound. *Nation* 139 (October 17, 1934): 458–59.

"The Universe Alive." Rev. of *Nature and Life*, by Alfred North Whitehead. *New Republic* 81 (November 14, 1934): 26.

"While Waiting." Rev. of *Those Who Perish*, by Edward Dahlberg. *New Republic* 81 (November 21, 1934): 53.

"Concern about English." Rev. of *Wine and Physic: A Poem and Six Essays on the Fate of Our Language*, by Alexander Laing. *Poetry* 45 (February 1935): 294–96.

"Goethe and the Jews." Rev. of *Goethe and the Jews*, by Mark Waldman. *New Masses* 14 (March 19, 1935): 25.

"One Who Wrestled." Rev. of *Dostoevsky: A Life*, by Avrahm Yarmolinsky. *New Republic* 82 (March 27, 1935): 192, 194.

"Change of Identity." Rev. of *Judgment Day*, by James T. Farrell. *New Republic* 83 (June 19, 1935): 171–72.

"Two Kinds of Against." Rev. of *No Thanks*, by E. E. Cummings, and *Poems*, by Kenneth Fearing. *New Republic* 83 (June 26, 1935): 198–99.

"The Impartial Essence." Rev. of *Lectures in America*, by Gertrude Stein. *New Republic* 83 (July 3, 1935): 227.

"Protective Coloration." Rev. of *Redder than the Rose*, by Robert Forsythe. *New Republic* 83 (July 10, 1935): 255–56.

"The Hope in Tragedy." Rev. of *Chorus for Survival*, by Horace Gregory. *Poetry* 46 (July 1935): 227–30.

"Recent Poetry." Omnibus review. *Southern Review* 1 (July 1935): 164–77.

"Renaming Old Directions." Rev. of *Redirecting Education: Volume I, The United States*, edited by Rexford G. Tugwell and Leon H. Keyserling. *Nation* 141 (August 7, 1935): 166.

"Storm Omens." Rev. of *Pittsburgh Memoranda*, by Haniel Long. *New Republic* 84 (August 28, 1935): 83.

"A Radical, But—." Rev. of *The Neurotic Nightingale*, by Vardis Fisher. *New Republic* 84 (October 2, 1935): 221.

"Coleridge Rephrased." Rev. of *On Imagination: Coleridge's Critical Theory*, by I. A. Richards. *Poetry* 47 (October 1935): 52–54.

Rev. of *Stalin: A New World Seen through One Man*, by Henri Barbusse. *Book Union Bulletin* (November 1935): 1–2.

"Return after Flight." Rev. of *Theory of Flight*, by Muriel Rukeyser. *New Masses* 18 (February 4, 1936): 26.

"Anatomy of the Mask." Rev. of *Propaganda: Its Psychology and Technique*, by Leonard W. Doob. *New Republic* 85 (February 5, 1936): 371–72.

"Liberalism's Family Tree." Rev. of *Liberalism and Social Action*, by John Dewey. *New Republic* 86 (March 4, 1936): 115–16.

"By Ice, Fire, or Decay?" Rev. of *Paradise Lost: A Play in 3 Acts*, by Clifford Odets. *New Republic* 86 (April 15, 1936): 283–84.

"A Sour Note on Literary Criticism." Rev. of *A Note on Literary Criticism*, by James T. Farrell. *New Republic* 87 (June 24, 1936): 211.

"Property as an Absolute." Rev. of *Who Owns America? A New Declaration of Independence*, edited by Herbert Agar and Allen Tate. *New Republic* 87 (July 1, 1936): 245–46.

"Without Benefit of Politics." Rev. of *Truth and Reality: A Life History of the Human Will* and *Will Therapy: An Analysis of the Therapeutic Process in Terms of Relationship*, by Otto Rank. *Nation* 143 (July 18, 1936): 78.

"Deft Plaintiveness." Rev. of *One Season Shattered*, by James Daly. *Poetry* 48 (August 1936): 282–85.

"Symbolic War." Rev. of *Proletarian Literature in the United States*, edited by Granville Hicks. *Southern Review* 2 (Summer 1936): 134–47.

"William James: Superlative Master of the Comparative." Rev. of *The Thought and Character of William James*, by Ralph Barton Perry. *Science and Society* 1 (Fall 1936): 122–25.

Rev. of *Reason and Emotion*, by John Macmurray. *American Journal of Sociology* 42 (September 1936): 283.

"Cautious Enlightenment." Rev. of *The Double Agent: Essays in Craft and Elucidation*, by R. P. Blackmur. *Poetry* 49 (October 1936): 52–54.

"Methodology of the Scramble." Rev. of *Politics: Who Gets What, When, How?*, by Harold D. Lasswell. *New Republic* 89 (December 23, 1936): 250.

"Synthetic Freedom." Rev. of *The Restoration of Property; An Essay on the Modern Crisis*, by Hilaire Belloc. *New Republic* 89 (January 20, 1937): 365.

"The Constants of Social Relativity." Rev. of *Ideology and Utopia*, by Karl Mannheim. *Nation* 144 (January 30, 1937): 131.

"Exceptional Improvisation." Rev. of *Some Versions of Pastoral*, by William Empson. *Poetry* 49 (March 19, 1937): 347–50.

"The Esthetic Instinct." Rev. of *Art and Society*, by Herbert Read. *New Republic* 90 (April 28, 1937): 363–64.

"Tentative Proposal." Rev. of *The Mediterranean, and Other Poems* and *Reactionary Essays on Poetry and Ideas*, by Allen Tate. *Poetry* 50 (May 1937): 96–100.

"A Gist of Gists of Gists." Rev. of *One Mighty Torrent: The Drama of Biography*, by Edgar Johnson. *Nation* 144 (May 29, 1937): 622–23.

"The Second Study of Middletown." Rev. of *Middletown in Transition*, by Robert S. and Helen Merrell Lynd. *New Masses* 9 (June 1937): 22, 24.

"Leave the Leaf Its Springtime." Rev. of *New Poems*, by Frederick Mortimer Clapp. *Poetry* 50 (July 1937): 226–29.

"Field Work in Bohemia." Rev. of *This Room and This Gin and These Sandwiches*, by Edmund Wilson. *Nation* 145 (July 31, 1937): 133–34.

"Spender's Left Hand." Rev. of *Forward from Liberalism*, by Stephen Spender. *New Republic* 92 (August 11, 1937): 24–25.

"A Recipe for Worship." Rev. of *The Hero*, by Lord Raglan. *Nation* 145 (August 21, 1937): 201–2.

"Thurber Perfects Mind Cure." Rev. of *Let Your Mind Alone! And Other More or Less Inspirational Pieces*, by James Thurber. *New Republic* 92 (September 29, 1937): 220–21.

Rev. of *The Ethics of Competition and Other Essays*, by Frank Hyneman Knight. *American Journal of Sociology* 43 (September 1937): 332–34.

"The 'Science' of Race-Thinking." Rev. of *Race: A Study in Modern Superstition*, by Jacques Barzun. *New Masses* 25 (October 5, 1937): 22.

"Responses to Pressure." Rev. of *Wordsworth and Milton, Poets and Prophets. A Study of Their Reactions to Political Events*, by Herbert J. C. Grierson. *Poetry* 51 (October 1937): 37–42.

"A Trail Trails Off." Rev. of *From These Roots: The Ideas That Have Made Modern Literature*, by Mary M. Colum. *New Republic* 93 (December 22, 1937): 205–6.

"Semantics in Demotic." Rev. of *The Tyranny of Words*, by Stuart Chase. *New Republic* 93 (January 26, 1938): 343–44.

"Weighted History." Rev. of *The Crisis of Civilization*, by Hilaire Belloc. *New Republic* 93 (February 2, 1938): 375–76.

"Corrosive without Corrective." Rev. of *The Folklore of Capitalism*, by Thurman W. Arnold. *New Masses* 26 (February 8, 1938): 22–24.

"Exceptional Book." Rev. of *English Pastoral Poetry*, by William Empson. *New Republic* 95 (May 25, 1938): 81.

Rev. of *La Poésie et le Principe de Transcendance: Essai sur la Création Poétique*, by Maurice Duval. *American Journal of Sociology* 44 (July 1938): 167–68.

"George Herbert Mead." Rev. of *The Works of George Herbert Mead*, edited by Charles W. Morris et al. *New Republic* 97 (January 11, 1939): 292–93.

"Fearing's New Poems." Rev. of *Dead Reckoning*, by Kenneth Fearing. *New Masses* 33 (February 1939): 27–28.

"Monads—on the Make." Rev. of *Reality*, by Paul Weiss. *New Republic* 98 (April 19, 1939): 314–15.

"The Book of Proverbs." Rev. of *Racial Proverbs: A Selection of the World's Proverbs Arranged Linguistically*, edited by S. G. Champion. *New Republic* 99 (June 28, 1939): 230.

"Why Coleridge?" Rev. of *Samuel Taylor Coleridge: A Biographical Study*, by E. K. Chambers, and *The Life of S. T. Coleridge: The Early Years*, by Lawrence Hanson. *New Republic* 100 (September 13, 1939): 163–64.

"On Poetry and Poetics." Rev. of *The World's Body: Foundations for Literary Criticism*, by John Crowe Ransom. *Poetry* 55 (October 1939): 51–54.

"Quantity and Quality." Rev. of *Modern Man in the Making*, by Otto Neurath. *New Republic* 101 (November 8, 1939): 22–23.

"The Sources of 'Christabel.'" Rev. of *The Road to Tryermaine: A Study of the History, Background, and Purposes of Coleridge's "Christabel,"* by Arthur N. Nethercot. *New Republic* 102 (May 6, 1940): 617.

"Key Words for Critics." Rev. of *The Intent of the Critic*, by Edmund Wilson, Norman Foerster, John Crowe Ransom, and W. H. Auden; *The New Criticism*, by John Crowe Ransom; and *Reason in Madness*, by Allen Tate. *Kenyon Review* 4 (Winter 1941–42): 126–32.

Secondary Studies and Primary Works by Others

Aaron, Daniel. *Writers on the Left.* New York: Oxford University Press, 1961, 1977.

Abbott, Don Paul. "Kenneth Burke's Secular Conversion." *Horns of Plenty: Malcolm Cowley and His Generation* 2 (1989): 39–52.

———. "Marxist Influences on the Rhetorical Theory of Kenneth Burke." *Philosophy and Rhetoric* 7 (1974): 217–33.

Addison, Gayle. *Richard Wright: Ordeal of a Native Son.* Garden City, N.Y.: Anchor, 1980.

Aldington, Richard, ed. *Imagist Anthology: New Poetry.* New York: Covici, Friede, 1930.

Ardzrooni, Leon, and Thorstein Veblen. *Essays in Our Changing Order.* New York: Viking, 1934.

Aune, James A. "Burke's Palimpsest: Rereading *Permanence and Change.*" *Communication Studies* 42 (1991): 234–37.

Bak, Hans. *Malcolm Cowley: The Formative Years.* Athens: University of Georgia Press, 1993.

Benét, William Rose. "The Poetry Session [at the Third Writers' Congress]." *Saturday Review of Literature* 20 (June 10, 1939): 10–11.

Blackmur, R. P. "The Critic's Job of Work." In *The Double Agent: Essays in Craft and Elucidation.* New York: Arrow Editions, 1935. 269–302.

Blakesley, David. "Kenneth Burke's Pragmatism—Old and New." In *Kenneth Burke and the Twenty-First Century,* edited by Bernard L. Brock, 71–95. Albany: SUNY Press, 1999.

Bloom, James D. *Left Letters: The Culture Wars of Mike Gold and Joseph Freeman.* New York: Columbia University Press, 1992.

"The Book Union." *New Masses* 15 (April 16, 1935): 6.

Booth, Wayne. "Between Two Generations: The Heritage of the Chicago School." In *Profession 82,* 19–26. New York: MLA, 1982.

Bourne, Randolph. "Twilight of the Idols." *Seven Arts* 2 (1917): 695, 697–99.

Boyle, Kay, et al. "The Revolution of the Word." *Transition* 14 (June 1929): n.pag.

Bremen, Brian. *William Carlos Williams and the Diagnostics of Culture.* New York: Oxford University Press, 1993.

Breslin, James E. *William Carlos Williams: An American Artist.* Chicago: University of Chicago Press, 1970.

Brinkley, Alan. *Voices of Protest: Huey Long, Father Coughlin, and the Great Depression.* New York: Knopf, 1982.

Brooks, Cleanth. "New Criticism." In *Princeton Encyclopedia of Poetry and Poetics,* edited by Alex Preminger, 567–68. Princeton: Princeton University Press, 1974.

Brooks, Cleanth, and Robert Penn Warren, eds. *Stories from the "Southern Review."* Baton Rouge: Louisiana State University Press, 1953.

Brooks, Van Wyck. "On Creating a Usable Past." *Dial* 66 (April 1918): 337–41.

———. *Three Essays on America.* New York: E. P. Dutton, 1934.

———. *The Wine of the Puritans.* London: Sisley's Ltd., 1908

Brown, Leonard. "Dialectical Materialism and Proletarian Literature." *Syracuse University Library Associates Courier* 29 (1994): 41–59.

Buhle, Paul. *Marxism in the United States.* London: Verso, 1987.

Burgchardt, Carl R. "Two Faces of American Communism: Pamphlet Rhetoric of the Third Period and the Popular Front." *Quarterly Journal of Speech* 66 (1980): 375–91.

Burks, Don M. "Kenneth Burke: The Agro-Bohemian 'Marxoid.'" *Communication Studies* 42 (1991): 219–33.

Burnham, James, and Philip Wheelwright. "Thirteen Propositions." *Symposium* 4 (1933): 127–34.

Bushman, Donald. "'A Conversation of Gestures': George Herbert Mead's Pragmatic Theory of Language." *Rhetoric Review* 16 (1998): 253–67.

Caldwell, Erskine. *God's Little Acre.* New York: Grosset & Dunlap, 1933.

———. *Tobacco Road.* New York: Grosset & Dunlap, 1932.

Calverton, V. F. "Critic on the Barricades." *New Masses* 20 (August 1936): 15.

Cantwell, Robert. "Four Hundred Million Borrowed Books." *Vanity Fair* 32 (April 1935): 56, 65.

Chamberlain, John. "The First American Writers' Congress." *Saturday Review of Literature* 12 (May 4, 1935): 4.

———. "The Literary Left Grows Up." *Saturday Review of Literature* 12 (May 11, 1935): 3–4, 17–18.

Chase, Stuart. *Men and Machines.* New York: Macmillan, 1929.

———. *The Promise of Power.* New York: John Day, 1933.

———. *Technocracy: An Interpretation.* New York: John Day, 1933.

Chesebro, James, ed. *Extensions of the Burkeian System.* Tuscaloosa: University of Alabama Press, 1993.

Coe, Richard. Posting to Burke-L. June 23, 2000.

Conkin, Paul K. *The Southern Agrarians.* Knoxville: University of Tennessee Press, 1988.

Conklin, Groff. "The Science of Symbology." Rev. of *Attitudes toward History. New Masses* 10 (August 10, 1937): 25–26.

Conroy, Jack. *The Disinherited.* New York: Covici-Friede, 1933.

Cooney, Terry A. *The Rise of the New York Intellectuals: Partisan Review and Its Circle.* Madison: University of Wisconsin Press, 1986.

Core, George. "Vanderbilt English and the New Criticism." In *The Vanderbilt Tradition: Essays in Honor of Thomas Daniel Young,* edited by Mark Winchell, 19–35. Baton Rouge: Louisiana State University Press, 1991.

Cork, Jim. "John Dewey and Karl Marx." In *John Dewey: Philosopher of Science and Freedom,* edited by Sidney Hook, 331–50. New York: Dial Press, 1950.

Cowan, Louise. *The Fugitive Group.* Baton Rouge: Louisiana State University Press, 1959.

Cowley, Malcolm. *After the Genteel Tradition.* New York: Norton, 1936.

———. *Blue Juniata.* New York: J. Campe & H. Smith, 1929.

———. *The Dream of the Golden Mountains: Remembering the 1930s.* New York: Viking, 1980.

———. *Exile's Return.* New York: Norton, 1934.

———. "In Memoriam." *New Republic* 103 (August 12, 1940): 219–20.

———. "Let's Build a Railroad." Rev. of *Road to Life. New Republic* 69 (February 10, 1932): 351.

———. "Notes on a Writers Congress." *New Republic* 99 (June 21, 1939): 192–93.

———. "The Poet and the World." Rev. of John Dos Passos's *1919*. *New Republic* 70 (April 27, 1932): 303–5.

———. "Red Ivory Tower." *New Republic* 97 (November 9, 1938): 22–23.

———. Rev. of *Towards a Better Life*. *New Republic* 70 (February 17, 1932): 23–24.

Crable, Bryan. "Ideology as 'Metabiology': Rereading Burke's *Permanence and Change*." *Quarterly Journal of Speech* 84 (1998): 303–19.

Crane, R. S. *A Census of British Newspapers and Periodicals 1620–1800*. London: Cambridge University Press, 1927.

———. "History versus Criticism in the University Study of Literature." *English Journal* (College Edition) 24 (1935): 645–67.

———. *New Essays by Oliver Goldsmith*. Chicago: University of Chicago Press, 1927.

Crane, R. S., and Richard McKeon, eds. *Critics and Criticism Ancient and Modern*. Chicago: University of Chicago Press, 1952.

Crossman, Richard, ed. *The God That Failed*. New York: Harper & Row, 1950.

Crowley, John. "Introduction: Remembering Leonard Brown." *Syracuse University Library Associates Courier* 29 (1994): 41–44.

———. "Introduction: Shirley Jackson on Ernest Hemingway: A Recovered Term Paper." *Syracuse University Library Associates Courier* 31 (1996): 33–39.

Crowley, John D., S.J. "Bibliography of Sidney Hook." In *Sidney Hook and the Contemporary World: Essays on the Pragmatic Intelligence*, edited by Paul Kurtz, 429–71. New York: John Day, 1968.

Crusius, Timothy. *Kenneth Burke and the Conversation after Philosophy*. Carbondale: Southern Illinois University Press, 1999.

———. "Kenneth Burke's *Auscultation:* A 'De-struction' of Marxist Dialectic and Rhetoric." *Rhetorica* 6 (1988): 355–79.

Cutrer, Thomas W. *Parnassus on the Mississippi: The "Southern Review" and the Baton Rouge Literary Community, 1935–1942*. Baton Rouge: Louisiana State University Press, 1984.

Denning, Michael. *The Cultural Front*. New York: Verso, 1996.

Dewey, John. *Art as Experience*. New York: Minton, Balch, 1934.

———. *Experience in Nature*. New York: Waverly, 1925.

———. "How Much Freedom in New Schools?" *New Republic* 62 (July 9, 1930): 204–6.

———. *Liberalism and Social Action*. New York: Putnam, 1935.

———. *The Philosophy of the Present*. Chicago: Open Court, 1932.

———. *The Public and Its Problems*. New York: Holt, 1927.

———. *The Quest for Certainty: A Study of the Relation of Knowledge and Action*. New York: Minton, Balch, 1929.

———. *School and Society*. Chicago: University of Chicago Press, 1899.

———. *Studies in Logical Theory*. Chicago: University of Chicago Press, 1903.

———. "Why I Am Not a Communist." *Modern Monthly* 8 (April 1934): 135–37.

Dexter, Lewis Anthony. *How Candidates Lend Strength to Tickets*. Privately printed, 1956.

Diggins, John Patrick. *The Bard of Savagery: Thorstein Veblen and Modern Social Theory*. New York: Seabury Press, 1978.

————. *The Promise of Pragmatism*. Chicago: University of Chicago Press, 1994.

Dorfman, Joseph. *Thorstein Veblen and His America*. New York: Viking, 1934.

Dos Passos, John. *The Big Money*. New York: Harcourt, Brace, 1936.

————. *Manhattan Transfer*. New York: Harper & Brothers, 1925.

————. *1919*. New York: Harcourt, Brace, 1932.

Dreiser, Theodore. *An American Tragedy*. New York: Boni & Liveright, 1925.

————. *Sister Carrie*. New York: Boni & Liveright, 1925.

Du Bois, W. E. B. "The Criteria of Negro Art." *Crisis* 32 (1926): 296.

Dykhuizen, George. *The Life and Mind of John Dewey*. Carbondale: Southern Illinois University Press, 1973.

Eastman, Max. *Artists in Uniform: A Study of Literature and Bureaucratism*. New York: Knopf, 1934.

Eddy, Mary Baker. *Science and Health*. Boston: Trustees under the Will of Mary Baker Eddy, 1934.

Eliot, T. S. *Ash Wednesday*. London: Faber & Faber, 1930.

————. "The Idea of a Literary Review." *Criterion* 4 (1926): 1–6.

Eliot, Thomas D. Rev. of *Permanence and Change*. *American Sociological Review* 2 (February 1937): 115–17.

Empson, William. *Seven Types of Ambiguity*. London: Chatto & Windus, 1930.

————. *Some Versions of Pastoral*. London: Chatto & Windus, 1935.

Enoch, Jessica. "Becoming Symbol-Wise: Kenneth Burke's Pedagogy of Critical Reflection." *College Composition and Communication* 56 (2004): 272–96.

Farrell, James T. "Dewey in Mexico." In *John Dewey: Philosopher of Science and Freedom*, edited by Sidney Hook, 351–77. New York: Dial Press, 1950.

————. *Judgment Day*. New York: Vanguard Press, 1935.

————. *A Note on Literary Criticism*. New York: Vanguard Press, 1936.

————. *Studs Lonigan: A Trilogy*. New York: Vanguard Press, 1935.

————. *Yet Other Waters*. New York: Vanguard Press, 1952.

Farrell, Kathleen. *Literary Integrity and Political Action: The Public Argument of James T. Farrell*. Boulder, Colo.: Westview, 2000.

Feehan, Michael. "Kenneth Burke and Mary Baker Eddy." In *Unending Conversations: New Writings by and about Kenneth Burke*, edited by Greig Henderson and David Cratis Williams, 206–24. Carbondale: Southern Illinois University Press, 2001.

Feffer, Andrew. *The Chicago Pragmatists and American Progressivism*. Ithaca: Cornell University Press, 1993.

Fisch, Max H. *Peirce, Semeiotic, and Pragmatism*. Edited by Kenneth L. Ketner and Christian J. W. Kloesel. Bloomington: Indiana University Press, 1986.

Foley, Barbara. *Radical Representations: Politics and Form in U.S. Proletarian Fiction, 1929–1941*. Durham: Duke University Press, 1993.

Folsom, Franklin. *Days of Anger, Days of Hope*. Boulder: University Press of Colorado, 1994.

Frank, Waldo. *City Block*. Darien, Conn.: Waldo Frank, 1922.

————. *Holiday*. New York: Boni & Liveright, 1923.

————. *Our America*. New York: Boni & Liveright, 1919.

Franklin, Jay. "What's Wrong with Our Radicals?" *Vanity Fair* 44 (April 1935): 33–34.

Frazer, James George, Sir. *The Golden Bough: A Study in Magic and Religion.* London: Macmillan, 1890. Abridged ed. New York: Macmillan, 1922.

Freeman, Joseph. Introduction to *Proletarian Literature in the United States.* Edited by Granville Hicks et al. New York: International Publishers, 1935.

George, Ann, ed. "Kenneth Burke's 'On *Must* and *Take Care.'"* *Rhetoric Society Quarterly* 29 (1999): 21–39.

———. "Kenneth Burke's *Permanence and Change:* Rhetoric and Culture." Ph.D. diss., Pennsylvania State University, 1997.

Givner, Joan. *Katherine Anne Porter: A Life.* Rev. ed. Athens: University of Georgia Press, 1991.

Gold, Mike. "Editorial: Go Left, Young Writers!" *New Masses* 5 (January 1929): 6.

———. "Editorial: On a Section Gang [A New Program for Writers]." *New Masses* 4 (July 1928): 8–9.

———. "Notes of the Month." *New Masses* 5 (December 1929): 23.

———. "Out of the Fascist Unconscious." Rev. of *Frescoes for Mr. Rockefeller's City,* by Archibald MacLeish. *New Republic* 75 (July 26, 1933): 295–96.

———. "Towards Proletarian Art." *Liberator* 4, no. 2 (February 1921): 20–24.

Grattan, Hartley. "New Voices: The Promise of Our Youngest Writers." *Forum* 88 (November 1932): 284–88.

Grattan, Hartley, ed. *The Critique of Humanism: A Symposium.* New York: Brewer & Warren, 1930.

Guterman, Norman. "Analysis of Communication." Rev. of *Permanence and Change.* by Kenneth Burke. *New Masses* 3 (April 16, 1935): 23.

Hampden, Paul. "The New Direction in Economics." *New Directions* 2 (1937): n.pag.

Harris, Wendell. "Critics Who Made Us: Kenneth Burke." *Sewanee Review* 96 (1988): 452–63.

Hart, Henry, ed. *American Writers' Congress.* New York: International Publishers, 1935.

———, ed. *The Writer in a Changing World.* New York: Equinox, 1937.

Hawhee, Debra. "Burke and Nietzsche." *Quarterly Journal of Speech* 85 (1999): 129–45.

———. "Burke on Drugs." *Rhetoric Society Quarterly* 34 (2004): 5–28.

Hayakawa, S. I. *Language in Action.* New York: Harcourt, Brace, 1941.

———. "The Meaning of Semantics." *New Republic* 99 (August 2, 1939): 354–57.

Hazlitt, Henry. "Kenneth Burke's Metaphysics" Rev. of *Permanence and Change, New York Times Book Review* (May 5, 1935): 19.

Henderson, Greig. "Aesthetic and Practical Frames of Reference: Burke, Marx, and the Rhetoric of Social Change." In *Extensions of the Burkeian System,* edited by James W. Chesebro, 173–85.

Hicks, Granville. "The Crisis in American Criticism." *New Masses* 5 (February 1933): 3–5.

———. *The Great Tradition: An Interpretation of American Literature since the Civil War.* New York: Macmillan, 1933. Rev. ed., 1935.

———. "In Defense of Eloquence." Rev. of *Counter-Statement. New Republic* 69 (December 2, 1931): 75–76.

———. *Part of the Truth.* New York: Harcourt, Brace & World, 1965.

———. "Response" [to Kenneth Burke's "Counter-Blasts on *Counter-Statement*"]. *New Republic* 69 (December 9, 1931): 101.

Hicks, Granville, Michael Gold, Isidor Schneider, Joseph North, Paul Peters, and Alan Calmer, eds. *Proletarian Literature in the United States: An Anthology.* New York: International Publishers, 1935.

Homberger, Eric. *American Writers and Radical Politics, 1900–1939.* New York: St. Martin's Press, 1986.

Hook, Sidney, "The Anatomy of the Popular Front." *Partisan Review* 6 (Spring 1939): 39–42.

―――. "Experimental Naturalism." In *American Philosophy Today and Tomorrow,* edited by Horace M. Kallen and Hook, 205–25. New York: L. Furman, 1935.

―――. "Is Mr. Burke Serious?" *Partisan Review* 4 (January 1938): 44–47.

―――. *John Dewey: An Intellectual Portrait.* New York: John Day, 1939.

―――. "Liberalism and the Case of Leon Trotsky." *Southern Review* 3 (Autumn 1937): 267–82.

―――. "The Metaphysics of Pragmatism." Ph.D. diss., Columbia University, 1927.

―――. *Out of Step.* New York: Harper & Row, 1987.

―――. "Saint Stalin." Rev. of *Stalin,* by Henri Barbusse. *Saturday Review of Literature* 13 (November 16, 1935): 7–8.

―――. "The Technique of Mystification." Rev. of *Attitudes toward History,* by Kenneth Burke. *Partisan Review* 4 (December 1937): 57–62.

―――. *Towards the Understanding of Karl Marx.* New York: John Day, 1933.

Hook, Sidney, ed. *John Dewey: Philosopher of Science and Freedom.* New York: Dial Press, 1950.

―――, ed. *The Meaning of Marx: A Symposium.* New York: Farrar & Rinehart, 1934.

Hummel, Beth. "Katherine Anne Porter's 'Growing Season' in Greenwich Village." Unpublished honors thesis, Pennsylvania State University, 2000.

Jack, Jordynn. "'The Piety of Degradation': Kenneth Burke, the Bureau of Social Hygiene, and *Permanence and Change.*" *Quarterly Journal of Speech* 90 (2004): 446–68.

Jaensch, E. R. *Eidetic Imagery and Typological Methods of Investigation; Their Importance for the Psychology of Childhood, the Theory of Education, General Psychology, and the Psychophysiology of Human Personality.* London: K. Paul, Trench, Trübner / New York: Harcourt, Brace, 1930.

James, William. "The Chicago School." *Psychological Bulletin* 1 (1904): 1.

―――. *Pragmatism: A New Name for Some Old Ways of Thinking: Popular Lectures on Philosophy.* New York: Longmans, Green, 1907.

Jameson, Fredric. "The Symbolic Inference; or, Kenneth Burke and Ideological Analysis." *Critical Inquiry* 4 (1978): 507–23.

Jay, Martin. *The Dialectical Imagination: A History of the Frankfurt School and the Institute of Social Research, 1923–1950.* Boston: Little, Brown, 1973.

Jay, Paul. *Contingency Blues.* Madison: University of Wisconsin Press, 1997.

―――. "Kenneth Burke and the Motives of Eloquence." *American Literary History* 1 (1989): 535–53.

―――, ed. *The Selected Correspondence of Kenneth Burke and Malcolm Cowley, 1915–1981.* New York: Viking, 1988.

Johnson, Edgar. "The Artist and His World." Rev. of "On Interpretation." *New Republic* 80 (September 5, 1934): 109–10.

————. *Charles Dickens, His Tragedy and Triumph.* New York: Simon & Schuster, 1952.

————. "Society and the Poetic Mind." Rev. of *Permanence and Change. Saturday Review of Literature* 12 (October 26, 1935): 22.

Josephson, Matthew. "For a Literary United Front." *New Masses* 7 (April 30, 1935): 22–23.

————. *Infidel in the Temple: A Memoir of the Nineteen-Thirties.* New York: Knopf, 1967.

————. *The Robber Barons: The Great American Capitalists, 1861–1901.* New York: Harcourt, Brace, 1934.

Kastely, James. "Kenneth Burke's Comic Rejoinder to the Cult of Empire." *College English* 58 (1996): 307–26.

Klehr, Harvey. *The Heyday of American Communism.* New York: Basic Books, 1984.

Klingender, F. D. "American Writers Congress." N.p., n.d. Included in Kenneth Burke Papers, 1936.

Korzybski, Alfred. *Science and Sanity: An Introduction to Non-Aristotelian Systems and General Semantics.* 3rd ed. Garden City, N.Y.: Country Life Press, 1948.

Krutch, Joseph Wood. "Marx as Metaphor." Rev. of *Permanence and Change. Nation* 140 (April 17, 1935): 453–54.

————. *Was Europe a Success?* New York: Farrar & Rinehart, 1932.

Kunitz, Joshua. "In Defense of a Term." *New Masses* 10 (July 12, 1938): 145–47.

Kutulas, Judy. "Becoming 'More Liberal': The League of American Writers, the Communist Party, and the Literary People's Front." *Journal of American Culture* 13 (1990): 71–80.

————. *The Long War: The Intellectual People's Front and Anti-Stalinism, 1930–1940.* Durham, N.C.: Duke University Press, 1995.

Laughlin, James. "Preface." *New Directions* 2 (1937): n.pag.

Lawrence, D. H. *Fantasia of the Unconscious.* New York: T. Seltzer, 1922.

"The League of American Writers." *New Masses* 15 (May 7, 1935): 7.

Leitch, Vincent. *American Literary Criticism from the Thirties to the Eighties.* New York: Columbia University Press, 1988.

Lentricchia, Frank. *Criticism and Social Change.* Chicago: University of Chicago Press, 1983.

————. "Reading History with Kenneth Burke." In *Representing Kenneth Burke*, edited by Hayden White and Margaret Brose, 119–49. Baltimore: Johns Hopkins University Press, 1982.

Logie, John. "The Author('s) Property: Rhetoric, Literature, and the Construction of Authorship." Ph.D. diss., Pennsylvania State University, 1999.

Lowenfels, Walter. Letter to the editor. *New Masses* 28 (July 12, 1938): 145.

Mailloux, Steven. "Rhetorical Paths of Thought: Burkean (Dis)Connections." Triennial Conference of the Kenneth Burke Society, Iowa City, 1999.

Malinowski, Bronislaw. "The Problem of Meaning in Primitive Languages." Supplement 1 to *The Meaning of Meaning: A Study of the Influence of Language upon Thought and of the Science of Symbolism*, by C. K. Ogden and I. A. Richards, 296–336. London: Kegan Paul, Trench, & Trübner / New York: Harcourt, Brace, 1923.

Mangione, Jerre. *An Ethnic at Large: A Memoir of America in the Thirties and Forties.* New York: Putnam, 1978.

Mariani, Paul. *William Carlos Williams: The Poet and His Critics.* Chicago: American Library Association, 1975.

Markey, Morris. "Adversity." *New Yorker* (April 27, 1935): 38–44.

———. "Relief." *New Yorker* (April 20, 1935): 40–43.

Mayer, Milton. *Robert Maynard Hutchins: A Memoir.* Berkeley: University of California Press, 1993.

McGill, V. S. "Comments on Burke's Propositions." *Science and Society* 2 (1938): 253–56.

McGowan, John. *Democracy's Children: Intellectuals and the Rise of Cultural Politics.* Ithaca: Cornell University Press, 2002.

———. "Kenneth Burke." *Minnesota Review* 58–60 (2003): 241–49.

———. "Literature as Equipment for Living: A Pragmatist Project." *Soundings: An Interdisciplinary Journal* 6 (2003): 119–48.

McKeon, Richard. *The Basic Works of Aristotle.* New York: Random House, 1941.

———. "Criticism and the Liberal Arts: The Chicago School of Criticism." In *Profession 82*, 1–18. New York: MLA, 1982.

———. *Selections from Medieval Philosophers.* New York: Charles Scribner's Sons, 1929.

McNeill, William H. *Hutchins' University.* Chicago: University of Chicago Press, 1991.

Mead, George Herbert. *Mind, Self, and Society from the Standpoint of a Social Behaviorist.* Chicago: University of Chicago Press, 1934.

———. *Movements of Thought in the Nineteenth Century.* Chicago: University of Chicago Press, 1936.

———. *The Philosophy of the Act.* Chicago: University of Chicago Press, 1938.

———. *The Philosophy of the Present.* Chicago: Open Court, 1932.

Menand, Louis. *The Metaphysical Club.* New York: Farrar, Straus & Giroux, 2001.

Meyers, Jeffrey. *Edmund Wilson: A Biography.* Boston & New York: Houghton Mifflin, 1995.

Miller, Carolyn. "Genre as Social Action." *Quarterly Journal of Speech* 70 (1984): 151–67.

Mitchell, Wesley Clair. *What Veblen Taught: Selected Writings of Thorstein Veblen.* New York: Viking, 1936.

Molesworth, Charles. *Marianne Moore: A Literary Life.* New York: Atheneum, 1990.

Monroe, Harriet. "Art and Propaganda." *Poetry* 44 (July 1934): 210–15.

Moore, Marianne. "The Cantos." Rev. of *A Draft of XXX Cantos*, by Ezra Pound. *Poetry* 39 (October 1931): 37–50.

———. *The Pangolin and Other Verse.* London: Brendin, 1936.

———. Rev. of *XXX Cantos*, by Ezra Pound. *Criterion* 13 (1934): 482–85.

———. *Selected Poems.* New York: Macmillan, 1935.

Moore, T. Sturge. "Style or Beauty in Literature." *Criterion* 9 (1930): 591–603.

Morris, Charles. *The Pragmatic Movement in American Philosophy.* New York: Braziller, 1970.

Mumford, Lewis. *The Golden Day: A Study in American Experience and Culture.* New York: Boni & Liveright, 1926.

———. *Technics and Civilization.* New York: Harcourt, Brace, 1934.

Munson, Gorham. *Destinations: A Canvass of American Literature since 1900.* New York: J. H. Sears, 1928.

Nelson, Cary. *Repression and Recovery: Modern American Poetry and the Politics of Cultural Memory, 1910–1945.* Madison: University of Wisconsin Press, 1989.

Nicotra, Jodie. "Kenneth Burke and General Semantics." Unpublished ms. N.d.

Nietzsche, Friedrich Wilhelm. *The Will to Power: An Attempted Translation of All Values.* Translated by Anthony Mario Ludovici. Edinburgh: T. N. Foulis, 1909.

Ogden, C. K., and I. A. Richards. *The Meaning of Meaning: A Study of the Influence of Language upon Thought and of the Science of Symbolism.* London: Kegan Paul, Trench, & Trübner / New York: Harcourt, Brace, 1923.

O'Neill, Eugene. *The Hairy Ape: A Comedy of Ancient and Modern Life in Eight Scenes.* New York: Boni & Liveright, 1922.

Oppenheimer, Judy. *Private Demons: The Life of Shirley Jackson.* New York: Putnam, 1988.

Orage, A. R. "Is Social Credit the Answer?" *New Republic* 32 (February 27, 1935): 66–71.

Osborn, Reuben. *Freud and Marx: A Dialectical Study.* New York: Equinox Cooperative Press, 1937.

Parker, Donald, and Warren Herenden. "KB and MC: An Interview." *Visionary Company* 2, no. 3 (1987): 87–98.

Parkes, Henry Bamford. Rev. of *Attitudes toward History. Southern Review* 3 (1938): 693–706.

Parrington, Vernon. *Main Currents in American Thought: An Interpretation of American Literature from the Beginnings to 1920.* New York: Harcourt, Brace, 1926.

Pauley, Garth. "Criticism in Context: Kenneth Burke's 'The Rhetoric of Hitler's "Battle."'" Triennial Conference of the Kenneth Burke Society, Iowa City, May 1999.

Phelps, Christopher. *Young Sidney Hook: Marxist and Pragmatist.* Ithaca: Cornell University Press, 1997.

Porter, Katherine Anne. "Bouquet for October." *Pagany* 3 (January–March 1932): 21–29.

———. "The Circus." *Southern Review* 1 (July 1935): 36–41.

———. *Flowering Judas and Other Stories.* New York: Harcourt, Brace, 1930.

———. "The Grave." *Virginia Quarterly Review* 11 (April 1935): 177–83.

———. *Ship of Fools.* Boston: Little, Brown, 1962.

Pound, Ezra. *A Draft of XXX Cantos.* New York: Farrar & Rinehart, 1933.

Quandahl, Ellen. "'More than Lessons in How to Read': Burke, Freud, and the Resources of Symbolic Transformation." *College English* 63 (2001): 633–54.

Rahv, Philip. "Two Years of Progress—From Waldo Frank to Donald Ogden Stewart." *Partisan Review* 4 (February 1938): 22–30.

Ransom, John Crowe. "Address to Kenneth Burke." *Kenyon Review* 4 (1942): 219–37.

———. "Criticism, Inc." *Virginia Quarterly Review* 13 (1937): 586–602.

———. "Fiction Harvest." *Southern Review* 2 (Autumn 1936): 399–418.

———. *God without Thunder: An Unorthodox Defense of Orthodoxy.* New York: Harcourt, Brace, 1930.

———. *The New Criticism.* Norfolk, Conn.: New Directions, 1941.

————. "The Pragmatics of Art." *Kenyon Review* 2 (1940): 76–87.

————. "The Tense of Poetry." *Southern Review* 1 (Autumn 1935): 221–38.

————. *The World's Body.* New York: Charles Scribner's Sons, 1938.

Richards, I. A. *Coleridge on Imagination.* London: Kegan Paul, Trench, Trübner, 1934.

————. *Practical Criticism: A Study of Literary Judgment.* London: Kegan Paul, Trench, Trübner / New York: Harcourt, Brace, 1929.

————. *The Principles of Literary Criticism.* London: Kegan Paul, Trench, Trübner / New York: Harcourt, Brace, 1924.

————. *Science and Poetry.* London: Kegan Paul, Trench, Trübner / New York: Norton, 1926.

Richter, David. "R. S. Crane." In *Dictionary of Literary Biography, Volume 63: Modern American Critics, 1920–1955,* edited by Gregory Jay, 87–98. Detroit: Gale, 1988.

Rideout, Walter B. *The Radical Novel in the United States 1900–1954.* Cambridge, Mass.: Harvard University Press, 1956.

Rosteck, Thomas, and Michael Leff. "Piety, Propriety, and Perspective: An Interpretation and Application of Key Terms in Kenneth Burke's *Permanence and Change.*" *Western Journal of Speech Communication* 53 (1989): 327–41.

Rountree, J. Clark. "The 'Literary' Period (Early Days through *Towards a Better Life.*)" In *Conversations with Kenneth Burke Vol. 1* [videorecording]. Iowa City: University of Iowa, 1987.

Rowse, A. L. "The Theory and Practice of Communism." *Criterion* 9 (April 1930): 451–69.

Rucker, Darnell. *The Chicago Pragmatists.* Minneapolis: University of Minnesota Press, 1969.

Rueckert, William H. "A Field Guide to Kenneth Burke—1990. In *Extensions of the Burkean System,* edited by James W. Chesebro, 3–41. Tuscaloosa: University of Alabama Press, 1993.

————. "Rereading Kenneth Burke." In *The Legacy of Kenneth Burke,* edited by Herbert W. Simons and Trevor Melia, 239–61. Madison: University of Wisconsin Press, 1989.

Rueckert, William H., ed. *Critical Responses to Kenneth Burke, 1924–1966.* Minneapolis: University of Minnesota Press, 1969.

Russell, Bertrand. *The Analysis of Mind.* New York: G. Allen & Unwin / Macmillan, 1921.

Schachner, E. A. "Revolutionary Literature in the United States Today." *Windsor Quarterly* 2 (Spring 1934): 27–64.

Schiappa, Edward, and T. Keenan, "The Lost Passages of *Permanence and Change.*" *Communication Studies* 42 (1991): 191–98.

Schlauch, Margaret. "A Reply to Kenneth Burke." *Science and Society* 2 (1938): 250–53.

————. Rev. of *Attitudes toward History. Science and Society* 2 (1937–38): 128–32.

Schulze, Robin. "Marianne Moore's 'Imperious Ox, Imperial Dish' and the Poetry of the Natural World." *Twentieth Century Literature* 44 (1988): 1–33.

————. *The Web of Friendship: Marianne Moore and Wallace Stevens.* Ann Arbor: University of Michigan Press, 1995.

Schwartz, Lawrence. *Marxism and Culture: The CPUSA and Aesthetics in the 1930s.* Port Washington, N.Y.: Kennikat Press, 1980.

Seaver, Edwin. "What Is a Proletarian Novel? Notes toward a Redefinition." *Partisan Review* 2 (April-May 1935): 5–8.

"The Second American Writers' Congress." In *The Writer in a Changing World*, edited by Henry Hart, 195–256. New York: Equinox, 1937.

Selzer, Jack. *Kenneth Burke in Greenwich Village: Conversing with the Moderns, 1915–1931*. Madison: University of Wisconsin Press, 1996.

Sharer, Wendy. "Rhetoric, Reform, and Political Activism: The Logic in U.S. Women's Organizations, 1920–1930." Ph.D. diss., Pennsylvania State University, 2001.

Sheriff, Stacey. "Situating Kenneth Burke's 'My Approach to Communism.'" *Rhetorica* 23 (2005): 281–96.

Shi, David E. *Matthew Josephson, Bourgeois Bohemian*. New Haven: Yale University Press, 1981.

Simpson, Louis, James Olney, and Jo Gulledge, eds. *The Southern Review and Modern Literature, 1935–1985*. Baton Rouge: Louisiana State University Press, 1988.

Singal, Daniel J. *The War Within: From Victorian to Modernist Thought in the South, 1919–1945*. Chapel Hill: University of North Carolina Press, 1982.

Skodnick, Roy. "CounterGridlock: An Interview with Kenneth Burke." *All Area* 2 (1983): 4–32.

Smith, Bernard. "The Liberals Grow Old." *Saturday Review of Literature* 10 (December 30, 1933): 1–2.

Smyth, Robert. "The Third Writers' Congress." *Saturday Review of Literature* 20 (June 10, 1939): 10.

Soule, George. "Psychology and Revolution." *New Republic* 92 (August 25, 1937): 66–72.

Spurgeon, Caroline. *Shakespeare's Imagery*. New York: Macmillan, 1935.

Stevens, Wallace. *Harmonium*. New York: Knopf, 1923.

———. *Ideas of Order*. New York: Knopf, 1936.

Stewart, Donald Ogden. *Fighting Words*. Rahway, N.J.: Quinn & Boden, 1940.

Strachey, John. *The Coming Struggle for Power*. New York: Covici, Friede, 1933

Stull, Bradford. *Religious Dialectics of Pain and Imagination*. Albany: SUNY Press, 1994.

Tashjian, Dickran. *William Carlos Williams and the American Scene, 1920–1940*. Berkeley: University of California Press, 1978.

Tate, Allen. *Essays of Four Decades*. Chicago: Swallow Press, 1968.

———. "The Function of a Critical Inquiry." *Southern Review* 1 (1936): 551–59.

———. "Mr. Burke and the Historical Environment." *Southern Review* 1 (1936): 363–72.

———. "Poetry and Politics." *New Republic* 75 (August 2, 1933): 308–11.

———. *The Poetry Reviews of Allen Tate, 1924–1944*. Edited by Ashley Brown and Frances Neel Cheney. Baton Rouge: Louisiana State University Press, 1983.

———. *Reactionary Essays on Poetry and Ideas*. New York: Charles Scribner's Sons, 1936.

———. "Three Types of Poetry." In Tate, *Reactionary Essays on Poetry and Ideas*, 83–112.

Tate, Allen, and Herbert Agar, eds. *Who Owns America? A New Declaration of Independence*. Boston & New York: Houghton Mifflin, 1936.

Tell, David. "'Four Master Tropes' and Rhetorical Action." *Rhetoric Society Quarterly* 34, no. 4 (2004): 33–54.

Thayer, H. S. *Meaning and Action: A Critical History of Pragmatism.* 2nd ed. Indianapolis: Hackett, 1981.

"There Was Once a Tea Party." *Congressional Record,* April 22, 1935, 6109–12.

"Thirty Years Later: Memories of the First American Writers' Congress" [symposium with Kenneth Burke, Malcolm Cowley, Granville Hicks, and William Phillips; moderated by Daniel Aaron]. *American Scholar* 35 (1966): 495–516.

Toomer, Jean. *Cane.* New York: Boni & Liveright, 1923.

Trotsky, Leon. *Literature and Revolution.* N.p., 1924.

Twelve Southerners. *I'll Take My Stand: The South and the Agrarian Tradition.* New York: Harper & Brothers, 1930. Reprint, Baton Rouge: Louisiana State University Press, 1977.

Veblen, Thorstein. *The Engineers and the Price System.* New York: Viking, 1921.

———. *The Instinct of Workmanship and the State of the Industrial Arts.* New York: Macmillan, 1914.

———. *The Theory of the Leisure Class: An Economic Study of Institutions.* New York: Macmillan, 1899.

Vinh, Alphonse, ed. *Cleanth Brooks and Allen Tate: Collected Letters, 1933–1976.* Columbia: University of Missouri Press, 1998.

Wais, Erin. "'Trained Incapacity': Thorstein Veblen and Kenneth Burke." *Kenneth Burke Journal* 2 (2005): n.pag.

Wald, Alan M. *James T. Farrell: The Revolutionary Socialist Years.* New York: New York University Press, 1978.

———. *The New York Intellectuals.* Chapel Hill: University of North Carolina Press, 1987.

Walker, Jeffrey. *Bardic Ethos and the American Epic Poem: Whitman, Pound, Crane, Williams, Olson.* Baton Rouge: Louisiana State University Press, 1989.

Wander, Philip. "At the Ideological Front." *Communication Studies* 42–43 (1991): 199–218.

Warren, Austin. *Becoming What One Is.* Ann Arbor: University of Michigan Press, 1995.

———. "The Sceptic's Progress." Rev. of *Permanence and Change. American Review* 6 (1936): 193–213.

Warren, Robert Penn. *All the King's Men.* New York: Harcourt, Brace, 1946.

———. "The Briar Patch." In Twelve Southerners, *I'll Take My Stand,* 246–64.

———. *The Circus in the Attic and Other Stories.* New York: Harcourt, Brace, 1947.

———. *John Brown: The Making of a Martyr.* New York: Payson & Clarke, 1929.

Weaver, Mike. *William Carlos Williams: The American Background.* Cambridge: Cambridge University Press, 1970.

Weaver, Richard. *Composition: A Course in Writing and Rhetoric.* New York: Holt, 1957.

———. *The Ethics of Rhetoric.* Chicago: Regnery, 1953.

———. *Language Is Sermonic: Richard M. Weaver on the Nature of Rhetoric.* Edited by Richard L. Johannesen, Rennard Strickland, and Ralph T. Eubanks. Baton Rouge: Louisiana State University Press, 1970.

Wess, Robert. *Kenneth Burke: Rhetoric, Subjectivity, Postmodernism.* Cambridge: Cambridge University Press, 1996.

"When Father Coughlin Comes to Washington." *Readers' Digest* 26 (April 1935): 3.

Wiggershaus, Rolf. *The Frankfurt School: Its Histories, Theories, and Political Significance.* Cambridge, Mass.: MIT Press, 1994.

Williams, David Cratis. "Toward Kenneth Burke's Philosophy of Rhetoric: An Intellectual History, 1897–1935." Ph.D. diss., University of Kansas, 1990.

Williams, William Carlos. *Adam & Eve in the City.* Peru, Vt.: Alcestis Press, 1936.

———. *The Autobiography of William Carlos Williams.* New York: Random House, 1948.

———. *Collected Poems, 1921–1931.* New York: Objectivist Press, 1934.

———. *An Early Martyr and Other Poems.* New York: Alcestis Press, 1935.

———. *The Embodiment of Knowledge.* New York: New Directions, 1974.

———. *In the American Grain.* New York: A & C Boni, 1925.

———. *The Knife of the Times.* Ithaca, N.Y.: Dragon Press, 1932.

———. "Letter to the Editor." *New Masses* 8 (December 1932): 22.

———. "A Night in June." *Blast: A Magazine of Proletarian Short Stories* 1, no. 5 (1934): 2–4.

———. *Selected Essays.* New York: New Directions, 1954.

———. *Sour Grapes: A Book of Poems.* Boston: Four Seas, 1921.

———. *The White Mule.* Norfolk, Conn.: New Directions, 1937.

Wilson, Edmund. *American Jitters: A Year of the Slump.* New York: Charles Scribner's Sons, 1932.

———. "An Appeal to Progressives." *New Republic* 65 (January 14, 1931): 234–38.

———. *Axel's Castle: A Study in the Imaginative Literature of 1870–1930.* New York: Charles Scribner's Sons, 1931.

———. *Letters on Literature and Politics, 1912–1972.* Edited by Elena Wilson. New York: Farrar, Straus & Giroux, 1977.

Wimsatt, William. "The Chicago Critics." *Comparative Literature* 5 (1953): 50–74.

Winchell, Mark Royden. *Cleanth Brooks and the Rise of Modern Criticism.* Charlottesville: University Press of Virginia, 1996.

———, ed. *The Vanderbilt Tradition: Essays in Honor of Thomas Daniel Young.* Baton Rouge: Louisiana State University Press, 1991.

Winters, Yvor. *In Defense of Reason.* Denver, Colo.: Swallow Press, 1943.

———. "Poetry, Morality, and Criticism." In *The Critique of Humanism: A Symposium,* edited by C. Hartley Grattan, 301–33. New York: Brewer & Warren, 1930.

———. *Primitivism and Decadence: A Study of American Experimental Poetry.* New York: Arrow Editions, 1937.

———. "Snow-Ghost." *Pagany* 1 (July–September 1930): 71.

Wirth, Louis. Rev. of *Permanence and Change. American Journal of Sociology* 43 (1937–38): 483–86.

Wolin, Ross. *The Rhetorical Imagination of Kenneth Burke.* Columbia: University of South Carolina Press, 2001.

Woodcock, John. "An Interview with Kenneth Burke." *Sewanee Review* 85 (1977): 704–18.

Wolfe, Cary. "Nature as Critical Concept: Kenneth Burke, the Frankfurt School, and 'Metabiology.'" *Cultural Critique* 18 (1991): 65–96.

Yagoda, Ben. "Kenneth Burke." *Horizon* 23 (June 1980): 66–69.

Young, Thomas Daniel. *Gentleman in a Dustcoat: The Biography of John Crowe Ransom.* Baton Rouge: Louisiana State University Press, 1976.

———. "Malcolm Cowley's Politics: A View of the Thirties." *Visionary Company* 2 & 3 (1987): 162–74.

Young, Thomas Daniel, and George Core. Introduction to *Selected Letters of John Crowe Ransom,* edited by Young and Core, 1–8. Baton Rouge: Louisiana State University Press, 1984.

Zabel, Morton. "The Harmonium of Wallace Stevens." Rev. of *Harmonium,* by Wallace Stevens. *Poetry* 39 (December 1931): 148–54.

Zaturenska, Marya. Unpublished diary. Bird Library, Syracuse University.

Zukofsky, Louis, and Charles Reznikoff. "Program." *Poetry* 37 (February 1931): 268–72.

Index